# PHILIP'S

CW01022668

# STREET
# Newcastle
# and Gateshead

First published 2007 by

Philip's, a division of
Octopus Publishing Group Ltd
2–4 Heron Quays
London E14 4JP

First edition 2007
First impression 2007

ISBN-10   0-540-09122-7
ISBN-13   978-0-540-09122-5
© Philip's 2007

This product includes mapping data licensed
from Ordnance Survey®, with the
permission of the Controller of Her Majesty's
Stationery Office.© Crown copyright 2007.
All rights reserved.
Licence number 100011710

Photographic acknowledgements:
VI Liz Boyd / Alamy
VII Stephen Dorey / Alamy

Printed by Toppan, China

## Contents

# Key to map symbols

## Roads

| | |
|---|---|
| (12) | **Motorway** with junction number |
| A34 | **Primary route** – dual, single carriageway |
| A40 | **A road** – dual, single carriageway |
| B1289 | **B road** – dual, single carriageway |
| | **Through-route** – dual, single carriageway |
| | **Minor road** – dual, single carriageway |
| | **Rural track, private road or narrow road in urban area** |
| | **Path, bridleway, byway open to all traffic, road used as a public path** |
| | **Road under construction** |
| | **Pedestrianised area** |
| | **Gate or obstruction to traffic** restrictions may not apply at all times or to all vehicles |
| P P&R | **Parking, Park and Ride** |

## Railways

 **Railway**

 **Miniature railway**

 **Metro station, private railway station**

## Emergency services

**Ambulance station, coastguard station**

**Fire station, police station**

**Hospital, Accident and Emergency entrance to hospital**

## General features

| | |
|---|---|
| + PO | **Place of worship, Post Office** |
| i | **Information centre** (open all year) |
| | **Bus or coach station, shopping centre** |
| | **Important buildings,** schools, colleges, universities and hospitals |
| | **Woods, built-up area** |
| Tumulus FORT | **Non-Roman antiquity, Roman antiquity** |

## Leisure facilities

 **Camping site, caravan site**

 **Golf course, picnic site**

## Boundaries

• • • • • • • • **Postcode boundaries**

━ • ━ **County and unitary authority boundaries**

## Water features

River Ouse **Tidal water, water name**

**Non-tidal water** – lake, river, canal or stream

< | **Lock, weir**

## Enlarged mapping only

**Railway or bus station building**

**Place of interest**

**Parkland**

## Scales

**Blue pages: 4½ inches to 1 mile   1:14 080**

| 0 | 220 yds | ¼ mile | 660 yds | ½ mile |
|---|---|---|---|---|

| 0 | 125m | 250m | 375m | ½ km |
|---|---|---|---|---|

**Red pages: 7 inches to 1 mile   1:9 051**

| 0 | 110 yds | 220 yds | 330 yds | ¼ mile |
|---|---|---|---|---|

| 0 | 125m | 250m | 375m | ½ km |
|---|---|---|---|---|

 62 **Adjoining page indicators** The colour of the arrow and the band indicates the scale of the adjoining page (see above)

## Abbreviations

| | | | | |
|---|---|---|---|---|
| Acad | Academy | | Mkt | Market |
| Allot Gdns | Allotments | | Meml | Memorial |
| Cemy | Cemetery | | Mon | Monument |
| C Ctr | Civic Centre | | Mus | Museum |
| CH | Club House | | Obsy | Observatory |
| Coll | College | | Pal | Royal Palace |
| Crem | Crematorium | | PH | Public House |
| Ent | Enterprise | | Recn Gd | Recreation Ground |
| Ex H | Exhibition Hall | | Resr | Reservoir |
| Ind Est | Industrial Estate | | Ret Pk | Retail Park |
| IRB Sta | Inshore Rescue Boat Station | | Sch | School |
| Inst | Institute | | Sh Ctr | Shopping Centre |
| Ct | Law Court | | TH | Town Hall/House |
| L Ctr | Leisure Centre | | Trad Est | Trading Estate |
| LC | Level Crossing | | Univ | University |
| Liby | Library | | Wks | Works |
| | | | YH | Youth Hostel |

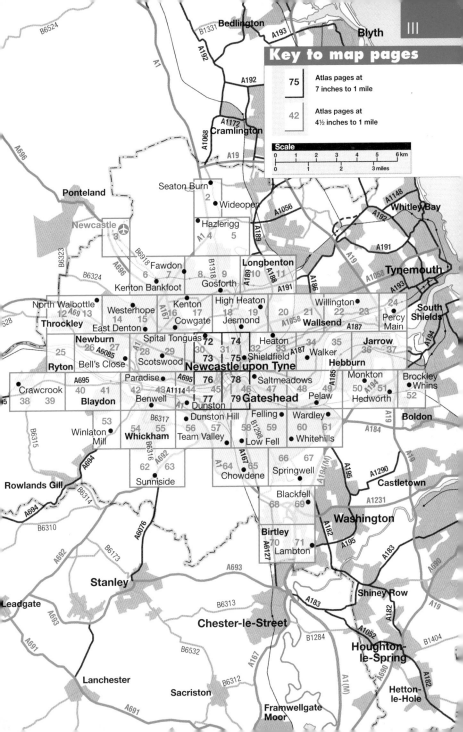

B6524

Bedlington

B1331

A193

Blyth

A192

A192

A1

A1172

A1068

Cramlington

A19

A696

Ponteland

Seaton Burn

2

Wideopen

A1056

A1148

Whitley Bay

A192

Newcastle

Hazlerigg

3

A1 4 5

A189

A191

Tynemouth

B6323

B6918

Fawdon

6 7

B1318

8 9

A189

A186

A191

A186

A1058

Tynemouth

A193

A696

Kenton Bankfoot

Gosforth

Longbenton

10 11

B6324

North Walbottle

12 A69 13

Westerhope

14 15

A167

Kenton

16 17

High Heaton

18 19

20

Willington

21 22 23

24

Percy Main

South Shields

B528

Throckley

East Denton

Cowgate

Jesmond

A1058

Wallsend

A187

A194

Newburn

26 A6085 27

28 29

Spital Tongues

72 74

Heaton

32 83

A187

34 35

Jarrow

36 37

25

Bell's Close

Scotswood

30 31

73 75

Shieldfield

Walker

Hebburn

Ryton

Newcastle upon Tyne

Paradise

A695

76 78

Saltmeadows

Monkton

50 A194 51

Brockley Whins

Crawcrook

40 41

42 43

A1114 44 45

46 47 48 49

Pelaw

Hedworth

52

38 39

Blaydon

Benwell

77

Dunston

79 Gateshead

A185

A19

Boldon

53

B6317

Dunston Hill

Felling

Wardley

A184

Winlaton Mill

54 55

56 57

58 59

60 61

Whitehills

B6315

Whickham

B6316

Team Valley

B1298

Low Fell

A167

A694

A692

62 63

A1

64 65

66 67

Springwell

A194(M)

A195

A1290

Castletown

Rowlands Gill

B6314

Sunniside

Chowdene

Blackfell

68 69

A1231

Washington

B6310

A694

A6076

Birtley

70 71

A182

A195

A183

A690

B6173

A6127

Lambton

Shiney Row

Stanley

A693

A183

A182

A19

Leadgate

A693

B6313

Chester-le-Street

B1284

A1052

Houghton-le-Spring

B1404

A691

B6532

A167

A690

Lanchester

Sacriston

B6312

Framwellgate Moor

A1(M)

Hetton-le-Hole

A182

A691

# Sights of Newcastle and Gateshead

## Museums and Galleries

**BALTIC Centre for Contemporary Art**
*Gateshead Quays, South Shore Road, Gateshead* Constant change of exhibitions presenting a dynamic, diverse and international programme of contemporary visual art. ☎0191 478 1922 🖳www.balticmill.com 78 C4

**Bede's World** *Church Bank, Jarrow* The Age of Bede exhibition, with pottery, stone carvings and early coloured window-glass from the 7th century. An Anglo-Saxon demonstration farm, herb garden and monastic site of St Paul's. 🖳www.bedesworld.co.uk ☎0191 489 2106 37 B3

**The Biscuit Factory** *Stoddart Street, Newcastle* Britain's biggest original art store. On-going displays with the pieces of art available to purchase. 🖳www.thebiscuitfactory.com ☎0191 261 1103 75 C2

**Centre for Life** *Times Square, Newcastle* Life Science Centre uncovering the secret language of DNA and our ancestors. Brain testing activities. 🖳www.life.org.uk ☎0191 243 8210 76 C4

**The Discovery Museum** *Blandford Square, Newcastle* Newcastle's colourful history from Romans and Knights to ship builders and pitmen. Scientific exhibitions and collections of maritime and social history. 🖳www.twmuseums.org.uk/discovery ☎0191 232 6789 76 C4

**Gateshead Central Library** *Prince Consort Road, Gateshead* Access to parish records, maps and photographs of the Gateshead area. 🖳www.gateshead.gov.uk/libraries ☎0191 433 8400 58 B4

**Globe Gallery** *Curtis Mayfield House, Carliol Square, Newcastle* Contemporary art gallery. ☎0191 222 1666 🖳www.globegallery.org 75 B1

**Hatton Gallery** *The Quadrangle, University of Newcastle* The permanent collection has over 3,500 paintings, drawings and sculptures from the 14th century to the present day. It also holds 5 or 6 temporary exhibitions each year, of historical and contemporary work. 🖳www.ncl.ac.uk/hatton ☎0191 222 6059 74 A3

**Laing Art Gallery** *New Bridge Street, Newcastle* Extensive collection of British oil paintings, watercolours and silver, of national and international significance. ☎0191 232 7734 🖳www.twmuseums.org.uk/laing 75 B2

**The Lit & Phil** *Westgate Road, Newcastle* The largest independent library collection outside of London, with over 150,000 books. Large music library. All stored in the Grade II listed building opened in 1825. ☎0191 232 0192 🖳www.litandphil.org.uk 78 A4

**Museum of Antiquities** *The Quadrangle, University of Newcastle* History of Hadrian's Wall and the Roman frontier. Artefacts, models and archives. Full scale reconstruction of the Temple to Mithras at Carrawburgh. 🖳http://museums.ncl.ac.uk ☎0191 222 7846 74 A3

**Newburn Hall Motor Museum** *Townfield Gardens, Newburn* Period buildings built for the 4th Northumberland Fusiliers. Now housing vintage cars and motorcycles. ☎0191 264 2977 26 A4

**Newcastle Arts Centre** *Westgate Road, nr Central Station, Newcastle* Exhibition centre, gallery and theatre with studios making music, photography and ceramics. Also has a large art store. ☎0191 261 5618 🖳www.newcastle-arts-centre.co.uk 75 A1

**Segedunum Roman Fort, Baths & Museum** *Buddle Street, Wallsend* The last outpost of Hadrian's Wall, once home to 600 Roman soldiers. ☎0191 236 9347 22 A1 🖳www.twmuseums.org.uk/segedunum

**Shefton Museum of Greek Art & Archaeology** *Armstrong Building, The Quadrangle, University of Newcastle* Collection uncovering the world of the ancient Greeks. ☎0191 222 8996 🖳www.ncl.ac.uk/shefton-museum 74 A3

**The Shipley Art Gallery** *Prince Consort Road, Gateshead* Broad range of contemporary craft and fine art. 🖳www.twmuseums.org.uk/shipley ☎0191 477 1495 58 B4

**Trinity House** *Broad Chare, Newcastle* Maritime buildings tour takes in the 1505 private Brethren's Chapel and 1721 Banqueting Hall. Viewing by appointment only. ☎0191 232 8226 🖳www.trinityhousenewcastle.org.uk 78 B4

**University Gallery, Northumbria University** *Library Building, Sandyford Road, Newcastle* Permanent and temporary exhibitions of photography, sculpture and prints. Art club and bookshop. 🖳http://northumbria.ac.uk/universitygallery ☎0191 227 4424 74 B3

**Workplace Gallery** *Ellison Street, Gateshead* A commercial gallery run by artists. Represents emerging and established artists through programmes of contemporary art. 🖳www.workplacegallery.co.uk 78 C3

## Historic Sites

**Bessie Surtees House** *Sandhill, Newcastle* One of a group of 18th century timber framed buildings, noted for its interesting period architecture. ☎0191 269 1200 🖳www.english-heritage.org.uk 78 B4

**Black Gate** *Castle Arch, St Nicholas Street, Newcastle* Medieval gatehouse to the Castle Keep surmounted by a 17th century house. Home to the Society of Antiquaries of Newcastle. ☎0191 261 5390 🖳http://museums.ncl.ac.uk/keep 78 A4

**Blackfriars** *Monk Street, Newcastle* A restored former monastery that dates from the 13th century. 🖳www.newcastle.gov.uk 73 C1

**Castle Keep** *St Nicholas Street, Castle Garth, Newcastle* Original starting point for Hadrian's Wall. ☎0191 232 7938 🖳http://museums.ncl.ac.uk/keep 78 A4

**Grey's Monument** *Grey Street, Newcastle* The focal point of the city centre, this is a towering monument featuring Earl Grey. 75 A1

**West Walls** *Bath Lane, Newcastle* Best remaining stretch of the original city walls, Newcastle's main medieval defence. 🖳www.newcastlegateshead.com 73 C1

## Places of Worship

**Cathedral Church of St Mary** *Clayton Street West, Newcastle* Roman Catholic Cathedral completed in 1844. Beautiful stained glass windows, five pipe organs and newly discovered underground crypt. ☎0191 232 6953 🖳www.stmaryscathedral.org.uk 78 C4

**St Nicholas' Anglican Cathedral** *St Nicholas Street, Newcastle* Mother Church of the most northerly diocese in England. Dates from 14th century. 🖳www.newcastle-ang-cathedralstnicholas.org.uk ☎0191 232 1939 75 B1

**St Paul's Monastery** *Church Bank, Jarrow* This Anglo-Saxon church has the oldest dedication stone in the country, dated 685AD. 🖳www.english-heritage.org.uk ☎0191 489 7052 37 B3

*Millennium Bridge and BALTIC Art Centre, Gateshead*

## Other Sights

**Angel of the North** *A1/Durham Road, Low Eighton, Gateshead* A 208-tonne Angel sculpture by artist Antony Gormley.
🖳www.angelofthenorth.org.uk 68 A4

**Assembly Rooms** *Fenkle Street, Newcastle* Georgian building now a conference and banqueting venue. ☎0191 232 8695
🖳www.assemblyrooms.co.uk 78 A4

**Chinese Arch** *Stowell Street, Newcastle* Based on a Chinese Royal Palace, bringing luck and prosperity to the city's Chinatown.
🖳www.newcastlechinatown.co.uk 73 C1

**Gateshead Millennium Bridge** *The Quayside, Newcastle* The world's first and only tilting bridge. It won the Outstanding Structure Award from IABSE in 2005. ☎0191 477 5380
🖳www.gateshead.gov.uk 78 C4

**Gateshead Quays** *South Shore Road, Gateshead* The site of the BALTIC Centre of Contemporary Art, the Gateshead Millennium Bridge, The Sage Gateshead and Gateshead Visitor Centre. ☎0191 477 5380
🖳www.gateshead-quays.com 78 C4

**Gateshead Visitor Centre** *St Mary's Church, Oakwellgate, Gateshead* Discover the history and regeneration of Gateshead. Panoramic views from St Mary's over both quaysides.
🖳www.gateshead-quays.com/visitor.htm
☎0191 477 5380 78 B4

**Grainger Town** *Grainger Street, Newcastle* The restored heart of Newcastle, mixing elegant architecture with cafe culture. 75 A1

**The Quayside** *Off Watergate and Queen Street, Newcastle* Restaurants and clubbing. Beautiful views of the Tyne, Baltic, Sage, Millennium Bridge and the Tyne Bridge.
🖳www.newcastlequayside.co.uk 78 B4

**The Tyne Bridge** *A167 Gateshead Highway* Completed and ceremonially opened in 1928 by King George V and Queen Mary. Based on the Sydney Harbour Bridge.
🖳www.tynebridgewebcam.com 78 B4

## Green Spaces

**Exhibition Park** *Claremont Road, Newcastle* Park with croquet lawns, tennis courts, boating lake, crazy golf and skate park.
🖳www.newcastle.gov.uk 74 A4

**Jesmond Vale** *Jesmond Vale Lane, High Heaton, Newcastle* Public park along a narrow steep sided valley. Located in woodland with crags, waterfalls and pools. Very tranquil.
🖳www.jesmonddene.org.uk 32 C3

**Leazes Park** *Richardson Road, Newcastle* The oldest city park in Newcastle, Leazes Park is a conservation area and is Grade II on the English Heritage Register of Parks and Gardens of Special Historic Interest.
🖳www.newcastle.gov.uk/leazes.nsf 73 C2

**Saltwell Park** *Saltwell Towers, West Park Road, Gateshead* Victorian park, awarded the Green Flag Award in 2006. With 55 acres of landscapes, woodland and ornamental gardens. Lake, play areas and bowling greens.
🖳www.gateshead.gov.uk
☎0191 433 5900 58 A3

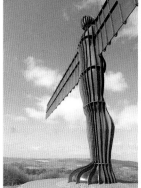

▲ *The Angel of the North*

**Walker Riverside Park** *Walker Road, Walker, Newcastle* Consists of wildflower meadows, woodlands, and fantastic views of the river.
☎0191 281 3833 🖳www.newcastle.gov.uk 48 B2

## Activities

**Bowes Railway** *Springwell Village, Gateshead* The site of a Scheduled Industrial Monument dedicated to showing the industrial heritage of the region. Has a collection of 80 colliery wagons. 🖳www.bowesrailway.co.uk
☎0191 416 1847 66 C2

**Eldon Garden** *Percy Street, Newcastle* Exclusive shopping centre, attached to Eldon Square, with extensive collection of designer brands. Specialist beauty salons and pavement-style cafes. 🖳www.newcastle.gov.uk 75 A2

**Eldon Square** *Northumberland Street and Percy Street* Large shopping centre with high street names, cafes, restaurants and leisure centre.
🖳www.eldon-square.co.uk
☎0191 261 1891 75 A2

**The Gate** *Newgate Street* Large indoor centre with restaurants, bars, clubs, cinema and casino. 🖳www.thegatenewcastle.co.uk
☎0191 223 5000 75 A1

**MetroCentre** *Hollinside Road, Newcastle Western Bypass, Gateshead* The largest shopping and leisure centre in Europe, with 330 shops and major department stores. Includes Metroland, the largest indoor theme park in Europe, Megabowl and a cinema.
🖳www.metrocentre-gateshead.co.uk
☎0191 493 0219 43 B2

**Metro Radio Arena** *Along A189 over Redheugh Bridge, Newcastle* The largest concert and exhibition venue in the North East. Home to Newcastle Eagles Basketball Team and Newcastle Vipers Ice Hockey Club. ☎0870 707 8000 🖳www.telewestarena.co.uk 76 C3

**Newcastle Carling Academy** *Westgate Road, Newcastle* Hosts variety of gigs from popular artists. 🖳www.newcastle-academy.co.uk
☎0870 771 2000 75 A1

**Newcastle City Hall** *Northumberland Road, Newcastle* Plays host to national and international performers from rock to musicals to comedy. 🖳www.newcastle.gov.uk/cityhall
☎0191 261 2606 75 B2

**Newcastle Racecourse** *High Gosforth Park, Great North Road, Newcastle* Premier racing course. 🖳www.newcastle-racecourse.co.uk
☎0191 236 2020 4 C3

**Newcastle United FC** *St James' Park, Barrack Road, Newcastle* Formed in 1892 and nick-named the 'Magpies'. ☎0191 201 8400
🖳www.nufc.premiumtv.co.uk 73 C2

**Northern Stage** *Barras Bridge, Newcastle* Presents local, national and international theatre. 🖳www.northernstage.co.uk
☎0871 700 0125 74 A3

**The Sage** *St Mary's Square, Gateshead Quays, Gateshead* Centre for musical education and performance. Offers a kaleidoscope of genres. 🖳www.thesagegateshead.org
☎0191 443 4661 78 C4

**Seven Stories** *Lime Street, Newcastle* Exhibition centre celebrating British children's literature. Original artwork, manuscripts and story-telling. ☎0845 271 0777
🖳www.sevenstories.org.uk 32 B1

**Tanfield Railway** *Andrewshouse, Sunniside, Gateshead* The world's oldest surviving working railway. Fleet of locomotives with train rides available. ☎0191 387 4784
🖳www.tanfield-railway.co.uk 62 C1

**Theatre Royal** *Grey Street, Newcastle* Variety of entertainment – drama, musicals, comedy, dance and music. ☎0870 905 5060
🖳www.theatreroyal.co.uk 75 A1

**Tyneside Cinema** *Old Town Hall, West Street, Gateshead* Independent cinema with a diverse choice of screenings. In-house cafe and coffee rooms. ☎0191 232 8289
🖳www.tynecine.org 78 B3

**Whickham Thorns Outdoor Centre** *Market Lane, Dunston, Gateshead* Skiing, snow boarding, indoor and outdoor climbing, assault courses, orienteering, mountain biking, archery and high ropes. ☎0191 433 5767
🖳www.gateshead.gov.uk 55 C4

## Information

**Tourist Information**
🛈*Newcastle: Grainger Street*
☎0191 277 8000 75 A1
🛈*Gateshead Visitor Centre: St Mary's Church*
☎0191 478 4222 78 B4

**Newcastle City Council**
*Civic Centre, Barras Bridge* ☎0191 232 8520
🖳www.newcastle.gov.uk 75 A2

**Gateshead Council**
*Civic Centre, Regent Street* ☎0191 433 3000
🖳www.gateshead.gov.uk 79 B2

**NCP Car Parking**
☎0870 606 7050 🖳www.ncp.co.uk

**National Rail Enquiries**
☎0845 748 4950 🖳www.nationalrail.co.uk

**Tyne & Wear Metro**
☎0191 203 3333 🖳www.nexus.org.uk

**Local Bus and Rail**
☎0870 608 2608 🖳www.traveline.org.uk

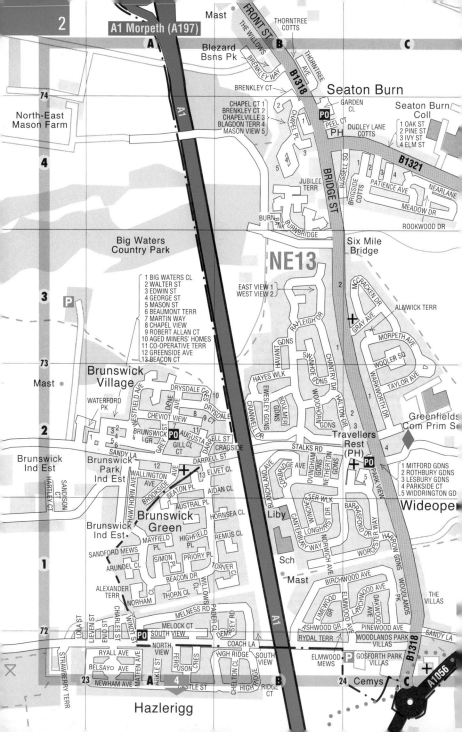

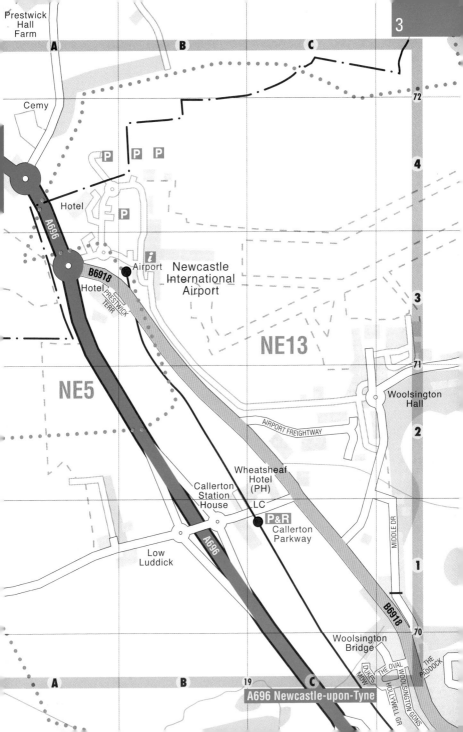

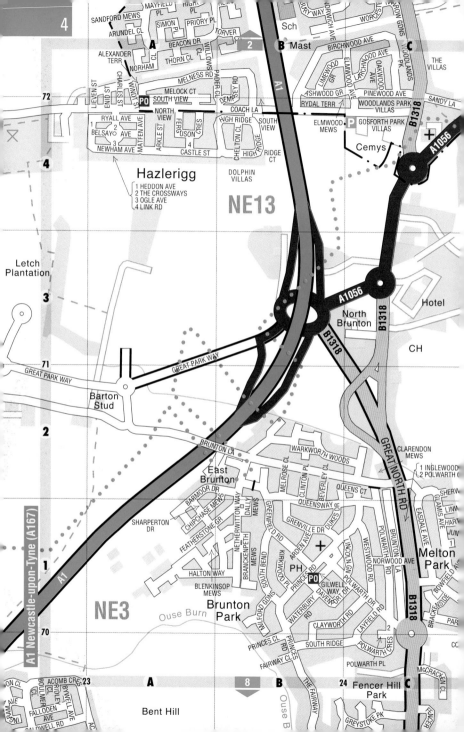

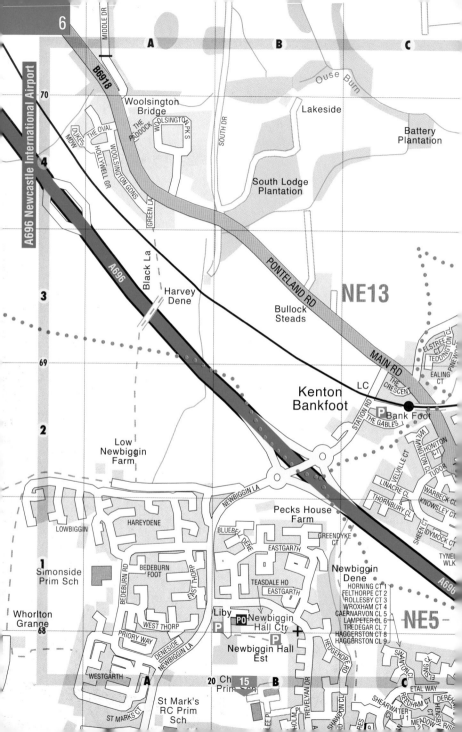

**6**

A    B    C

MIDDLE DR

B6918

A696 Newcastle International Airport

70

THE OVAL
DUKES MDW
HOLLYWELL GR
WOOLSINGTON GDNS
THE PADDOCK
WOOLSINGTON PKS
SOUTH DR

Woolsington
Bridge

Lakeside

Battery
Plantation

4

A696

Black La

GREEN LA

South Lodge
Plantation

PONTELAND RD

NE13

3

Harvey
Dene

Bullock
Steads

MAIN RD

ELSTREE CT
TEDDINGTON CT
PINEWOOD

69

LC
THE CRESCENT

EALING CT

2

Low
Newbiggin
Farm

Kenton
Bankfoot

P Bank Foot
STATION RD
THE GABLES

WELLINGTON CT
HONITON CT
TUDOR

LINACRE CL
VELVILLE CT
THORNBURY CL
SHEEN CT
KNOWSLEY CT
WARBECK CL
DYMOCK CT

NEWBIGGIN LA

HAREYDENE

LOWBIGGIN

Pecks House
Farm

BLUEBELL DENE

EASTGARTH

GREENDYKE CT

TYNE
WLK

1

Simonside
Prim Sch

BEDEBURN RD
BEDEBURN
FOOT
EAST THORP

TEASDALE HO
EASTGARTH

Newbiggin
Dene

HORNING CT 1
FELTHORPE CT 2
ROLLESBY CT 3
WROXHAM CT 4
CAERNARVON CL 5
LAMPETER CL 6
TREDEGAR CT 7
HAGGERSTON CT 8
HAGGERSTON CL 9

NE5

Whorlton
Grange

68

WEST THORP
PRIORY WAY
DENESIDE
NEWBIGGIN LA

Liby
P PO
Newbiggin
Hall Ctr

P

Newbiggin Hall
Est

HEDGEHOPE RD

SHANNON CL

A696

WESTGARTH

ST MARKS

St Mark's
RC Prim
Sch

A

DENESIDE

20 Ch
Prim Sch

**15**

B

HOLM
LEE PL
TREVELYAN DR
SHANNON CL
REDHAM RD
DEREHAM CT

SHEARWATER
ETAL WAY
MENDOW
C

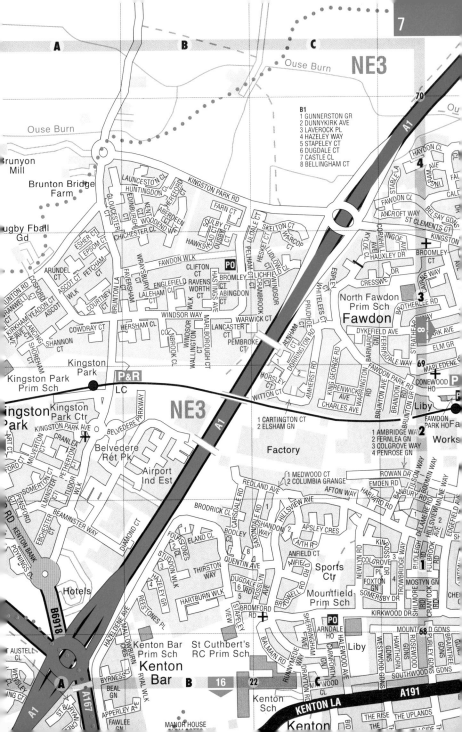

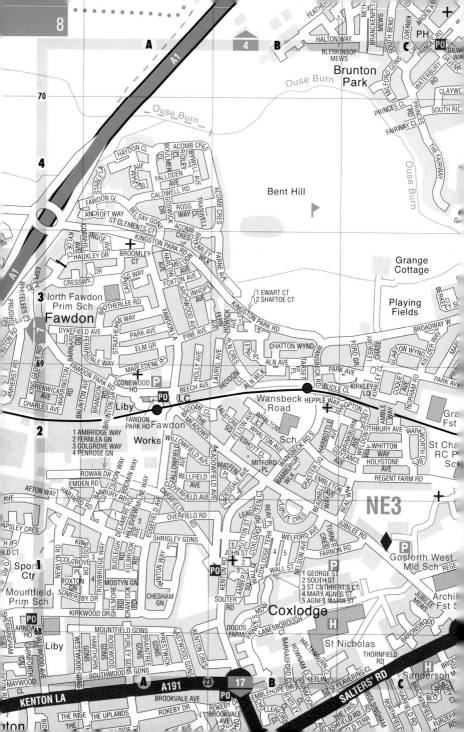

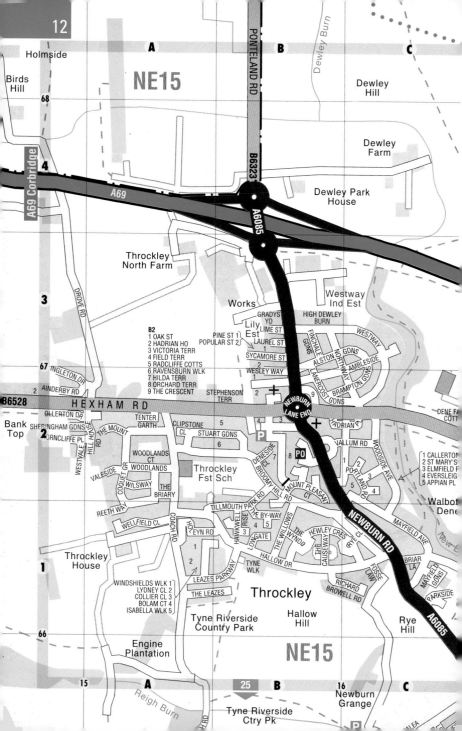

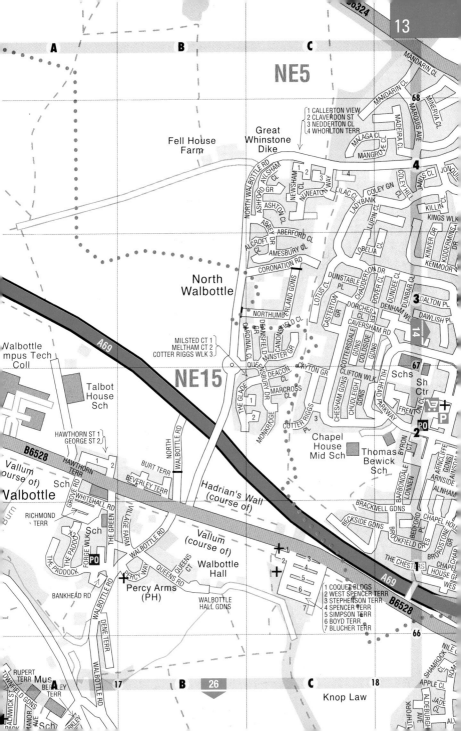

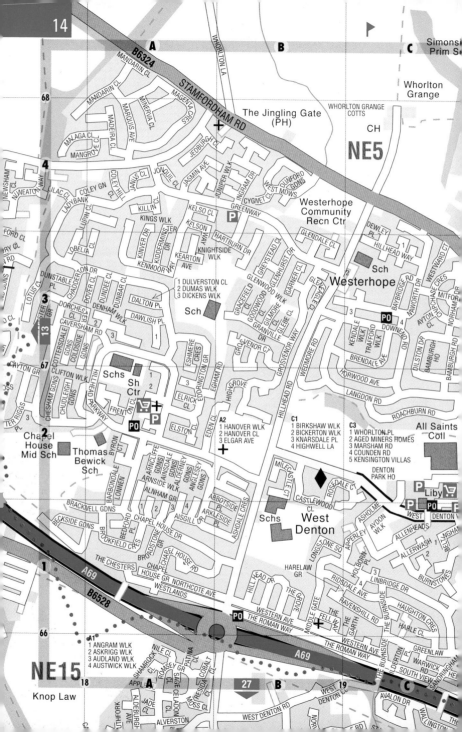

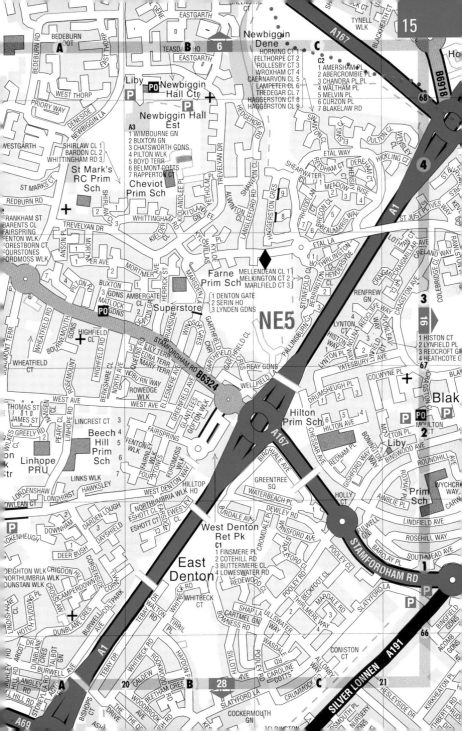

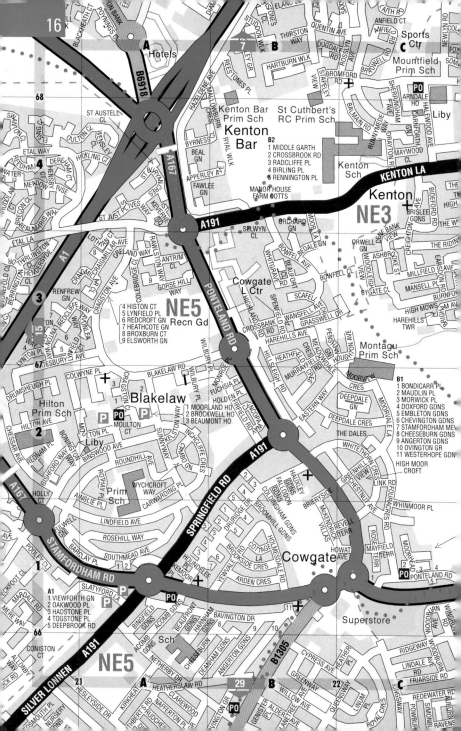

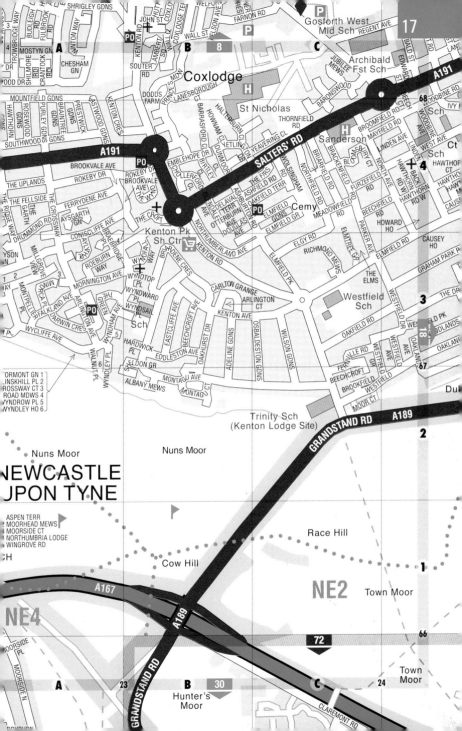

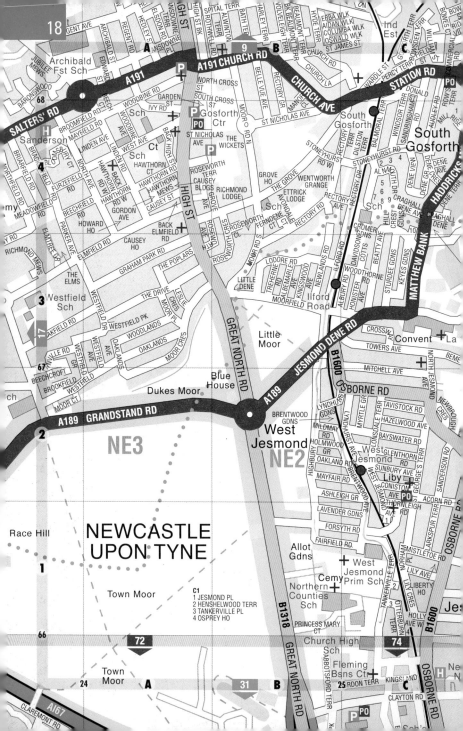

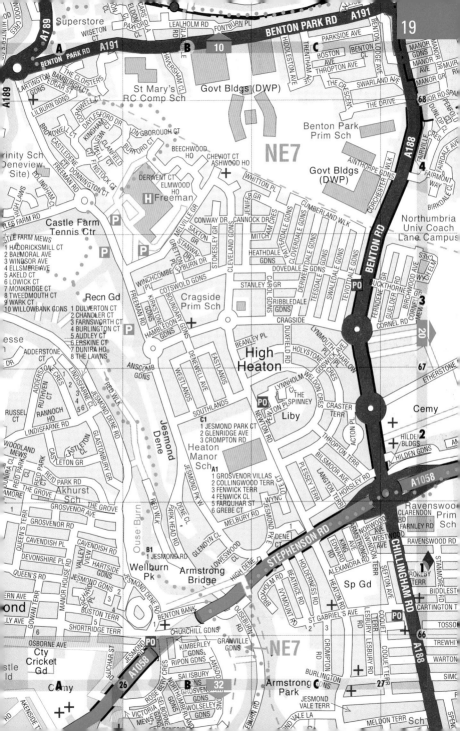

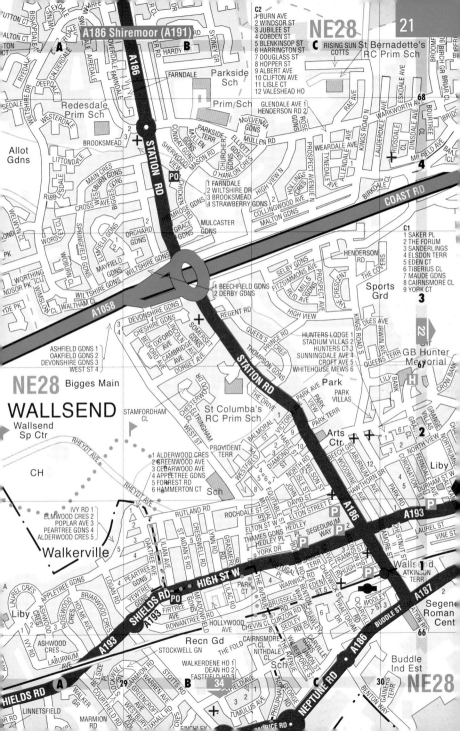

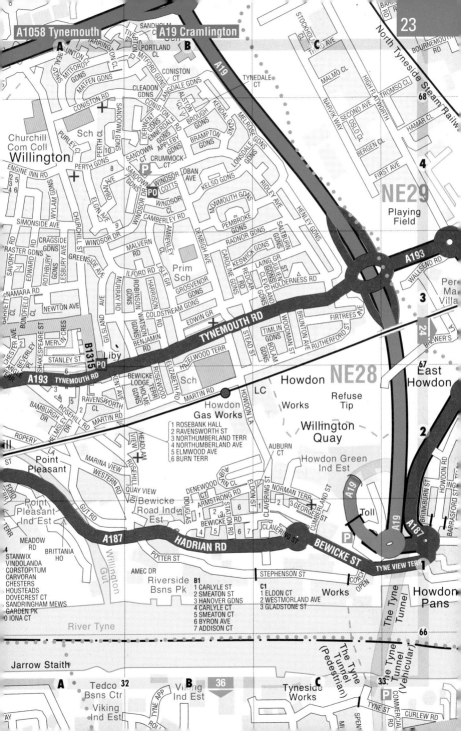

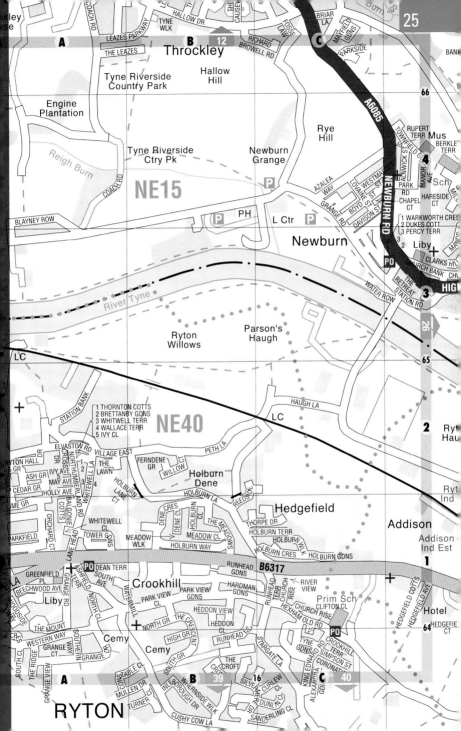

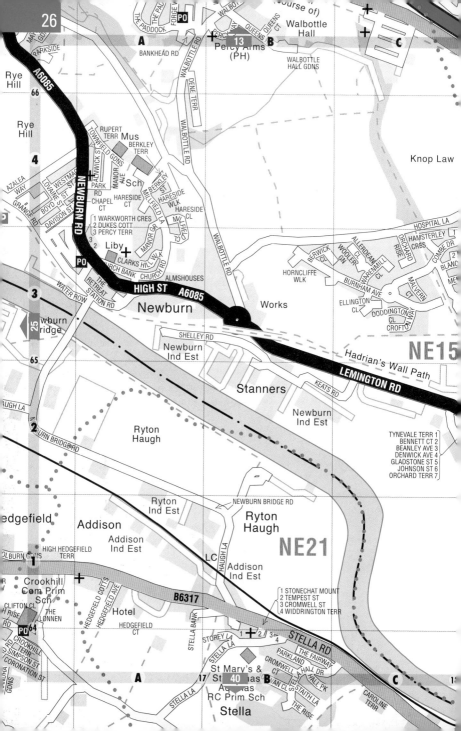

A6085

Rye Hill

66

Rye Hill

4

THE PADDOCK

THE PALL

FORGE CT

PO

WALBOTTLE RD

BROXHOLM

QUEENS CT

QUEENS CT

Walbottle Hall

WALBOTTLE HALL GDNS

A

BANKHEAD RD

13

Percy Arms (PH)

B

C

DENE TERR

WALBOTTLE RD

Knop Law

PARKSIDE

MAY GDNS

AZALEA WAY

GRANGE RD

WESTMAC

LOAINE ST

BOYD ST

DAVISON ST

RUPERT TERR

TOWNFIELD GDNS

ALNWICK GDNS

PARK RD

Mus

BERKLEY TERR

MANOR AVE

Sch

BERKLEY ST

MILLFIELD LA

CHAPEL CT

HARESIDE CT

HARESIDE

HARESIDE WLK

HARESIDE CL

1 WARKWORTH CRES
2 DUKES COTT
3 PERCY TERR

MILLFIELD LA

NEWBURN RD

3 2

Liby

CLARKS

PO

CHURCH BANK

MANOR GR

CLARKS HILL WLK

CHURCH BANK

THE RETREAT

STATION RD

ALMSHOUSES

WALBOTTLE RD

HOSPITAL LA

HAMSTERLEY CRES

ORCHARD RISE

COMBE DR

BERWICK CL

WOOLER GDN

ALLERDEAN CL

WARENMILL CL

MALVERN CT

BLANC

ME

HIGH ST A6085

Newburn

Works

HORNCLIFFE WLK

BURNHAM AVE

ELLINGTON CL

DODDINGTON CL

CROFTON

3

25

wburn ridge

WATER ROW

65

SHELLEY RD

Newburn Ind Est

Hadrian's Wall Path

NE15

KEATS RD

LEMINGTON RD

Stanners

Newburn Ind Est

TYNEVALE TERR 1
BENNETT CT 2
BEANLEY AVE 3
DENWICK AVE 4
GLADSTONE ST 5
JOHNSON ST 6
ORCHARD TERR 7

HAUGH LA

2

N BURN BRIDGE RD

Ryton Haugh

Ryton Ind Est

NEWBURN BRIDGE RD

Ryton Haugh

NE21

edgefield

Addison

HIGH HEDGEFIELD TERR

OLBURN GDNS

1

Crookhill Com Prim Sch

CLIFTON CL

H RISE

RD

PO 64

CROOKHILL TERR

SIMPSON ST

CORONATION ST

Addison Ind Est

HEDGEFIELD COTTS

HEDGEFIELD AVE

THE LONNEN

Hotel

HEDGEFIELD CT

B6317

STELLA BANK

HAUGH LA

LC

Addison Ind Est

1 STONECHAT MOUNT
2 TEMPEST ST
3 CROMWELL ST
4 WIDDRINGTON TERR

1 2 3 4

STELLA RD

THE FAIRWAY

PARKLAND

CROMWELL

HALL DR

HALL PK

STAITH LA

CAROLINE TERR

STOREY LA

STELLA LA

STELLA LA

STELLA LA

A

17

B

40

St Mary's & St mas Aquinas RC Prim Sch

Stella

VAN CL

THE RISE

C

18

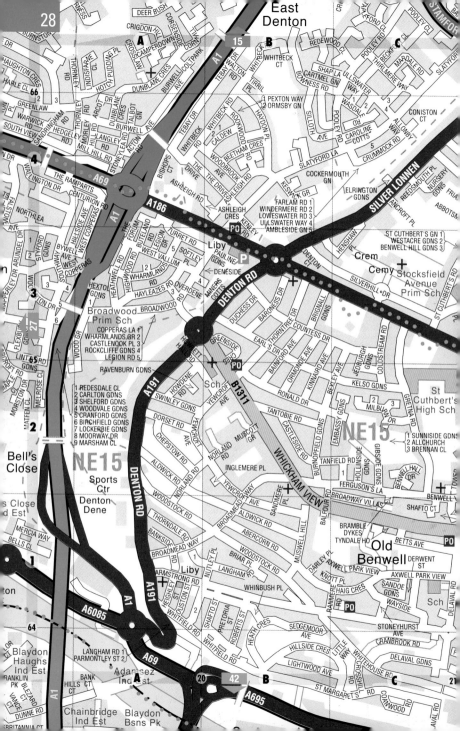

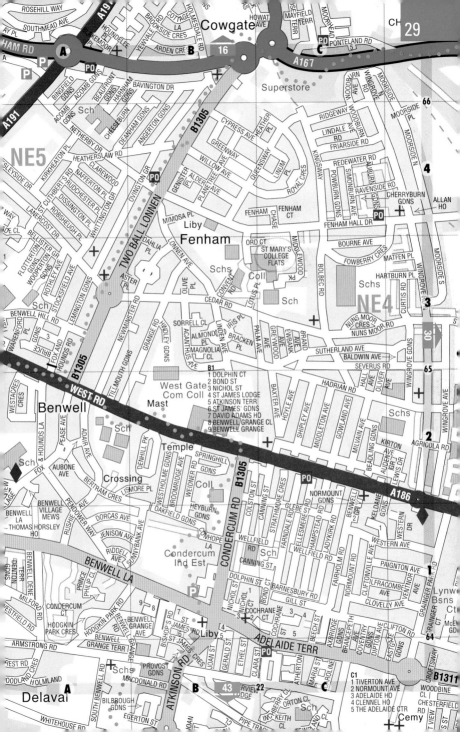

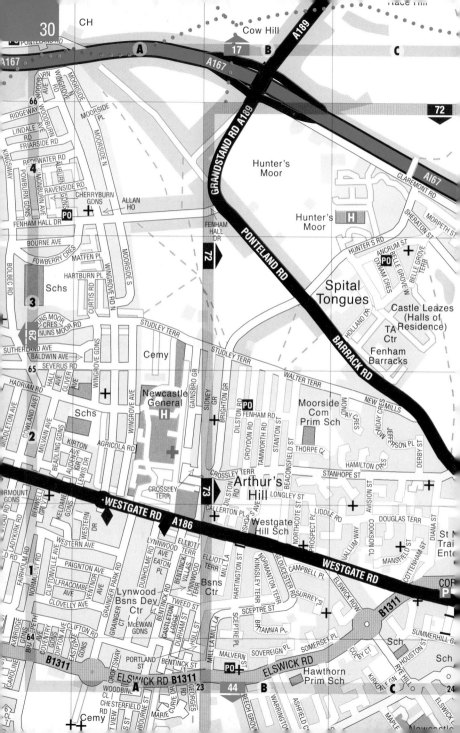

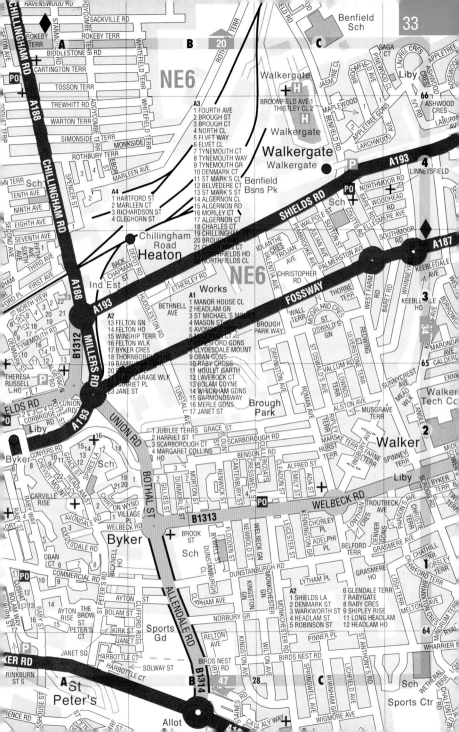

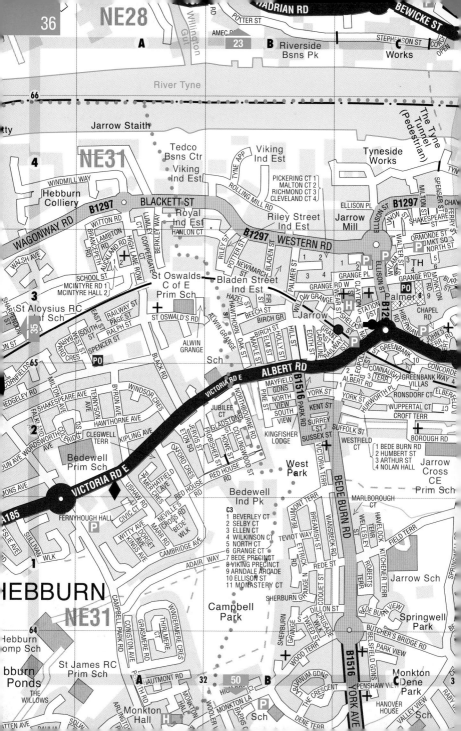

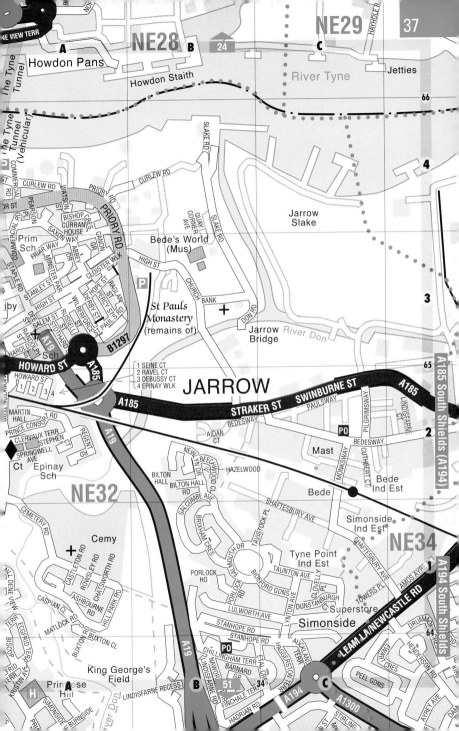

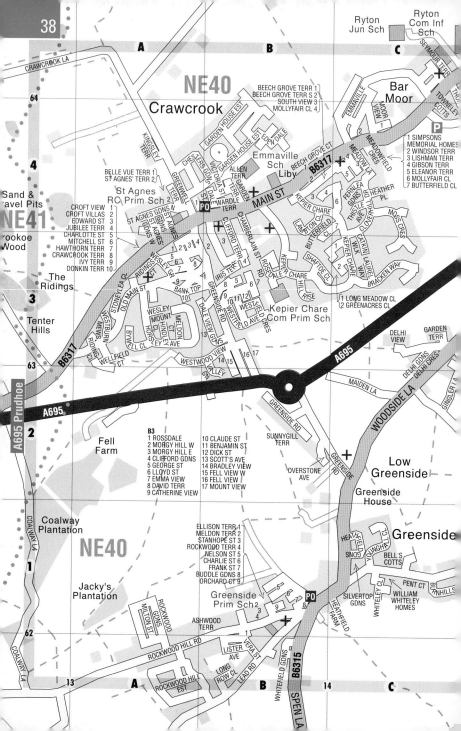

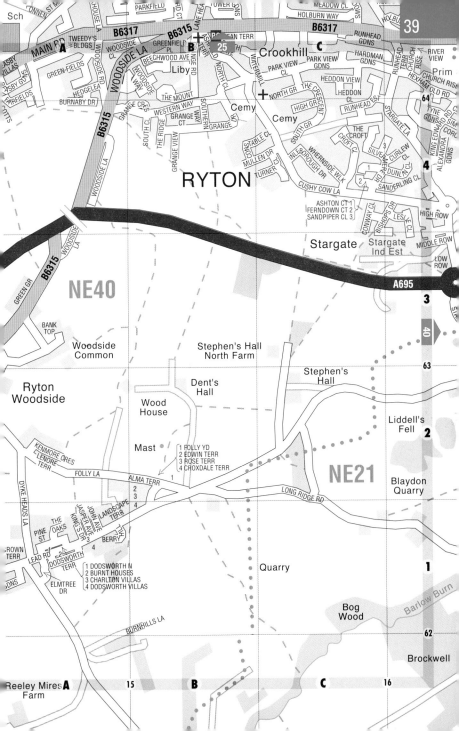

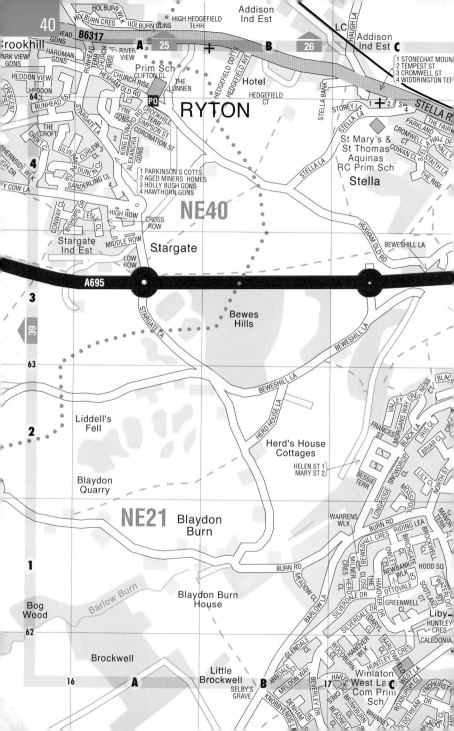

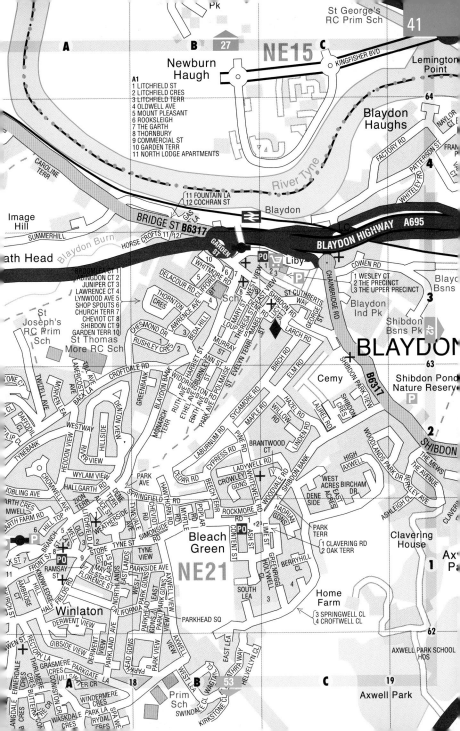

St George's
RC Prim Sch

A    B    27    NE15    C    KINGFISHER BVD    Lemington
Point

Newburn
Haugh

64

A1
1 LITCHFIELD ST
2 LITCHFIELD CRES
3 LITCHFIELD TERR
4 OLDWELL AVE
5 MOUNT PLEASANT
6 ROOKSLEIGH
7 THE GARTH
8 THORNBURY
9 COMMERCIAL ST
10 GARDEN TERR
11 NORTH LODGE APARTMENTS

Blaydon
Haughs

FACTORY RD
PATTERSON ST
WHITELEY RD
NAYLOR ST
FRAN

Image
Hill

SUMMERHILL
CAROLINE TERR

River Tyne

11 FOUNTAIN LA
12 COCHRAN ST

Blaydon

ath Head

Blaydon Burn

BRIDGE ST
B6317

HORSE CROFTS 11/12

BLAYDON HIGHWAY    A695

GARDEN TERR

Blaydon

Liby
COWEN RD

1 WESLEY CT
2 THE PRECINCT
3 THE UPPER PRECINCT

Blayd
Bsns

BROOMLEA CT 1
ABINGDON CT 2
JUNIPER CT 3
LAWRENCE CT 4
LYNWOOD AVE 5
SHOP SPOUTS 6
CHURCH TERR 7
CHEVIOT CT 8
SHIBDON CT 9
GARDEN TERR 10

St
Joseph's
RC Prim
Sch

St Thomas
More RC Sch

WHITMORE RD
DELACOUR RD
CLIFFORDS
THORNTON CRES
LAWRENCE AVE
CHESMOND DR
RUSHLEY CRES
BEDA HILL

WEST VIEW
MARY ST
THERESA ST
ST EVELYN TERR
 MABEL ST
ST CUTHBERTS WAY
CHAINBRIDGE RD
ST GEORGE

LOUP
MURRAY
ANN ST
HARRIET ST

LUCY ST
LARCH RD

BIRCH RD
ELM RD

Blaydon
Ind Pk

3

Shibdon
Bsns Pk    42

BLAYDON

63

Cemy

B6317

Shibdon Pond
Nature Reserv

TWIZELL AVE
IMOGEN LEA
BACK LA
LANECROSS RD
CROFTDALE RD
GREENBANK
BLAYDON BANK
WIDDRINGTON RD
RUTH AVE
ETHEL AVE
EDITH AVE
PARK AVE
ST EVELYN TERR
POLMAISE

MONARCH TERR
DENTON AVE

LABURNUM RD
CYPRESS RD
SYCAMORE RD
MAPLE RD
PINE RD
LINDEN RD
WILLOW RD

HAZEL RD
LAUREL RD

SHIBDON PARK VIEW
SHIBDON CRES

WOODLANDS PARK DR
BEXLEY CL
ASHLEIGH CL

SHIBDON
THE MEWS
THE AVENUE

2

WESTWAY
HEDDON VIEW
RIVER VIEW
HILLSIDE
WYLAM VIEW
HALLGARTH RD
ZION TERR
CROMWELL AVE
TOBLING AVE

PARK
AVE

SPRINGFIELD RD
HAWTHORN RD
CEDAR RD
BEECH TERR
LADYWELL RD
CROWLEY GDNS
WHITEWELL RD
WOODVALE RD
SHIBDON BANK

BRANTWOOD
CT

HIGH
AXWELL

WEST
ACRES
DENE
SIDE

BIRCHAM
DR

EAST
ACRES

CLAVERI

LANGDALE
CL
DAFODIL
CL
TULIP
CL
TYNEBANK

WEATHERSIDE
OLD LICHFIELD LA
STORE
MAY ST
CLARA ST
SIMONSIDE
TYNE ST
TYNE VIEW
PARKSIDE AVE

MYRTLE RD
POPLAR
ROCKMORE
RD

ASH ST
CONTENT ST

HADRIAN
GDNS

LIME ST
GREENRIGG
HOLYWELL

PARK
TERR

1 CLAVERING RD
2 OAK TERR

Clavering
House

Ax
P

ARTH CRES
MWELL
ARTH FARM RD
HILL TOP
BRANCH

6    5
8    4
PO
FRONT ST
RAMSAY ST

7
KNOWLEDGE
FLORENCE ST
WEST
NORTHLANDS
CALIFORNIA

Bleach
Green

NE21

FLORENCE ST
MAY ST
CLARA ST
EAST

PARKHEAD PARK GDNS
PARKHEAD PARK GDNS
EAST
PARKHEAD SQ

SOUTH
LEA

BERRYHILL
CL

3

Home
Farm

3 SPRINGWELL CL
4 CROFTWELL CL

62

1

CLAVER

Ax
Pa

GIBSIDE VIEW
DERWENT VIEW

Winlaton

RECTORY LA
THIRLMERE CRES
GRASMERE CRES
EMERDALE CRES
ESKDALE CRES
CONISTON CR
BUTTERM
CRES
WASKDALE CRES
WINDERMERE CRES
PARK LA
RYDAL CRES
SPA

A    18    B    53    C    19

Prim
Sch

SWINDALE CL
KIRKSTONE CL
WAGTAIL
CATHRA WAY
HELVELLYN CL
EAST LEA

Axwell Park

AXWELL PARK SCHOOL
HOS

WEST VIEW
DERWENT VIEW
PARKLAND AVE
PARK

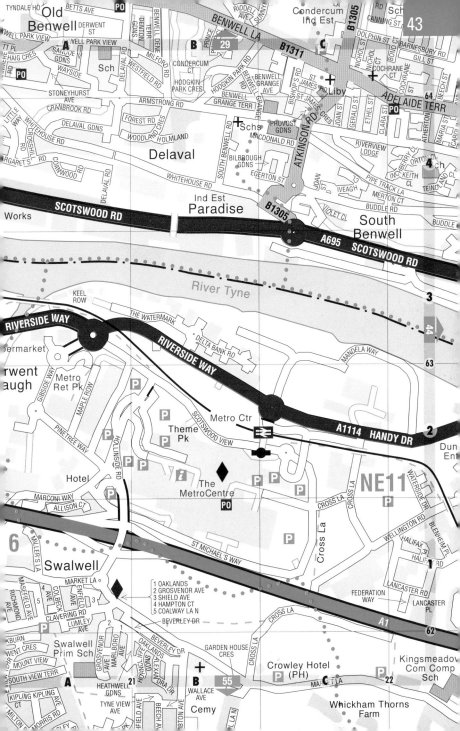

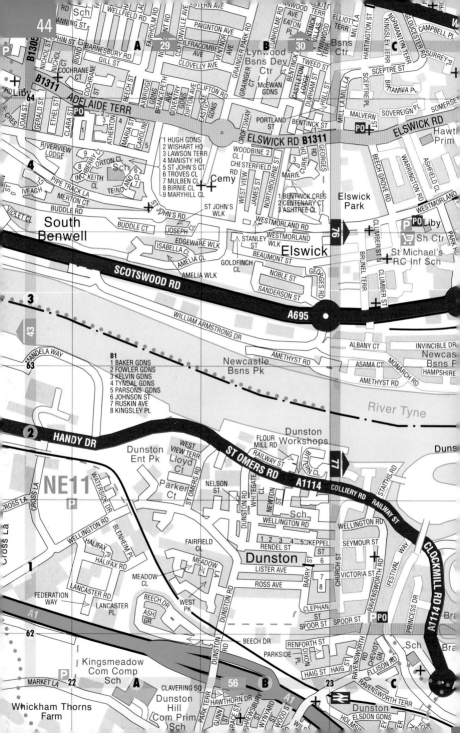

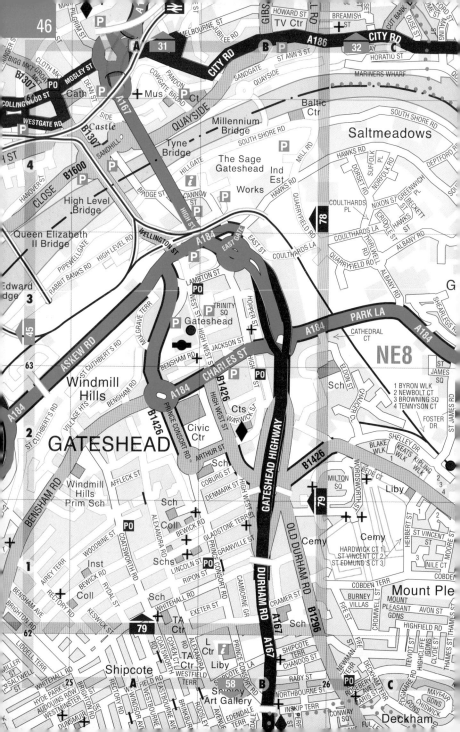

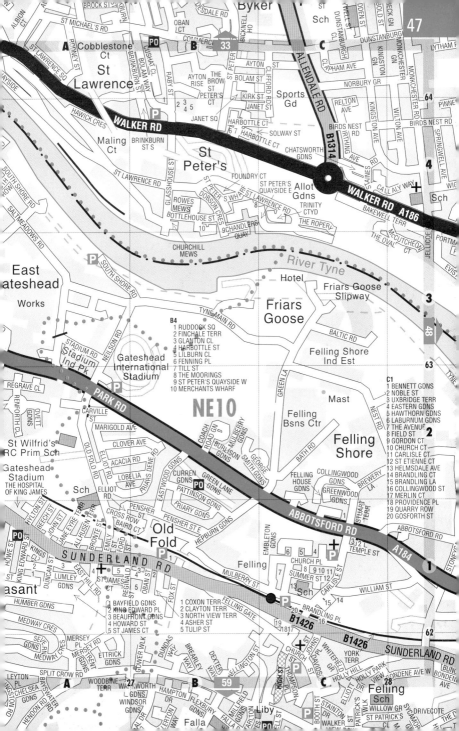

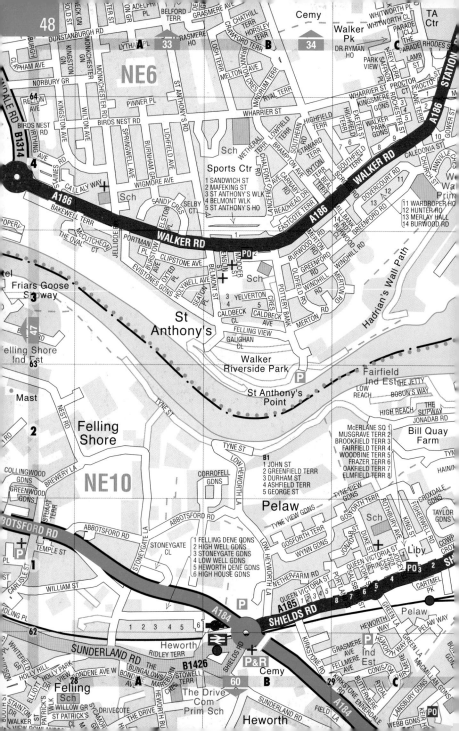

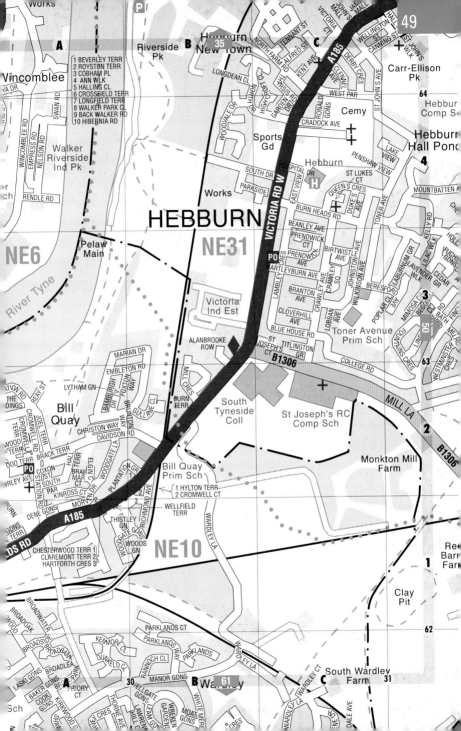

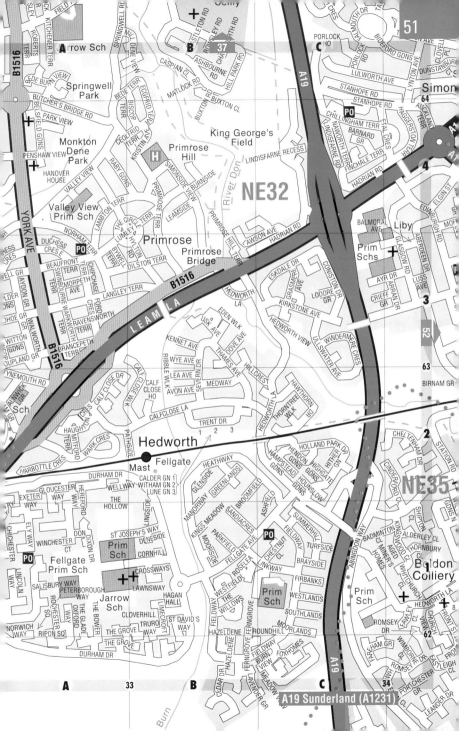

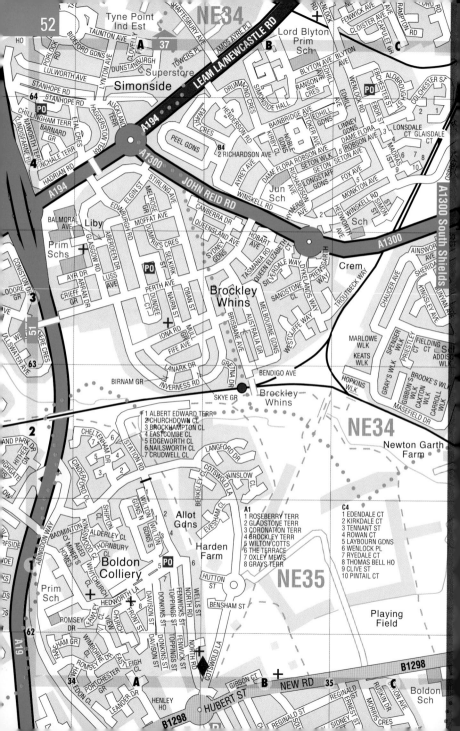

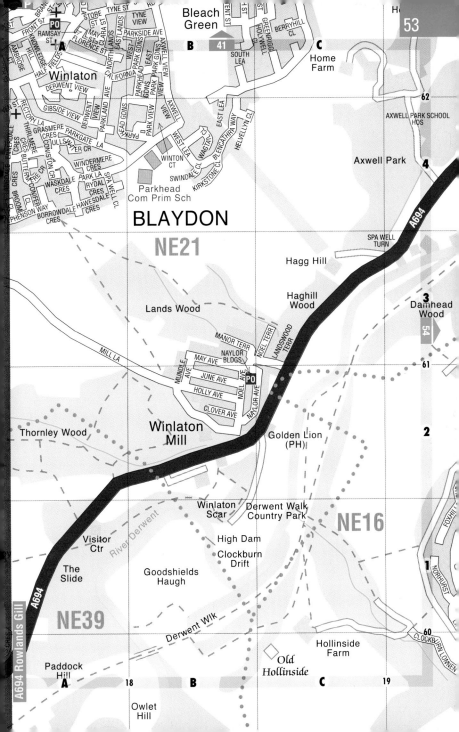

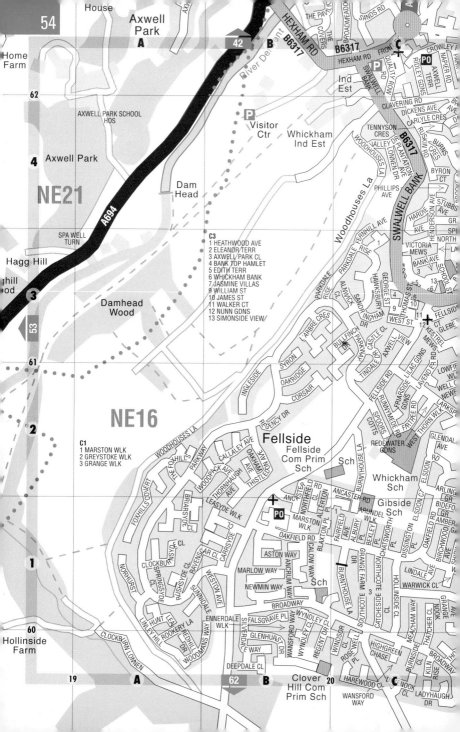

House
Axwell
Park
**A**
Home
Farm

62

**4** Axwell Park

**NE21**

Axwell Park School
Hos

SPA WELL
TURN

Hagg Hill

3

ghill
od

53

61

2

**NE16**

C1
1 MARSTON WLK
2 GREYSTOKE WLK
3 GRANGE WLK

1

60

Hollinside
Farm

19

42

River Derwent

B6317

HEXHAM RD

B6317
Hexham Rd

Ind
Est

P

Visitor
Ctr

Whickham
Ind Est

Dam
Head

Damhead
Wood

C3
1 HEATHWOOD AVE
2 ELEANOR TERR
3 AXWELL PARK CL
4 BANK TOP HAMLET
5 EDITH TERR
6 WHICKHAM BANK
7 JASMINE VILLAS
9 WILLIAM ST
10 JAMES ST
11 WALKER CT
12 NUNN GDNS
13 SIMONSIDE VIEW

THE PAV

THE COVERS

SANDS RD

QUALITY ROW

FRON

**C**

CROWLEY P

PO

NAPIER RD

RIDLEY GDNS

AXWELL
TERR

DICKENS AVE

CLAVERING RD

CARLYLE CRES

AVE

TENNYSON
CRES

VALLEY
DR

RUSKIN RD

BURNS
CRES

BYRON
CT

Woodhouses La

PLANTATION

LONNEN DR

WOODHOUSES LA

Phillips
Ave

HARDIE
AVE

HENDERSON AVE

STUBBS
AVE

GR

SP

NORTH

FERNHILL AVE

PARKDALE RISE

Victoria
Mews

BANK AVE

SCHOOL

SWALWELL BANK

PARKDALE
RISE

HAWKSBURY

SANDRINGHAM

GEORGE ST

THOMAS ST

WEST ST

5
6

10

12

FELLSID
CT GLEBE

KESTREL
MEWS

LOWFIR

WELL

NEWF

ALNWICK

ARBRE CRES

SYRON

OAKRIDGE

CORSAIR

BULLFINCH
DR

CASTLE CL

PARKWAY

AXWELL
VIEW

TINDALE DR

LILAC GDNS

LAVENDER RD

FRIARSIDE RD

FRITPEE RD

FELLSIDE RD

RUNNYMEDE RD

WEST THORN WLK

LARKSP

WEST
WELL

LOWFIR

INGLESIDE

REGENCY DR

Fellside

Fellside
Com Prim
Sch

REDEWATER
GDNS

SPOORS
COTTS

Sch

Whickham
Sch

Gibside
Sch

GLENDAL
AVE

RD

ARLING
GR

WOODHOUSES LA

PARKWAY

THE FOXHILLS

CALLALEY AVE

OAKHAM
AVE

THISTLE AVE

WOODPACK AVE

THORNHAUGH
AVE

LEASYDE WLK

ANCASTER
RD

NORTHFIELD CL

ALLERTON PL

ANCASTER RD

ARUNDEL
WLK

CHATSWORTH

DISSINGTON
DR

OAKFIELD RD

BIDEFO
GR

AMBER
G

BIRCHWOOD
AVE

FOXHILLS COVERT

BRIARSYDE

CL

BRIARSYDE

RUSHSYDE
CL

RAVENSCAR CL

CARRSYDE

OAKFIELD RD

BLAXTON PL

FAIRFIELD
DR

ALBURY
PL

BEXLEY
PL

Aston Way

MARSTON
WLK

Sch

CALOW WAY

ANGRUM
WAY

GRANGE FARM
DR

NORTHCOTE

LINDALE
DR

WARWICK CL

MEACHAM WAY

THATCHER CL

BROADWAY

CLOCKBURN

CL

SPRINGSYDE

SUNNIDALE

WESTON AVE

MARLOW WAY

NEWMIN WAY

BROADWAY

HOLLINSIDE RD

HOLLINSIDE WAY

CATCHWELL RD

SOUTHCOTE

KILN
RISE

BURNISDALE

NORTHURST

LINLEY HILL

HUNT LEA

ROOKERY LA

REDHILL

WOODMANS WAY

ENNERDALE
WLK

FALSGRAVE PL

SILVERDALE

GLENHURST
WAY

WYNDLEY CL

WINDSOR
CL

ROSE WELL
PL

HIGHGREEN
CHASE

GRANGE

NOOK

CLOCKBURN LONNEN

DEEPDALE CL

Clover
Hill Com
Prim Sch

WANSFORD
WAY

20

HAREWOOD CL

NOOK
CL

LADYHAUGH
DR

62

**B**

**C**

60

2

1

A694

Dam
Head

A

A

A

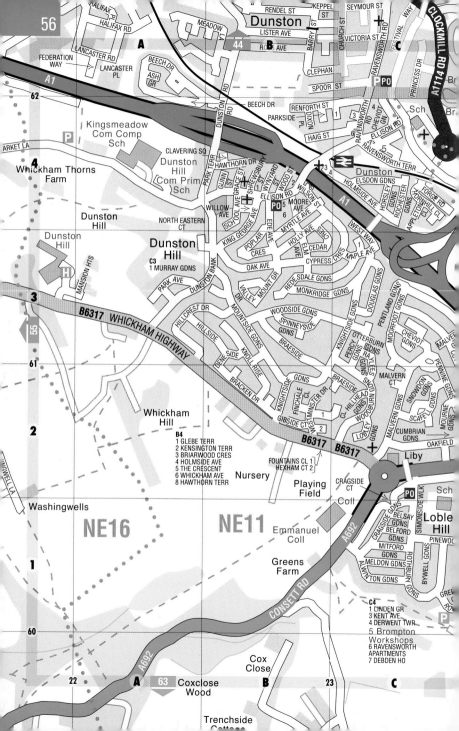

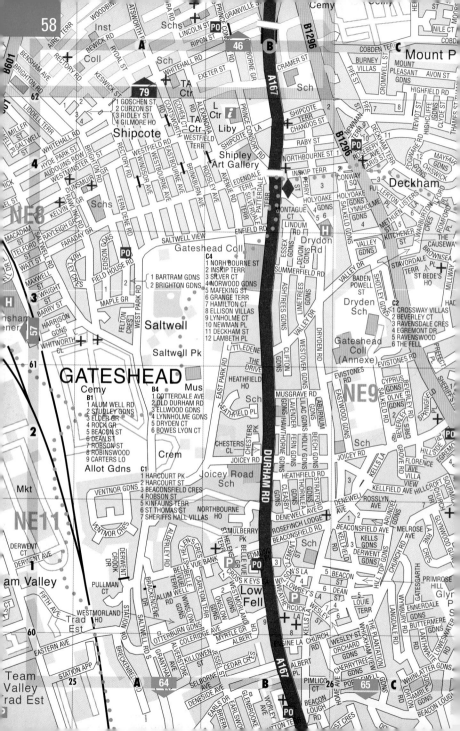

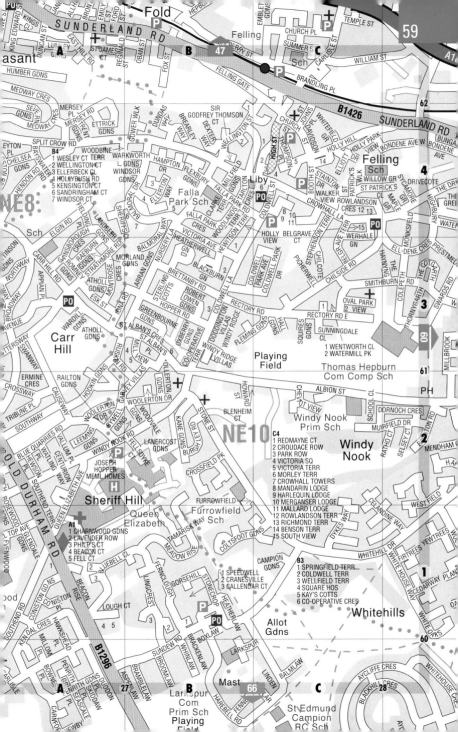

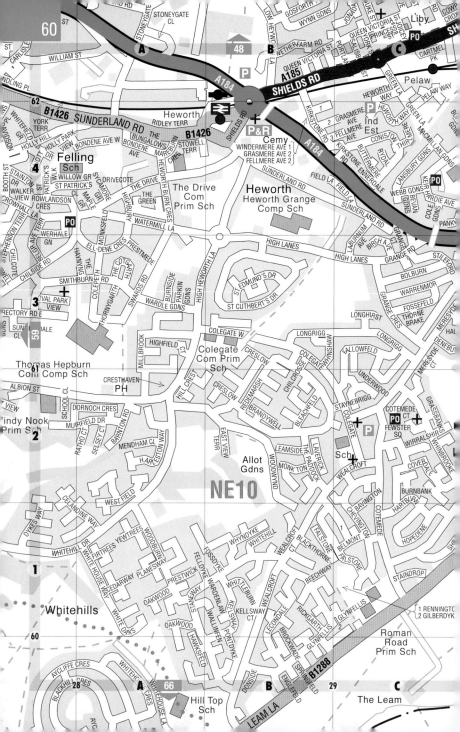

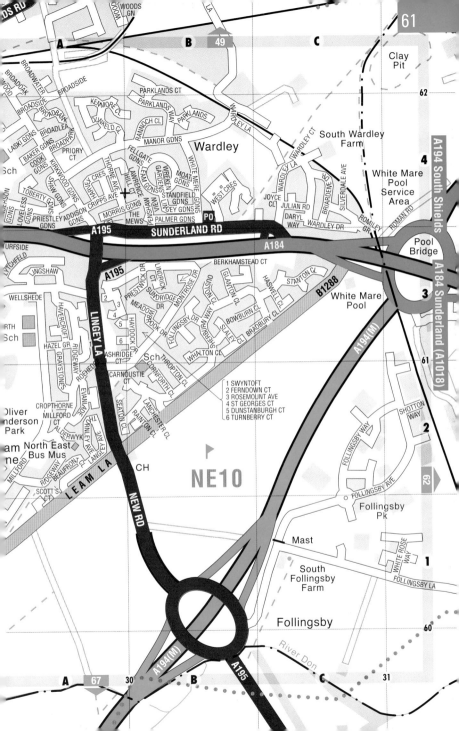

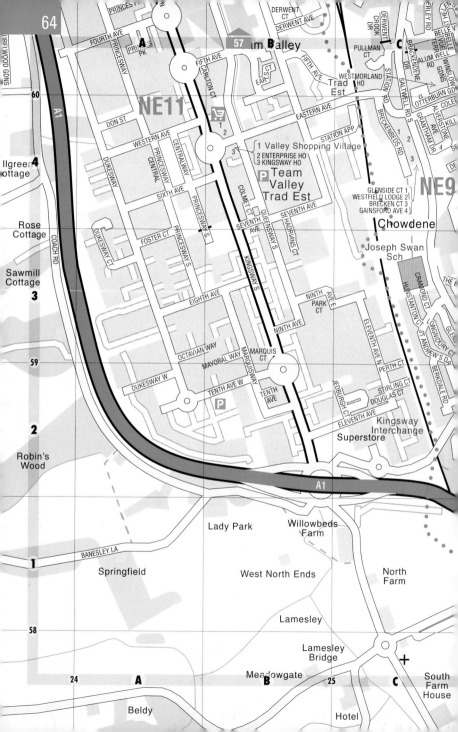

NE11

NE9

Team Valley Trad Est

1 Valley Shopping Village
2 ENTERPRISE HO
3 KINGSWAY HO

GLENSIDE CT 1
WESTFIELD LODGE 2
BRECKEN CT 3
GAINSFORD AVE 4

Chowdene

Joseph Swan Sch

Kingsway Interchange
Superstore

Robin's Wood

Lady Park

Willowbeds Farm

West North Ends

North Farm

Springfield

Lamesley

Lamesley Bridge

Meadowgate

Beldy

Hotel

South Farm House

Rose Cottage

Sawmill Cottage

llgreen Cottage

Team Balley

Westmorland Ho

Trad Est

A1

FOURTH AVE

FIFTH AVE

PRINCESWAY

DON ST

WESTERN AVE

CENTRALWAY

CENTRAL

DUKESWAY

PRINCESWAY

SIXTH AVE

PRINCESWAY S

FOSTER CT

DUKESWAY CT

DUKESWAY

EIGHTH AVE

OCTAVIAN WAY

DUKESWAY W

MAYORAL WAY

MARQUISWAY

TENTH AVE W

COACH RD

CARLTON CT

COLMET CT

SEVENTH AVE

QUEENSWAY S

KINGSWAY S

HADRIANS CT

SEVENTH AVE

NINTH AVE

NINTH PARK CT

MARQUIS CT

TENTH AVE

ELEVENTH AVE N

ELEVENTH AVE

PERTH CT

STIRLING CT

DOUGLAS CT

JEDBURGH CT

EASTERN AVE

STATION APP

STATION RD

SALTWELL RD S

BRECKENBEDS RD

HUNSTANTON CT

CRAMOND CT

LONGRIDDY CT

ST ANDREW'S DR

BERKDALE RD

DERWENT CT

DERWENT AVE

PULLMAN CT

DERWENT CROOK DR

BRACKENDENE

ALUM WELL RD

OTTERBURN GD

COLE

GRANTHAM DR

AVERSTONE

BANESLEY LA

60

59

58

4

3

2

1

24

A

B

25

C

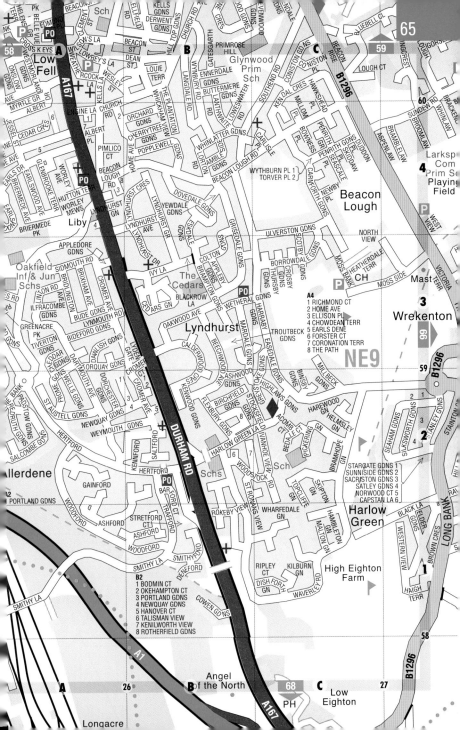

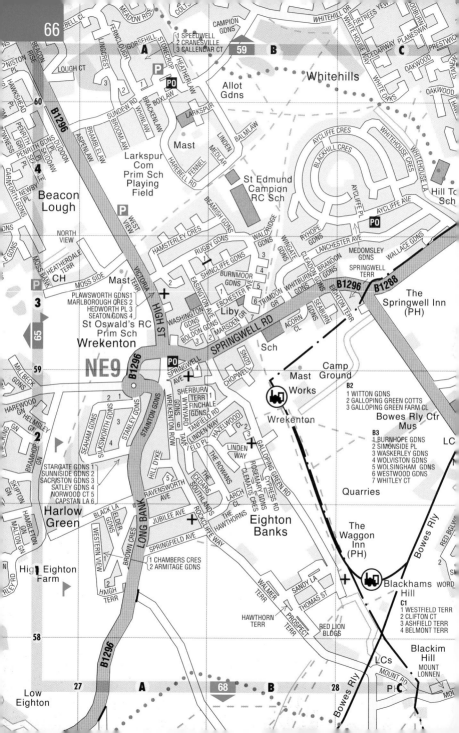

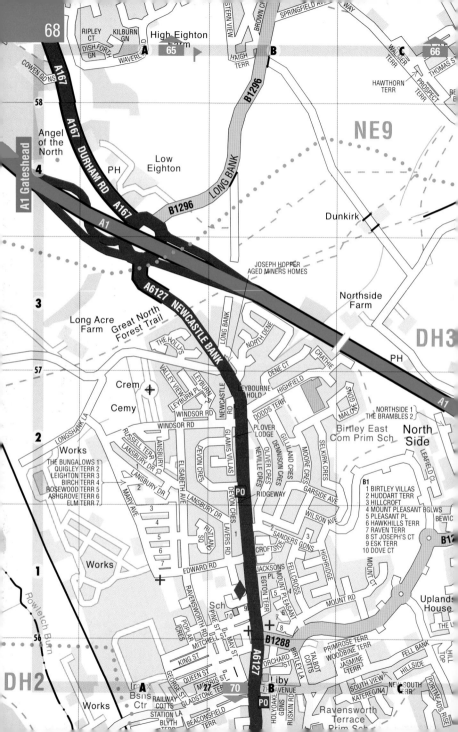

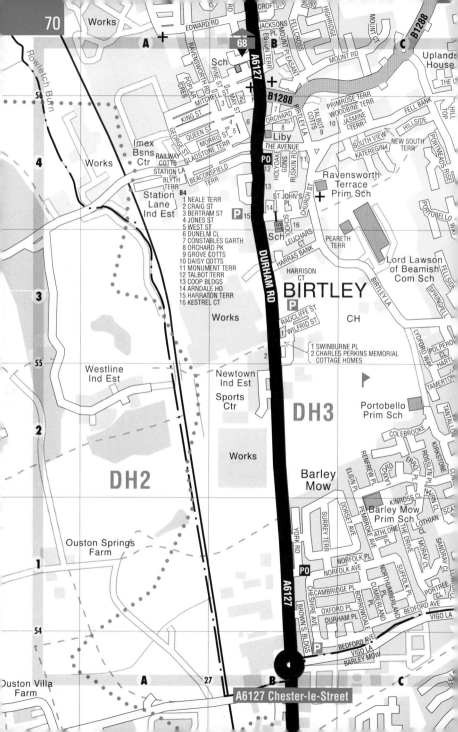

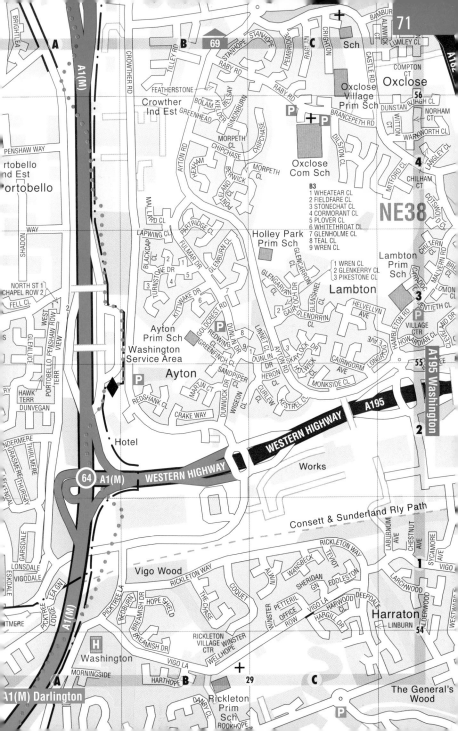

Scale: 7 inches to 1 mile

0 — 110 yards — 220 yards
0 — 125 m — 250 m

655

3

A167

B1318

P

CLAREMONT PL

NORTH TERR

Royal Victoria H

NEWCASTLE UPON TYNE

C 18

Town Moor

CLAREMONT TERR

FRAMLINGTON PL

FRAMLINGTON HO

RICHARDSON RD

NE2

1 CHIPPENDALE PL
2 CROSS SHERATON ST
3 CALANDRA CHASE
4 ASHTREE HO

CLAREMONT RD

WINDMILL CT

CLAREMONT ST

WALLACE ST

CHIMNEY MILLS

WINDMILL

5

4

3

2

1

MARRIS HO 1
OWEN CT 2
GOLDSBROUGH CT 3
LOWDON CT 4
ESTHER CAMPBELL CT 5

LIMEWOOD CT

MORPETH ST

CROSBY ST

MYERS ST

BURNSIDE

240

MILL HO

SHERATON ST

MAGDALENE CT

BELLE GROVE TERR

BELLE GROVE VILLAS

BELLE GROVE PL

Castle Leazes
(Halls of Residence)

B

MARY MAGDALENE BGLWS

HUNTER'S PL

SHERATON TERR

ANCRUM ST

PO

BELLE GROVE W

OXNAM CRES

BELLE GROVE

TA Ctr

Fenham Barracks

HOLY JESUS BGLWS

HUNTER'S MOOR CL

HUNTER'S RD

FOUNTAIN ROW

Spital Tongues

HOLLAND DR

BARRACK R

H

HUNTSMOOR HO

Hunter's Moor

Broadcasting Ctr

235 17

A167

Hunter's Moor

PONTELAND RD

GRANDSTAND RD

A189

FENHAM HALL DR

NE4

STUDLEY TERR

129

140

151

A

655

3

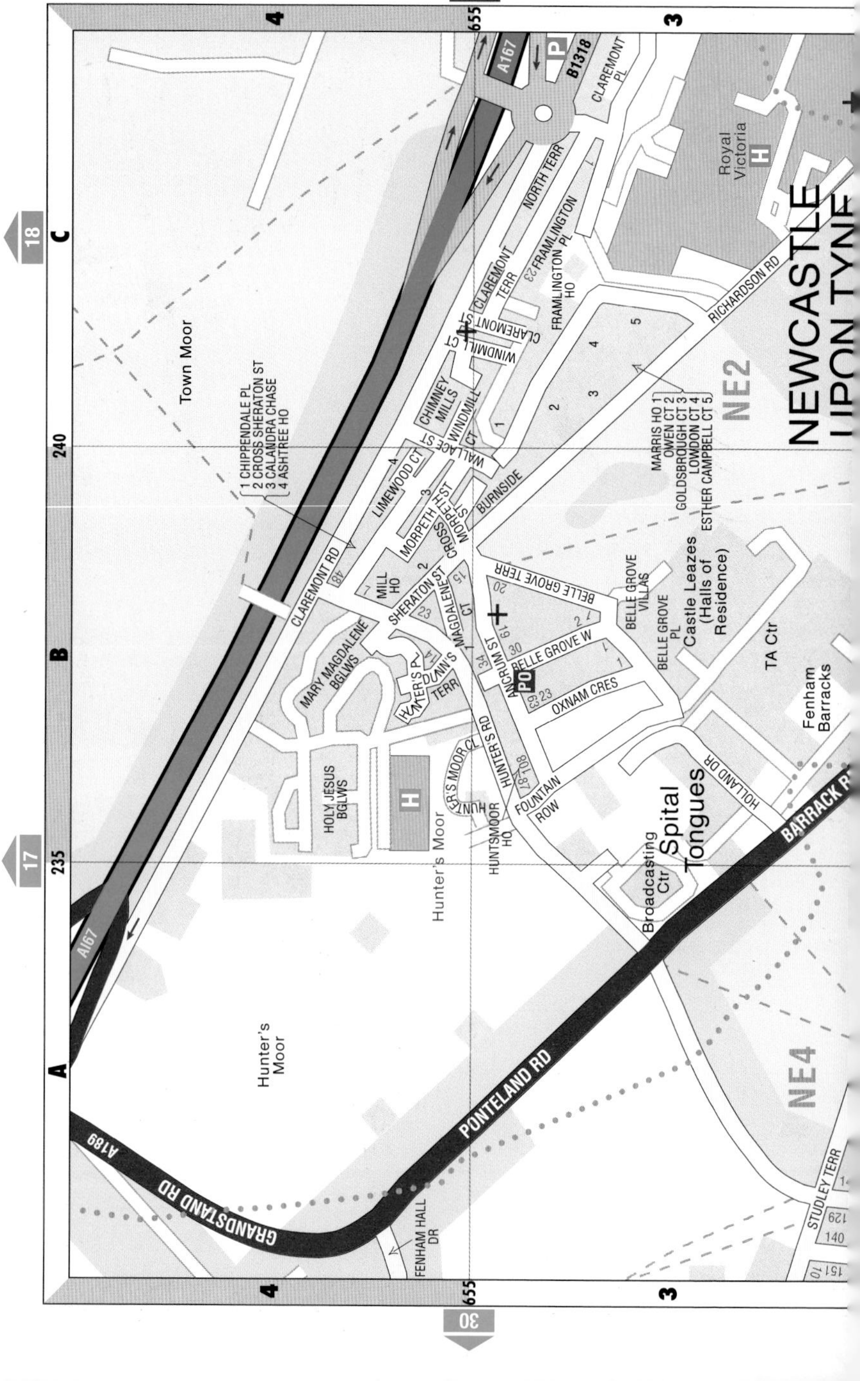

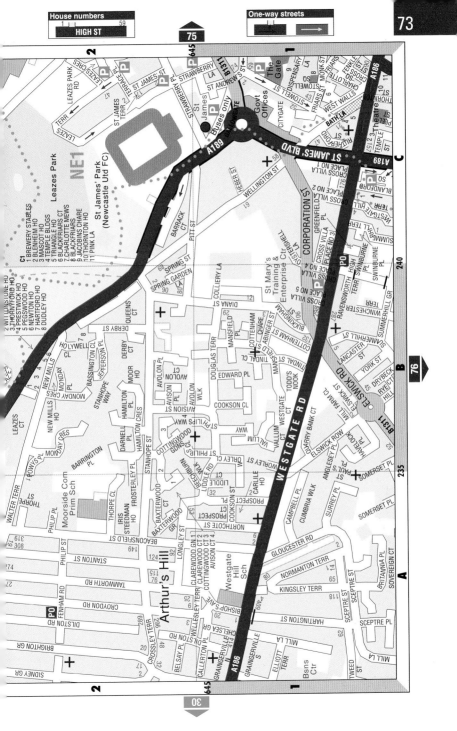

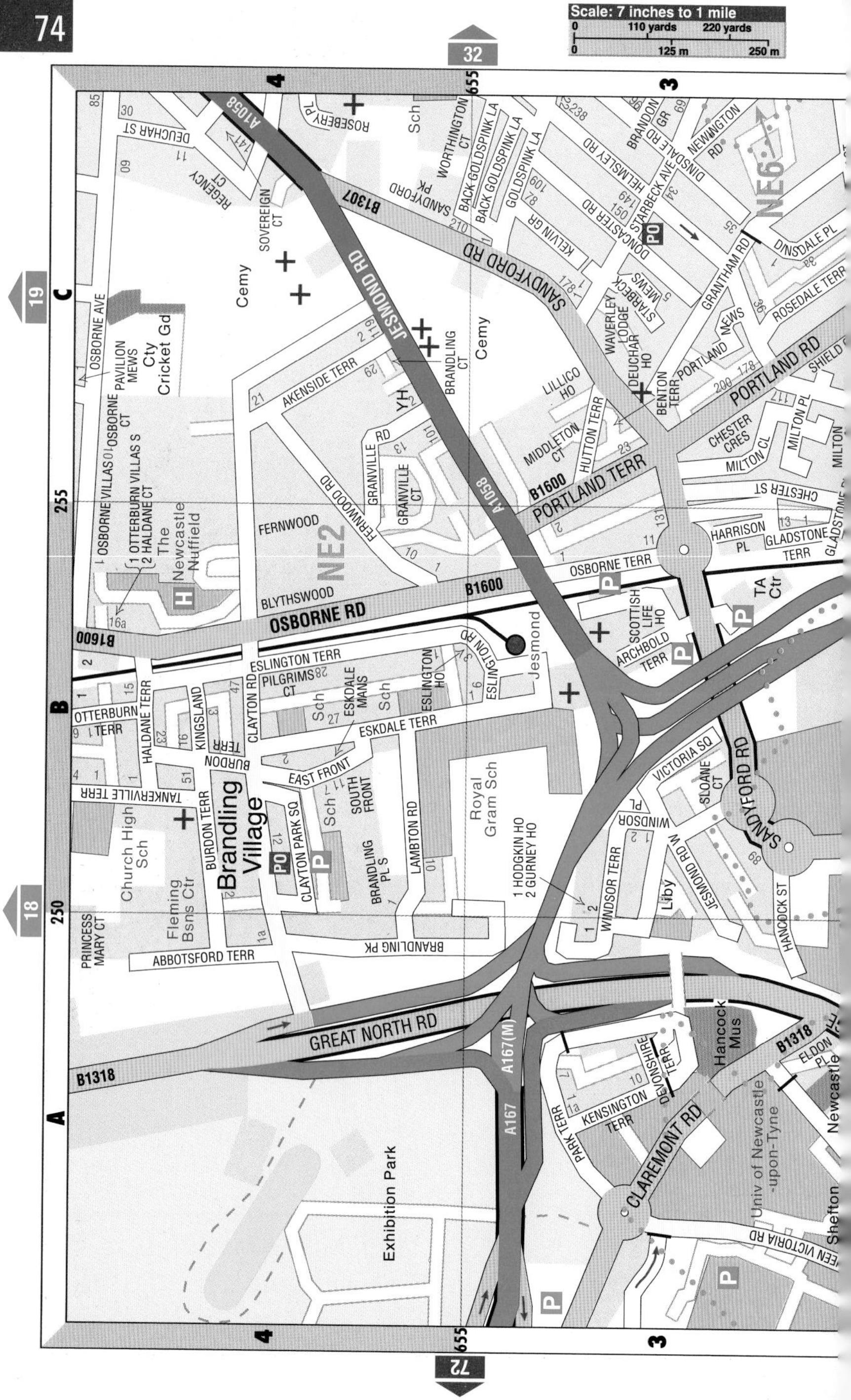

Scale: 7 inches to 1 mile
0
110 yards
220 yards
0
125 m
250 m
32
19
18
72
A
B
C
3
4
250
255
655
NE2
NE6
OSBORNE RD
B1600
JESMOND RD
A1058
B1307
SANDYFORD RD
PORTLAND TERR
PORTLAND RD
OSBORNE TERR
GREAT NORTH RD
B1318
A167(M)
A167
CLAREMONT RD
Brandling Village
Exhibition Park
Royal Gram Sch
Church High Sch
Fleming Bsns Ctr
The Newcastle Nuffield
Cty Cricket Gd
Cemy
Jesmond
Hancock Mus
Univ of Newcastle -upon-Tyne
Liby
TA Ctr
ABBOTSFORD TERR
BRANDLING PK
LAMBTON RD
BRANDLING PL S
SOUTH FRONT
EAST FRONT
ESKDALE TERR
ESKDALE MANS
CLAYTON PARK SQ
CLAYTON RD
PILGRIMS CT
ESLINGTON TERR
ESLINGTON RD
ESLINGTON HO
BURDON TERR
KINGSLAND
HALDANE TERR
OTTERBURN TERR
TANKERVILLE TERR
PRINCESS MARY CT
OSBORNE VILLAS
OTTERBURN VILLAS S
OSBORNE AVE
PAVILION MEWS
OSBORNE CT
1 OTTERBURN CT
2 HALDANE CT
BLYTHSWOOD
FERNWOOD
FERNWOOD RD
GRANVILLE RD
GRANVILLE CT
AKENSIDE TERR
BRANDLING CT
YH
SOVEREIGN CT
REGENCY CT
DEUCHAR ST
ROSEBERY PL
WORTHINGTON CT
BACK GOLDSPINK LA
GOLDSPINK LA
SANDYFORD PK
KELVIN GR
DONCASTER RD
HELMSLEY RD
BRANDON GR
DINSDALE RD
STARBECK AVE
STARBECK MEWS
NEWINGTON RD
GRANTHAM RD
DINSDALE PL
ROSEDALE TERR
WAVERLEY LODGE
DEUCHAR HO
LILLICO HO
MIDDLETON CT
HUTTON TERR
BENTON TERR
PORTLAND MEWS
CHESTER CRES
MILTON CL
MILTON PL
CHESTER ST
HARRISON PL
GLADSTONE TERR
SCOTTISH LIFE HO
ARCHBOLD TERR
VICTORIA SQ
SLOANE CT
WINDSOR PL
WINDSOR TERR
JESMOND RD W
1 HODGKIN HO
2 GURNEY HO
HANCOCK ST
DEVONSHIRE TERR
KENSINGTON TERR
PARK TERR
ELDON PL
Newcastle
QUEEN VICTORIA RD
Shefton
PO
P
H
Sch

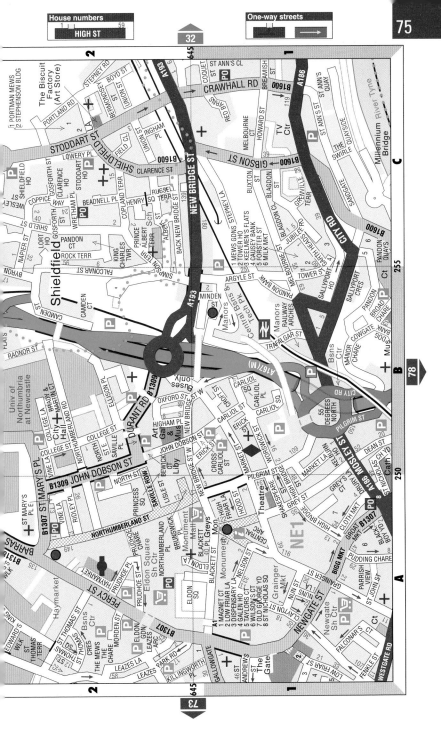

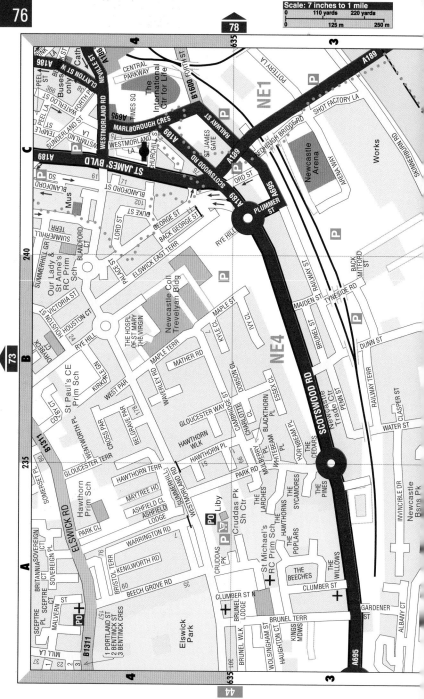

Scale: 7 inches to 1 mile

0   110 yards   220 yards
0   125 m   250 m

78

635

**C**  **4**  **3**

NE1

A189

POTTERY LA

SHOT FACTORY LA

Works

SKINNERBURN RD

SUNDERLAND

CLAYTON ST

A186

NEVILLE ST

A186

PEEL ST

WATERFORD ST

PEEL LA

TEMPLE ST

WESTMORLAND RD

Cath

CENTRAL PARKWAY

The International Ctr for Life

FORTH ST

B1600

RAILWAY ST

TIMES SQ

MARLBOROUGH CRES

WESTMORLAND LA

WESTMORLAND

WESTMORLAND RD

A695

CHURCHILL ST

A189

A189

ST JAMES GATE

REDHEUGH BRIDGE RD

A695

Newcastle Arena

ARENA WAY

BACK MITFORD ST

A189

SCOTSWOOD RD

ORD ST

A189

A695

PLUMMER ST

BLANDFORD SQ

Mus

BLANDFORD ST

DUKE ST

LORD ST

GEORGE ST

BACK GEORGE ST

RYE HILL

MAIDEN ST

RAILWAY ST

BRUNEL ST

TYNESIDE RD

DUNN ST

SUMMERHILL GR

SUMMERHILL TERR

BLANDFORD CT

PALACE ST

ELSWICK EAST TERR

Newcastle Coll Trevelyan Bldg

MAPLE CL

KYLE CL

IVY CL

NE4

RAILWAY TERR

CLASPER ST

WATER ST

Our Lady & St Anne's RC Prim Sch

VICTORIA ST

HOUSTON CT

DRECK ST

HOLISTON ST

RYE HILL

KIRKALE GN

THE HOSPL OF ST MARY THE VIRGIN

MAPLE TERR

MATHER RD

WAVERLEY RD

DOBSON CL

ESSEX CL

Newcastle Trade Ctr

PENN ST

**B**  **73**

235  240

COG CT

St Paul's CE Prim Sch

WENTWORTH PL

WEST PAR

BELGRANE PAR

CROSS PAR

GLOUCESTER WAY ST

CAMBRIDGE ST

CHARLOTTE CL

BLACKTHORN PL

WHITEBEAM PL

MULBERRY PL

HORNBEAM PL

THE CEDARS

THE PINES

INVINCIBLE DR

Newcastle Bsns Pk

SOMERSET PL

Hawthorn Prim Sch

GLOUCESTER TERR

HAWTHORN WLK

HAWTHORN PL

HAWTHORN TERR

SUMMERHILL ST

WESTMORLAND ST

PARK RD

THE LARCHES

THE HAWTHORNS

THE SYCAMORES

B1311

ELSWICK RD

PARK CL

MAYTREE HO

ASHFIELD CL

ASHFIELD LODGE

Liby

P0

Cruddas Pk Sh Ctr

WARRINGTON RD

BRISTOL TERR

KENILWORTH RD

BEECH GROVE RD

St Michael's RC Prim Sch

CRUDDAS PK

THE POPLARS

THE WILLOWS

GARDENER ST

**A**  **4**  **3**

SCEPTRE PL

BRITANNIA CT

SOVEREIGN CT

SOVEREIGN PL

MALVERN ST

SCEPTRE ST

PORTLAND ST

BENTINCK ST

BENTINCK CRES

P0

B1311

MILL LA

CLUMBER ST N

BRUNEL LODGE

Elswick Park

BRUNEL WLK

WOLSINGHAM ST

HAUGHTON CT

BRUNEL ST

BRUNEL TERR

KINGS MDWS

CLUMBER ST

THE BEECHES

A695

ALBANY CT

1 PORTLAND ST
2 BENTINCK ST
3 BENTINCK CRES

44

635

**3**

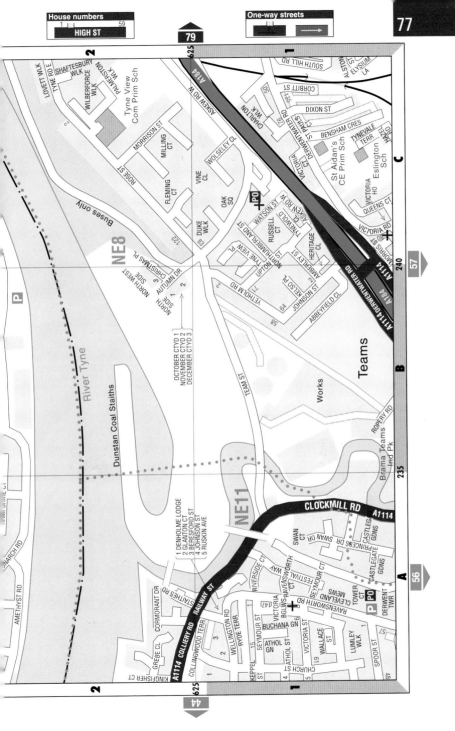

**Scale: 7 inches to 1 mile**

0  110 yards  220 yards
0  125 m  250 m

46

635

NEWCASTLE UPONTYNE

NE1

1 PINK LA
2 BEWICK ST

Baltic Ctr for Contemporary Art

Baltic Quay

BALTIC SQ

Millennium Bridge

SOUTH SHORE RD

QUARRYFIELD RD

MILL RD

HAWKS RD

Ind Est

Works

Works

PARK LA

A184

1 PRIORY CT
2 PARK CT
3 PEARETH CT

CLOISTER CT

LYCHGATE

MINSTER

The Sage Gateshead

EAST ST

East St

EAST GATE

A184

COULTHARDS

HOPPER LA

HOPPER PL

TRINITY

TRINITY SQ

191

242

NUNS LA

JACKSON ST

HIGH WE

34

HIGH WES

OAKWELLGATE

CANNON

Cts

B1600

QUAYSIDE

BROAD CHARE

BankMus

DOG

PEPPERCORN

BROAD GARTH

KING ST

LOMBARD ST

ST MARTINS CT

PILGRIM ST

A167

HILLGATE

Blue Anchor

Tyne Bridge

Swing Bridge

CHURCH ST

HIGH ST

BOTTLE BANK

WILLIAM

MIRK LA

BRIDGE ST

Hotel

WELLINGTON ST

HUDSON ST

B1307

HIGH LEVEL RD

PIPEWELLGATE

GRAND HOTEL ST

ASKEW RD

SWINBURNE PL

SWINBURNE ST

NELSON ST

LAMBTON ST

WEST ST

PO

ELLISON ST

SWAN ST

A184

MULGRAVE TERR

NITHBERT'S RD

ASKEW RD

Gateshead

Guildhall

WATERGATE

SANDHILL

ALL HALLOWS LA

SIDE

DEAN ST

AMEN CNR

Castle Mus

CASTLE GARTH

AKENSIDE

B1307

B1600

High Level Bridge

THE TURNBULL

QUEEN'S LA

CLAVERING PL

River Tyne

RABBIT BANKS RD

MELBOURNE CT 1
ADELAIDE CT 2
SYDNEY CT 3
BRISBANE CT 4

Greenesfield Bsns Ctr

Queen Elizabeth II Bridge

King Edward Bridge

New Redheugh Bridge

Buses only

250

255

i Cath

ST NICHOLAS' ST

A186

COLLINGWOOD ST

DENTON CHARE

STAMP EXCHANGE

14

WESTGATE RD

ORCHARD

ST

23

FORTH ST

ORCHARD ST

STEPHENSON'S ST

HANOVER ST

SOUTH ST

FORTH BANKS

FORTH PL

SKINNERBURN RD

COOKSON'S LA

POTTERY LA

GRAINGER ST

A186

NEVILLE ST

Newcastle Upon Tyne Central

Central

Newcastle Central

FORTH LA

36

2

75

4

635

3

250

4

635

3

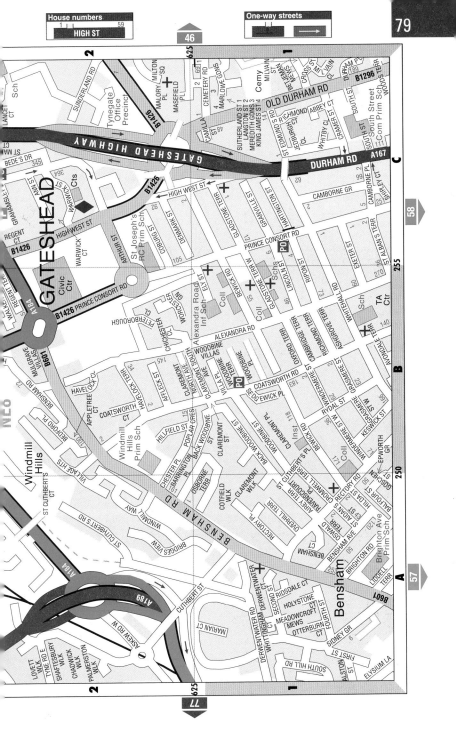

Street names are listed alphabetically and show the locality, the Postcode district, the page number and a reference to the square in which the name falls on the map page

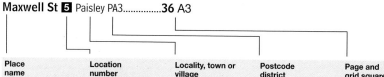

| Place name | Location number | Locality, town or village | Postcode district | Page and grid square |
|---|---|---|---|---|
| May be abbreviated on the map | Present when a number indicates the place's position in a crowded area of mapping | Shown when more than one place has the same name | District for the indexed place | Page number and grid reference for the standard mapping |

**Towns and villages** are listed in CAPITAL LETTERS

**Public and commercial buildings** are highlighted in magenta. **Places of interest** are highlighted in blue with a star ★

## Abbreviations used in the index

| | | | | | | | |
|---|---|---|---|---|---|---|---|
| Acad | **Academy** | Ct | **Court** | Hts | **Heights** | Pl | **Place** |
| App | **Approach** | Ctr | **Centre** | Ind | **Industrial** | Prec | **Precinct** |
| Arc | **Arcade** | Ctry | **Country** | Inst | **Institute** | Prom | **Promenade** |
| Ave | **Avenue** | Cty | **County** | Int | **International** | Rd | **Road** |
| Bglw | **Bungalow** | Dr | **Drive** | Intc | **Interchange** | Recn | **Recreation** |
| Bldg | **Building** | Dro | **Drove** | Junc | **Junction** | Ret | **Retail** |
| Bsns, Bus | **Business** | Ed | **Education** | L | **Leisure** | Sh | **Shopping** |
| Bvd | **Boulevard** | Emb | **Embankment** | La | **Lane** | Sq | **Square** |
| Cath | **Cathedral** | Est | **Estate** | Liby | **Library** | St | **Street** |
| Cir | **Circus** | Ex | **Exhibition** | Mdw | **Meadow** | Sta | **Station** |
| Cl | **Close** | Gd | **Ground** | Meml | **Memorial** | Terr | **Terrace** |
| Cnr | **Corner** | Gdn | **Garden** | Mkt | **Market** | TH | **Town Hall** |
| Coll | **College** | Gn | **Green** | Mus | **Museum** | Univ | **University** |
| Com | **Community** | Gr | **Grove** | Orch | **Orchard** | Wk, Wlk | **Walk** |
| Comm | **Common** | H | **Hall** | Pal | **Palace** | Wr | **Water** |
| Cott | **Cottage** | Ho | **House** | Par | **Parade** | Yd | **Yard** |
| Cres | **Crescent** | Hospl | **Hospital** | Pas | **Passage** | | |
| Cswy | **Causeway** | HQ | **Headquarters** | Pk | **Park** | | |

## Index of towns, villages, streets, hospitals, industrial estates, railway stations, schools, shopping centres, universities and places of interest

### 80    Abb–Ale

**A**

Abbey Ct NE8 . . . . . . . . . 79 C1
**Abbey Dr**
  Jarrow NE32 . . . . . . . . . . 37 A3
  Newcastle-u-T NE5 . . . . . 13 C4
Abbeyfield Cl NE8 . . . . . 77 B1
Abbeyvale Dr NE6 . . . . . 34 C3
Abbot Ct NE8 . . . . . . . . . 78 C3
Abbotsford Rd NE10 . . . 47 C1
Abbotside Pl NE5 . . . . . . 14 B2
Abbotsmeade Cl NE5 . . . 29 A4
Abbots Way NE16 . . . . . 55 A3
Abercorn Rd NE15 . . . . . 28 B1
Abercrombie Pl **2** NE15 . 15 C2
Aberdeen Ct NE3 . . . . . . . 7 B4
Aberdeen Dr NE32 . . . . . 52 A3
Aberford Cl NE15 . . . . . . 13 C3
Abigail Ct NE3 . . . . . . . . . 9 C1
**Abingdon Ct**
  Blaydon NE21 . . . . . . . . 41 B3
  Newcastle-u-T NE7 . . . . . 7 B3
Abingdon Rd NE6 . . . . . . 34 C3
Acacia Gr NE31 . . . . . . . 50 A4

Acacia Rd NE10 . . . . . . . 47 A2
Acanthus Ave NE4 . . . . . 29 B3
Acomb Cres NE3 . . . . . . . 8 B4
Acomb Ct NE9 . . . . . . . . 65 C2
Acomb Gdns NE5 . . . . . . 16 A1
Acorn Ave NE8 . . . . . . . . 57 B4
Acorn Cl NE9 . . . . . . . . . 66 B3
Acorn Rd NE2 . . . . . . . . . 18 C2
Acton Pl NE7 . . . . . . . . . . 19 C2
Acton Rd NE5 . . . . . . . . . 28 A4
Adair Ave NE15 . . . . . . . 29 A2
Adair Way NE31 . . . . . . . 36 B1
Adamsez Ind Est NE15 . . 42 B4
Adderstone Cres NE2 . . . 19 A2
Adderstone Ct NE2 . . . . . 19 A3
**ADDISON** . . . . . . . . . . . 26 A1
Addison Cl **2** NE6 . . . . . 32 C2
Addison Ct **7** NE28 . . . . 23 B1
Addison Gdns NE10 . . . . 61 A4
**Addison Ind Est**
  Ryton NE21 . . . . . . . . . . 26 A1
  Ryton NE21 . . . . . . . . . . 26 B1
**Addison Rd**
  Newcastle-u-T, Lemington
  NE15 . . . . . . . . . . . . . . 28 A3
  **15** Newcastle-u-T NE6 . . 32 C2
Addison Wlk NE34 . . . . . 52 C3

Addycombe Terr NE6 . . . 20 A1
Adelaide Ct NE8 . . . . . . . 78 B3
**Adelaide Ctr The 5**
  NE4 . . . . . . . . . . . . . . . 29 C1
Adelaide Ho **3** NE4 . . . 29 C1
Adelaide Gdns NE1 . . . . 17 B3
Adelaide Terr NE4 . . . . . 44 A4
Adeline Gdns NE3 . . . . . 17 B3
Adelphi Pl NE6 . . . . . . . . 33 C1
Affleck St NE8 . . . . . . . . 79 B2
Afton Way NE3 . . . . . . . . . 7 C2
**Aged Miners' Homes**
  Boldon Colliery NE35 . . . 51 C1
  Brunswick Village NE13 . . 2 A2
  **2** Newcastle-u-T NE5 . . 14 C3
  Ryton NE40 . . . . . . . . . . 40 A4
  Sunniside NE16 . . . . . . . 62 B1
Agincourt NE31 . . . . . . . 35 B3
Agnes Maria St NE3 . . . . . 8 B1
Agricola Rd NE4 . . . . . . . 30 A2
Aidan Cl NE13 . . . . . . . . . 2 A2
**Aidan Ct**
  Jarrow NE32 . . . . . . . . . 37 B2
  Longbenton NE7 . . . . . . 11 A1
Aidan Wlk NE3 . . . . . . . . . 9 C1
Ainsdale Gdns NE5 . . . . 14 A2
Ainslie Pl NE5 . . . . . . . . 16 A2
Ainsworth Ave NE34 . . . 52 C3
Ainthorpe Gdns NE7 . . . 20 A4

Aintree Gdns NE8 . . . . . 57 B3
**Airey Terr**
  Gateshead NE8 . . . . . . . 79 A1
  Newcastle-u-T NE6 . . . . 34 B1
Airport Freightway NE13  3 C2
Airport Ind Est NE3 . . . . . 7 B2
Airport Sta NE13 . . . . . . . 3 B3
Aisgill Dr NE5 . . . . . . . . . 14 A1
Akeld Ct NE3 . . . . . . . . . 18 C4
Akenside Hill NE1 . . . . . 78 B4
Akenside Ho NE1 . . . . . . 78 B4
Akhurst Sch NE2 . . . . . . 19 A2
Alanbrooke Row NE31 . . 49 B3
Albany Ave NE12 . . . . . . 11 B3
Albany Ct NE4 . . . . . . . . 76 A3
Albany Mews NE3 . . . . . 17 B2
Albany Rd NE8 . . . . . . . . 46 C3
Albemarle Ave NE2 . . . . 18 B3
Albert Ave **9** NE28 . . . . 21 C2
Albert Dr NE9 . . . . . . . . . 65 A4
**Albert Edward Terr**
  NE35 . . . . . . . . . . . . . . 52 A2
Albert Pl NE9 . . . . . . . . . 65 A4
**Albert Rd**
  Jarrow NE32 . . . . . . . . . 36 B2
  Jarrow NE32 . . . . . . . . . 36 C2
Albert St NE31 . . . . . . . . 35 B2
Albion Ct NE6 . . . . . . . . . 32 C1

**Albion Row**
  Newcastle-u-T NE6 . . . . 32 C2
  Newcastle-u-T, St Lawrence
  NE6 . . . . . . . . . . . . . . . 32 C1
Albion St NE10 . . . . . . . . 59 C2
Albion Terr **6** NE9 . . . . 67 A1
Albury Pl NE16 . . . . . . . . 54 C1
Albury Rd NE2 . . . . . . . . 18 C3
Alcroft Ct NE5 . . . . . . . . 13 C3
Alder Ave NE4 . . . . . . . . 29 B4
Alderburgh Ave NE15 . . . 27 A4
Alderley Cl NE35 . . . . . . 52 A1
Alderley Rd NE9 . . . . . . . 58 A1
Alderney Gdns NE5 . . . . 14 A2
Alderwood Cres NE6 . . . 21 A1
Alderwyk NE10 . . . . . . . . 61 A2
Aldsworth Cl NE9 . . . . . . 67 B1
Aldwick Rd NE15 . . . . . . 28 B1
Alexander Terr NE13 . . . . 2 A1
Alexandra Dr NE16 . . . . . 55 B4
Alexandra Gdns NE40 . . . 40 A4
**Alexandra Rd**
  Gateshead NE8 . . . . . . . 79 B1
  Newcastle-u-T NE6 . . . . 19 C1
**Alexandra Road Inf Sch**
  NE8 . . . . . . . . . . . . . . . 79 B1
Alexandra St NE28 . . . . . 22 A2

**Alexandra Terr**
15 Springwell NE9 . . . . . .67 A1
Sunniside NE16 . . . . . . . .63 A2
Alford Gn NE12 . . . . . . . .11 A3
**Alfred St**
Hebburn NE31 . . . . . . . . .9 A1
Newcastle-u-T NE6 . . . . . .33 C2
Algernon Cl 14 NE6 . . . . .33 A3
Algernon Ct 17 NE6 . . . . .33 A3
**Algernon Rd**
15 Newcastle-u-T, Heaton
NE6 . . . . . . . . . . . . . . . .33 A3
Newcastle-u-T, Lemington
NE15 . . . . . . . . . . . . . .27 A2
Alice St NE21 . . . . . . . . . .41 A1
Alison Ct 4 NE6 . . . . . . . .32 C3
Allandale Ave NE12 . . . . .11 B3
Allan Ho NE4 . . . . . . . . . .30 A4
Allchurch NE15 . . . . . . . .28 C2
Allen Ave NE11 . . . . . . . .57 C3
Allendale Ave NE6 . . . . . .21 C4
Allendale Rd NE6 . . . . . . .33 B1
Allendale Terr NE6 . . . . . .34 A1
Allenheads NE5 . . . . . . . .14 C1
Allen Terr NE40 . . . . . . . .38 B4
Allerdean Cl NE15 . . . . . .28 C4
**ALLERDENE** . . . . . . . . .65 A2
Allerdene Wlk NE16 . . . . .55 A2
Allerton Gdns NE6 . . . . . .20 B2
Allerton Pl NE16 . . . . . . . .54 B1
Alerwash NE5 . . . . . . . . .14 C1
All Hallows La NE1 . . . . . .78 B4
Allhusen Terr NE8 . . . . . . .47 A1
Allingham Ct NE7 . . . . . . .20 C3
Allison Ct NE16 . . . . . . . .43 A1
Allonby Way NE5 . . . . . . .28 C4
All Saints Coll NE5 . . . . . .14 C2
Allwork Terr NE16 . . . . . .55 A3
Alma Terr NE40 . . . . . . . .39 B2
Almond Cres NE8 . . . . . . .67 B4
Almond Pl NE4 . . . . . . . . .29 B3
Almshouses NE15 . . . . . .26 A3
Aln Ave NE3 . . . . . . . . . . .8 B3
Aln Cres NE3 . . . . . . . . . .8 B3
Aln Gr NE15 . . . . . . . . . . .27 A3
Aln Gr NE15 . . . . . . . . . . .27 A3
Alnham Ct NE3 . . . . . . . . .7 C3
Alnham Gr NE5 . . . . . . . .14 A2
Almouth Ave NE29 . . . . . .24 B4
Alnmouth Dr NE3 . . . . . . .18 C4
Aln St NE31 . . . . . . . . . . .35 B2
Alnwick Ave NE29 . . . . . .24 B4
Alnwick Cl NE16 . . . . . . . .54 C3
Alnwick Gr NE32 . . . . . . . .51 A2
**Alnwick St**
Newburn NE15 . . . . . . . .26 A4
Wallsend NE28 . . . . . . . .22 A2
Alnwick Terr NE13 . . . . . . .2 C3
Aln Wlk NE3 . . . . . . . . . . .8 B2
Alston Ave NE6 . . . . . . . .33 C2
Alston Cl NE28 . . . . . . . . .23 B4
Alston Gdns NE15 . . . . . .12 B3
Alston St NE8 . . . . . . . . . .79 A1
Altan Pl NE12 . . . . . . . . . .10 C3
**Alum Well Rd**
1 Gateshead, Low Fell
NE9 . . . . . . . . . . . . . . . .58 B1
Gateshead NE9 . . . . . . . .58 A1
Alverston Cl NE15 . . . . . .27 A4
Alverstone Ave NE9 . . . . .64 C4
Alwin NE38 . . . . . . . . . . .71 C1
**Alwin Grange**
Hebburn NE31 . . . . . . . .36 A3
Jarrow NE32 . . . . . . . . . .36 B3
Alwinton Cl NE5 . . . . . . . .15 B4
Alwinton Gdns NE11 . . . . .56 C1
Alwinton Terr NE3 . . . . . . .9 B1
Ambergate Cl NE5 . . . . . .15 B3
Amberley Cl NE28 . . . . . .23 B3
Amberley Gdns NE7 . . . . .20 A2
Amberley St NE8 . . . . . . .77 C1
Amberley Wlk NE16 . . . . .55 A1
Amble Cl NE29 . . . . . . . . .24 C4
Amble Gr NE2 . . . . . . . . . .32 B3
Ambleside NE15 . . . . . . . .12 C3
Ambleside Gdns NE9 . . . .65 B4
Ambleside Gn NE5 . . . . . .28 C4
Amble Way NE3 . . . . . . . . .8 A1
Ambridge Way NE3 . . . . . .8 A1
Ambrose Ct NE21 . . . . . . .41 A1
Ambrose Pl NE6 . . . . . . . .34 C2

Amec Dr NE28 . . . . . . . . .23 B1
Amec Way NE28 . . . . . . . .22 C1
Amelia Cl NE4 . . . . . . . . .44 A3
Amelia Wlk NE4 . . . . . . . .44 A3
Amen Cnr NE1 . . . . . . . . .78 B4
Amersham Pl 1 NE5 . . . .15 C2
Amesbury Cl NE5 . . . . . . .13 C3
Amethyst Rd NE4 . . . . . . .77 A2
Amherst Rd NE3 . . . . . . . .7 C2
Ancaster Ave NE12 . . . . .10 C2
Ancaster Rd NE16 . . . . . .54 B2
Ancroft Pl NE5 . . . . . . . . .28 C4
Ancroft Way NE3 . . . . . . . .8 A4
Ancrum Way NE16 . . . . . .54 B1
Andrew Ct 4 NE6 . . . . . .34 B2
Anfield Ct NE3 . . . . . . . . . .7 C1
Anfield Rd NE3 . . . . . . . . .7 C1
Angerton Gdns 9 NE5 . .29 B4
Anglesey Gdns NE5 . . . . .14 A2
Angle Terr NE28 . . . . . . . .23 A2
Angram Wlk 1 NE5 . . . . .14 A1
Angus Cres NE29 . . . . . . .24 B3
Angus Rd NE8 . . . . . . . . .57 B4
**Ann St**
Blaydon NE21 . . . . . . . . .41 B3
Gateshead NE8 . . . . . . . .79 C2
Hebburn NE31 . . . . . . . .35 A3
Annville Cres NE6 . . . . . .48 C4
Ann Wlk NE6 . . . . . . . . . .48 C4
Anscomb Gdns NE7 . . . . .19 B2
Anson Pl NE5 . . . . . . . . . .15 A3
Antrim Cl NE5 . . . . . . . . .16 A3
Apperley Cl NE5 . . . . . . . .14 C1
Apperley Ave NE3 . . . . . .16 A4
**Appian Pl**
Gateshead NE9 . . . . . . . .59 A3
Throckley NE15 . . . . . . . .12 C2
Appleby Ct NE12 . . . . . . .10 C2
**Appleby Gdns**
Gateshead NE9 . . . . . . . .65 B3
Wallsend NE28 . . . . . . . .23 B4
Apple Cl NE15 . . . . . . . . .27 A4
Appledore Gdns NE9 . . . .65 A3
Appleton Cl NE11 . . . . . . .56 C4
Appletree Ct NE8 . . . . . . .79 B2
Appletree Gdns NE6 . . . . .21 A1
Apsley Cres NE3 . . . . . . . .7 C1
**Archbishop Runcie CE Fst**
Sch NE3 . . . . . . . . . . . . . .9 B1
Archer St NE28 . . . . . . . .22 C3
Archer Villas NE28 . . . . . .22 B3
Archibald Fst Sch NE3 . . . .9 A1
Archibald St NE3 . . . . . . . .9 A1
Arcot Dr NE5 . . . . . . . . . .28 A4
Arden Ave NE3 . . . . . . . . .4 B1
Arden Cres NE5 . . . . . . . .16 B1
Arena Way NE4 . . . . . . . .76 C3
Argus Cl NE11 . . . . . . . . .57 A3
Argyle St NE31 . . . . . . . . .35 B3
Arkleside Pl NE5 . . . . . . . .14 B1
**Arkle St**
Gateshead NE8 . . . . . . . .57 B4
Hazlerigg NE13 . . . . . . . . .4 A4
Arkwright St NE8 . . . . . . .57 C3
Arlington Ave NE3 . . . . . .17 A3
Arlington Ct NE3 . . . . . . . .17 B3
Arlington Gr NE16 . . . . . .54 C2
Arlington Rd NE31 . . . . . .50 B4
Arlott Ho NE7 . . . . . . . . . .20 B3
Armitage Gdns NE9 . . . . .66 A1
Armstrong Ave NE6 . . . . .19 C1
Armstrong Ind Est NE37 . .60 C2
**Armstrong Rd**
Newcastle-u-T NE15,
NE4 . . . . . . . . . . . . . . . .43 B4
Wallsend NE28 . . . . . . . .23 B1
Washington NE37 . . . . . .69 C3
Armstrong St NE8 . . . . . . .57 C3
Arncliffe Gdns NE5 . . . . . .14 A2
Arndale Arc 9 NE32 . . . .36 C3
**Arndale Ho**
14 Birtley DH3 . . . . . . .70 B4
Newcastle-u-T NE3 . . . . . .7 C1
Arndale Sq NE12 . . . . . . .10 B2
Arnside Wlk NE5 . . . . . . .14 A2
Arran Dr NE32 . . . . . . . . .52 A3
Arran Gdns NE10 . . . . . . .59 B3
Arthur Cook Ave NE16 . . .55 B2
**Arthur St**
Gateshead NE8 . . . . . . . .79 C2
Jarrow NE32 . . . . . . . . . .36 C2
Arundel Cl NE13 . . . . . . . .2 A1

**Arundel Ct**
Longbenton NE12 . . . . . .10 B2
Newcastle-u-T NE3 . . . . . .7 A3
Arundel Dr NE15 . . . . . . .27 C3
Arundel Gdns NE5 . . . . . .8 C1
Arundel Wlk NE16 . . . . . .54 C1
Asama Ct NE4 . . . . . . . . .76 A3
Ascham House Sch NE3 . .18 A4
Ascot Cres NE8 . . . . . . . .57 B3
Ascot Ct NE3 . . . . . . . . . . .7 A3
Ascott Ct NE12 . . . . . . . . .10 C2
Ascot Wlk NE3 . . . . . . . . .7 A3
Ashbourne Ave NE6 . . . . .34 A2
Ashbourne Rd NE32 . . . . .37 A1
Ashbrooke Gdns NE28 . . .22 C3
Ashbrooke St NE3 . . . . . .16 C3
Ashburton Rd NE3 . . . . . .17 B4
Ashcroft Dr NE12 . . . . . . .11 C3
Ashdale Cres NE5 . . . . . .14 B1
Ashdown Cl NE12 . . . . . . .10 C3
Ashdown Way NE12 . . . . .10 C3
Asher St NE10 . . . . . . . . .47 B1
Ashfield NE32 . . . . . . . . . .51 C2
Ashfield Ave NE16 . . . . . .55 B4
Ashfield Cl NE4 . . . . . . . .76 A4
Ashfield Gdns NE28 . . . . .21 B3
Ashfield Lodge NE4 . . . . .76 A4
Ashfield Pk NE5 . . . . . . . .55 A4
**Ashfield Rd**
Newcastle-u-T NE3 . . . . . .17 B4
Whickham NE16 . . . . . . .55 A1
Ashfield Rise NE16 . . . . . .55 A1
**Ashfield Terr**
4 Gateshead NE10 . . . . .48 B1
Ryton NE40 . . . . . . . . . . .25 A1
3 Springwell NE9 . . . . . .66 C1
Ashford NE9 . . . . . . . . . . .65 B1
Ashford Gr NE5 . . . . . . . .13 C4
**Ash Gr**
Dunston NE11 . . . . . . . . .44 A1
Ryton NE40 . . . . . . . . . . .25 A2
Wallsend NE28 . . . . . . . .22 B1
**Ashgrove Terr**
Birtley DH3 . . . . . . . . . . .68 A1
Gateshead NE8 . . . . . . . .79 B1
Ashleigh Cl NE21 . . . . . . .42 A1
Ashleigh Cres NE5 . . . . . .28 B4
**Ashleigh Gr**
Longbenton NE12 . . . . . .11 B3
Newcastle-u-T NE2 . . . . . .18 B2
Ashleigh Rd NE5 . . . . . . .28 B4
Asholme NE5 . . . . . . . . .14 C1
Ashridge Ct NE10 . . . . . . .61 B3
Ash St NE21 . . . . . . . . . . .41 B1
Ashton Cl NE5 . . . . . . . . .13 C4
Ashton Ct NE40 . . . . . . . .39 C4
Ashtree Cl NE4 . . . . . . . . .44 B4
Ashtrees Gdns NE9 . . . . .58 B3
Ashwood Cl NE12 . . . . . .11 C4
Ashwood Cres NE6 . . . . .21 C4
Ashwood Croft NE31 . . . .35 B3
Ashwood Gdns NE9 . . . . .65 B2
Ashwood Gr NE13 . . . . . . .2 B1
Ashwood Ho NE7 . . . . . . .19 B4
Ashwood Terr NE40 . . . . .38 B1
Askew Rd NE8 . . . . . . . . .78 B3
Askew Rd W NE8 . . . . . . .77 C1
Askrigg Wlk 2 NE5 . . . . .14 A1
Aspenlaw NE9 . . . . . . . . .66 A4
Aspen Terr NE5 . . . . . . . .16 C1
Aster Pl NE4 . . . . . . . . . . .29 A3
Aston Way NE16 . . . . . . .54 B1
Aston Wlk 6 NE6 . . . . . .34 B2
Atherton Dr NE4 . . . . . . . .44 A4
Athlone Pl DH3 . . . . . . . . .70 C1
Athol Dr NE11 . . . . . . . . .77 A1
Atholl Gdns NE9 . . . . . . . .59 A3
Athol St NE11 . . . . . . . . . .77 A1
Atkinson Rd NE4 . . . . . . .43 C4
**Atkinson Road Prim Sch**
NE4 . . . . . . . . . . . . . . . .43 C4
Atkinson St NE28 . . . . . . .21 C1
**Atkinson Terr**
5 Newcastle-u-T NE4 . . .29 B1
Wallsend NE28 . . . . . . . .21 C1
Aubone Ave NE15 . . . . . .29 A2
Auburn Cl NE28 . . . . . . . .23 B2
Auburn Ct NE28 . . . . . . . .23 B2
Auburn Gdns NE4 . . . . . .29 C4
Auckland NE38 . . . . . . . . .71 C1
Auckland Rd NE31 . . . . . .36 A3
Auckland Terr NE32 . . . . .52 A4
Auden Gr NE4 . . . . . . . . .29 C2

Audland Wlk 3 NE5 . . . .14 A1
Audley Ct NE2 . . . . . . . . .19 A2
Audley Rd NE3 . . . . . . . . .18 C4
Audouins Row NE8 . . . . . .58 A4
Augusta Cl NE13 . . . . . . . .2 A1
Augusta Gr NE34 . . . . . . .52 B3
Australia Gr NE34 . . . . . . .52 B3
Austral Pl NE13 . . . . . . . . .2 A1
Austwick Wlk 4 NE5 . . . .14 A1
Autumn Dr NE8 . . . . . . . .77 B2
Avalon Dr NE15 . . . . . . . .27 C4
Avenue Rd NE8 . . . . . . . .58 B4
**Avenue The**
Birtley DH3 . . . . . . . . . . .70 B4
Blaydon NE21 . . . . . . . . .42 A2
Gateshead, Carr Hill NE9 .59 A3
7 Gateshead, Felling
NE10 . . . . . . . . . . . . . . .47 C1
Wallsend NE28 . . . . . . . .21 C1
**Avon Ave**
Hedworth NE32 . . . . . . . .51 B2
North Shields NE29 . . . . .24 C4
Avondale Ave NE12 . . . . .11 B4
Avondale Cl NE31 . . . . . .35 C4
Avondale Rd NE6 . . . . . . .33 A1
Avondale Rise 5 NE6 . . .33 A1
Avondale Terr NE8 . . . . . .79 B1
Avonlea Way NE5 . . . . . . .16 A3
Avon Rd NE31 . . . . . . . . .50 B4
Avon St NE8 . . . . . . . . . . .46 A2
Axbridge Gdns NE4 . . . . .29 C1
**AXWELL PARK** . . . . . . .42 A2
Axwell Park Cl 3 NE16 . .54 C3
Axwell Park Rd NE15 . . . .42 C1
**Axwell Park School Hos**
NE21 . . . . . . . . . . . . . . .42 A2
Axwell Park View NE15 . . .28 C1
Axwell Terr NE16 . . . . . . .42 C1
**Axwell View**
Blaydon NE21 . . . . . . . . .41 B1
Whickham NE16 . . . . . . .54 C3
Aycliffe Ave NE9 . . . . . . . .66 C4
Aycliffe Cres NE9 . . . . . . .66 B4
Aycliffe Pl NE9 . . . . . . . . .66 C4
Aydon Gdns NE12 . . . . . .10 A2
Aydon Gr NE32 . . . . . . . .51 A3
Aydon Wlk NE5 . . . . . . . .14 C1
Aylesbury Pl NE12 . . . . . .10 C3
Aylsham Cl NE5 . . . . . . . .13 C4
Aylyth Pl NE3 . . . . . . . . . .17 A3
Ayr Dr NE32 . . . . . . . . . . .52 A3
Ayrey Ave NE34 . . . . . . . .52 B4
Aysgarth Gn NE3 . . . . . . .17 A4
**AYTON** . . . . . . . . . . . . . .71 B2
Ayton Cl NE5 . . . . . . . . . .14 A1
Ayton Prim Sch NE38 . . . .71 B3
Ayton Rd NE38 . . . . . . . . .71 B4
Ayton Rise NE6 . . . . . . . . .33 A1
Ayton St NE6 . . . . . . . . . .33 B1
Azalea Way NE15 . . . . . . .25 C4

## B

Back Beaumont Terr NE3 .9 B1
Back Chapman St NE6 . . .33 A3
Back Elmfield Rd NE3 . . . .18 A4
Back George St NE4 . . . . .76 C4
**Back Hawthorn Rd W**
NE3 . . . . . . . . . . . . . . . .18 A4
**Back Heaton Park Rd** 9
NE6 . . . . . . . . . . . . . . . .33 C2
Back High St NE13 . . . . . .18 A4
Back La NE21 . . . . . . . . . .41 A2
Back Maling St NE6 . . . . .32 B1
Back Mitford St NE4 . . . . .76 B3
Back Row NE16 . . . . . . . .55 A3
Back St NE21 . . . . . . . . . .41 A1
Back Stephen St 6 NE6 .32 B2
Back Walker Rd NE6 . . . . .48 C4
Back Woodbine St NE8 . . .79 B1
Baden Powell St NE9 . . . .58 C3
Badger Mews NE9 . . . . . .67 A2
Badminton Cl NE35 . . . . .52 A1
Baildon Cl NE28 . . . . . . . .23 A4
Bainbridge Ave NE34 . . . .52 B4
Bainford Ave NE15 . . . . . .28 B3
Baird Ave NE28 . . . . . . . .24 A2
Baird Ct NE8 . . . . . . . . . . .47 A1
**Baker Gdns**
1 Dunston NE11 . . . . . .44 B1
Gateshead NE10 . . . . . . .61 A4
Bakewell Terr NE6 . . . . . .47 C4
Baldwin Ave NE4 . . . . . . .30 A3

Balfour Rd NE15 . . . . . . . .28 B2
Balfour St NE8 . . . . . . . . .79 A1
Balgonie Cotts NE40 . . . . .25 A1
Balliol Bsns Pk NE12 . . . .10 B3
Balliol Gdns NE7 . . . . . . .10 C1
Balliol Prim Sch NE12 . . .10 C2
Balmain Rd NE6 . . . . . . . .16 C4
Balmlaw NE9 . . . . . . . . . .66 B4
**Balmoral Ave**
Brockley Whins NE32 . . . .52 A3
Newcastle-u-T NE3 . . . . . .18 C4
Balmoral Dr NE10 . . . . . . .59 B4
Balmoral Dr NE28 . . . . . .21 C2
**Balmoral Terr**
Newcastle-u-T, Heaton
NE6 . . . . . . . . . . . . . . . .32 C4
Newcastle-u-T, South
Gosforth NE3 . . . . . . . . .18 C4
Balmoral Way NE10 . . . . .59 B4
Balroy Ct NE12 . . . . . . . . .11 C3
**Baltic Ctr for**
**Contemporary Art***
NE8 . . . . . . . . . . . . . . . .78 C4
Baltic Ind Pk NE28 . . . . . .24 C3
Baltic Quay NE8 . . . . . . . .78 C4
Baltic Rd NE10 . . . . . . . . .47 C3
Baltic Sq NE8 . . . . . . . . . .78 C4
**Bamburgh Ct**
Gateshead NE8 . . . . . . . .57 B3
Newcastle-u-T NE7 . . . . .10 A1
**Bamburgh Dr**
Gateshead NE10 . . . . . . .49 A2
Wallsend NE28 . . . . . . . .23 A2
Bamburgh Gr NE32 . . . . .50 C3
Bamburgh Ho NE5 . . . . . .14 C3
Bamburgh Rd NE5 . . . . . .14 C3
Bamburgh Terr 18 NE6 . .33 A2
Bamburgh Wlk NE3 . . . . . .8 B2
Banbury NE37 . . . . . . . . . .8 A2
Banbury Way NE29 . . . . . .24 B4
Bangor Sq NE32 . . . . . . .50 C1
Bank Ave NE16 . . . . . . . .54 C3
Bank Ct NE21 . . . . . . . . . .42 B4
Bankhead Rd NE15 . . . . . .6 C2
Bankside Rd NE15 . . . . . .28 A1
**Bank Top**
Crawcrook NE40 . . . . . . .38 A3
Greenside NE40 . . . . . . .39 A3
**Bank Top Hamlet** 4
NE16 . . . . . . . . . . . . . . .54 C3
Bankwell La NE8 . . . . . . .78 B4
**Barbondale Lonnen**
NE5 . . . . . . . . . . . . . . . .14 A2
Barclay Pl NE5 . . . . . . . . .15 A4
Bardon Cl NE5 . . . . . . . . .15 A4
Bardsey Pl NE12 . . . . . . .10 C3
Barents Cl 2 NE5 . . . . . .15 A4
**Baret Rd**
Newcastle-u-T, Walkergate
NE6 . . . . . . . . . . . . . . . .33 C4
Newcastle-u-T, Walker
NE6 . . . . . . . . . . . . . . . .34 A3
Barford Ct NE9 . . . . . . . . .65 B2
**BARLEY MOW** . . . . . . . .70 B2
**Barley Mow Prim Schs**
DH3 . . . . . . . . . . . . . . . .70 C1
Barmoor Dr NE3 . . . . . . . .4 A2
Barnard Cres NE31 . . . . . .35 C3
Barnard Gn NE3 . . . . . . . .7 C3
Barnard Gr NE32 . . . . . . .51 C4
Barnesbury Rd NE4 . . . . .29 C1
Barns Cl NE32 . . . . . . . . .50 C1
Barnton Rd NE10 . . . . . . .60 A2
Baroness Dr NE15 . . . . . .28 B3
Baronswood NE3 . . . . . . . .8 C1
Barrasford Cl NE3 . . . . . .17 B4
Barrasford Dr NE13 . . . . . .2 C1
Barrasford St NE28 . . . . . .24 A1
Barrington Pl NE3 . . . . . . .79 A2
**Barry St**
Dunston NE11 . . . . . . . . .44 B1
Gateshead NE8 . . . . . . . .57 C3
Bartram Gdns NE8 . . . . . .58 A3
Barwell Ct NE7 . . . . . . . . .20 C3
Basingstoke Pl NE12 . . . .11 A3
Bates La NE21 . . . . . . . . .42 B2
**Bath Rd**
Gateshead NE10 . . . . . . .47 C2

**Bath Rd** *continued*
Hebburn NE31 . . . . . . . . . . .50 A3
**Bath Sq** NE32 . . . . . . . . . . . .50 C1
**Bath St** NE6 . . . . . . . . . . . . .34 C2
**Bath Terr** NE3 . . . . . . . . . . . . .9 B1
**Baugh Cl** NE37 . . . . . . . . . . .69 C3
**Bavington** NE10 . . . . . . . . . .60 C1
**Bavington Dr** NE5 . . . . . . . .16 B1
**Baxter Ave** NE4 . . . . . . . . . .29 C2
**Baybridge Rd** NE5 . . . . . . .14 C3
**Bayfield Gdns** NE8 . . . . . .47 A1
**Bayswater Rd**
Gateshead NE8 . . . . . . . . . . .59 A4
Newcastle-u-t NE2 . . . . . . . .18 C2
**Beaches The** NE4 . . . . . . . .76 A3
**Beacon Ct**
Brunswick Village NE13 . . . .2 A2
  **4** Gateshead NE9 . . . . . .59 A1
**Beacon Dr** NE13 . . . . . . . . . .2 A1
**BEACON LOUGH** . . . . . . . .65 C4
**Beacon Lough Rd** NE9 . . .65 B4
**Beacon Rise** NE9 . . . . . . . . .59 A1
**Beaconsfield Ave** NE9 . . .58 C1
**Beaconsfield Cres 3**
  NE9 . . . . . . . . . . . . . . . . . . . .58 C1
**Beaconsfield Rd** NE9 . . . .58 B1
**Beaconsfield Terr** DH3 . .70 A4
**Beacon St** NE9 . . . . . . . . . . .58 C1
**Beadling Gdns** NE4 . . . . . .29 C2
**Beadnell Ave** NE29 . . . . . . .24 B4
**Beadnell Way** NE3 . . . . . . . .8 B2
**Beal Gn** NE5 . . . . . . . . . . . . .16 A4
**Beal Terr** NE6 . . . . . . . . . . . .48 B4
**Beal Way** NE3 . . . . . . . . . . . .8 C2
**Beaminster Way** NE3 . . . . .7 A1
**Beamish Gdns** NE9 . . . . . . .66 B4
**Beamish View** DH3 . . . . . . .69 A1
**Beanley Ave**
Hebburn NE31 . . . . . . . . . . .49 C4
Newcastle-u-t NE15 . . . . . . .27 A2
**Beanley Pl** NE7 . . . . . . . . . .19 B3
**Beatrice Rd** NE6 . . . . . . . . .19 C1
**Beatty Ave** NE2 . . . . . . . . . .18 C3
**Beaufort Cl** NE10 . . . . . . . . .61 A2
**Beaufront Cl** NE10 . . . . . . .61 A2
**Beaufront Gdns**
Gateshead NE8 . . . . . . . . . . .47 A1
Newcastle-u-t NE5 . . . . . . . .16 A1
**Beaufront Terr** NE32 . . . . .51 A3
**Beaumaris Ct** NE12 . . . . . . .10 B2
**Beaumaris Way** NE5 . . . . .15 C4
**Beaumont Ho** NE6 . . . . . . . .16 A2
**Beaumont St** NE4 . . . . . . . .44 B3
**Beaumont Terr**
Brunswick Village NE13 . . . .2 A2
Jarrow NE32 . . . . . . . . . . . . .36 B1
Newcastle-u-t, Gosforth
  NE3 . . . . . . . . . . . . . . . . . . . . .9 B1
Newcastle-u-t NE3 . . . . . . . .9 B1
**Beckenham Gdns** NE28 . . .22 A4
**Beckett St** NE8 . . . . . . . . . . .46 C4
**Beckfoot Cl** NE5 . . . . . . . . .15 C1
**Beckside Gdns** NE5 . . . . . .13 C1
**Beda Hill** NE21 . . . . . . . . . . .41 B3
**Bedale Ct** NE9 . . . . . . . . . . .65 C2
**Bedale Gn** NE5 . . . . . . . . . . .16 B3
**Bedburn** NE38 . . . . . . . . . . .71 B1
**Bedeburn Foot** NE5 . . . . . . .6 A1
**Bede Burn Prim Sch**
  NE32 . . . . . . . . . . . . . . . . . . .50 C4
**Bedeburn Rd** NE5 . . . . . . . . .6 A1
**Bede Burn Rd** NE32 . . . . . .36 C1
**Bede Burn View** NE32 . . . .36 C1
**Bede Com Prim Sch**
  NE10 . . . . . . . . . . . . . . . . . . .47 A2
**Bede Cres** NE28 . . . . . . . . . .22 C3
**Bede Ct** NE8 . . . . . . . . . . . . .46 C2
**Bede Ind Est** NE32 . . . . . . .37 C2
**Bede Precinct 7** NE32 . . .36 C3
**Bede Sta** NE32 . . . . . . . . . . .37 C2
**Bedesway** NE32 . . . . . . . . . .37 C2
**Bede's World (Mus)★**
  NE32 . . . . . . . . . . . . . . . . . . .37 B3
**Bede Terr** NE32 . . . . . . . . . .37 A1
**Bedewell Ind Pk** NE31 . .36 B1
**Bedewell Prim Sch**
  NE31 . . . . . . . . . . . . . . . . . . .36 A2
**Bede Wlk**
Hebburn NE31 . . . . . . . . . . .36 A1

**Bede Wlk** *continued*
Newcastle-u-t NE3 . . . . . . . .9 C1
**Bedford Ave**
Birtley DH3 . . . . . . . . . . . . .70 C1
Wallsend NE28 . . . . . . . . . . .21 B3
**Bedford Pl**
Gateshead NE8 . . . . . . . . . . .79 B2
Newcastle-u-t NE5 . . . . . . . .14 A1
**Beech Ave**
Newcastle-u-t NE3 . . . . . . . .8 A2
Whickham NE16 . . . . . . . . . .55 B4
**Beech Cl** NE3 . . . . . . . . . . . . .4 C1
**Beechcroft**
Newcastle-u-t NE3 . . . . . . . .17 C2
Washington NE37 . . . . . . . . .67 C2
**Beechcroft Ave** NE3 . . . . .17 B3
**Beech Ct** NE3 . . . . . . . . . . . .18 A4
**Beech Dr** NE11 . . . . . . . . . . .44 A1
**Beeches The** NE12 . . . . . . .11 B2
**Beechfield Gdns** NE28 . . .21 B3
**Beechfield Rd** NE3 . . . . . . .17 C4
**Beech Gdns** NE9 . . . . . . . . .58 B2
**Beech Gr**
Longbenton NE12 . . . . . . . .11 B2
Springwell NE9 . . . . . . . . . .67 A1
Wallsend NE9 . . . . . . . . . . . .21 C2
**BEECHGROVE** . . . . . . . . . . .15 B3
**Beech Grove** NE40 . . . . . . .38 B4
**Beech Grove Rd** NE4 . . . . .44 C4
**Beech Grove Terr** NE40 . .38 B4
**Beech Grove Terr S**
  NE40 . . . . . . . . . . . . . . . . . . .38 B4
**Beech Hill Prim Sch**
  NE5 . . . . . . . . . . . . . . . . . . . .15 A2
**Beech St**
Gateshead NE8 . . . . . . . . . . .47 A1
Jarrow NE32 . . . . . . . . . . . . .36 B3
Newcastle-u-t NE4 . . . . . . . .29 C1
  **1** Sunniside NE16 . . . . . .62 C2
**Beech Terr** NE21 . . . . . . . . .41 B2
**Beechway** NE10 . . . . . . . . . .60 B1
**Beechwood Ave**
Gateshead NE8 . . . . . . . . . . .65 B3
Newcastle-u-t NE3 . . . . . . . .9 C2
Ryton NE40 . . . . . . . . . . . . . .25 A1
**Beechwood Cl** NE32 . . . . .37 B2
**Beechwood Gdns** NE11 . .57 A1
**Beechwood Ho** NE7 . . . . . .19 B4
**Beetham Cres** NE5 . . . . . . .28 B4
**Begonia Cl** NE31 . . . . . . . . .50 A3
**Belford Gdns** NE11 . . . . . . .56 C1
**Belford Terr** NE6 . . . . . . . . .33 C1
**Belgrave Ct** NE10 . . . . . . . .59 C4
**Belgrave Par** NE4 . . . . . . . .76 B4
**Belgrave Terr** NE10 . . . . . .59 C3
**Belle View Terr 13** NE9 . .67 A1
**Belle Vue Ave** NE8 . . . . . . .58 A1
**Belle Vue Bank** NE9 . . . . . .58 B1
**Belle Vue Gr** NE9 . . . . . . . . .58 B1
**Belle Vue Terr**
Crawcrook NE40 . . . . . . . . . .38 B4
Gateshead NE8 . . . . . . . . . . .58 A1
**Bellfield Ave** NE3 . . . . . . . . .8 A2
**Bellgreen Ave** NE3 . . . . . . . .5 A1
**Bellingham Ct** NE28 . . . . . .22 B4
**Bellingham Ct 8** NE3 . . . .7 B1
**Bellister Gr** NE5 . . . . . . . . . .29 A3
**Bells Cl** NE15 . . . . . . . . . . . .27 C1
**BELL'S CLOSE** . . . . . . . . . . .27 C2
**Bells Close Ind Est**
  NE15 . . . . . . . . . . . . . . . . . . .27 C1
**Bell's Cotts** NE40 . . . . . . . .38 C1
**Bell St** NE31 . . . . . . . . . . . . .35 B2
**Belmont** NE10 . . . . . . . . . . . .60 C1
**Belmont Cotts 6** NE5 . . .15 A3
**Belmont St** NE6 . . . . . . . . . .48 B3
**Belmont Terr 4** NE6 . . . . .66 C1
**Belmont Wlk** NE6 . . . . . . . . .48 B3
**Belmount Ave** NE3 . . . . . . . .5 A1
**Belsay** NE38 . . . . . . . . . . . . .71 B4
**Belsay Ave** NE13 . . . . . . . . . .4 A4
**Belsay Gdns**
Dunston NE11 . . . . . . . . . . . .56 C1
Newcastle-u-t NE3 . . . . . . . .8 A1
**Belsfield Gdns** NE32 . . . . .51 A4
**Belsize Pl** NE6 . . . . . . . . . . .34 A4
**Beltingham** NE5 . . . . . . . . . .14 C1
**Belvedere Ct 12** NE6 . . . .33 A3
**Belvedere Gdns** NE12 . . . .11 B2
**Belvedere Ho 10** NE6 . . . .32 C2
**Belvedere Parkway** NE3 . .7 B2
**Belvedere Ret Pk** NE3 . . .7 A2

**Bemersyde Dr** NE2 . . . . . .18 C3
**Bendigo Ave** NE34 . . . . . . .52 B3
**Benfield Bsns Pk** NE6 . . .33 C4
**Benfield Rd** NE6 . . . . . . . . . .20 C1
**Benfield Sch** . . . . . . . . . . . . .20 C1
**Benjamin Rd** NE28 . . . . . . .23 B3
**Benjamin St 11** NE40 . . . . .38 B3
**Bennett Ct** NE15 . . . . . . . . .27 A2
**Bennett Gdns 1** NE10 . . .47 C1
**BENSHAM** . . . . . . . . . . . . . . .79 A1
**Bensham Ave** NE8 . . . . . . . .79 A1
**Bensham Cres** NE8 . . . . . . .77 C1
**Bensham Ct** NE8 . . . . . . . . .79 A1
**Bensham General Hospl**
  NE8 . . . . . . . . . . . . . . . . . . . .57 C3
**Bensham Rd**
Gateshead, Bensham
  NE8 . . . . . . . . . . . . . . . . . . . .79 A1
Gateshead NE8 . . . . . . . . . . .78 B2
Gateshead, Windmill Hills
  NE8 . . . . . . . . . . . . . . . . . . . .79 B2
**Bensham St** NE35 . . . . . . . .52 B1
**Bensham Trad Est** NE8 . .57 C4
**Benson Pl 20** NE6 . . . . . . .33 A2
**Benson Rd** NE6 . . . . . . . . . .33 A2
**Benson Terr 14** NE10 . . . .59 C4
**Bentinck Cres** NE4 . . . . . . .44 B4
**Bentinck Rd** NE4 . . . . . . . . .30 A1
**Bentinck St** NE4 . . . . . . . . .30 A1
**Bentinck Villas** NE4 . . . . . .30 A1
**Benton Bank** NE2 . . . . . . . .19 B1
**Benton Cl** NE7 . . . . . . . . . . .10 C1
**Benton Hall Wlk** NE7 . . . .20 B2
**Benton La** NE12 . . . . . . . . . .12 A3
**Benton Lodge Ave** NE7 . .10 C1
**Benton Park Prim Sch**
  NE7 . . . . . . . . . . . . . . . . . . . .10 B1
**Benton Park Rd** NE7 . . . . .10 B1
**Benton Rd** NE7 . . . . . . . . . . .19 C3
**Benton Sta** NE12 . . . . . . . . .11 B2
**Benton Way**
Wallsend NE28 . . . . . . . . . . .21 C1
Wallsend NE28 . . . . . . . . . . .34 C4
**BENWELL** . . . . . . . . . . . . . . .29 A2
**Benwell Dene Terr**
  NE15 . . . . . . . . . . . . . . . . . . .29 A1
**Benwell Gr** NE4 . . . . . . . . . .29 C1
**Benwell Grange 9**
  NE15 . . . . . . . . . . . . . . . . . . .29 B1
**Benwell Grange Ave**
  NE15 . . . . . . . . . . . . . . . . . . .29 B1
**Benwell Grange Cl 6**
  NE15 . . . . . . . . . . . . . . . . . . .29 B1
**Benwell Grange Rd**
  NE15 . . . . . . . . . . . . . . . . . . .29 A1
**Benwell Grange Terr**
  NE15 . . . . . . . . . . . . . . . . . . .29 A1
**Benwell Hall Dr** NE15 . . . .28 C2
**Benwell Hill Gdns** NE5 . . .28 C2
**Benwell Hill Rd** NE5 . . . . . .29 A3
**Benwell La**
Newcastle-u-t NE15 . . . . . . .29 A1
Newcastle-u-t, Old Benwell
  NE15 . . . . . . . . . . . . . . . . . . .28 C1
**Benwell Roman Temple★**
  NE15 . . . . . . . . . . . . . . . . . . .29 B2
**Benwell Vallum Crossing★**
  NE15 . . . . . . . . . . . . . . . . . . .29 B2
**Benwell Village** NE15 . . . .28 C2
**Benwell Village Mews**
  NE15 . . . . . . . . . . . . . . . . . . .29 A2
**Berberis Way** NE15 . . . . . .25 C4
**Beresford Ave** NE31 . . . . . .50 A3
**Beresford Gdns 7** NE6 . .33 A1
**Beresford St** NE11 . . . . . . . .77 A1
**Bergen Cl** NE29 . . . . . . . . . .23 C4
**Berkdale Rd** NE9 . . . . . . . . .64 C2
**Berkeley Cl** NE35 . . . . . . . . .52 A2
**Berkeley Sq** NE3 . . . . . . . . . .9 B3
**Berkhamstead Ct** NE10 . .61 B3
**Berkley Ave** NE21 . . . . . . . .42 A2
**Berkley St** NE15 . . . . . . . . . .26 A4
**Berkley Terr** NE15 . . . . . . . .26 A4
**Berkley Way** NE31 . . . . . . . .36 A4
**Berkshire Cl** NE5 . . . . . . . . .15 A2
**Bernard St** NE6 . . . . . . . . . .49 A4
**Berrington Dr** NE5 . . . . . . . .15 C3
**Berry Cl** NE6 . . . . . . . . . . . . .34 B2
**Berry Hill** NE40 . . . . . . . . . .39 A1
**Berryhill Cl** NE21 . . . . . . . . .41 C1
**Bertram Cres** NE15 . . . . . . .29 A2
**Bertram St 3** DH3 . . . . . . .70 B4

**Berwick** NE38 . . . . . . . . . . . .71 B4
**Berwick Cl** NE15 . . . . . . . . .26 B3
**Berwick Terr** NE29 . . . . . . .24 B4
**Bessie Surtees House
  Mus★** . . . . . . . . . . . . . . . . .78 A1
**Bessie Terr** NE21 . . . . . . . . .40 C2
**Bethnal Ave** NE6 . . . . . . . . .33 B3
**Betjeman Mews** NE8 . . . . .79 C1
**Betts Ave** NE15 . . . . . . . . . .28 C1
**Bevan Dr** NE12 . . . . . . . . . . .10 A2
**Bevan Gdns** NE10 . . . . . . . .61 C4
**Beverley Cl** NE3 . . . . . . . . . .4 B2
**Beverley Cres** NE9 . . . . . . .58 C2
**Beverley Ct**
  **2** Gateshead NE9 . . . . . .58 C2
  **1** Jarrow NE32 . . . . . . . .36 C3
**Beverley Dr** NE16, NE21 . .55 B4
**Beverley Pl** NE28 . . . . . . . . .23 A3
**Beverley Rd** NE9 . . . . . . . . .58 C2
**Beverley Terr**
Newcastle-u-t NE6 . . . . . . . .34 B1
Walbottle NE15 . . . . . . . . . . .13 C3
**Beweshill Cres** NE21 . . . . .40 C1
**Beweshill La** NE21 . . . . . . . .40 C3
**Bewick Cres** NE15 . . . . . . . .27 B3
**Bewick Lodge** NE28 . . . . . .23 B2
**Bewicke Rd** NE28 . . . . . . . . .23 B1
**Bewicke Road Ind Est**
  NE28 . . . . . . . . . . . . . . . . . . .23 B1
**Bewicke St** NE28 . . . . . . . . .23 C1
**Bewicke View** DH3 . . . . . . .68 C1
**Bewick Rd** NE8 . . . . . . . . . . .79 B1
**Bewick St** NE1 . . . . . . . . . . .78 A4
**Bexley Ave** NE15 . . . . . . . . .28 C2
**Bexley Pl** NE16 . . . . . . . . . . .54 C1
**Bickerton Wlk 2** NE5 . . . .14 C1
**Bicknell Ho** NE6 . . . . . . . . . .33 A1
**Biddick Hall Inf Sch**
  NE34 . . . . . . . . . . . . . . . . . . .52 C3
**Biddlestone Rd** NE6 . . . . . .20 A1
**Bideford Gdns**
Gateshead NE9 . . . . . . . . . . .65 A3
Jarrow NE32 . . . . . . . . . . . . .37 C1
**Bideford Rd** NE16 . . . . . . . .54 C1
**Bideford Rd** NE3 . . . . . . . . .16 C4
**Bigges Gdns** NE28 . . . . . . .21 A4
**Big Waters Cl** NE13 . . . . . . .2 B3
**Big Waters Ctry Pk★**
  NE13 . . . . . . . . . . . . . . . . . . . .2 A3
**Bilbrough Gdns** NE4 . . . . .43 C4
**BILL QUAY** . . . . . . . . . . . . . .49 A2
**Bill Quay Prim Sch**
  NE10 . . . . . . . . . . . . . . . . . . .49 B2
**Bilsdale Pl** NE12 . . . . . . . . .10 A2
**Bilsmoor Ave** NE7 . . . . . . . .19 C2
**Bilton Hall Rd** NE32 . . . . . .37 B2
**Bilton Hall Rd** NE32 . . . . . .37 B2
**Bingfield Gdns** NE5 . . . . . .16 A1
**Bink Moss** NE37 . . . . . . . . . .69 C2
**Binsby Gdns** NE9 . . . . . . . . .65 C2
**Binswood Ave** NE5 . . . . . . .16 A2
**Bircham Dr** NE21 . . . . . . . . .41 C1
**Birch Ave** NE10 . . . . . . . . . .60 C3
**Birches The** NE16 . . . . . . . .63 A3
**Birchfield** NE16 . . . . . . . . . .55 A1
**Birchfield Gdns**
Gateshead NE9 . . . . . . . . . . .65 B2
Newcastle-u-t NE15 . . . . . . .27 C3
**Birchgate Cl** NE21 . . . . . . . .40 C1
**Birch Gr** NE32 . . . . . . . . . . . .36 B3
**Birch Rd** NE21 . . . . . . . . . . .41 C3
**Birch St** NE32 . . . . . . . . . . . .36 B3
**Birch Terr**
Birtley DH3 . . . . . . . . . . . . .68 A1
Newcastle-u-t NE6 . . . . . . . .34 B1
**Birchvale Ave** NE5 . . . . . . .15 C2
**Birchwood Ave**
Newcastle-u-t NE7 . . . . . . . .20 A3
Whickham NE16 . . . . . . . . . .54 C1
Wideopen NE13 . . . . . . . . . .2 C1
**Birds Nest Rd**
Newcastle-u-t NE6 . . . . . . . .47 C4
Newcastle-u-t NE6 . . . . . . . .48 A4
**Birkdale Cl**
Newcastle-u-t NE7 . . . . . . . .20 A4
Wallsend NE28 . . . . . . . . . . .22 A4
Washington NE37 . . . . . . . . .67 C2
**Birkshaw Wlk 1** NE5 . . . .14 C1
**Birling Pl 4** NE5 . . . . . . . . .16 B2
**Birnam Gr** NE32 . . . . . . . . . .52 A2
**Birnham Pl** NE3 . . . . . . . . . .17 A3
**Birnie Cl** NE4 . . . . . . . . . . . .44 A4

**BIRTLEY** . . . . . . . . . . . . . . . .70 B3
**Birtley Cl** NE3 . . . . . . . . . . . .17 B4
**Birtley East Com Prim Sch**
  DH3 . . . . . . . . . . . . . . . . . . . .68 B2
**Birtley Golf Course** DH3 .70 C2
**Birtley La** DH3 . . . . . . . . . . .70 C3
**Birtley Villas 1** DH3 . . . . .68 B1
**Birtwistle Ave** NE31 . . . . . .49 C3
**Biscop Terr** NE32 . . . . . . . . .51 B4
**Bishop Cres** NE32 . . . . . . . .37 A4
**Bishop Rock Dr** NE12 . . . .10 B2
**Bishops Cl** NE28 . . . . . . . . . .22 C2
**Bishops Ct** NE5 . . . . . . . . . .28 A4
**Bishops Dr** NE40 . . . . . . . . .39 C4
**Bishop's Rd** NE15 . . . . . . . .29 B1
**Bittern Cl** NE11 . . . . . . . . . .44 B2
**Blackberries The 18**
  NE9 . . . . . . . . . . . . . . . . . . . .67 A1
**Blackburn Gn** NE10 . . . . . . .59 B3
**Blackcap Cl** NE38 . . . . . . . .71 B3
**Blackett St** NE1, NE32 . . . .36 A4
**BLACKFELL** . . . . . . . . . . . . . .69 C2
**Blackfell Prim Sch**
  NE37 . . . . . . . . . . . . . . . . . . .69 C2
**Blackfell Rd** NE37 . . . . . . . .69 B2
**Blackfriars Way** NE12 . . . .10 B2
**Blackhams Hill Sta★**
  NE9 . . . . . . . . . . . . . . . . . . . .66 C1
**Blackheath Ct** NE5 . . . . . . . .6 C1
**Blackhill Cres** NE9 . . . . . . .66 B4
**Black La**
Blaydon NE21 . . . . . . . . . . . .40 C2
Gateshead NE9 . . . . . . . . . . .66 A1
**Blackpool Par** NE31 . . . . . .50 C3
**Black Rd** NE31 . . . . . . . . . . .36 A2
**Blackrow La** NE9 . . . . . . . . .65 B3
**Blackstone Ct** NE21 . . . . . .40 C2
**Blackthorn Cl** NE16 . . . . . .62 B2
**Blackthorne** NE10 . . . . . . . .60 B1
**Blackthorn Pl** NE4 . . . . . . .76 B3
**Blackwell Ave** NE6 . . . . . . .34 B2
**Bladen St** NE32 . . . . . . . . . .36 B3
**Bladen Street Ind Est**
  NE32 . . . . . . . . . . . . . . . . . . .36 B3
**Blagdon Terr** NE13 . . . . . . .2 B4
**Blake Ave** NE16 . . . . . . . . . .55 A3
**BLAKELAW** . . . . . . . . . . . . . .16 A2
**Blakelaw Rd**
  **7** Newcastle-u-t NE15 . .15 C2
Newcastle-u-t NE5 . . . . . . . .16 A2
**Blakemoor Pl** NE5 . . . . . . . .16 A1
**Blake Wlk** NE8 . . . . . . . . . . .46 C2
**Blanchland Ave**
Newcastle-u-t NE15 . . . . . . .27 A3
Wideopen NE13 . . . . . . . . . .2 B2
**Blandford Ct** NE4 . . . . . . . .76 C4
**Blandford Sq** NE1 . . . . . . . .76 C4
**Blandford St** NE1 . . . . . . . .76 C4
**Blaxton Pl** NE16 . . . . . . . . . .54 B1
**BLAYDON** . . . . . . . . . . . . . . .42 A3
**Blaydon Bank** NE21 . . . . . .41 B2
**Blaydon Bsns Ctr** NE21 . .42 A3
**Blaydon Bsns Pk** NE21 . .42 A3
**BLAYDON BURN** . . . . . . . . .40 A1
**BLAYDON HAUGHS** . . . . . .42 A4
**Blaydon Haughs Ind Est**
  NE21 . . . . . . . . . . . . . . . . . . .41 B3
**Blaydon Highway** NE21 . .41 C3
**Blaydon Ind Pk** NE21 . . . .41 C3
**Blaydon Trad Pk** NE21 . . .42 B3
**Blaydon West Prim Sch**
  NE21 . . . . . . . . . . . . . . . . . . .41 B3
**Blayney Row** NE15 . . . . . . .25 A4
**Bleachfield** NE10 . . . . . . . . .60 B2
**BLEACH GREEN** . . . . . . . . . .41 B1
**Blencathra Way** NE21 . . . .53 B4
**Blenheim Ct** NE10 . . . . . . . .59 B2
**Blenheim Pl** NE11 . . . . . . . .44 A1
**Blenkinsop Gr** NE32 . . . . . .51 A3
**Blenkinsop Mews** NE5 . . . .4 A1
**Blenkinsop St 5** NE28 . . .21 C2
**Blezard Ct** NE21 . . . . . . . . . .41 B4
**Bloomsbury Ct** NE3 . . . . . .17 C4
**Blount St** NE6 . . . . . . . . . . . .33 B2
**Blucher Terr** NE15 . . . . . . . .13 C1
**Blue Anchor Ct** NE8 . . . . . .78 B4
**Bluebell Cl** NE9 . . . . . . . . . .59 A1
**Bluebell Dene** NE5 . . . . . . . .6 B1
**Blue House Rd** NE31 . . . . . .49 C3
**Blue Quarries Rd** NE9 . . . .59 A2
**Blyth Ct** NE15 . . . . . . . . . . . .27 A3
**Blyth Terr** DH3 . . . . . . . . . . .70 A4

Bodley Cl NE3 . . . . . . . . 7 B1
Bodmin Cl ⬛1 NE9 . . . . . 65 B2
Bodmin Way NE3 . . . . . . 8 A2
Bolam NE38 . . . . . . . . . . 71 B4
Bolam Coyne ⬛13 NE6 . . . 33 A1
Bolam Ct NE15 . . . . . . . . 12 B1
Bolam Gdns NE28 . . . . . . 23 C3
Bolam St
  Gateshead NE8 . . . . . . . 57 A4
  Newcastle-u-T NE6 . . . . 33 A1
Bolam Way NE6 . . . . . . . 33 A1
Bolbec Rd NE4 . . . . . . . . 29 C3
Bolburn NE10 . . . . . . . . . 60 C3
BOLDON COLLIERY . . . . 52 A1
Boldon Gdns NE9 . . . . . . 66 A3
Bolingbroke St NE6 . . . . . 32 B3
Bond Ct NE4 . . . . . . . . . . 29 C1
Bondene Ave NE10 . . . . . 60 A4
Bondene Ave W NE10 . . . 60 A4
Bondfield Cl NE28 . . . . . . 23 A3
Bondfield Gdns NE10 . . . 61 C4
Bondicarr Pl ⬛1 NE5 . . . 16 B1
Bond St ⬛2 NE4 . . . . . . . 29 B1
Bonington Way NE5 . . . . 15 C2
Booth St NE10 . . . . . . . . 59 C4
Border Rd NE28 . . . . . . . 21 C1
Borough Rd NE32 . . . . . . 36 C2
Borrowdale
  Birtley DH3 . . . . . . . . . . 70 C1
  Whickham NE16 . . . . . . 55 C3
Borrowdale Ave NE6 . . . 34 A3
Borrowdale Cres NE21 . . 53 A4
Borrowdale Gdns NE9 . . 65 C3
Boscombe Dr NE28 . . . . . 22 A4
Boston Ave NE7 . . . . . . . 10 C1
Bosun's Way NE10 . . . . . 48 C2
Bosworth Gdns NE6 . . . . 20 B2
Bothal St NE6 . . . . . . . . . 33 B2
Botham Ho NE29 . . . . . . 24 B3
Bottle Bank NE8 . . . . . . . 78 B4
Bottlehouse St NE6 . . . . . 47 B4
Boulevard The NE12 . . . . 10 B2
Boulmer Cl NE3 . . . . . . . 8 A4
Boulmer Gdns NE13 . . . . 2 B2
Boundary Gdns NE7 . . . . 19 B3
Bourne Ave NE4 . . . . . . . 29 C3
Bournemouth Gdns
  NE5 . . . . . . . . . . . . . . . 15 A3
Bournemouth Par NE31 . 50 C3
Bourtree Cl NE28 . . . . . . 22 A4
Bowburn Cl NE10 . . . . . . 61 B3
Bowes Cl NE16 . . . . . . . . 62 C2
Bowes Ct NE3 . . . . . . . . . 9 C1
Bowes Lyon Ct ⬛6 NE9 . 58 B4
Bowes Rly* NE9 . . . . . . . 69 A4
Bowes Rly Ctr Mus*
  NE9 . . . . . . . . . . . . . . . 66 C2
Bowes St NE3 . . . . . . . . . 9 C1
Bowes Wlk NE12 . . . . . . 11 A3
Bowfell Ave NE5 . . . . . . . 16 B3
Bowfell Cl NE5 . . . . . . . . 16 B3
Bowfield Ave NE3 . . . . . . 4 C1
Bowness Pl NE9 . . . . . . . 65 C4
Bowness Rd
  Newcastle-u-T NE15 . . . 15 B1
  Whickham NE16 . . . . . . 55 C3
Bowsden Cl NE3 . . . . . . . 9 C1
Bowsden Terr NE3 . . . . . 9 C1
Boxlaw NE9 . . . . . . . . . . 59 B1
Boyd Cres NE28 . . . . . . . 22 A2
Boyd Rd NE28 . . . . . . . . 22 B2
Boyd St NE15 . . . . . . . . . 25 C4
Boyd Terr
  Newcastle-u-T, Walbottle
  NE15 . . . . . . . . . . . . . . 13 C1
  ⬛5 Newcastle-u-T,
  Westerhope NE5 . . . . . . 15 A3
Brackendene Dr NE9 . . . 58 A1
Bracken Dr NE11 . . . . . . 56 B2
Brackenfield Rd NE3 . . . 17 C4
Brackenlaw NE9 . . . . . . . 66 A3
Bracken Pl NE4 . . . . . . . 29 B3
Brackenside NE3 . . . . . . 4 C1
Bracken Way NE40 . . . . . 38 C3
Brackley Gr NE29 . . . . . . 24 B4
Bracknell Gdns NE5 . . . . 16 A1
Brack Terr NE10 . . . . . . . 49 A2
Bradbury Cl NE11 . . . . . . 61 C3
Bradley View ⬛14 NE40 . . 38 B3
Bradwell Rd NE3 . . . . . . 7 C1
Braebridge Pl NE3 . . . . . 17 A3
Braemar Ct NE10 . . . . . . 49 A2

Braeside NE11 . . . . . . . . 56 B3
Brahman Ave NE29 . . . . 24 B4
Braintree Gdns NE3 . . . . 17 A4
Brama Teams Ind Pk
  NE8 . . . . . . . . . . . . . . . 57 A4
Bramble Dykes NE15 . . . 28 C2
Bramblelaw NE9 . . . . . . 66 A4
Brambles The DH3 . . . . . 68 C2
Bramhope Gn NE9 . . . . . 65 C2
Bramley Ct NE7 . . . . . . . 20 C3
Brampton Ave NE6 . . . . . 48 B4
Brampton Gdns
  Gateshead NE9 . . . . . . . 65 B3
  Throckley NE15 . . . . . . 12 C2
  Wallsend NE28 . . . . . . . 23 B4
Bramwell Ct NE3 . . . . . . 9 C1
Brancepeth Ave NE4 . . . 29 C1
Brancepeth Cl NE15 . . . . 27 A3
Brancepeth Rd
  Hebburn NE31 . . . . . . . 36 A3
  Washington NE38 . . . . . 71 C4
Brancepeth Terr NE32 . . 51 A3
Branch St NE21 . . . . . . . 41 A1
Branckenpeth Mews NE3 4 B1
Brand Ave NE4 . . . . . . . . 29 C2
Brandling Ct ⬛14 NE10 . . 47 C1
Brandling Dr NE3 . . . . . . 5 A1
Brandling La ⬛15 NE10 . . 47 C1
Brandling Mews NE3 . . . 5 A1
Brandling Pl NE10 . . . . . 47 C1
Brandling Prim Sch
  NE10 . . . . . . . . . . . . . . 47 C1
Brandling St NE8 . . . . . . 78 C4
Brandon Gdns NE9 . . . . . 66 B3
Brandon Rd NE3 . . . . . . . 8 A2
Brandywell NE10 . . . . . . 60 B2
Branton Ave NE31 . . . . . 49 C3
Brantwood Ct NE21 . . . . 41 C2
Branxton Cres NE6 . . . . . 34 A1
Braydon Dr NE29 . . . . . . 24 C3
Brayside NE32 . . . . . . . . 51 C1
Breamish Ho NE1 . . . . . . 32 B1
Breamish St
  Jarrow NE32 . . . . . . . . . 36 B1
  Newcastle-u-T NE1 . . . . 32 B1
Brearley Way NE10 . . . . 59 B4
Breckenbeds Rd NE9 . . . 64 C4
Brecken Ct NE9 . . . . . . . 64 C4
Brecon Cl NE5 . . . . . . . . 15 C4
Brendale Ave NE5 . . . . . 14 C3
Brenkley Ct NE13 . . . . . . 2 B4
Brennan Cl NE15 . . . . . . 28 C2
Brentwood Ave NE2 . . . . 18 C2
Brentwood Gdns
  Newcastle-u-T NE2 . . . . 18 B2
  Whickham NE16 . . . . . . 55 A1
Brentwood Gr NE28 . . . . 22 B1
Brettanby Gdns NE40 . . . 25 A2
Brettanby Rd NE10 . . . . . 59 B3
Brett Cl NE7 . . . . . . . . . . 20 B3
Bretton Gdns NE7 . . . . . 20 A2
Brewer's La NE28, NE29 . 24 A3
Brewery Bank ⬛6 NE16 . 42 C1
Brewery La
  Gateshead NE10 . . . . . . 47 C2
  ⬛5 Whickham NE16 . . . 42 C1
Briar Cl NE21 . . . . . . . . . 40 C2
Briardene Cres NE3 . . . . 17 B3
Briardene Dr NE10 . . . . . 61 C4
Briar Edge NE12 . . . . . . . 11 B4
Briarfield Rd NE3 . . . . . . 17 C4
Briar La NE15 . . . . . . . . . 12 C1
Briar Pl NE15 . . . . . . . . . 28 B1
Briarside NE5 . . . . . . . . . 15 B3
Briarsyde NE12 . . . . . . . 11 C2
Briarsyde Cl NE16 . . . . . 54 A1
Briarwood Ave NE3 . . . . 9 C2
Briarwood Cres
  ⬛3 Dunston NE11 . . . . . 56 B4
  Newcastle-u-T NE6 . . . . 21 A1
Briary The NE15 . . . . . . . 12 A2
Bridge Pk NE3 . . . . . . . . 9 A3
Bridge Road S NE29 . . . . 24 C3
Bridge St
  Blaydon NE21 . . . . . . . . 41 B4
  Gateshead NE8 . . . . . . . 78 B4
  Seaton Burn NE13 . . . . . 2 B4
Bridges View NE8 . . . . . 79 A2
Bridgewater Cl
  Newcastle-u-T NE15 . . . 27 A3
  Wallsend NE28 . . . . . . . 22 A4
Bridlington Ave NE9 . . . 65 A3

Bridlington Par NE31 . . . 50 C3
Briermede Ave NE9 . . . . 65 A4
Briermede Pk NE9 . . . . . 65 A4
Brieryside NE5 . . . . . . . . 16 B2
Brigham Ave NE3 . . . . . . 16 C3
Brightlea DH3 . . . . . . . . . 69 A1
Brighton Ave Prim Sch
  NE8 . . . . . . . . . . . . . . . 79 A1
Brighton Gdns NE8 . . . . 58 A3
Brighton Par NE31 . . . . . 50 C3
Brighton Rd NE8 . . . . . . 58 A4
Brignall Gdns NE15 . . . . 28 B3
Brigside Cotts NE13 . . . . 2 C4
Brinkburn Ave
  Gateshead NE8 . . . . . . . 58 A4
  Newcastle-u-T NE3 . . . . 8 C2
  Whickham NE16 . . . . . . 55 A1
Brinkburn Cl NE6 . . . . . . 32 C2
Brinkburn Ct NE6 . . . . . . 32 C2
Brinkburn La ⬛21 NE6 . . 32 C2
Brinkburn Pl ⬛28 NE6 . . 32 C2
Brinkburn St S NE6 . . . . 47 B4
Brinkburn Sq ⬛7 NE6 . . 32 C1
Brinkburn St
  ⬛17 Newcastle-u-T NE6 . . 32 C2
  Newcastle-u-T, St Lawrence
  NE6 . . . . . . . . . . . . . . . 32 C1
  North Shields NE28 . . . . 24 A1
Brisbane Ave NE34 . . . . . 52 B3
Brisbane Ct NE8 . . . . . . . 78 B3
Brislee Gdns NE3 . . . . . . 16 C4
Bristol Terr NE4 . . . . . . . 76 A4
Britannia Ct NE4 . . . . . . 76 A4
Brittania Ho NE28 . . . . . 23 A1
Brixham Ave NE9 . . . . . . 65 A3
Brixham Cres NE32 . . . . 37 B1
Broadbank NE10 . . . . . . 61 A4
Broad Chare NE1 . . . . . . 78 B4
Broadlea NE10 . . . . . . . . 61 A4
Broad Mdws NE3 . . . . . . 17 A3
Broadmeadows Cl NE16 . 62 C1
Broadmead Way NE15 . . 28 B1
Broadoak NE10 . . . . . . . 49 A1
Broadpark NE10 . . . . . . . 61 A4
Broadpool Gn NE16 . . . . 55 B2
Broadpool Terr NE16 . . . 55 B2
Broadside NE10 . . . . . . . 60 B2
Broadstone Gr NE5 . . . . . 14 A1
Broadsway ⬛ NE28 . . . . 22 A4
Broadwater NE10 . . . . . . 49 A1
Broadway
  Gateshead NE9 . . . . . . . 59 A3
  Newcastle-u-T NE15 . . . 27 B3
  Whickham NE16 . . . . . . 62 B4
Broadway Ct NE3 . . . . . . 9 A3
Broadway E NE3 . . . . . . . 9 A3
Broadway East Fst Sch
  NE3 . . . . . . . . . . . . . . . 9 B3
Broadway Villas NE15 . . 28 C2
Broadway W NE3 . . . . . . 8 C3
Broadwell Ct NE3 . . . . . . 19 A4
Broadwood Prim Sch
  NE15 . . . . . . . . . . . . . . 28 A3
Broadwood Rd NE15 . . . 28 A3
Brockhampton Cl NE35 . 52 A2
Brockley Terr ⬛4 NE35 . . 52 A1
BROCKLEY WHINS . . . . 52 B3
Brockley Whins Sta
  NE32 . . . . . . . . . . . . . . 52 B3
Brock Sq S NE6 . . . . . . . 32 C1
Brock St NE6 . . . . . . . . . 32 C1
Brockwade NE10 . . . . . . 67 A4
Brockwell Cl NE21 . . . . . 40 C1
Brockwell Ho NE5 . . . . . 16 A2
Brockwell Rd NE38 . . . . . 69 B1
Brodrick Cl NE3 . . . . . . . 7 B1
Brokenheugh NE5 . . . . . 15 A1
Bromford Rd NE3 . . . . . . 7 B1
Bromley Ct NE3 . . . . . . . 7 B3
Brompton Workshops S
  NE11 . . . . . . . . . . . . . . 56 C4
Bronte St NE8 . . . . . . . . . 47 A1
Brooke Ave NE16 . . . . . . 54 C4
Brooke's Wlk NE34 . . . . 52 C2
Brookfield NE3 . . . . . . . . 17 C2
Brookfield Cres NE5 . . . . 14 A1
Brookfield Terr NE10 . . . 48 C1
Brookside Ave NE13 . . . . 2 A2
Brookside Cres NE5 . . . . 16 B1
Brooksmead NE28 . . . . . 21 B4
Brook St NE6 . . . . . . . . . 33 B1

Brookvale Ave NE3 . . . . . 17 B4
Broom Cl
  Blaydon NE21 . . . . . . . . 53 A4
  Whickham NE16 . . . . . . 55 B2
Broom Ct NE9 . . . . . . . . 69 B4
Broome Cl NE3 . . . . . . . . 8 A2
Broomfield NE32 . . . . . . 51 B2
Broomfield Ave NE6 . . . 20 C1
Broomfield Rd NE3 . . . . 17 C4
Broom Gn NE16 . . . . . . . 55 B2
Broomhill Gdns NE5 . . . 16 B1
Broom La NE16 . . . . . . . 55 B2
Broomlaw NE9 . . . . . . . . 66 A4
Broomlea Ct NE21 . . . . . 41 B3
Broomlee Cl NE7 . . . . . . 20 B3
Broomley Ct NE3 . . . . . . 8 A3
Broomley Wlk NE3 . . . . . 8 A3
Broomridge Ave NE15 . . 29 B2
Broom Terr NE16 . . . . . . 55 B2
Broomy Hill Rd NE15 . . . 12 B2
Brotherlee Rd NE3 . . . . . 8 A3
Brough Ct S NE6 . . . . . . 33 A3
Brough Gdns NE28 . . . . . 23 B4
Brough Park Way NE3 . . 33 B3
Brough St S NE6 . . . . . . 33 A3
Brough Way ⬛20 NE6 . . 33 A3
Brown Cres NE9 . . . . . . . 66 A1
Browning Sq NE8 . . . . . . 46 C2
Brownlow Cl NE7 . . . . . . 20 C3
Brown's Bldgs DH3 . . . . 70 B1
Brownsea Pl NE9 . . . . . . 58 C3
Brow The NE6 . . . . . . . . . 33 A1
Broxburn Ct NE5 . . . . . . 16 A3
Broxholm Rd NE6 . . . . . . 19 C1
Bruce Cl NE5 . . . . . . . . . 15 A2
Bruce Gdns NE5 . . . . . . . 29 A3
Brunel Lodge NE4 . . . . . 76 A3
Brunel St
  Gateshead NE8 . . . . . . . 57 C4
  Newcastle-u-T NE4 . . . . 76 B3
Brunel Terr NE4 . . . . . . . 76 B3
Brunel Wlk NE4 . . . . . . . 76 A3
Brunswick Gr NE13 . . . . 2 A2
BRUNSWICK GREEN . . . 2 A1
Brunswick Park Ind Est
  NE13 . . . . . . . . . . . . . . 2 A2
BRUNSWICK VILLAGE . . 2 A2
Brunton Ave
  Newcastle-u-T NE3 . . . . 8 A2
  Wallsend NE28 . . . . . . . 23 C3
Brunton Gr NE3 . . . . . . . 8 A2
Brunton La
  Newcastle-u-T, Brunton
  Park NE3, NE13 . . . . . . 4 B2
  Newcastle-u-T, Kingston Park
  NE3 . . . . . . . . . . . . . . . 7 A3
BRUNTON PARK . . . . . . 4 B1
Brunton Rd NE3 . . . . . . . 7 A3
Brunton St NE29 . . . . . . 24 B3
Brunton Way NE10 . . . . . 49 A2
Brussels Rd NE28 . . . . . . 21 C1
Buchanan Gn NE11 . . . . 77 A1
Buchanan St NE31 . . . . . 35 B1
Buckthorne Gr NE7 . . . . 20 A3
Buddle Cl NE4 . . . . . . . . 44 A4
Buddle Ind Est NE28 . . . 35 A4
Buddle Rd NE4 . . . . . . . . 43 C4
Buddle St NE28 . . . . . . . 22 A1
Bude Ct NE28 . . . . . . . . . 22 A4
Bude Gdns NE9 . . . . . . . 65 A3
Budle Cl NE3 . . . . . . . . . 8 B2
Budleigh Rd NE3 . . . . . . 8 A1
Bullfinch Dr NE16 . . . . . . 54 C2
Bungalows The
  Birtley DH3 . . . . . . . . . . 68 A2
  Gateshead NE10 . . . . . . 60 A4
  Wallsend NE28 . . . . . . . 23 A3
Bunyan Ave NE34 . . . . . 52 C3
Burdale Ave NE5 . . . . . . 15 B1
Burdon Lodge NE16 . . . . 63 A2
Burdon Pk NE16 . . . . . . . 63 A2
Burdon St NE29 . . . . . . . 24 B3
Burford Ct NE7 . . . . . . . . 19 B4
Burghley Rd NE10 . . . . . 59 B2
Burlington Ct NE2 . . . . . . 19 A2
Burlington Gdns NE6 . . . 32 C4
Burlison Gdns NE10 . . . . 47 B2
Burnaby Dr NE40 . . . . . . 39 A4
Burn Ave
  ⬛2 Longbenton NE12 . . 11 B4
  ⬛1 Wallsend NE28 . . . . 21 C2

Burnbank
  Gateshead NE10 . . . . . . 60 C2
  Seaton Burn NE13 . . . . . 2 B4
Burnbridge NE13 . . . . . . 2 B4
Burn Closes Cres NE28 . . 22 C3
Burney Villas NE8 . . . . . 46 C1
Burnfoot Way NE3 . . . . . 16 C3
Burnham Ave NE15 . . . . 26 C3
Burnham Gr NE6 . . . . . . 48 A4
Burn Heads Rd NE31 . . . 49 C4
Burnhills Gdns NE40 . . . 38 C1
Burnhope Gdns ⬛1 NE9 . 66 B3
Burnley St NE21 . . . . . . . 41 B2
Burnmoor Gdns NE9 . . . 66 B3
Burnopfield Gdns NE15 . 28 B2
Burn Rd NE21 . . . . . . . . . 40 C1
Burnside NE11 . . . . . . . . 55 A1
Burns Cres NE16 . . . . . . 54 C4
Burnside
  Gateshead NE10 . . . . . . 60 A3
  Jarrow NE32 . . . . . . . . . 51 B4
  NE28 . . . . . . . . . . . . . . 22 B2
Burnside Cl NE16 . . . . . . 62 B4
Burnside Rd NE3 . . . . . . 9 A3
Burnside The NE5 . . . . . 14 C1
Burns St NE32 . . . . . . . . 36 C3
Burnstones NE5 . . . . . . . 14 C1
Burn Terr
  Hebburn NE31 . . . . . . . 49 B2
  Wallsend NE28 . . . . . . . 23 A2
Burnthouse La
  Whickham NE16 . . . . . . 54 C1
  Whickham NE16 . . . . . . 54 C2
  Whickham, Whickham Fell
  NE16 . . . . . . . . . . . . . . 62 B4
Burnt Houses NE40 . . . . 39 A1
Burnville Rd NE6 . . . . . . 36 B3
Burstow Ave NE6 . . . . . . 48 A3
Burt Terr NE15 . . . . . . . . 13 B2
Burwell Ave NE5 . . . . . . 28 A4
Burwood Cl NE6 . . . . . . . 48 C4
Burwood Rd NE6 . . . . . . 48 B3
Buston Terr NE2 . . . . . . . 19 A1
Butcher's Bridge Rd
  NE32 . . . . . . . . . . . . . . 51 A4
Buteland Rd NE15 . . . . . 28 A3
Butterburn Cl NE7 . . . . . 20 C4
Butterfield Cl NE40 . . . . 38 B4
Buttermere NE10 . . . . . . 61 C4
Buttermere Ave NE16 . . . 54 A1
Buttermere Cl S NE5 . . . 15 C1
Buttermere Cres NE21 . . 53 A4
Buttermere Gdns NE9 . . 58 C1
Buxton Cl NE32 . . . . . . . 37 A1
Buxton Gdns NE5 . . . . . . 15 A3
Buxton Gn ⬛2 NE5 . . . . 15 A3
Buxton Rd NE32 . . . . . . . 37 A1
Byeways The NE12 . . . . . 10 C2
Bygate Cl NE3 . . . . . . . . 16 C3
BYKER . . . . . . . . . . . . . . 33 A1
Byker Bank NE6 . . . . . . . 14 C1
Byker Bridge NE1, NE6 . . 32 B2
Byker Bsns Development
  Ctr ⬛9 NE6 . . . . . . . . . 32 C1
Byker Cres ⬛17 NE6 . . . 33 A2
Byker Prim Sch NE6 . . . . 32 C1
Byker St NE6 . . . . . . . . . 34 A2
Byker Sta NE6 . . . . . . . . 33 A2
Byker Terr NE6 . . . . . . . . 34 A2
Byland Rd NE12 . . . . . . . 10 A2
Byrness NE5 . . . . . . . . . . 14 C1
Byrness Cl NE3 . . . . . . . . 16 A4
Byron Ave
  Hebburn NE31 . . . . . . . 36 A2
  ⬛6 Wallsend NE28 . . . . 23 B1
Byron Ct
  Newcastle-u-T NE5 . . . . 14 A2
  Whickham NE16 . . . . . . 54 C4
Byron Wlk NE8 . . . . . . . . 46 C2
By-Way The NE15 . . . . . . 12 B1
Bywell Ave
  Newcastle-u-T, Denton
  Burn NE15 . . . . . . . . . . 27 C3
  Newcastle-u-T, Fawdon
  NE3 . . . . . . . . . . . . . . . 8 A4
Bywell Cl NE40 . . . . . . . . 38 A3
Bywell Gdns
  Dunston NE11 . . . . . . . . 56 C1

**Bywell Gdns** continued
Gateshead NE9. . . . . . . . . . .**59** A2
**Bywell St** NE6 . . . . . . . . . . . .**33** B1
**Bywell Terr** NE32. . . . . . . . .**51** A3

## C

**Caedmon Com Prim Sch**
NE8. . . . . . . . . . . . . . . . . . . .**79** B1
**Caernarvon Cl** NE5 . . . . . . .**15** C4
**Caesar Way** NE28 . . . . . . . . .**22** C4
**Cairngorm Ave** NE38. . . . . .**71** C2
**Cairnsmore Cl** NE6 . . . . . . .**34** C4
**Cairns Way** NE3 . . . . . . . . . . .**8** A3
**Caldbeck Ave** NE6 . . . . . . . .**48** B3
**Caldbeck Cl** NE6 . . . . . . . . . .**48** B3
**Calderdale Ave** NE6. . . . . . .**34** A3
**Calder Gn** NE32. . . . . . . . . . .**51** B2
**Calder Wlk**
Sunniside NE16 . . . . . . . . . .**62** B2
Sunniside NE16 . . . . . . . . . .**62** B3
**Calderwood Cres** NE9. . . .**65** B3
**Caldew Cres** NE5 . . . . . . . . .**28** B4
**Caldwell Rd** NE3. . . . . . . . . . .**8** A4
**Caledonia St** NE31. . . . . . . .**35** B3
**Caledonia St** NE6 . . . . . . . . .**48** C4
**Calf Close Dr** NE32. . . . . . . .**51** A2
**Calf Close Rd** NE32 . . . . . . .**51** B2
**Calfclose La** NE32 . . . . . . . .**51** B2
**Calf Close Wlk** NE32 . . . . . .**51** B2
**California** NE21. . . . . . . . . . . .**41** A1
**Callaley Ave** NE16. . . . . . . . .**54** B2
**Callaly Way** NE6 . . . . . . . . . .**47** C4
**Callendar Ct** NE9 . . . . . . . . .**59** B1
**Callerton Parkway Sta**
NE13. . . . . . . . . . . . . . . . . . . . .**3** C1
**Callerton Rd** NE15 . . . . . . . .**12** C2
**Callerton View** NE5 . . . . . . .**13** C4
**Calow Way** NE16. . . . . . . . . .**54** B1
**Camberley Rd** NE28. . . . . . .**23** B4
**Camberwell Cl** NE11 . . . . . .**57** A2
**Cambo Cl** NE3 . . . . . . . . . . . . .**9** B1
**Cambo Gn** NE5 . . . . . . . . . . .**16** A2
**Camborne Gr** NE8 . . . . . . . .**79** C1
**Camborne Pl** NE8 . . . . . . . . .**79** C1
**Cambridge Ave**
Hebburn NE31 . . . . . . . . . . . .**36** A1
Longbenton NE12. . . . . . . . .**11** B4
Wallsend NE28. . . . . . . . . . . .**21** B3
**Cambridge Pl** DH3. . . . . . . .**70** B1
**Cambridge St** NE4 . . . . . . . .**76** B4
**Cambridge Terr** NE8 . . . . . .**79** B1
**Camelford Ct** NE15 . . . . . . .**27** A4
**Camilla St** NE8 . . . . . . . . . . .**79** C1
**CAMPBELL PARK** . . . . . . . .**36** A1
**Campbell Park Rd** NE31 . . .**36** A1
**Campbell St** NE31 . . . . . . . .**35** C3
**Camperdown** NE5 . . . . . . . .**15** A1
**Campion Gdns** NE10 . . . . . .**59** C1
**Camsey Cl** NE12 . . . . . . . . . .**10** A3
**Camsey Pl** NE12 . . . . . . . . . .**10** A3
**Canberra Dr** NE34 . . . . . . . .**52** B4
**Candelford Cl** NE7 . . . . . . . .**20** B3
**Canning St**
Hebburn NE31 . . . . . . . . . . . .**35** C1
Newcastle-u-T NE4 . . . . . . . .**29** C1
**Canning Street Prim Sch**
NE4. . . . . . . . . . . . . . . . . . . . .**29** B1
**Cannock Dr** NE7 . . . . . . . . . .**19** B4
**Cannon St** NE8 . . . . . . . . . . .**78** B4
**Canon Gr** NE32 . . . . . . . . . . .**37** A3
**Canonsfield Cl** NE15 . . . . . .**13** C3
**Canterbury Cl** NE12 . . . . . . .**10** B3
**Canterbury St** NE6 . . . . . . . .**33** B2
**Canterbury Way**
Hedworth NE32 . . . . . . . . . . .**50** C1
Wideopen NE13 . . . . . . . . . . .**2** B1
**Capstan La** NE6 . . . . . . . . . .**66** A2
**Cardigan Terr** NE6 . . . . . . . .**32** C3
**Cardinal Cl**
Longbenton NE12 . . . . . . . . .**10** B2
Newcastle-u-T NE15 . . . . . . .**13** C3
**Carham Cl** NE3 . . . . . . . . . . . .**9** B2
**Caris St** NE8, NE9. . . . . . . . .**58** C4
**Carlisle Ct** 11 NE10 . . . . . . .**47** C1
**Carlisle Pl** NE7 . . . . . . . . . . .**65** C4
**Carlisle St** NE10 . . . . . . . . . .**47** C1
**Carlton Ct** NE11 . . . . . . . . . .**57** B1
**Carlton Gdns** NE15 . . . . . . .**27** C3

**Carlton Grange** NE3 . . . .**17** B3
**Carlton Rd** NE12. . . . . . . . . .**11** B2
**Carlton Terr**
Gateshead NE9. . . . . . . . . . . .**58** B1
24 Springwell NE9 . . . . . . . .**67** A1
**Carlyle Cres** NE16. . . . . . . . .**54** C4
**Carlyle Ct** 4 NE28 . . . . . . . .**23** B1
**Carlyle St** 1 NE28 . . . . . . . .**23** B1
**Carnaby Rd** NE6 . . . . . . . . . .**48** B4
**Carnation Terr** 5 NE16. .**55** A3
**Carnforth Gdns** NE9 . . . . . .**65** C4
**Carnforth Gn** NE31 . . . . . . .**16** C4
**Carnoustie Cl** NE7 . . . . . . . .**20** A4
**Carnoustie Ct** NE10 . . . . . . .**61** A2
**Carol Gdns** NE7 . . . . . . . . . .**19** C3
**Caroline Cotts** NE5 . . . . . . .**28** C4
**Caroline Gdns** NE28. . . . . . .**23** B3
**Caroline St**
Jarrow NE32 . . . . . . . . . . . . . .**36** B3
Newcastle-u-T NE4 . . . . . . . .**44** A4
**Caroline Terr** NE21. . . . . . . .**41** A4
**Carolyn Cl** NE12 . . . . . . . . . .**11** A2
**Carrfield Rd** NE3. . . . . . . . . . .**8** A1
**CARR HILL**. . . . . . . . . . . . . . .**59** A3
**Carr Hill Com Prim Sch**
NE9. . . . . . . . . . . . . . . . . . . . .**59** A3
**Carr Hill Rd** N10, NE9. . . . . .**59** A3
**Carrigill Dr** NE12 . . . . . . . . . .**10** B2
**Carroll Wlk** NE34 . . . . . . . . .**52** C2
**Carr St** NE31. . . . . . . . . . . . . .**35** B3
**Carrsyde Cl** NE16 . . . . . . . . .**54** B1
**Carsdale Rd** NE3. . . . . . . . . . .**7** B1
**Carter Ave** NE31 . . . . . . . . . .**35** C2
**Carters Lo** 9 NE5 . . . . . . . . .**58** B1
**Cartington Ct** NE3 . . . . . . . . .**7** C3
**Cartington Terr** NE6. . . . . . .**20** A1
**Cartmel Gn** NE5 . . . . . . . . . .**15** B1
**Cartmel Gr** NE8. . . . . . . . . . .**57** C3
**Cartmel Pk** NE10 . . . . . . . . .**48** C1
**Carville Gdns** NE28 . . . . . . .**24** B1
**Carville Prim Sch** NE28 . . .**34** C4
**Carville Rd** NE28. . . . . . . . . .**21** C1
**Carville Rise** NE6 . . . . . . . . .**33** A2
**Carville St** NE10 . . . . . . . . . .**47** A2
**Carville Station Cotts**
NE28. . . . . . . . . . . . . . . . . . . .**22** A1
**Carvoran** 4 NE28. . . . . . . . .**23** A4
**Carwarding Pl** NE5 . . . . . . . .**16** A2
**Caspian Cl** NE32 . . . . . . . . . .**37** A1
**Casterton Gr** NE5 . . . . . . . . .**13** C3
**Castle Cl**
7 Newcastle-u-T NE3. . . . . . .**7** B1
Whickham NE16 . . . . . . . . . . .**54** C3
**Castledene Ct** NE3. . . . . . . .**19** A4
**Castle Farm Mews** NE2 .**19** A3
**Castle Garth** NE1 . . . . . . . . .**78** B4
**Castlegate Gdns** NE8 . . . . .**77** A1
**Castlenook Pl** NE15. . . . . . .**28** A3
**Castle Rd** NE38 . . . . . . . . . . .**69** C1
**Castles Farm Rd** NE2,
NE7. . . . . . . . . . . . . . . . . . . . .**19** A4
**Castleside Rd** NE15 . . . . . . .**28** B2
**Castle St** NE11. . . . . . . . . . . . .**4** A4
**Castleton Cl** NE2 . . . . . . . . .**19** A2
**Castleton Gr** NE2 . . . . . . . . .**19** A2
**Castleton Lodge** NE4 . . . . .**30** A1
**Castleton Rd** NE32. . . . . . . .**37** A1
**Castlewood Cl** NE15 . . . . . .**14** B2
**Catcheside Cl** NE16. . . . . . .**54** C1
**Cathedral Ct** NE8 . . . . . . . . .**46** C3
**Catherine View** 9 NE40 .**38** A3
**Catkin Wlk** NE40. . . . . . . . . .**38** C3
**Catton Gr** NE16 . . . . . . . . . . .**62** C3
**Causeway** NE9. . . . . . . . . . . .**59** A2
**Causeway The**
Gateshead NE9. . . . . . . . . . . .**58** C4
Throckley NE15 . . . . . . . . . . .**12** B1
**Causey Bldgs** NE3 . . . . . . . .**18** A4
**Causey Ho** NE3 . . . . . . . . . . .**18** A3
**Causey St** NE3 . . . . . . . . . . . .**18** A4
**Cavalier View** NE31 . . . . . . .**35** B3
**Cavendish Pl** NE2. . . . . . . . .**19** A1
**Cavendish Rd** NE2 . . . . . . . .**19** A1
**Caversham Rd** NE5 . . . . . . .**13** C3
**Cawburn Cl** NE7 . . . . . . . . . .**20** C3
**Cawfields Ct** NE12 . . . . . . . .**10** A2
**Caxton Wlk** NE34 . . . . . . . . .**52** C2
**Cayton Gr** NE5. . . . . . . . . . . .**13** C2
**Cecil Ct** NE28. . . . . . . . . . . . .**34** C4
**Cedar Cres**
Dunston NE11. . . . . . . . . . . . .**56** B3
Gateshead NE9. . . . . . . . . . . .**65** A4

**Cedar Gr**
Hebburn NE31. . . . . . . . . . . .**50** A3
Ryton NE40. . . . . . . . . . . . . . .**25** A2
Wallsend NE28. . . . . . . . . . . .**22** B2
**Cedar Rd**
Blaydon NE21. . . . . . . . . . . . .**41** B2
Newcastle-u-T NE4 . . . . . . . .**29** B3
**Cedars Gn** NE9. . . . . . . . . . . .**65** B3
**Cedars Sch The** NE9 . . . . . .**65** B3
**Cedars The**
Gateshead NE9. . . . . . . . . . . .**66** A2
Newcastle-u-T NE4 . . . . . . . .**76** B3
Whickham NE16 . . . . . . . . . .**62** C4
**Cedarway** NE10 . . . . . . . . . .**60** A1
**Cedarwood Ave** NE6 . . . . . .**21** B1
**Celadon Cl** NE15. . . . . . . . . .**27** A4
**Celandine Cl** NE3 . . . . . . . . . .**9** B3
**Celandine Way** NE10. . . . . .**60** A1
**Cemetery Rd**
Gateshead NE8. . . . . . . . . . . .**79** C1
Jarrow NE32 . . . . . . . . . . . . . .**37** A1
**Centenary Ct** NE4. . . . . . . . .**44** B4
**Central Newcastle High**
Sch (Jun Dept) NE3 . . . . . .**18** A4
**Central Parkway** NE1 . . .**76** C4
**Central Sta (Metro)**
NE1. . . . . . . . . . . . . . . . . . . . .**78** A4
**Centralway** NE11 . . . . . . . . .**64** A4
**Centurion Rd** NE15 . . . . . . .**28** A4
**Centurion Way** NE9 . . . . . . .**59** A2
**Ceolfrid Terr** NE32 . . . . . . . .**51** B4
**Chadderton Dr** NE5. . . . . . .**13** C3
**Chadwick Sch** NE28 . . . . . .**21** C1
**Chadwick Wlk** NE8 . . . . . . .**79** A2
**Chainbridge Ind Est**
NE21. . . . . . . . . . . . . . . . . . . .**42** B4
**Chainbridge Rd**
Blaydon, Derwenthaugh
NE21. . . . . . . . . . . . . . . . . . . .**42** B4
Blaydon NE21. . . . . . . . . . . . .**41** C3
**Chainbridge Road Ind Est**
NE21. . . . . . . . . . . . . . . . . . . .**42** B4
**Chalfont Rd** NE6 . . . . . . . . . .**48** B4
**Chamberlain Rd** NE40. . . . .**38** B4
**Chambers Cres** NE9 . . . . . . .**66** A1
**Chandler Ct** NE2. . . . . . . . . .**19** A2
**Chandlers Quay** NE6 . . . . . .**47** B4
**Chandless St** NE8 . . . . . . . . .**78** C3
**Chandos St** NE8 . . . . . . . . . .**58** B4
**Chandra Pl** 3 NE5. . . . . . . . .**15** C2
**Chantry Dr** NE13. . . . . . . . . . .**2** B2
**Chapel Cl** NE3 . . . . . . . . . . . . .**5** A1
**Chapel Ct**
Newburn NE15 . . . . . . . . . . .**25** C4
Seaton Burn NE13 . . . . . . . . .**2** B4
**Chapel House Dr** NE5 . . . . .**14** A1
**Chapel House Gr** NE5 . . . . .**14** A1
**Chapel House Mid Sch**
NE5. . . . . . . . . . . . . . . . . . . . .**13** C2
**Chapel House Rd** NE5. . . . .**14** A1
**Chapel Park Mid Sch**
NE5. . . . . . . . . . . . . . . . . . . . .**14** A3
**Chapel Pl** NE13 . . . . . . . . . . . .**2** B4
**Chapel Rd** NE32 . . . . . . . . . .**36** C3
**Chapel Row** DH3. . . . . . . . . .**71** A3
**Chapel View** NE13. . . . . . . . .**2** A2
**Chapelville** NE13 . . . . . . . . . .**2** B4
**Charlbury Rd** NE15 . . . . . . . .**67** A1
**Charles Ave**
Longbenton NE12 . . . . . . . . .**11** B4
Newcastle-u-T NE3 . . . . . . . . .**7** C2
**Charles Ct** 18 NE6 . . . . . . . .**33** A3
**Charles Perkins Memorial**
**Cottage Homes** DH3 . . .**70** B3
**Charles St**
Gateshead NE8. . . . . . . . . . . .**79** C2
Hazlerigg NE13 . . . . . . . . . . . .**2** A1
**Charleswood** NE9 . . . . . . . . .**9** B4
**Charlie St** NE40. . . . . . . . . . .**38** B1
**Charlotte Cl** NE4. . . . . . . . . .**76** B3
**Charlotte St**
Crawcrook NE40. . . . . . . . . . .**38** A3
Wallsend NE28. . . . . . . . . . . .**22** A2
**Charlton Mews** NE15. . . . . .**27** B2
**Charlton St** NE15 . . . . . . . . .**27** B2
**Charlton Villas** NE40 . . . . . .**39** A1
**Charlton Wlk** NE8 . . . . . . . . .**77** C1
**Charminster Gdns** NE6. .**20** A1
**Charnwood Ave** NE12 . . . . .**10** B2
**Charnwood Gdns** 1
NE9. . . . . . . . . . . . . . . . . . . . .**59** A1
**Chase Ct** NE16. . . . . . . . . . . .**55** A3

**Chase Sch** NE16 . . . . . . . . .**55** A3
**Chase The** NE38 . . . . . . . . . .**71** B1
**Chathill Terr** NE6 . . . . . . . . .**34** A1
**Chatsworth Gdns**
3 Newcastle-u-T NE5 . . . . . .**15** A3
Newcastle-u-T, Walker
NE6. . . . . . . . . . . . . . . . . . . . .**47** C4
**Chatsworth Pl** NE16. . . . . . .**54** C3
**Chatsworth Rd** NE32 . . . . . .**37** A1
**Chatton St** NE28 . . . . . . . . . .**24** A1
**Chatton Wynd** NE3. . . . . . . . .**8** B3
**Chaucer Ave** NE34 . . . . . . . .**52** C3
**Chaucer Cl** NE8. . . . . . . . . . .**46** C2
**Chaucer Rd** NE16 . . . . . . . . .**55** A4
**Chaytor St** NE32 . . . . . . . . . .**36** C4
**Cheam Cl** NE16 . . . . . . . . . . .**55** A1
**Cheddar Gdns** NE6. . . . . . . .**65** A3
**Cheeseburn Gdns** 8
NE5. . . . . . . . . . . . . . . . . . . . .**16** B1
**Chelmsford Gr** NE2 . . . . . . .**32** B3
**Chelsea Gdns** NE8 . . . . . . . .**59** A4
**Cheltenham Dr** NE35. . . . . .**52** A2
**Cheltenham Terr** NE6 . . . . .**32** C3
**Chelton Cl** NE13 . . . . . . . . . . .**4** B4
**Chepstow Gdns** NE8 . . . . . .**57** C3
**Chepstow Rd** NE15. . . . . . . .**28** A2
**Cherryburn Gdns** NE4 . . . .**29** C4
**Cherrytree Dr** NE16. . . . . . .**55** B4
**Cherrytree Gdns** NE9 . . . . .**65** A3
**Cherry Tree Wlk** NE31. . . . .**50** A4
**Cherrywood** NE6 . . . . . . . . .**20** C1
**Chesham Gdns** NE5. . . . . . .**13** C2
**Chesham Gn** NE3 . . . . . . . . . .**8** A1
**Cheshire Ave** DH3 . . . . . . . .**70** B1
**Cheshire Ct** NE31 . . . . . . . . .**35** B1
**Cheshire Gdns** NE28 . . . . . .**21** B3
**Chesmond Dr** NE21 . . . . . . .**41** B3
**Chessar Ave** NE5 . . . . . . . . .**15** C3
**Chester Ave** NE31 . . . . . . . . .**35** B1
**Chesterfield Rd** NE4 . . . . . .**44** B4
**Chester Pl** NE8 . . . . . . . . . . .**79** B2
**Chesters** 5 NE28 . . . . . . . . .**23** A4
**Chesters Ave** NE12. . . . . . . .**10** B1
**Chesters Ct** NE9 . . . . . . . . . .**58** B2
**Chesters Ct** NE12 . . . . . . . . .**10** C2
**Chesters Gdns** NE40 . . . . . .**38** A4
**Chesters Pk** NE9 . . . . . . . . . .**58** B2
**Chesters The** NE5. . . . . . . . .**14** A1
**Chester Way** NE32 . . . . . . . .**51** C2
**Chesterwood Dr** NE28 . . . .**20** C2
**Chesterwood Terr** NE10 .**49** A1
**Chestnut Ave**
Newcastle-u-T NE16 . . . . . . .**55** A1
Whickham NE16 . . . . . . . . . . .**55** A1
**Chestnut Cl** NE32. . . . . . . . .**51** C1
**Chestnut Gdns** NE8 . . . . . . .**57** B4
**Chestnut St** NE28 . . . . . . . . .**22** A1
**Cheswick Dr** NE3 . . . . . . . . . .**9** B2
**Chevin Cl** NE6 . . . . . . . . . . . .**21** C1
**Chevington** NE10 . . . . . . . . .**60** C1
**Chevington Gdns** 6
NE5. . . . . . . . . . . . . . . . . . . . .**16** B1
**Cheviot Cl** NE37 . . . . . . . . . .**69** C2
**Cheviot Ct**
Blaydon NE21. . . . . . . . . . . . .**41** B3
Newcastle-u-T NE7 . . . . . . . .**19** B4
**Cheviot Gdns** NE11 . . . . . . .**56** C3
**Cheviot Gn** NE11. . . . . . . . . .**56** C4
**Cheviot Mount** NE6 . . . . . . .**33** A2
**Cheviot Prim Sch** NE5 . . . .**15** B4
**Cheviot Rd**
Blaydon NE21. . . . . . . . . . . . .**41** B3
Hebburn NE32 . . . . . . . . . . . .**50** C4
**Cheviot View**
Brunswick Village NE13. . . . .**2** A2
Gateshead NE10. . . . . . . . . . .**59** C2
Longbenton NE12. . . . . . . . .**11** A2
**Chevron The** 4 NE6 . . . . .**32** C1
**Chichester Cl**
Gateshead NE8. . . . . . . . . . . .**79** B2
Newcastle-u-T NE3 . . . . . . . . .**9** B2
**Chichester Way** NE32. . . . . .**51** A1
**Chicken Rd** NE28 . . . . . . . . .**21** B4
**Chilcote Cl** NE10 . . . . . . . . . .**59** C3
**Chilcrosse** NE10 . . . . . . . . . .**60** B2
**Chillingham Ct** NE19 . . .**33** A3
**Chillingham Dr** NE29. . . . . .**24** B4
**Chillingham Ind Est**
NE6. . . . . . . . . . . . . . . . . . . . .**33** A3
**Chillingham Rd** NE6 . . . . . . .**33** A4

**Chillingham Road Prim**
**Sch** NE6. . . . . . . . . . . . . . .**33** A4
**Chillingham Road Sta**
NE6. . . . . . . . . . . . . . . . . . . . .**33** B3
**Chillingham Terr** NE32 .**51** C4
**Chilside Rd** NE10 . . . . . . . . .**59** C3
**Chiltern Gdns** NE11. . . . . . .**57** B3
**Chiltern Rd** NE29 . . . . . . . . .**38** B4
**Chipchase** NE38 . . . . . . . . . .**71** B4
**Chipchase Cres** NE5 . . . . . .**14** C3
**Chipchase Mews** NE3 . . . . . .**4** A1
**Chipchase Terr** NE32 . . . . . .**51** B3
**Chirton Wynd** NE6 . . . . . . . .**33** A1
**Chiswick Gdns** NE8 . . . . . . .**58** C4
**Chollerford Cl** NE3. . . . . . . .**17** B4
**Chopwell Gdns** NE9 . . . . . . .**66** B2
**Chorley Pl** NE6 . . . . . . . . . . .**33** C1
**Chowdean Terr** 4 NE9 . .**65** A4
**CHOWDENE** . . . . . . . . . . . . .**64** C4
**Chowdene Bank** NE11,
NE9. . . . . . . . . . . . . . . . . . . . .**65** B3
**Christie Terr** NE6 . . . . . . . . .**34** A1
**Christmas Pl** NE8 . . . . . . . . .**77** B2
**Christon Cl** NE3 . . . . . . . . . . .**9** C1
**Christon Rd** NE3. . . . . . . . . . .**9** B1
**Christon Way** NE10 . . . . . . .**49** A2
**Christopher Rd** NE6 . . . . . . .**33** C3
**Chudleigh Gdns** NE5 . . . . . .**13** C2
**Church Ave** NE3 . . . . . . . . . . .**9** B1
**Church Bank**
Jarrow NE32 . . . . . . . . . . . . . .**37** B3
Newburn NE15 . . . . . . . . . . .**26** A3
Wallsend NE28. . . . . . . . . . . .**22** B2
**Church Chare** NE16 . . . . . . .**55** A3
**Church Cl** 10 NE10 . . . . . . .**47** C1
**Churchdown** NE35 . . . . . . . .**52** A2
**Church Dr** NE9 . . . . . . . . . . . .**58** C2
**Churcher Gdns** NE28 . . . . . .**21** B4
**Church Gn** 1 NE21 . . . . . . .**41** B3
**Churchill Com Coll**
NE28. . . . . . . . . . . . . . . . . . . .**23** A4
**Churchill Gdns** NE2. . . . . . .**19** B1
**Churchill Mews** NE6 . . . . . .**47** B4
**Churchill St**
Newcastle-u-T NE1 . . . . . . . .**76** C4
Wallsend NE28. . . . . . . . . . . .**23** C4
**Church La**
Gateshead NE9. . . . . . . . . . . .**59** A2
Newcastle-u-T NE3 . . . . . . . . .**9** B1
Newcastle-u-T NE10 . . . . . . .**47** C1
**Church Pl** NE10. . . . . . . . . . .**47** C1
**Church Rd**
Gateshead NE9. . . . . . . . . . . .**58** C1
Newburn NE15 . . . . . . . . . . .**26** A3
Newcastle-u-T NE3 . . . . . . . . .**9** B1
**Church Rise**
Ryton NE40. . . . . . . . . . . . . . .**25** C1
Whickham NE16 . . . . . . . . . . .**55** A3
**Church St**
Birtley DH3 . . . . . . . . . . . . . . .**70** B4
Blaydon NE21. . . . . . . . . . . . .**41** A1
Dunston NE11. . . . . . . . . . . . .**77** A1
Gateshead, Felling NE10 . . . .**59** C2
Gateshead NE8. . . . . . . . . . . .**78** B4
Hebburn NE31 . . . . . . . . . . . .**35** B3
Newcastle-u-T NE6 . . . . . . . .**48** C4
Sunniside NE16 . . . . . . . . . . .**62** B1
**Church Terr** NE21 . . . . . . . . .**41** B3
**Church View**
Boldon Colliery NE35 . . . . . .**52** A1
Wallsend NE28. . . . . . . . . . . .**22** B2
**Churchwalk Ho** NE6 . . . . . .**34** B1
**Church Wlk** NE6 . . . . . . . . . .**34** B1
**Cinderford Cl** NE35 . . . . . . .**52** A2
**Circle The** NE32. . . . . . . . . . .**51** B4
**Civic Ctr** NE31 . . . . . . . . . . . .**36** A1
**Clanfield Ct** NE3 . . . . . . . . . .**19** A4
**Clapham Ave** NE6 . . . . . . . . .**33** B1
**Clarance Pl** NE3 . . . . . . . . . . .**9** C1
**Clara St**
Blaydon NE21. . . . . . . . . . . . .**41** A1
Newcastle-u-T NE4 . . . . . . . .**43** C4
**Claremont Ave** NE15 . . . . . .**27** B3
**Claremont North Ave**
NE8. . . . . . . . . . . . . . . . . . . . .**79** B2
**Claremont Pl** NE8 . . . . . . . . .**79** B1
**Claremont South Ave**
NE8. . . . . . . . . . . . . . . . . . . . .**79** B1
**Claremont St** NE8 . . . . . . . . .**79** B1
**Claremont Terr**
Gateshead NE8. . . . . . . . . . . .**49** A1
9 Springwell NE9 . . . . . . . . .**67** A1
**Claremont Wlk** NE8. . . . . . .**79** A1
**Clarendon Mews** NE3 . . . . . .**4** C1

Clarendon Rd NE6 ......20 A1
Clarewood PI NE5 ......29 A4
Clarke Terr NE10 ......59 B4
Clarks Hill Wlk NE15 ....26 A3
Clasper Ct NE4 ......76 B3
Clasper Way NE16 ......42 C3
Claude St **10** NE40 ......38 B3
Claverdon St NE5 ......13 C4
Clavering PI NE1 ......78 A4
Clavering Rd
  Blaydon NE21 ..........41 B1
  Whickham NE16 ........43 A1
Clavering Sq NE11 ......56 B4
Clavering St NE28 ......23 C1
Clavering Way NE21 ....42 A2
Claypath NE10 ........67 A4
Claypath St **4** NE6 ....32 B2
Clayton St W NE1 ......76 C4
Clayton St NE32 ......36 C3
Clayton Terr NE8 ......47 B1
Clayworth Rd NE3 ....4 B1
Cleadon Gdns NE9 ....66 B3
Cleadon St NE6 ......33 C2
Cleasby Gdns NE9 ....58 B2
Cleghorn St **5** NE4 ....33 A4
Clegwell Terr NE31 ....36 A2
Clematis Cres NE9 ....66 B2
Clement St NE9 ......58 B1
Clennel Ave NE31 ....35 B1
Clennel Ho **4** NE4 ....29 C1
Clent Way NE12 ......10 B2
Clephan St NE11 ......44 B1
Clervaux Terr NE32 ....37 A2
Cleveland Ct NE32 ....36 B3
Cleveland Gdns
  Newcastle-u-T NE7 ....19 B3
  Wallsend NE28 ........23 C3
Cleveland Mews NE1 ..77 A1
Clifford Gdns **4** NE40 ..38 B3
Clifford Rd NE6 ......33 B1
Clifford St
  Blaydon NE21 ..........41 B3
  Newcastle-u-T NE6 ....32 C2
Clifford Terr NE40 ....38 B3
Clifton Ave **10** NE28 ....21 C2
Clifton Ct NE40 ......40 A4
Clifton Ct
  **2** Gateshead NE9 ....66 C1
  Newcastle-u-T NE3 ......7 B3
Clifton Gdns
  Gateshead NE9 ........58 B3
  North Shields NE29 ....24 C3
Clifton Rd NE4 ......30 A1
Clifton Terr NE12 ....11 B3
Cliftonville Ave NE4 ..29 C1
Clifton Wlk NE15 ......13 C2
Clinton PI NE3 ......4 B2
Clipsham Cl NE12 ....10 C2
Clipstone Ave NE6 ....48 A3
Clipstone Cl NE15 ....12 A2
Clive PI NE6 ......32 C1
Clive St **9** NE34 ......52 C4
Clockburnsyde Cl NE16 .54 A1
Clockmill Rd NE11, NE8 .77 A1
Cloister Ct NE8 ......78 C3
Cloister Garth NE7 ....10 A1
Cloisters The NE7 ....10 A1
Cloister Wlk NE32 ....37 A3
Close NE1 ......78 A4
Close The
  Blaydon NE21 ..........40 C1
  Newcastle-u-T NE5 ....27 C4
Clovelly Ave NE4 ......29 C1
Clovelly PI NE32 ......37 C1
Clover Ave
  Gateshead NE10 ......47 A2
  Winlaton Mill NE21 ....53 B2
Cloverdale Gdns
  Newcastle-u-T NE7 ....19 C3
  Whickham NE16 ......55 A1
Cloverfield Ave NE3 ..8 A2
Cloverhill NE12 ......51 B1
Clover Hill NE16 ....62 C2
Cloverhill Ave NE31 ..43 A4
Clover Hill Com Prim Sch
  NE16 ......62 A4
Cloverhill Dr NE40 ..38 C4
Clumber St N NE4 ....76 A3
Clumber St NE4 ......76 A3
Clyde Ave NE31 ......50 A3
Clydedale Ave NE12 ..11 B4

Clydesdale Mount **8**
  NE6 ......33 A1
Clydesdale Rd NE6 ....33 A1
Clyde St NE8 ......58 C4
Coach La
  Hazlerigg NE13 ........4 B4
  Newcastle-u-T NE7 ....20 A4
Coach Open NE28 ....23 C1
Coach Rd
  Throckley NE15 ........12 A1
  Wallsend NE28 ........22 A1
Coach Road Gn NE10 ..47 B2
Coalway Dr NE16 ....55 A4
Coalway La NE16 ....55 A3
Coalway La N NE16 ....55 A3
Coanwood Gdns NE11 .57 A1
Coanwood Rd NE15 ...43 A4
Coanwood Way NE16 ..62 C3
Coast Rd
  Newcastle-u-T NE6, NE7,
    NE28 ......20 C2
  Wallsend NE28, NE29 ..22 A4
Coatsworth Ct NE8 ....79 B2
Coatsworth Rd NE8 ...79 B1
Cobalt Cl NE15 ......27 A4
Cobblestone Ct NE6 ..32 C1
Cobden St
  Gateshead NE8 ........46 C1
  **4** Wallsend NE28 ....21 C2
Cobden Terr NE8 ......46 C1
Cobham PI NE6 ......48 C4
Coble Dene NE29 ....24 C2
Coburg St NE8 ......79 C2
Cochrane Ct NE4 ......29 C1
Cochrane Park Ave NE7 20 A2
Cochrane St NE4 ......29 C1
Cochran St NE21 ......41 B4
Cockburn Terr NE29 ..24 B3
Cockermouth Gn NE5 ..28 B4
Cohen Ct NE8 ......58 A4
Colbeck Ave NE16 ....43 A1
Colby Ct NE4 ......76 B4
Coldingham Gdns NE5 .16 B2
Coldside Gdns NE5 ...13 C3
Coldstream Gdns NE28 .23 B3
Coldstream Rd NE15 ..28 C3
Coldwell La NE10 ....59 B3
Coldwell Park Ave NE10 59 C3
Coldwell Park Dr NE10 .59 C3
Coldwell St NE10 ....59 C4
Coldwell Terr **2** NE10 .59 B3
Colebridge Cl NE5 ....16 A3
Colebrooke DH3 ......70 C2
Colegate NE10 ......60 B3
Colegate Com Prim Sch
  NE10 ......60 B3
Colegate W NE10 ....60 B3
Cole Gdns NE10 ....61 C4
Colepeth NE10 ......60 A3
Coleridge Ave NE9 ....64 C4
Coleridge Sq NE31 ...35 C2
Coley Gn NE5 ......13 C4
Coley Hill Cl NE5 ....14 A4
Colgrove PI NE3 ....7 C1
Colgrove Way NE3 ....8 A1
Colin PI NE6 ......34 B4
College La NE1 ......11 A2
College Rd NE31 ....49 C2
Collier Cl NE15 ......12 B1
Colliery Rd NE11 ....44 B2
Collingwood Ave NE28 .23 A3
Collingwood Gdns NE10 47 C2
Collingwood Mews NE3 .9 A1
Collingwood St
  **10** Gateshead NE10 ..47 C1
  Hebburn NE31 ........36 B2
  Newcastle-u-T NE1 ....78 A4
Collingwood Terr
  Dunston NE11 ........77 A1
  **2** Newcastle-u-T NE2 .19 A1
Colmet Ct NE11 ......64 B4
Colnbrook Cl NE3 ....7 B3
Colston St NE4 ......29 B2
Colton Gdns NE9 ....65 B3
Coltpark NE5 ......15 A1
Coltsfoot Gdns NE10 ..59 B2
Columba Wlk NE3 ....9 C1
Columbia Grange NE3 ..7 C1
Colwell PI NE5 ......28 C3
Colwyne PI NE5 ......15 C2
Colwyn Par NE31 ....50 C2
Combe Dr NE15 ......26 C3

Comma Ct NE11 ......57 A3
Commercial Rd
  Jarrow NE32 ..........37 A4
  Newcastle-u-T, Byker
    NE6 ......33 A1
  Newcastle-u-T, South
    Gosforth NE3 ........9 C1
Commercial St **9** NE21 .41 A1
Concorde Way NE32 ...36 C2
Condercum Ct NE15 ..29 A1
Condercum Ind Est NE4 29 B1
Condercum Rd NE4 ....29 B1
Conewood Ho NE15 ...8 A2
Conhope La NE15, NE4. .29 A2
Conifer Cl NE21 ......53 A4
Coniscliffe Ave NE3 ...17 A4
Coniston
  Birtley DH3 ..........70 C2
  Gateshead NE10 ......61 C4
Coniston Ave
  Hebburn NE31 ........50 B4
  Newcastle-u-T NE2 ...18 C2
  Whickham NE16 ......55 C3
Coniston Cl NE15 ....25 C3
Coniston Cres NE21 ..53 A4
Coniston Ct
  Newcastle-u-T NE5 ...28 C4
  Wallsend NE28 ......23 B4
Coniston Dr NE32 ....51 C3
Coniston Gdns NE9 ...59 A1
Coniston PI NE9 ....59 A1
Coniston Rd NE28 ....23 B4
Connaught Gdns NE12 .11 B3
Connaught Terr NE32 ..36 C2
Conningsby Cl NE3 ...9 A4
Consett Rd NE11 ....56 C1
Constable Cl NE40 ...39 B4
Constables Garth **7**
  DH3 ......70 B4
Content St NE21 ......41 B1
Convent Rd NE4 ......29 B3
Conway Cl NE40 ....39 C4
Conway Dr NE7 ......19 B4
Conway Gdns NE28 ..21 B4
Conway Sq NE9 ....58 C4
Conyers Rd NE6 ....33 A2
Cook Gdns NE10 ....61 A4
Cookson's La NE1 ....77 A4
Coop Bldgs **13** DH3 ....70 B4
Co-operative Cres **6**
  NE10 ......59 B3
Co-operative Terr
  Brunswick Village NE13 .2 A2
  Gateshead NE10 ......59 B3
Copperas La NE15 ....28 A3
Coppergate Ct NE31 ..36 A3
Coppers Cl NE11 ....57 A3
Copse The
  Blaydon NE21 ..........42 B2
  Newcastle-u-T NE3 ...9 B4
  Washington NE37 ....67 C2
Coquet NE38 ......71 B1
Coquet Ave NE3 ....8 C2
Coquet Bldgs NE15 ...13 C1
Coquetdale Ave NE6 ..34 B2
Coquet Gr NE15 ....12 A2
Coquet St
  Hebburn NE31 ........35 B2
  Jarrow NE32 ..........36 B1
  Newcastle-u-T NE1 ...32 B2
Coquet Terr NE6 ....32 C4
Corbitt St NE8 ......77 C1
Corbridge Ave NE13 ..2 B2
Corbridge Ct NE12 ...10 A2
Corbridge Rd NE6 ....33 A2
Corbridge St NE6 ....32 C2
Corby Gdns NE6 ....34 A2
Corchester Wlk NE7 ..20 A4
Cormorant Cl **4** NE38 .71 B3
Cormorant Dr NE11 ...77 A2
Cornel Mews NE7 ....20 A3
Cornel Rd NE7 ......20 A3
Cornfields The NE31 ..35 C2
Cornforth Cl NE10 ....61 B2
Cornhill
  Hedworth NE32 ......51 B1
  Newcastle-u-T NE5 ...15 A1
Cornhill Ave NE3 ....4 B3
Cornmoor Gdns NE16 .55 A1
Cornmoor Rd NE16 ...55 A2
Cornwall Rd NE31 ....50 B3
Cornwall Ct NE3 ....19 A4

Coronation Ave NE16 ..62 C2
Coronation Bglws NE3 ..9 B1
Coronation Rd
  Newcastle-u-T NE5 ...13 C3
  Sunniside NE16 ......62 C2
Coronation St
  Ryton NE40 ..........40 A4
  Wallsend NE28 ......22 A2
Coronation Terr
  **3** Boldon Colliery
    NE35 ......52 A1
  **7** Gateshead NE9 ...65 A4
  **21** Springwell NE9 ...67 A2
Corpus Christi RC Prim
  Sch NE8 ......58 A4
Corrofell Gdns NE10 ..48 B1
Corsair NE16 ......54 B2
Corsenside NE5 ......15 A1
Corstopitum **3** NE28 ..23 A4
Cosford Ct NE3 ......8 B3
Cosserat PI NE31 ....35 B3
Cosyn St NE6 ......32 B1
Cotehill Rd **2** NE5 ....15 C1
Cotemede Ct NE10 ...60 C1
Cotemede Ct NE10 ...60 C2
Cotfield Wlk NE8 ....79 A1
Cotgarth The NE10 ...60 A3
Cotswold Gdns
  Dunston NE11 ........56 C3
  Newcastle-u-T NE7 ...19 B3
Cotswold La NE35 ...52 B2
Cotswold PI NE8 ....58 B4
Cotterdale Ave **1** NE8 .58 B4
Cotter Riggs PI NE5 ..13 C2
Cotter Riggs Wlk NE5 .13 C2
Cottersdale Gdns NE5 .13 C3
Coulthards La NE8 ...78 C3
Coulthards PI NE8 ....46 C4
Counden Rd **4** NE5 ....14 C3
Countess Dr NE15 ...28 B3
Coupland Gr NE32 ...51 A3
Courtfield Rd NE6 ....34 A4
Courtney Ct NE3 ....7 B3
Court The NE16 ......55 B2
Coutts Rd NE6 ......33 C4
Coventry Gdns
  Newcastle-u-T NE4 ...44 A4
  North Shields NE29 ..24 C4
Coventry Way NE32 ...51 A1
Coverdale NE10 ....60 C2
Covers The
  Longbenton NE12 ....11 C2
  Wallsend NE28 ......21 C3
  Whickham NE16 ......42 B1
Cowan Cl NE21 ......40 C4
Cowans Ho NE15 ....27 A2
Cowdray Ct NE3 ....7 A3
Cowdrey Ho NE29 ...24 B3
Cowen Gdns NE9 ....65 B1
Cowen Rd NE21 ....41 C3
Cowen St
  Blaydon NE21 ..........53 A4
  Newcastle-u-T NE6 ...34 A2
COWGATE ......30 B4
Cowpath Gdns NE10 ..48 C1
COXLODGE ......8 B1
Coxlodge Rd NE3 ....8 B1
Coxlodge Terr NE3 ...8 B1
Coxon St NE10 ......49 A2
Coxon Terr NE8 ....47 B1
Cradock Ave NE31 ...49 C4
Craggyknowe NE37 ...69 B2
Craghall Dene NE2 ...18 C4
Craghall Dene Ave NE2 .18 C4
Cragside
  Brunswick Village NE13 .2 B2
  Newcastle-u-T NE7 ...19 B3
Cragside Cl NE11 ....56 C2
Cragside Gdns
  Dunston NE11 ........56 C1
  Wallsend NE28 ......21 C3
Cragside Prim Sch NE7 19 B3
Cragside Rd NE37 ...69 C3
Cragston Ave NE5 ...16 A3
Cragston Ct NE5 ....16 A2
Craigmillar Ave NE5 ..16 A3
Craigmillar Cl NE5 ...16 A3
Craigmont Ct NE12 ...11 B2
Craig St **2** DH3 ....70 B4
Crake Way NE38 ....71 B2
Cramer St NE8 ......79 C1

Cramond Ct NE9 ......64 C3
Cranbrook Ave NE3 ....9 A3
Cranbrook Ct NE3 ....7 C3
Cranbrook Rd NE15 ...43 A4
Cranesville NE9 ......59 B1
Cranfield PI NE15 ....27 A3
Cranford Gdns NE15 ..27 C3
Cranlea NE3 ......7 A2
Cranleigh Ave NE3 ...7 A3
Crantock Rd NE3 ....8 A1
Cranwell Ct NE3 ....7 A3
Cranwell Dr NE13 ....2 B2
Craster Ct NE11 ....57 B2
Craster Gdns NE28 ...23 A3
Craster Sq NE3 ....8 B2
Craster Terr NE7 ....19 C2
Crathie DH3 ......68 B3
CRAWCROOK ......38 A4
Crawcrook Terr NE40 ..38 A3
Crawford Terr NE6 ...34 A1
Crawley Ave NE31 ...49 C3
Crawley Gdns NE16 ..55 B3
Crawley Rd NE28 ....21 C1
Crawley Sq NE31 ...49 C3
Craythorne Gdns NE6..20 B2
Creighton Ave NE3 ..16 C4
Creland Way NE5 ....16 A3
Crescent The
  **5** Dunston NE11 ....56 B4
  Jarrow NE32 ..........50 C4
  Newcastle-u-T, Kenton
    Bankfoot NE13 ......6 C2
  Newcastle-u-T NE7 ...10 C1
  Ryton NE40 ..........25 B1
  Sunniside NE16 ......62 C2
  **9** Throckley NE15 ...12 B2
  Wallsend NE28 ......21 C3
  Whickham NE16 ......55 B2
Crescent Way NE12 ...11 C4
Crescent Way N NE12 .11 C4
Crescent Way S NE12 .11 C4
Creslow NE10 ......60 B2
Cresswell Dr NE3 ....7 C3
Cresswell Rd NE28 ...21 B1
Cresswell St NE6 ....33 B2
Cresthaven NE10 ....60 A2
Criddle St NE8 ......46 C4
Crieff Gr NE32 ......51 C3
Crigdon Hill NE5 ....15 A1
Crighton NE38 ......69 C1
Cripps Ave NE10 ....61 A4
Crocus Cl NE21 ......40 C2
Croft Ave
  Longbenton NE12 ....11 C3
  Wallsend NE28 ......22 A2
Croft Cl NE40 ......39 C4
Croftdale Rd NE21 ...41 A2
Croft Dale Way NE15 .26 C3
Croftside DH3 ......68 B1
Croftsway NE4 ......44 B4
Croft Terr NE32 ....36 C2
Croft The
  Newcastle-u-T NE3 ...17 B4
  Ryton NE40 ..........39 C4
Croft View NE40 ....38 A3
Croft Villas NE40 ....38 A3
Croftwell Cl NE21 ...41 C1
Cromdale PI NE5 ....15 C1
Cromer Ave NE9 ....65 A3
Cromer Ct NE9 ......65 B3
Cromer Gdns NE2 ...18 C3
Crompton Rd NE6 ...32 C4
Cromwell Ave NE21 ..41 A2
Cromwell Ct
  Newcastle-u-T NE10 ..49 B2
  Ryton NE21 ..........40 C1
Cromwell PI NE21 ...40 C1
Cromwell Rd
  Gateshead NE10 ......49 A2
  Whickham NE16 ......55 B4
Cromwell St
  Gateshead NE8 ......46 C1
  Ryton NE21 ..........40 C1
Cromwell Terr
  Gateshead NE8 ......79 A1
  Newcastle-u-T NE10 ..49 A2
CROOKHILL ......25 B1
Crookhill Com Prim Sch
  NE40 ......25 C1

Crookhill Terr NE40 . . . . . . . .**40** A4
Cropthorne NE10 . . . . . . . . . . .**61** A2
Crosby Gdns NE9 . . . . . . . . . .**65** C3
Cross Ave NE28 . . . . . . . . . . .**21** A4
Crossbank Rd NE5 . . . . . . . . .**16** B3
Crossbrook Rd **2** NE6 . . . . .**16** B2
Cross Dr NE40 . . . . . . . . . . . .**25** A2
Crossfield Pk NE10 . . . . . . . .**59** B2
Crossfield Terr NE6 . . . . . . . .**48** C4
Crosshill Rd NE15 . . . . . . . . . .**43** A4
Cross Keys La NE9 . . . . . . . . .**58** B1
Cross La NE11 . . . . . . . . . . . .**43** C2
Crosslaw NE5 . . . . . . . . . . . . .**15** A1
Cross Par NE4 . . . . . . . . . . . .**76** B4
Cross Row
  Gateshead NE8 . . . . . . . . . .**47** A1
  Ryton NE40 . . . . . . . . . . . . .**40** A4
Cross St
  Gateshead NE8 . . . . . . . . . .**79** C1
  Newcastle-u-T, St Ann's
  NE6 . . . . . . . . . . . . . . . . . .**32** B1
Crossway
  Gateshead NE9 . . . . . . . . . .**59** A2
  Newcastle-u-T NE2 . . . . . . .**18** C3
Crossway Ct NE17 . . . . . . . . .**17** A3
Crossways NE32 . . . . . . . . . . .**51** B1
Crossways The NE13 . . . . . . .**4** A4
Crossway The
  Newcastle-u-T, Kenton
  NE3 . . . . . . . . . . . . . . . . . .**17** A4
  Newcastle-u-T, Lemington
  NE15 . . . . . . . . . . . . . . . . .**53** C3
Crossway Villas **1** NE9 . . . .**58** C2
Croudace Row **2** NE10 . . .**59** C4
Crow Bank NE28 . . . . . . . . . . .**22** A2
Crowhall La NE10 . . . . . . . . . .**59** C4
Crowhall Towers **7**
  NE10 . . . . . . . . . . . . . . . . .**59** C4
Crowley Ave NE16 . . . . . . . . .**55** B4
Crowley Gdns NE21 . . . . . . . .**41** B2
Crowley Rd NE16 . . . . . . . . . .**42** C1
Crowley Villas **2** NE16 . . . .**42** C1
Crown Terr NE40 . . . . . . . . . .**39** A1
Crowther Ind Est
  Birtley NE37 . . . . . . . . . . . .**71** B4
  Washington NE38 . . . . . . . . .**69** B1
Crowther Rd NE38 . . . . . . . . .**69** B1
Croxdale Gdns NE10 . . . . . . .**48** C2
Croxdale Terr
  Gateshead NE10 . . . . . . . . .**48** C1
  Greenside NE40 . . . . . . . . . .**39** B1
Cruddas Pk NE4 . . . . . . . . . . .**76** A4
Cruddas Pk Sh Ctr NE4 .**76** A4
Crudwell Cl NE35 . . . . . . . . . .**52** A2
Crummock Ct NE28 . . . . . . . .**23** B4
Crummock Rd NE5 . . . . . . . . .**28** C4
Crusade Wlk NE32 . . . . . . . . .**36** B1
Cullercoats St NE6 . . . . . . . . .**33** C2
Cumberland Pl DH3 . . . . . . . .**70** C1
Cumberland St
  Wallsend NE28 . . . . . . . . . .**22** A2
  Wallsend, Willington Quay
  NE28 . . . . . . . . . . . . . . . . .**23** C1
Cumberland Wlk NE7 . . .**19** C4
Cumbrian Gdns NE11 . . . .**56** C2
Curlew Cl
  Longbenton NE12 . . . . . . . .**10** B3
  Ryton NE40 . . . . . . . . . . . . .**40** A4
  Washington NE38 . . . . . . . . .**71** C2
Curlew Rd
  Jarrow NE32 . . . . . . . . . . . .**37** A4
  Jarrow NE32 . . . . . . . . . . . .**37** A4
Curran House NE32 . . . . . . . .**37** A4
Curren Gdns NE10 . . . . . . . . .**47** B2
Curtis Rd NE4 . . . . . . . . . . . . .**30** A3
Curzon Pl **6** NE5 . . . . . . . . .**15** C2
Curzon Rd W NE28 . . . . . . . .**21** C1
Curzon St NE8 . . . . . . . . . . . .**58** A4
Cushat Cl NE6 . . . . . . . . . . . .**33** A1
Cushy Cow La NE40 . . . . . . . .**39** C4
Cut Bank NE1 . . . . . . . . . . . . .**79** C2
Cuthbert Ct NE32 . . . . . . . . . .**37** C2
Cuthbert St
  Gateshead NE8 . . . . . . . . . .**79** A2
  Hebburn NE31 . . . . . . . . . . .**35** B3
  Sunniside NE16 . . . . . . . . . .**62** B1
Cuthbert Wlk NE3 . . . . . . . . .**9** C1
Cygnet Cl NE5 . . . . . . . . . . . .**14** B4
Cyncopa Way NE5 . . . . . .**16** B2

Cypress Ave NE4 . . . . . . . . . .**29** B4
Cypress Cres NE11 . . . . . . . . .**56** C3
Cypress Gr NE40 . . . . . . . . . .**25** A2
Cypress Rd
  Blaydon NE21 . . . . . . . . . . .**41** B2
  Gateshead NE9 . . . . . . . . . .**66** B2
Cyprus Gdns NE9 . . . . . . . . . .**58** C2

## D

Daffodil Cl NE21 . . . . . . . . . . .**41** A2
Dahlia Rd NE4 . . . . . . . . . . . . .**29** B3
Dahlia Way NE31 . . . . . . . . . .**50** A4
Dairnbrook **7** NE37 . . . . . . .**69** C2
Daisy Cotts **10** DH3 . . . . . . .**70** B4
Dale St NE40 . . . . . . . . . . . . . .**38** B4
Dales The NE5 . . . . . . . . . . . .**16** C2
Dale View Gdns NE40 . . . . . . .**38** B3
Dally Mews NE3 . . . . . . . . . . .**4** B1
Dalton Cres **2B** NE6 . . . . . . .**32** C2
Dalton Pl NE5 . . . . . . . . . . . . .**14** A3
Dalton St
  Newcastle-u-T NE6 . . . . . . .**32** C1
  Newcastle-u-T NE6 . . . . . . .**32** C2
Dame Allan's Boys Sch
  NE4 . . . . . . . . . . . . . . . . . .**29** C3
Dame Allan's Girls Sch
  NE4 . . . . . . . . . . . . . . . . . .**29** C3
Dame Flora Robson Ave
  NE34 . . . . . . . . . . . . . . . . .**52** B4
Danby Gdns NE6 . . . . . . . . . .**20** B1
Darden Lough NE5 . . . . . . . . .**15** A1
Darley Pl NE5 . . . . . . . . . . . . .**28** B1
Darrell St NE13 . . . . . . . . . . . .**2** A2
Dartmouth Ave NE9 . . . . . . . .**65** A2
Darwin Cres NE3 . . . . . . . . . .**17** A3
Daryl Cl NE21 . . . . . . . . . . . . .**40** C1
Daryl Way NE10 . . . . . . . . . . .**61** C4
Davenport Dr NE3 . . . . . . . . .**4** B1
David Adams Ho **7**
  NE15 . . . . . . . . . . . . . . . . .**29** B1
Davidson Cotts NE2 . . . .**18** C3
Davidson Rd NE10 . . . . . . . . .**49** A2
Davidson St NE10 . . . . . . . . . .**59** C4
David St NE28 . . . . . . . . . . . . .**21** C2
David Terr **8** NE40 . . . . . . . .**38** B3
Davison St
  Boldon Colliery NE35 . . . . . .**52** A1
  Newburn NE15 . . . . . . . . . .**25** C4
Davy Bank NE28 . . . . . . . . . . .**22** B1
Dawlish Gdns NE9 . . . . . . . . .**65** A3
Dawlish Pl NE5 . . . . . . . . . . . .**14** A3
Dawson St **6** NE6 . . . . . . . . .**34** B2
Daylesford Dr NE3 . . . . . . . . .**19** A4
Dayshield NE5 . . . . . . . . . . . .**15** A1
Deacon Cl NE15 . . . . . . . . . . .**13** C2
Deacon Ct NE12 . . . . . . . . . . .**10** B3
Deanham Gdns NE5 . . . . . . . .**29** B4
Dean Ho NE6 . . . . . . . . . . . . .**34** B4
Deans Cl **1** NE16 . . . . . . . . .**55** A3
Deansfield Gr NE15 . . . . . . . . .**13** C3
Dean St NE9 . . . . . . . . . . . . . .**58** C1
Dean Terr NE40 . . . . . . . . . . .**25** A1
Debden Ho **7** NE11 . . . . . . .**56** C4
Debdon Gdns NE6 . . . . . . . . .**20** B1
Debussy Ct NE32 . . . . . . . . . .**37** A2
December Ctyd NE8 . . . .**77** B2
DECKHAM . . . . . . . . . . . . . . .**58** C4
Deckham St **11** NE8 . . . . . .**58** C4
Deckham Terr NE8, NE9 . .**58** C4
Deepbrook Rd **6** NE5 . . .**16** A1
Deepdale NE38 . . . . . . . . . . . .**71** C1
Deepdale Cl NE16 . . . . . . . . .**62** A4
Deepdale Cres NE5 . . . . . . . . .**16** C2
Deepdale Gn NE5 . . . . . . . . . .**16** C2
Deerbolt **7** NE11 . . . . . . . . . .**11** A3
Deer Bush NE5 . . . . . . . . . . . .**15** A1
Dee Rd NE31 . . . . . . . . . . . . .**50** B3
Deer Park Way NE21 . . . . . . . .**42** A1
Dees Ave NE28 . . . . . . . . . . . .**21** C3
Dee St NE32 . . . . . . . . . . . . . .**37** A3
Deighton Wlk NE5 . . . . . . . . .**15** A1
Delacour Rd NE21 . . . . . . . . . .**41** B3
Delamere Rd NE3 . . . . . . . . . .**8** A1
DELAVAL . . . . . . . . . . . . . . . .**43** B4
Delaval Com Prim Sch
  NE15 . . . . . . . . . . . . . . . . .**28** C1
Delaval Gdns NE15 . . . . . . . . .**43** A4
Delaval Rd
  Newcastle-u-T, Delaval
  NE15 . . . . . . . . . . . . . . . . .**43** A4

Delaval Rd continued
  Newcastle-u-T, Old Benwell
  NE15 . . . . . . . . . . . . . . . . .**28** C1
Delaval Terr NE3 . . . . . . . . . . .**17** B4
Delhi Cres NE40 . . . . . . . . . . .**38** C3
Delhi Gdns NE40 . . . . . . . . . .**38** C3
Delhi View NE40 . . . . . . . . . . .**38** C3
Delta Bank Rd NE11 . . . . . .**43** B3
Dempsey Rd NE13 . . . . . . . . .**4** B4
Denbeigh Pl NE12 . . . . . . . . .**11** A3
Denbigh Ave NE28 . . . . . . . . .**23** B3
Denbigh Com Prim Sch
  NE28 . . . . . . . . . . . . . . . . .**23** B3
Dene Ave
  Brunswick Village NE13 . . . .**2** A2
  Newcastle-u-T, Denton Burn
  NE15 . . . . . . . . . . . . . . . . .**27** B3
  Newcastle-u-T, South
  Gosforth NE3 . . . . . . . . . . .**18** C4
Dene Bank View NE3 . . . . . . .**16** C3
Deneburn NE10 . . . . . . . . . . .**60** C3
Dene Cl
  Newcastle-u-T NE7 . . . . . . .**19** B1
  Ryton NE40 . . . . . . . . . . . . .**25** B1
Dene Cres
  Newcastle-u-T NE3 . . . . . . .**18** C4
  Ryton NE40 . . . . . . . . . . . . .**25** B1
  Wallsend NE28 . . . . . . . . . .**22** B2
Dene Ct
  Birtley DH3 . . . . . . . . . . . . .**68** B3
  Newcastle-u-T NE7 . . . . . . .**19** C1
Dene Farm Cotts NE15 .**12** C2
Deneford NE9 . . . . . . . . . . . . .**65** B1
Dene Gdns
  Gateshead NE10 . . . . . . . . .**49** A1
  Newcastle-u-T NE15 . . . . . .**27** B2
Dene Gr NE3 . . . . . . . . . . . . . .**18** C4
Deneholm NE28 . . . . . . . . . . .**22** B3
Dene Rd NE21 . . . . . . . . . . . . .**41** C3
Deneside
  Dunston NE11 . . . . . . . . . . .**56** B3
  Hedworth NE32 . . . . . . . . . .**51** B1
  Newcastle-u-T, Denton Burn
  NE15 . . . . . . . . . . . . . . . . .**28** B3
  Newcastle-u-T NE5 . . . . . . .**15** A4
Dene Side NE21 . . . . . . . . . . .**41** C2
Deneside Ave NE9 . . . . . . . . .**65** A4
Deneside Cl NE15 . . . . . . . . . .**12** B2
Deneside Ct NE2 . . . . . . . . . . .**32** B4
Dene Terr
  Blaydon NE21 . . . . . . . . . . .**41** A2
  Jarrow NE32 . . . . . . . . . . . .**50** C4
  Newburn NE15 . . . . . . . . . .**26** A4
  Newcastle-u-T NE3 . . . . . . .**18** C4
Dene View NE3 . . . . . . . . . . . .**18** C4
Denewell Ave
  Gateshead NE9 . . . . . . . . . .**58** B1
  Newcastle-u-T NE7 . . . . . . .**19** B3
Denewood Ct NE28 . . . . . . . .**23** B2
Denham Wlk NE5 . . . . . . . . . .**14** A3
Denhill Pk NE15 . . . . . . . . . . .**28** A3
Denholme Lodge NE11 . .**77** A1
Denmark Ct **10** NE6 . . . . . . .**33** A3
Denmark St
  Gateshead NE8 . . . . . . . . . .**79** C2
  Newcastle-u-T NE6 . . . . . . .**33** A3
Dennison Cres DH3 . . . . . . . .**68** B2
Denton Ave NE15 . . . . . . . . . .**27** B2
DENTON BURN . . . . . . . . .**27** C3
Denton Chare NE1 . . . . . . . . .**78** A4
Denton Ct NE5 . . . . . . . . . . . .**28** B3
Denton Gate NE5 . . . . . . . . . .**15** B3
Denton Gdns NE15 . . . . . . . . .**29** A1
Denton Gr NE5 . . . . . . . . . . . .**15** B3
Denton Park Ho NE5 . . . .**14** C2
Denton Park Sh Ctr
  NE5 . . . . . . . . . . . . . . . . . .**14** C2
Denton Rd NE15 . . . . . . . . . . .**28** A2
Denton View NE21 . . . . . . . . .**41** A2
Denver Gdns NE6 . . . . . . . . . .**33** C1
Denwick Ave NE15 . . . . . . . . .**27** A2
Depot Rd NE6 . . . . . . . . . . . . .**33** B3
Deptford Rd NE8 . . . . . . . . . .**46** C4
Derby Cres NE31 . . . . . . . . . .**35** B1
Derby Gdns NE28 . . . . . . . . . .**21** B3
Derby St NE32 . . . . . . . . . . . .**37** A3
Dereham Ct NE5 . . . . . . . . . . .**15** C4
Derwent Ave
  Gateshead NE11 . . . . . . . . .**57** C1
  Hebburn NE31 . . . . . . . . . . .**50** A3
  Newburn NE15 . . . . . . . . . .**25** C3
Derwent Cres NE16 . . . . . . . . .**55** A4

Derwent Crook Dr NE9 . .**58** A1
Derwent Ct
  Gateshead NE11 . . . . . . . . .**57** C1
  Newcastle-u-T NE7 . . . . . . .**19** B4
Derwentdale Gdns NE7 .**19** C3
Derwent Gdns
  Gateshead NE8 . . . . . . . . . .**58** C1
  Wallsend NE28 . . . . . . . . . .**23** B4
DERWENT HAUGH . . . . . .**43** A2
Derwenthaugh Ind Est
  NE16 . . . . . . . . . . . . . . . . .**42** B3
Derwenthaugh Marina
  NE21 . . . . . . . . . . . . . . . . .**42** C3
Derwenthaugh Rd NE21 **42** C3
Derwent St NE15 . . . . . . . . . .**28** C1
Derwent Tower NE11 . . . .**77** A1
Derwent Twr **4** NE11 . . .**56** C3
Derwent View NE21 . . . . . . . .**41** A1
Derwent Walk Cty Pk*
  NE16, NE31, NE39 . . . . . . .**53** B1
Derwentwater St NE8 . .**79** A1
Derwentwater Gdns
  NE16 . . . . . . . . . . . . . . . . .**55** C3
Derwentwater Rd
  Gateshead NE8 . . . . . . . . . .**77** C1
  Gateshead NE9 . . . . . . . . . .**57** A4
Derwent Way NE21 . . . . . . . . .**42** A1
Devon Ave NE16 . . . . . . . . . . .**55** B3
Devon Cres DH3 . . . . . . . . . . .**68** A2
Devon Gdns NE9 . . . . . . . . . .**58** B3
Devon Rd NE31 . . . . . . . . . . .**50** B3
Devonshire Gdns NE28 . .**21** B3
Devonshire Pl NE2 . . . . . . . . .**19** A1
Dewhurst Terr **5** NE16 .**62** C2
Dewley Pl NE5 . . . . . . . . . . . .**14** C4
Dewley Rd NE5 . . . . . . . . . . . .**15** C1
Dexter Ho NE29 . . . . . . . . . . .**24** B3
Dexter Way NE10 . . . . . . . . . .**59** B4
Diamond Ct NE3 . . . . . . . . . . .**7** B1
Diamond St NE28 . . . . . . . . . .**21** C2
Dibley Sq **5** NE6 . . . . . . . . . .**32** C1
Dibley St **6** NE6 . . . . . . . . . .**32** C1
Dickens Ave NE16 . . . . . . . . . .**54** C4
Dickens Wlk NE5 . . . . . . . . . .**14** A3
Dick St **12** NE40 . . . . . . . . . .**38** B3
Didcot Ave NE29 . . . . . . . . . . .**24** C4
Dillon St NE32 . . . . . . . . . . . .**36** B1
Dilston Cl NE38 . . . . . . . . . . .**71** C4
Dilston Dr NE5 . . . . . . . . . . . .**14** C3
Dilston Terr
  Jarrow NE32 . . . . . . . . . . . .**51** B3
  Newcastle-u-T NE3 . . . . . . .**18** C4
Dimbula Gdns NE7 . . . . . . . . .**20** B2
Dinsdale Ave NE28 . . . . . . . . .**22** A4
Dipton Ave NE4 . . . . . . . . . . .**44** A4
Dishforth Gn NE9 . . . . . . . . . .**65** C1
Dissington Pl
  Newcastle-u-T NE5 . . . . . . .**29** A4
  Whickham NE16 . . . . . . . . .**54** C1
Dixon Pl NE11 . . . . . . . . . . . .**56** B4
Dixon St NE8 . . . . . . . . . . . . . .**77** C1
Dobson Cl NE4 . . . . . . . . . . . .**76** B3
Dobson Cres NE6 . . . . . . . . . .**47** B4
Dockendale La NE16 . . . . . . . .**55** B3
Dockendale Mews NE16 **55** B3
Doddfell St **17** NE37 . . . . . .**69** C2
Doddington Cl NE15 . . . . . . . .**26** C3
Doddington Villas NE10 .**59** B3
Dodds Farm NE3 . . . . . . . . . . .**8** B1
Dodds Terr DH3 . . . . . . . . . . .**68** B2
Dodsworth N NE40 . . . . . . . . .**39** A1
Dodsworth Terr NE40 . . . . . . .**39** A1
Dodsworth Villas NE40 . .**39** A1
Dog Bank NE1 . . . . . . . . . . . .**78** B4
Dolphin Ct **1** NE4 . . . . . . . . .**29** B1
Dolphin St NE4 . . . . . . . . . . . .**29** B1
Dolphin Villas NE13 . . . . . . . .**4** B4
Donald St NE3 . . . . . . . . . . . . .**9** C1
Doncrest Rd NE37 . . . . . . . . . .**67** C1
Don Dixon Dr NE32 . . . . . . . .**51** A1
Donkin Rd **1** NE37 . . . . . . . .**69** B3
Donkins St NE35 . . . . . . . . . . .**52** A1
Donkin Terr NE40 . . . . . . . . . .**38** A3
Donnington Ct NE3 . . . . . . . . .**19** A4
Don Rd NE32 . . . . . . . . . . . . .**37** B3
Donridge NE37 . . . . . . . . . . . .**67** C1
Donside NE10 . . . . . . . . . . . . .**67** A4
Don St NE11 . . . . . . . . . . . . . .**44** A4
Donvale Rd NE37 . . . . . . . . . .**67** B1
DONWELL . . . . . . . . . . . . . . .**67** C1
Dorcas Ave NE15 . . . . . . . . . .**29** A1
Dorchester Cl NE5 . . . . . . . . .**13** C3

Dorchester Gdns NE9 . . . .**65** A2
Doris Wilkes Ho NE6 . . . .**32** C2
Dorking Ave NE29 . . . . . . . . .**24** C4
Dornoch Cres NE10 . . . . . . . .**60** A2
Dorrington Rd NE3 . . . . . . . . .**7** C3
Dorset Ave
  Birtley DH3 . . . . . . . . . . . . .**70** C1
  Hebburn NE31 . . . . . . . . . . .**36** A1
  Wallsend NE28 . . . . . . . . . .**21** B3
Dorset Rd
  Gateshead NE8 . . . . . . . . . .**46** C4
  Newcastle-u-T NE15 . . . . . .**28** A2
Douglas Ave NE3 . . . . . . . . . .**17** B4
Douglas Cl NE11 . . . . . . . . . . .**64** C2
Douglas Gdns NE11 . . . . . . . .**56** C3
Douglas Par NE31 . . . . . . . . . .**50** C2
Douglass St **7** NE28 . . . . . . .**21** C2
Douglas St NE28 . . . . . . . . . . .**23** B1
Doulting Cl NE12 . . . . . . . . . . .**10** C2
Dove Ave NE32 . . . . . . . . . . . .**51** B3
Dovecote Rd NE12 . . . . . . . . .**11** C3
Dovecrest Ct **7** NE28 . .**23** A4
Dove Ct **10** DH3 . . . . . . . . . .**68** B1
Dovedale Gdns
  Gateshead NE9 . . . . . . . . . .**65** B4
  Newcastle-u-T NE7 . . . . . . .**19** C3
Dover Cl NE5 . . . . . . . . . . . . . .**14** A3
Dovercourt Rd NE6 . . . . . . . . .**48** C4
Downend Rd NE5 . . . . . . . . . .**14** C3
Downham NE5 . . . . . . . . . . . .**15** A1
Doxford Gdns **4** NE5 . . .**16** B1
Drayton Rd NE3 . . . . . . . . . . .**16** C4
Drive Com Prim Sch The
  NE10 . . . . . . . . . . . . . . . . .**60** A4
Drivecote NE10 . . . . . . . . . . . .**60** A4
Drive The
  Birtley DH3 . . . . . . . . . . . . .**70** C1
  Gateshead, Felling NE10 . . .**49** B2
  Gateshead, Saltwell NE9 . . .**58** B2
  Newcastle-u-T, East Denton
  NE5 . . . . . . . . . . . . . . . . . .**28** B4
  Newcastle-u-T, Gosforth
  NE3 . . . . . . . . . . . . . . . . . .**18** A3
  Newcastle-u-T NE7 . . . . . . .**19** C4
  Wallsend NE28 . . . . . . . . . .**21** C2
  Whickham NE16 . . . . . . . . .**55** A1
Dr Ryman Ho NE6 . . . . . . . . .**34** B1
Drumaldrace **5** NE37 . .**69** C2
Drummond Rd NE3 . . . . . . . . .**17** A4
Drumsheugh Pl NE5 . . . . . . . .**15** C2
Druridge Dr NE5 . . . . . . . . . . .**16** B1
Dryden Ct **8** NE9 . . . . . . . . .**58** B4
Dryden Rd NE9 . . . . . . . . . . . .**58** B3
Dryden Road Hospl NE9 **58** C3
Dryden Sch NE9 . . . . . . . . . . .**58** C3
Drysdale Cres NE13 . . . . . . . .**2** A2
Drysdale Ct NE13 . . . . . . . . . .**2** B2
Duchess Cres NE32 . . . . . . . . .**51** A3
Duchess Cres E NE32 . . . . . . .**51** A3
Duchess Dr NE15 . . . . . . . . . .**28** B3
Duckpool La NE16 . . . . . . . . . .**55** B3
Duckpool La N NE16 . . . . . . . .**55** B4
Duddon Pl NE9 . . . . . . . . . . . .**65** C4
Dudley Lane Cotts NE13 .**2** C4
Dugdale Ct **6** NE3 . . . . . . . . .**7** B1
Dugdale Rd NE3 . . . . . . . . . . .**7** B1
Duke's Ave NE31 . . . . . . . . . .**49** C4
Dukes Cott NE15 . . . . . . . . . .**26** A3
Dukes Dr NE3 . . . . . . . . . . . . .**4** B1
Duke St
  Gateshead NE8 . . . . . . . . . .**48** C1
  Newcastle-u-T NE1 . . . . . . .**76** C4
Dukesway NE11 . . . . . . . . . . .**64** A4
Dukesway Ct NE11 . . . . . . . . .**64** A3
Dukesway W NE11 . . . . . . . . .**64** A2
Duke Wlk NE8 . . . . . . . . . . . .**77** C1
Dulverston Cl NE5 . . . . . . . . .**14** A3
Dulverton Ct NE2 . . . . . . . . . .**19** A2
Dumas Wlk NE5 . . . . . . . . . . .**14** A3
Dumfries Cres NE32 . . . . . . . .**52** A3
Dunbar Cl NE5 . . . . . . . . . . . .**14** A4
Dunblane Cres NE5 . . . . . . . . .**15** A1
Duncan St
  Gateshead NE8 . . . . . . . . . .**47** A1
  Newcastle-u-T NE6 . . . . . . .**34** B1
Dundas Way NE10 . . . . . . . . .**59** B4
Dundee Cl NE5 . . . . . . . . . . . .**14** A3
Dundee Ct NE32 . . . . . . . . . . .**52** A3
Dunelm Cl **6** DH3 . . . . . . . . .**70** B4
Dunford Gdns NE5 . . . . . . . . .**14** A4
Dunholme Rd NE4 . . . . . . . . .**30** A1
Dunira Cl NE2 . . . . . . . . . . . . .**19** A2

Dunira Ho NE2 . . . . . . . . .19 A2
Dunkeld Cl NE10 . . . . . . . .61 A4
Dunlin Cl NE40 . . . . . . . . .40 A4
Dunlin Dr NE38 . . . . . . . . .71 B3
Dunlop Cl NE7 . . . . . . . . . .20 A4
Dunmoor Cl NE3 . . . . . . . .17 B4
Dunmorlie St NE6 . . . . . . .33 B2
Dunne Rd NE21 . . . . . . . . .42 A4
Dunnock Dr
  Sunniside NE16 . . . . . . . .62 B3
  Washington NE38 . . . . . . .71 B2
Dunnock Lodge NE15 . .27 B2
Dunn St NE4 . . . . . . . . . . .76 B3
Dunn Street Prim Sch
  NE32 . . . . . . . . . . . . . . . .37 A3
Dunn Terr NE6 . . . . . . . . .32 C2
Dunnykirk Ave 2 NE3 . . .7 B1
Dunsmuir Gr NE8 . . . . . . .57 C4
Dunstable Pl NE5 . . . . . . .13 C3
Dunstanburgh Cl NE6 . .33 B1
Dunstanburgh Ct
  Gateshead NE10 . . . . . . . .61 A3
  Jarrow NE32 . . . . . . . . . . .37 A1
Dunstanburgh Rd NE6 . .33 B1
Dunstan Wlk NE5 . . . . . . .15 A1
DUNSTON . . . . . . . . . . . . .44 B1
Dunston Bank NE11 . . . . .56 B3
Dunston Ent Pk NE11 . . .44 A2
DUNSTON HILL . . . . . . . .56 A3
Dunston Hill Com Prim
  Sch NE11 . . . . . . . . . . . . .56 B4
Dunston Hill Hospl
  NE11 . . . . . . . . . . . . . . . .55 C3
Dunston Rd NE11 . . . . . . .44 B1
Dunston Riverside Prim
  Sch NE11 . . . . . . . . . . . . .44 C4
Dunston Sta NE11 . . . . . .56 C4
Dunston Workshops
  NE11 . . . . . . . . . . . . . . . .44 B2
Dunvegan DH3 . . . . . . . . .71 A2
Durham Ct NE31 . . . . . . . .35 B1
Durham Dr NE32 . . . . . . . .51 A2
Durham Gr NE32 . . . . . . . .51 A2
Durham Pl
  Birtley DH3 . . . . . . . . . . . .70 C1
  Gateshead NE8 . . . . . . . . .79 C1
Durham Rd
  Birtley DH3 . . . . . . . . . . . .70 B3
  Gateshead NE8, NE9 . . . .58 B2
Durham St
  3 Gateshead NE10 . . . . .48 B1
  Newcastle-u-T NE4 . . . . .30 A1
  Wallsend NE28 . . . . . . . . .40 A4
Durham Street W NE28 .22 A2
Dutton Ct NE21 . . . . . . . . .42 A4
Duxfield Rd NE7 . . . . . . . .19 C3
Dykefield Ave NE3 . . . . . . .7 C3
Dyke Heads La NE40 . . . .39 A1
Dykelands Way NE34 . . . .52 B3
Dykenook Cl NE16 . . . . . . .62 B4
Dykes Way NE10 . . . . . . . .59 C1
Dymock Cl NE3 . . . . . . . . . .6 C1

E

Eaglescliffe Dr NE7 . . . . .20 B2
Ealing Ct NE3 . . . . . . . . . . .6 C2
Earls Ct DH98 . . . . . . . . . .57 C1
Earls Dene 5 NE9 . . . . . .65 A4
Earls Dr NE15 . . . . . . . . . .65 A4
Earl's Dr NE15 . . . . . . . . .28 B3
Earls Pk N Trad Est
  NE11 . . . . . . . . . . . . . . . .57 B3
Earlsway DH98, NE11,
  NE82 . . . . . . . . . . . . . . . .57 C1
Earlswood Ave NE9 . . . . .65 A4
Earlswood Pk NE9 . . . . . .65 A4
Earsdon Cl NE5 . . . . . . . . .15 B1
Earsdon Rd NE3 . . . . . . . .16 C3
Easby Cl NE3 . . . . . . . . . . . .9 B4
Easdale Ave NE3 . . . . . . . . .4 C1
Easedale Gdns NE9 . . . . .65 C3
Easington Ave NE9 . . . . . .66 A3
East Acres NE21 . . . . . . . .41 C1
East Ave NE12 . . . . . . . . . .11 B2
East Benton Cotts NE12 11 C1
Eastbourne Ave
  Gateshead NE8 . . . . . . . . .58 A4
  Newcastle-u-T NE6 . . . . .34 B2
Eastbourne Ct 1 NE6 . .34 B2
Eastbourne Gdns NE6 . .34 B2
Eastbourne Par NE31 . . .50 C2

Eastburn Gdns NE10 . . . .49 A2
Eastcheap NE6 . . . . . . . . .20 A1
Eastcliffe Ave NE3 . . . . . .17 B3
Eastcombe Cl NE35 . . . . .52 A2
Eastcote Terr NE6 . . . . . . .48 B4
EAST DENTON . . . . . . . . .15 B1
Easten Terr NE26 . . . . . . .24 A1
Eastern Ave NE11, NE9 . .64 B4
Eastern Gdns 4 NE10 . .47 C1
Eastern Way NE5 . . . . . . .16 B2
East Farm Ct NE16 . . . . . .54 B3
Eastfield Ave NE28, NE6. .34 B4
Eastfield Ho NE6 . . . . . . . .34 B4
Eastfield Rd NE12 . . . . . . .11 B2
Eastfield Terr NE12 . . . . . .11 B2
East Forest Hall Rd
  NE12 . . . . . . . . . . . . . . . .11 C4
Eastgarth NE5 . . . . . . . . . . .6 B1
East Gate NE8 . . . . . . . . . .78 C3
Eastgate Gdns NE4 . . . . . .44 A4
EAST GATESHEAD . . . . .47 A3
East Hill Rd NE8 . . . . . . . .47 A1
EAST HOWDON . . . . . . . .24 A2
Eastlands
  Blaydon NE21 . . . . . . . . . .41 C3
  Newcastle-u-T NE7 . . . . .19 B3
East Lea NE21 . . . . . . . . . .53 B4
East Park Gdns NE21 . . . .41 B1
East Park Rd NE9 . . . . . . .58 B2
East St
  Gateshead NE8 . . . . . . . . .78 C3
  Hebburn NE31 . . . . . . . . .36 A3
East Thorp NE5 . . . . . . . . . .6 A1
East View
  Blaydon NE21 . . . . . . . . . .41 C3
  Hebburn NE31 . . . . . . . . .49 C4
  Wideopen NE13 . . . . . . . . .2 B3
East View Terr
  Gateshead NE10 . . . . . . . .60 B2
  Whickham NE16 . . . . . . . .55 A4
Eastwood Ct NE12 . . . . . .11 B3
Eastwood Gdns
  Gateshead, Low Fell
    NE9 . . . . . . . . . . . . . . . . .58 C2
  Gateshead, Old Fold
    NE10 . . . . . . . . . . . . . . . .47 B2
  Newcastle-u-T NE3 . . . . .17 A4
Eaton Pl NE4 . . . . . . . . . . .30 A1
Ebba Wlk NE3 . . . . . . . . . . .9 B1
Ebchester Ave NE7 . . . . . .66 B3
Ebchester Ct NE3 . . . . . . . .7 A1
Ebor St
  Newcastle-u-T NE6 . . . . .33 A4
  South Shields NE34 . . . . .52 C4
Ecgfrid Terr NE32 . . . . . . .51 B4
Eddleston NE38 . . . . . . . . .71 C1
Eddleston Ave NE3 . . . . . .17 B3
Eddrington Gr NE5 . . . . . .14 A2
Ede Ave NE11 . . . . . . . . . . .56 B4
Edenbridge Cres NE12 . .10 C3
Eden Cl NE5 . . . . . . . . . . . .14 A2
Eden Ct 5 NE28 . . . . . . . .21 C1
Eden Dale NE40 . . . . . . . . .38 B4
Edendale Ct 1 NE34 . . .52 C4
Edendale Terr NE8 . . . . . .58 B4
Eden St NE28 . . . . . . . . . . .21 C1
Eden Wlk NE32 . . . . . . . . .51 B3
Edgar St NE13 . . . . . . . . . .10 A1
Edgefield Ave NE3 . . . . . . .8 A1
Edgeware Wlk NE4 . . . . . .44 A3
Edgeworth Cl NE35 . . . . .52 A2
Edgware Rd NE8 . . . . . . . .58 C4
Edhill Ave NE34 . . . . . . . . .52 C4
Edhill Gdns NE34 . . . . . . .52 B4
Edinburgh Ct NE3 . . . . . . .7 B4
Edinburgh Rd NE32 . . . . .52 A4
Edison Gdns NE8 . . . . . . . .58 A3
Edith Ave NE21 . . . . . . . . .41 B2
Edith St NE32 . . . . . . . . . . .36 B3
Edith Terr 5 NE16 . . . . . .54 C3
Edlingham Cl NE12 . . . . . .19 A4
Edmund Pl NE9 . . . . . . . . .58 B1
Edna Terr NE5 . . . . . . . . . .15 B3
Edrich Ho NE29 . . . . . . . . .24 B3
Edward Rd
  Birtley DH3 . . . . . . . . . . . .68 A1
  Wallsend NE28 . . . . . . . . .23 A3
Edward St
  Crawcrook NE40 . . . . . . . .38 A3
  Hebburn NE31 . . . . . . . . .35 A2
  Newcastle-u-T NE3 . . . . . .9 A1

Edwin Gr NE28 . . . . . . . . .23 B3
Edwins Ave NE12 . . . . . . .11 C4
Edwin's Ave S NE12 . . . . .11 C4
Edwin St
  Brunswick Village NE13 . . . .2 A2
  14 Newcastle-u-T NE6 . .32 C2
Edwin Terr NE40 . . . . . . . .39 B2
Egerton St NE4 . . . . . . . . .43 C4
Egham Rd NE5 . . . . . . . . .14 A2
Egremont Dr 4 NE9 . . . .58 C2
Egremont Gdns NE9 . . . .58 C2
Egton Terr DH3 . . . . . . . . .68 B1
Eighth Ave
  Gateshead NE11 . . . . . . . .64 B3
  Newcastle-u-T NE6 . . . . .33 A4
EIGHTON BANKS . . . . . .66 B1
Eighton Terr NE9 . . . . . . .66 C3
Eishort Way NE12 . . . . . . .10 C2
Eland Cl NE3 . . . . . . . . . . . .7 B1
Elberfeld Ct NE32 . . . . . . .36 C2
Elder Gdns NE9 . . . . . . . . .66 A1
Elder Gr 3 NE9 . . . . . . . .58 B1
Elderwood Gdns NE11 . .57 A1
Eldon Ct 1 NE28 . . . . . . .23 C1
Eldon Pl NE15 . . . . . . . . . .27 B3
Eldon Rd NE15 . . . . . . . . .27 B3
Eldon St
  Gateshead NE8 . . . . . . . . .46 C2
  Wallsend NE28 . . . . . . . . .23 C2
Eleanor Terr
  Crawcrook NE40 . . . . . . . .38 C4
  2 Whickham NE16 . . . . .54 C3
Eleventh Ave NE11 . . . . . .64 C2
Eleventh Ave N NE11 . . .64 C3
Elgar Ave 3 NE5 . . . . . . .14 A2
Elgin Ave NE28 . . . . . . . . .23 A4
Elgin Cl NE10 . . . . . . . . . . .49 A2
Elgin Gdns NE6 . . . . . . . . .34 A2
Elgin Pl DH3 . . . . . . . . . . . .70 C2
Elgin Rd NE9 . . . . . . . . . . .59 A4
Elgin St NE32 . . . . . . . . . . .52 A4
Elgy Rd NE3 . . . . . . . . . . . .17 C3
Elisabeth Ave DH3 . . . . . .68 A2
Elizabeth Rd NE28 . . . . . .23 B2
Elizabeth St NE6 . . . . . . . .32 B2
Ell-Dene Cres NE10 . . . . .60 A3
Ellen Ct 3 NE32 . . . . . . . .36 C3
Ellerbeck Cl 3 NE10 . . . .59 B4
Ellerton Way NE10 . . . . . .59 B4
Ellesmere Ave
  Newcastle-u-T, South
    Gosforth NE3 . . . . . . . . .18 C4
  Newcastle-u-T, Walkergate
    NE6 . . . . . . . . . . . . . . . . .33 C4
  Newcastle-u-T, Westerhope
    NE5 . . . . . . . . . . . . . . . . .15 B2
Ellesmere Rd NE4 . . . . . . .29 C1
Ellington Cl NE15 . . . . . . .26 C3
Elliot Rd NE10 . . . . . . . . . .47 A1
Elliott Dr NE10 . . . . . . . . .59 C4
Elliott Gdns NE28 . . . . . . .21 B4
Ellison Pl
  3 Gateshead NE9 . . . . . .65 A4
  Jarrow NE32 . . . . . . . . . . .36 C4
Ellison Rd NE11, NE8 . . . .56 B4
Ellison St
  Gateshead NE8 . . . . . . . . .78 C3
  Hebburn NE31 . . . . . . . . .35 A3
Ellison Terr NE40 . . . . . . .38 B1
Ellison Villas 8 NE8 . . . .58 C4
Ellwood Gdns 3 NE9 . . .58 B4
Elm Ave
  Dunston NE11 . . . . . . . . . .56 B3
  Whickham NE16 . . . . . . . .55 B4
Elmcroft Rd NE12 . . . . . . .11 C3
Elm Ct NE16 . . . . . . . . . . . .55 A1
Elmfield Gdns
  Newcastle-u-T NE3 . . . . .17 C4
  Wallsend NE28 . . . . . . . . .21 A4
Elmfield Gr NE3 . . . . . . . . .17 C4
Elmfield Pk NE3 . . . . . . . . .17 C3
Elmfield Rd
  Hebburn NE31 . . . . . . . . .50 B3
  Newcastle-u-T NE3 . . . . .18 A3
  Throckley NE15 . . . . . . . .12 C2
Elmfield Terr
  Gateshead NE10 . . . . . . . .48 C1
  Hebburn NE31 . . . . . . . . .50 B4
Elm Gr NE3 . . . . . . . . . . . . .8 A3
Elm Rd NE21 . . . . . . . . . . .41 C2

Elm St W NE16 . . . . . . . . .62 C2
Elmsford Gr NE12 . . . . . . .10 C2
Elm St
  Jarrow NE32 . . . . . . . . . . .36 B3
  Seaton Burn NE13 . . . . . . .2 C4
  Sunniside NE16 . . . . . . . .62 C2
Elms The NE3 . . . . . . . . . .17 C3
Elm Terr DH3 . . . . . . . . . . .68 A1
Elmtree Dr NE40 . . . . . . . .39 A1
Elmtree Gr NE3 . . . . . . . . .17 C3
Elmwood NE15 . . . . . . . . .27 A4
Elmwood Ave
  Wallsend NE28 . . . . . . . . .23 A2
  Wideopen NE13 . . . . . . . . .2 C1
Elmwood Cres NE6 . . . . . .21 A1
Elmwood Gdns NE11 . . . .57 A2
Elmwood Ho NE7 . . . . . . .19 B4
Elmwood Mews NE13 . . . .4 B4
Elrick Cl NE5 . . . . . . . . . . .14 A2
Elrington Gdns NE5 . . . . .28 C4
Elsdon Ct NE16 . . . . . . . . .54 C1
Elsdon Gdns NE11 . . . . . .56 C4
Elsdon Rd
  Newcastle-u-T NE3 . . . . . .9 A1
  Whickham NE16 . . . . . . . .54 C2
Elsdon Terr
  North Shields NE29 . . . . .24 B4
  4 Wallsend NE28 . . . . . .21 C1
Elsham Gn NE3 . . . . . . . . . .7 C2
Elsing Cl NE5 . . . . . . . . . . .15 C4
Elstob Pl NE6 . . . . . . . . . . .48 A4
Elston Cl NE5 . . . . . . . . . . .14 A2
Elstree Ct NE3 . . . . . . . . . .6 C3
ELSWICK . . . . . . . . . . . . . .44 B3
Elswick East Terr NE4 . .76 B4
Elswick Rd
  Newcastle-u-T NE4 . . . . .76 A4
  Washington NE37 . . . . . . .69 C3
Elsworth Gn NE5 . . . . . . . .16 A3
Elton St E NE28 . . . . . . . . .21 C1
Elton St W NE28 . . . . . . . .21 C1
Eltringham Cl NE28 . . . . .21 B2
Elvaston Rd NE40 . . . . . . .25 A2
Elvet Cl
  Brunswick Village NE13 . . . .2 B2
  6 Newcastle-u-T NE6 . . .33 A3
Elvet Ct NE6 . . . . . . . . . . . .33 A3
Elvet Way 5 NE6 . . . . . . .33 A3
Ely Cl NE12 . . . . . . . . . . . . .20 B4
Elysium La NE8 . . . . . . . . .79 A1
Ely St NE8 . . . . . . . . . . . . . .79 B1
Ely Way NE32 . . . . . . . . . . .51 A2
Embassy Gdns NE15 . . . .28 C2
Emblehope NE37 . . . . . . . .69 C2
Emblehope Dr NE3 . . . . . .17 B4
Embleton Ave NE3 . . . . . . .8 B2
Embleton Gdns
  Gateshead NE10 . . . . . . . .47 C1
  5 Newcastle-u-T NE5 . . .16 B1
Embleton Rd NE10 . . . . . .49 A2
Emden Rd NE3 . . . . . . . . . .8 A2
Emily St
  Gateshead NE8 . . . . . . . . .47 A1
  Newcastle-u-T NE6 . . . . .33 C2
Emmanuel Coll NE11 . . .56 C1
Emma View 7 NE40 . . . .38 B3
Emmaville NE40 . . . . . . . .38 C4
Emmaville Prim Sch
  NE40 . . . . . . . . . . . . . . . .38 B4
Empress Rd NE6 . . . . . . . .49 A4
Enfield Ave NE16 . . . . . . . .43 A1
Enfield Gdns NE16 . . . . . .55 A1
Enfield Rd NE9 . . . . . . . . .58 B4
Engine Inn Rd NE28 . . . . .23 A4
Engine La NE9 . . . . . . . . . .65 A4
Englefield NE10 . . . . . . . . .67 A4
Englefield Cl NE3 . . . . . . . .7 A3
English Martyrs' RC Prim
  Sch NE5 . . . . . . . . . . . . . .29 A4
Enid St NE13 . . . . . . . . . . . .4 A4
Ennerdale
  Birtley DH3 . . . . . . . . . . . .70 C2
  Gateshead NE10 . . . . . . . .61 C4
Ennerdale Cres NE21 . . .53 A4
Ennerdale Gdns
  Gateshead NE9 . . . . . . . . .58 C1
  Wallsend NE28 . . . . . . . . .23 B4
Ennerdale Rd NE6 . . . . . . .33 A3
Ennerdale Wlk NE16 . . . .54 B1
Ennismore Ct NE12 . . . . .11 B2
Enslin St NE6 . . . . . . . . . . .48 B3
Enterprise Ho NE11 . . . . .64 B4

Epinay Sch NE32 . . . . . . .37 A2
Epinay Wlk NE32 . . . . . . .37 A2
Epsom Ct NE3 . . . . . . . . . . .7 A3
Epworth Gr NE8 . . . . . . . .79 B1
Equitable St NE28 . . . . . . .21 C1
Ermine Cres NE9 . . . . . . . .59 A2
Errol Pl DH3 . . . . . . . . . . . .70 C2
Erskine Ct NE2 . . . . . . . . .19 A2
Esher Ct NE3 . . . . . . . . . . . .7 A3
Eshmere Cres NE5 . . . . . .14 A3
Eshott Cl
  Newcastle-u-T, East
    Denton NE5 . . . . . . . . . .15 B1
  Newcastle-u-T, Fawdon
    NE3 . . . . . . . . . . . . . . . . .8 B2
Eshott Ct NE5 . . . . . . . . . .15 B1
Eskdale DH3 . . . . . . . . . . .71 A1
Eskdale Cres NE37 . . . . . .67 C1
Eskdale Dr NE32 . . . . . . . .51 C3
Eskdale Gdns NE9 . . . . . .65 B3
Esk St N10, NE9 . . . . . . . .59 A3
Esk Terr 9 DH3 . . . . . . . . .68 B1
Eslington Ct NE8 . . . . . . . .57 A4
Eslington Sch NE8 . . . . . .77 C1
Espley Ct NE3 . . . . . . . . . . .7 A3
Essex Cl NE4 . . . . . . . . . . .76 B3
Essex Gdns
  Gateshead NE8 . . . . . . . . .58 B3
  Wallsend NE28 . . . . . . . . .22 C3
Etal Ave NE29 . . . . . . . . . .24 B4
Etal Cres NE32 . . . . . . . . .52 A4
Etal La NE5 . . . . . . . . . . . .15 C3
Etal Pl NE3 . . . . . . . . . . . . .8 B3
Etal Way NE5 . . . . . . . . . . .15 C4
Ethel Ave NE21 . . . . . . . . .41 B2
Ethel St NE4 . . . . . . . . . . .43 C4
Etherley Rd NE6 . . . . . . . .33 B3
Etherstone Ave NE7 . . . . .20 A3
Eton Sq NE31 . . . . . . . . . . .36 A2
Ettrick Gdns NE8 . . . . . . .59 A4
Ettrick Lodge NE3 . . . . . .18 B4
Ettrick Rd NE32 . . . . . . . .36 B1
Evanlade NE10 . . . . . . . . . .61 A2
Eva St NE15 . . . . . . . . . . . .27 A2
Evelyn Terr NE21 . . . . . . .41 B3
Evenwood Gdns NE9 . . . .59 A1
Eversleigh Pl NE15 . . . . . .12 C2
Eversley Pl
  7 Newcastle-u-T NE6 . . .32 C2
  Wallsend NE28 . . . . . . . . .23 A3
Evesham Cl NE35 . . . . . . .52 B1
Evesham Garth NE3 . . . . .16 C3
Evistones Gdns NE6 . . . . .48 A3
Evistones Rd NE9 . . . . . . .58 C3
Ewart Cres NE34 . . . . . . . .52 A4
Ewart Ct NE3 . . . . . . . . . . . .8 B3
Ewbank Ave NE4 . . . . . . . .29 C3
Ewesley Cl NE5 . . . . . . . . .15 B1
Ewesley Gdns NE13 . . . . . .2 B2
Exelby Cl NE3 . . . . . . . . . . .9 B4
Exeter Ct NE31 . . . . . . . . .35 B1
Exeter St
  Gateshead NE8 . . . . . . . . .79 C1
  Newcastle-u-T NE6 . . . . .48 C4
Exeter Way NE32 . . . . . . .51 A2

F

Factory Rd NE21 . . . . . . . .41 C4
Fairburn Ave NE7 . . . . . . .20 A4
Fairdale Ave NE7 . . . . . . . .20 A4
Fairfield NE12 . . . . . . . . . . .10 A2
Fairfield Ave
  3 Longbenton NE12 . . . .11 B4
  Whickham NE16 . . . . . . . .54 C1
Fairfield Cl NE15 . . . . . . . .44 A1
Fairfield Ind Est NE10 . .48 C2
Fairfield Rd NE2 . . . . . . . .18 B1
Fairfield Terr NE10 . . . . . .48 C1
Fairhaven NE9 . . . . . . . . . .67 A2
Fairhaven Ave NE6 . . . . . .34 B2
Fairhill Cl NE7 . . . . . . . . . .20 A4
Fairholm Rd NE4 . . . . . . . .29 C1
Fairmont Way NE7 . . . . . .20 A4
Fairnley Wlk NE5 . . . . . . .15 B2
Fairspring 3 NE5 . . . . . . .15 B2
Fairview Gn NE7 . . . . . . . .20 A4
Fairville Cres NE7 . . . . . . .20 A4
Fairway Cl NE3 . . . . . . . . . .8 C4

Fairways Ave NE7....20 A4
**Fairway The**
Newcastle-u-T NE3 ....8 C3
Ryton NE21.............40 C4
Falcon Pl NE12 ........10 B3
Faldonside NE6........20 B2
**Falkland Ave**
Hebburn NE31.........35 C2
Newcastle-u-T NE3 ...17 A3
Falla Park Com Prim Sch
NE10.................59 B4
Falla Park Cres NE10...59 B4
Falla Park Rd NE10 ...59 B4
Falloden Ave NE3 .....8 A4
Fallodon Gdns NE5 ...16 B2
Fallowfield NE10 ......60 C3
Fallowfield Ave NE3 ..8 A2
Falmouth Dr NE32 ....37 B1
Falmouth Rd NE6 .....32 C3
Falsgrave Pl NE16 ....54 B1
Falstone NE10..........60 C1
Falstone Ave NE15....27 C4
Falstone Sq NE3.......8 B2
Faraday Gr NE8........58 A3
Farlam Ct NE3 .........28 C4
**Farm Cl**
Sunniside NE16........62 C2
Washington NE37......67 C1
Farn Ct NE3 ...........7 B4
Farndale Rd NE4 ......29 C1
Farne Ave NE3 ........8 B3
Farne Prim Sch NE5 ..15 B3
Farne Terr NE6........33 C2
Farnham Cl NE15 .....27 B2
Farnham Rd NE15.....27 B2
Farnley Rd NE20.....20 A1
Farnon Rd NE3 ........8 B1
Farnsworth Ct NE2 ...19 A2
Farquhar St **9** NE2...19 A1
Farrfield NE10.........67 A4
Farthings The NE37 ..67 C2
Faversham Ct NE3 ....7 B3
**FAWDON** ..............7 C3
Fawdon Cl NE3 ........8 A4
Fawdon La NE3.........8 A3
Fawdon Park Ho NE3 .8 A2
Fawdon Park Rd NE3 ..8 A2
Fawdon Sta NE3........8 A2
Fawdon Wlk NE3 ......7 B3
Fawlee Gn NE5 ........16 A4
Fawley Cl NE35 .......52 A1
Featherstone NE38 ...69 B1
**Featherstone Gr**
Jarrow NE32 ..........50 C3
Newcastle-u-T NE3 ....4 A1
Federation Way NE11 ..44 A1
Felixstowe Dr NE7 ....20 B3
Fell Bank DH3 .........70 C4
**Fell Cl**
Birtley DH3...........71 A3
Sunniside NE16........62 C2
Fellcross DH3 .........68 B1
Fell Ct **5** NE9 ........59 A1
Felldyke NE10 ........60 B1
Fell Dyke Com Prim Sch
NE9.................66 B3
Fellgate Ave NE32 ...51 B1
Fellgate Gdns NE10 ..61 B2
Fellgate Prim Sch NE32 51 A1
Fellgate Sta NE32 ...51 B2
**FELLING**..............59 C4
Felling Bsns Ctr NE10...47 C2
Felling Dene Gdns
NE10.................48 A1
Felling Gate NE10 ....47 B1
Felling House Gdns
NE10.................47 C2
**FELLING SHORE** .......48 A2
Felling Shore Ind Est
NE10.................47 C3
Felling Sta NE10......47 C1
Felling View NE6......48 B3
Fellmere Ave NE10....61 C4
Fell Pl **7** NE9 .........67 A1
Fell Rd NE9............67 A1
Fellsdyke Ct NE9.....59 B2
**FELLSIDE** .............54 B2
Fellside DH3 ..........70 C3
Fellside Ave NE16....62 C3

Fellside Com Prim Sch
NE16.................54 C2
Fellside Ct NE16.......54 C3
Fellside Rd NE16 .....62 A3
Fellside The NE3......17 A4
Fells Rd NE11..........57 C3
Fells The **6** NE9 ......58 C2
Fell View **15** NE40 ....38 B3
Fell View W **15** NE40 ..38 B3
Fell Way The NE5 .....14 B1
Felthorpe Ct NE5 .....15 C4
Felton Ave NE3 .......8 B2
Felton Cres NE8 ......58 A3
Felton Gn **18** NE6 ....33 A2
Felton Ho **14** NE6 ....33 A2
Felton Wlk **18** NE6 ..33 A2
Fencer Ct NE3.........9 A4
**FENHAM** ..............29 B3
Fenham Chase NE4 ..29 C4
Fenham Ct NE4........29 C4
Fenham Hall Dr NE4 ..29 C4
Fennel NE9.............66 A4
Fenning Pl **6** NE6 ...47 B4
Fenton Wlk **4** NE5 ..15 B2
Fenwick Cl **4** NE2 ...19 A1
Fenwicks St NE35....52 A1
Fenwick Terr **3** NE2 ..19 A1
Ferguson Cres NE13 ...4 A4
Ferguson's La NE15...28 C2
**Fern Ave**
Newcastle-u-T, Fawdon
NE3...................8 B3
Newcastle-u-T, Jesmond
NE2...................19 A1
Fernclough NE9 .......59 B1
**Ferndale Ave**
Newcastle-u-T NE3 ....5 A1
Wallsend NE28........22 A2
Ferndale Terr **5** NE9...67 A1
**Ferndene**
Longbenton NE12......11 B3
Wallsend NE28........22 C4
Ferndene Ct NE3 .....18 B4
**Ferndene Gr**
Newcastle-u-T NE7 ...20 A3
Ryton NE40............25 B2
Fern Dene Rd NE8....58 A4
**Ferndown Ct**
Gateshead NE10.......61 A3
Ryton NE40............39 C4
Fern Gdns NE9........58 B2
Fernhill Ave NE16....54 C3
Fernlea Gdns NE40 ...38 C4
Fernlea Gn NE3.......8 A1
Fernville Ave NE16....62 C2
Fernville Rd NE3......17 C3
Fernwood Ave NE3 ....9 B2
Fernwood Rd NE15 ...27 B2
Fernyhough Hall NE31 ..36 A1
Ferriby Cl NE3 ........9 B4
Ferrisdale Way NE3 ...8 A3
Ferrydene Ave NE3 ..17 A4
Ferry St NE32..........36 C4
Festival Park Dr NE11 ...57 A3
Festival Way NE11, NE8 ..77 A1
Fetcham Ct NE3.......7 A3
Fewster Sq NE10 .....60 C2
Fieldfare Cl **2** NE28...71 B3
Field House Rd NE8 ..58 A3
Fielding Ct NE34......52 C3
Fielding Pl NE9........59 A4
Field La NE10..........61 C4
**Field St**
**8** Gateshead NE10......47 C1
Newcastle-u-T NE3 ...36 C1
**Field Terr**
Jarrow NE32 ..........36 C1
**2** Throckley NE15....12 B2
Fife Ave NE32..........52 A3
Fife St NE8 ............46 C1
**Fifth Ave**
Gateshead DH98,
NE11.................57 C1
Newcastle-u-T NE6 ...33 A3
Finchale Cl NE11 .....56 B2
**Finchale Gdns**
Gateshead NE9........66 A2
Throckley NE15.......12 B3
Finchale Rd NE31....50 A3
**Finchale Terr**
Jarrow NE32 ..........51 C4
**2** Newcastle-u-T NE6 ..47 B4

Finchley Cres NE6 ....34 B4
Finchley Ct NE6.......34 B4
Findon Gr NE29.......24 C4
Finsbury Ave NE6 ....33 C2
Finsmere Pl **1** NE5 ...15 C1
Finstock Ct NE3 ......19 A4
Firbanks NE32.........51 C1
Firfield Rd NE5 .......16 B2
Fir St NE32............36 B3
**First Ave**
Gateshead NE11.......57 B2
**1** Newcastle-u-T NE6 ...33 A3
North Shields NE29 ...24 A4
Firs The NE3...........17 C4
First St NE8............79 A1
Firtree Ave NE6.......21 B1
Firtree Rd NE16......54 C2
Firtrees NE10..........60 A1
Firtrees Ave NE28....23 C3
Firwood Gdns NE11...57 A1
Fisher Ind Est NE6....34 C3
Fisher St NE6..........34 C3
Fisherwell Rd NE10 ..48 C1
Fitzsimmons Ave NE28 ..21 C3
Flaxby Cl NE3..........9 B4
Fleming Ct NE8........77 C2
Fleming Gdns NE10...59 C2
Fletcher Ho NE29.....24 C3
**Flexbury Gdns**
Gateshead, Lyndhurst
NE9.................65 B2
Gateshead, Mount Pleasant
NE9.................59 B4
Newcastle-u-T NE15 ...27 C3
Flodden St NE6........33 B1
Flora St **12** NE6 ......32 C2
Florence Ave NE9.....58 C2
Florence St NE11.....41 A1
Flotterton Gdns NE5 ..29 A3
Flour Mill Rd NE11.....44 B2
Fold The NE6..........34 B4
**FOLLINGSBY** ..........61 C1
Follingsby Ave NE10 ..61 C2
Follingsby Dr NE10 ..61 B3
Follingsby Pk NE10...61 C1
Follingsby Way NE10..61 C2
**Folly La**
Blaydon NE21 .........41 A1
Boldon Colliery NE35 ...52 A1
Longbenton NE7, NE12...11 A1
Whickham NE16.......55 A3
Whickham, Swalwell
NE16.................42 C1
Front Street Com Prim
Sch NE16.............54 C3
Frosterley Wlk NE16 ..62 C3
Fuchsia Gdns NE31 ...50 A3
Fuchsia Pl NE5 .......16 B2
Fulbrook Rd NE3 .....8 A1
Fullerton Pl NE9......58 C4
Fulmar Dr NE38 ......71 B3
Fulwell Gn NE15 ......15 C1
Furrowfield NE10 .....59 B2
Furrowfield Jun Sch
DH3.................46 C4
Furrowfield Sch NE10 ..59 B2
Furzefield Rd NE3 ....17 C4

Fountain La NE21.....41 B3
Fountains Cl NE11 ....58 B2
Fountains Cres NE31...50 A3
Fouracres Rd NE5 ....16 C2
**Four Lane Ends Sta**
NE7.................11 A1
**Fourstones 6** NE5...15 B2
Fourstones Cl NE3 ...7 B1
**Fourth Ave**
Gateshead NE11.......57 B1
**1** Newcastle-u-T NE6 ...33 A3
Fourth St NE8.........79 A1
Fowberry Cres NE4 ...29 C3
Fowberry Rd NE15....42 B4
Fowler Gdns **2** NE11 ..44 B1
**Fox and Hounds La**
NE5.................29 A2
**Fox and Hounds Rd**
NE5.................29 A2
Fox Ave NE34..........52 C4
Foxhills Covert NE16...54 A1
Foxhills The NE16 ....54 A1
Fox St NE10............47 B1
Foxton Ave NE3.......8 A3
Foxton Cl NE29 .......24 C3
Foxton Gn NE3 .......7 C1
Foxton Way NE10.....49 A2
Frances St NE21......40 C2
Frankham St **1** NE5 ...15 A2
Franklin Pk NE21.....42 A4
**Frank St**
Greenside NE40.......38 B1
Wallsend NE28........21 C1
Frazer Terr NE10......48 C1
Freeman Hospl NE7 ...19 B4
Freeman Rd NE3, NE7 ...19 A4
Frenton Cl NE5........14 A2
Friars Dene Rd NE10...47 B2
**FRIARS GOOSE**........47 C3
Friarside Gdns NE16 ...54 C2
Friarside Rd NE4 .....29 C4
Friars Way NE5 .......15 A2
Friar Way NE32 .......37 A3
Friary Gdns NE10 ....47 B3
Frobisher St NE31 ...36 B2
Frome Gdns NE9......65 A2
**Front St**
Blaydon NE21 .........41 A1
Boldon Colliery NE35 ...52 A1
Longbenton NE7, NE12...11 A1
Whickham NE16.......55 A3
Whickham, Swalwell
NE16.................42 C1

**Garden Pk 9** NE28....23 A4
**Garden St**
Blaydon NE21 .........41 B3
Newcastle-u-T NE3 ...18 A4
**Garden Terr**
**10** Blaydon NE21 ......41 A1
Crawcrook NE40.......38 B4
Crawcrook, Ryton Woodside
NE40.................38 C3
Garmondsway **15** NE6...33 A1
Garner Cl NE5 ........14 B3
Garrett Cl NE28.......23 A3
Garsdale DH3 .........71 A1
Garside Ave DH3.....68 B2
Garston Cl NE7.......20 C3
Garth Cres NE21......41 A1
Garth Farm Rd NE21...41 A1
Garthfield Cl NE5.....15 B3
Garthfield Cnr NE5 ...15 B3
Garthfield Cres NE5...15 B3
**Garth The**
**7** Blaydon NE21 .......41 A1
Newcastle-u-T, Kenton
NE3...................17 A4
Newcastle-u-T NE5 ...14 C1
Garvey Villas N10, NE9...59 B2
Gatesgarth NE9 ......58 C1
Gateshead Coll NE9 ..58 B3
**Gateshead Coll (Annexe)**
NE9.................58 C3
**Gateshead Highway**
NE8.................79 C2
**Gateshead International
Stad (Athletics Gd)**
NE10.................47 B3
**Gateshead Jewish
Boarding Sch** NE8....79 B1
**Gateshead Jewish Prim
Sch** NE8.............79 B1
**Gateshead Jewish
Teachers Training Coll**
NE8.................79 B1
Gateshead Rd NE16...63 A3
Gateshead Sta NE8 ...78 B3
**Gateshead Stadium Sta**
NE8.................46 C2
**Gateshead Talmudical Coll**
NE8.................79 B1
Gatwick Ct NE3 .......7 A3
Gaughan Cl NE6......48 B3
Gellesfield Chare NE16...62 C4
Genister Pl NE4.......29 B4
**George Rd** NE28......34 C4
**George Smith Gdns**
NE10.................47 B2
**Georges Rd**
Newcastle-u-T, Elswick
NE4.................44 B3
Newcastle-u-T NE4 ...44 B4
**George St**
Birtley DH3...........70 A4
Blaydon NE21 .........41 C3
Brunswick Village NE13...3 A2
**5** Crawcrook NE40....38 B3
**5** Gateshead NE10....48 B1
Newcastle-u-T, Coxlodge
NE3...................8 B1
Newcastle-u-T, NE1, NE4 ..76 C4
Walbottle NE15 ......13 A2
Wallsend NE28........23 C1
Whickham NE16.......54 C3
Gerald St NE4 ........43 C4
Gibbon's Wlk NE34 ...52 C2
Gibside Ct NE11 ......56 B2
Gibside Gdns NE15 ...28 C2
Gibside Sch NE16.....54 C1
Gibside View NE21....53 A4
Gibside Way NE11 ....43 A2
Gibson Terr NE40 ....38 C4
Gilberdyke NE10......60 C1
Gill Ct NE13 ...........2 A2
Gillies St NE6..........33 B2
Gilliland Cres DH3 ...68 B2
Gill St NE4 ............29 C1
Gilmore Cl NE5 .......14 B4
Gilmore Ho NE8......58 A4
Gisland Ave NE28 ....23 A3
Gilwell Way NE3 ......4 B1
Gingler La NE40 ......38 C2
Gishford Way NE5 ...15 C2
Gladeley Way NE16 ...62 C2

**Fox and Hounds La**
**Foundation Way**
Foundry Ct NE6.......47 B4
Foundry St NE6.......47 B4
Foundry La NE6 ......32 B2

**Forum The**
Newcastle-u-T NE15 ...28 A3
**2** Wallsend NE28 ......21 C1
Fossdyke NE10.........60 B1
Fossefeld NE10........60 C3
Fosse Law NE15 ......12 C1
Fosse Terr NE9 .......59 A2
Fossway NE6 ..........33 C3
Foster Ct NE11 .......64 A3
Foster Dr NE8 ........47 A2
**Foster St**
Newcastle-u-T, Low Walker
NE6.................34 C1
Newcastle-u-T, Wincombe
NE6.................34 C1

**G**
**Gables The** NE13......6 C2
Gainers Terr NE28....35 A4
Gainford NE9..........65 A2
Gainsborough Cres NE9 53 A3
Gainsbro Gr NE4......30 A2
Gainsford Ave NE9...59 A2
Gairloch Dr NE38....71 C3
Gallalaw Terr NE3....10 A1
Gallant Terr NE28 ....24 A1
**Galloping Green Cotts 2**
NE9.................66 B2
**Galloping Green Farm Cl**
**3** NE9.................66 B2
**Galloping Green Rd**
NE9.................66 B2
Garden Cl NE13........2 B4
Garden Croft NE12....11 C4
Garden Dr NE31 ......49 C4
Gardener St NE4 .....76 A3
**Garden House Cres**
NE16.................55 B4
**Garden House Est** NE40 38 A4

Glade The NE15 . . . . . . . . .13 B2
Gladstonbury Pl NE12 . . . .11 A3
Gladstone St
Hebburn NE31, NE32 . . . . .36 B2
Newcastle-u-T NE15 . . . . . .27 A2
**3** Wallsend NE28 . . . . . . .23 C1
Gladstone Terr
Birtley DH3 . . . . . . . . . . . . .70 A4
**2** Boldon Colliery NE35 . .52 A1
Gateshead NE8 . . . . . . . . . .79 C1
Gladstone Terr W NE8 . .79 B1
Glaisdale Cl NE34 . . . . . . .52 C2
Glaisdale Rd NE7 . . . . . . . .10 B1
Glamis Ave NE3 . . . . . . . . . .4 C1
Glamis Terr NE16 . . . . . . . .62 B1
Glamis Villas DH3 . . . . . . .68 B2
Glantlees NE15 . . . . . . . . .15 B2
Glanton Cl
Gateshead NE10 . . . . . . . . .61 B3
**3** Newcastle-u-T NE6 . . .47 B4
Wallsend NE28 . . . . . . . . . .22 C3
Glanton Ct NE11 . . . . . . . .77 A1
Glanton Wynd NE3 . . . . . . .8 B4
Glanville Cl NE11 . . . . . . . .57 A3
Glasgow Rd NE32 . . . . . . . .52 A3
Glasshouse St NE6 . . . . . .47 B4
Glastonbury Gr NE2 . . . . .19 A2
Glebe Ave
Longbenton NE12 . . . . . . . .11 B3
Whickham NE16 . . . . . . . . .55 A3
Glebe Cl NE5 . . . . . . . . . . .14 B3
Glebe Rise NE16 . . . . . . . .55 A3
Glebe St NE4 . . . . . . . . . . .22 A3
Glebe Terr **1** NE11 . . . . . .56 B4
Glebe Wlk NE16 . . . . . . . . .54 C3
Glenbrooke Terr NE9 . . . .65 A4
Glenburn Cl NE38 . . . . . . .71 B3
Glencarron Cl NE38 . . . . .71 C3
Glen Ct NE31 . . . . . . . . . . .35 B1
Glendale Ave
Newcastle-u-T NE3 . . . . . . .17 B4
Wallsend NE28 . . . . . . . . . .21 C4
Whickham NE16 . . . . . . . . .54 C2
Glendale Cl NE5 . . . . . . . .14 B3
Glendale Gdns NE9 . . . . .59 A1
Glendale Terr **5** NE6 . . .33 A2
Glendyn Cl NE7 . . . . . . . . .19 B1
Gleneagle Cl NE5 . . . . . . .14 A3
Gleneagles Cl NE7 . . . . . .11 A1
Gleneagles Rd NE9 . . . . .64 C3
Glenfield Rd
Longbenton NE12 . . . . . . . .10 C3
Longbenton NE12 . . . . . . . .11 A3
Glengarvan Cl NE38 . . . . .71 C3
Glenholme Cl **7** NE38 . .71 B3
Glenhurst Dr
Newcastle-u-T NE5 . . . . . . .14 B3
Whickham NE16 . . . . . . . . .55 A1
Glenkerry Cl NE38 . . . . . .71 C3
Glenmoor NE31 . . . . . . . . .35 B3
Glenorrin Cl NE38 . . . . . . .71 C3
Glenridge Ave **2** NE6 . .19 C1
Glenshiel Cl NE38 . . . . . . .71 C3
Glenside NE32 . . . . . . . . . .51 B2
Glenside Ct NE9 . . . . . . . .64 C4
Glen St NE31 . . . . . . . . . . .35 B1
Glenthorn Rd NE2 . . . . . . .18 C2
Glenuce DH3 . . . . . . . . . . .71 A3
Glenwood Wlk NE5 . . . . . .14 B3
Gloucester Ct NE3 . . . . . . .7 A4
Gloucester Terr NE4 . . . .76 A4
Gloucester Way
Hedworth NE32 . . . . . . . . .51 A2
Newcastle-u-T NE4 . . . . . . .76 B4
Glynfellis NE10 . . . . . . . . .67 A4
Glynfellis Ct NE10 . . . . . . .60 B1
Glynwood Com Prim Sch
NE9 . . . . . . . . . . . . . . . . . . .58 C1
Glynwood Gdns NE9 . . . .58 C1
Goathland Ave NE12 . . . . .11 A2
Goathland Prim Sch
NE12 . . . . . . . . . . . . . . . . . .11 A2
Gofton Wlk NE5 . . . . . . . . .15 B2
Goldcrest Rd NE11 . . . . . .71 B3
Goldfinch Cl NE4 . . . . . . . .44 B4
Goldspink La NE2 . . . . . . .22 C3
Goodwood Ave NE8 . . . . .57 B4
Goodwood Cl NE5 . . . . . . .14 B3
Gordon Ave NE3 . . . . . . . .18 A4
Gordon Ct **9** NE10 . . . . . .47 C1
Gordon Ho **2** NE6 . . . . . .32 C1
Gordon Rd **3** NE6 . . . . . .32 C1

Gordon Sq NE6 . . . . . . . . .32 C1
Gorsehill NE9 . . . . . . . . . . .59 B1
Gorse Hill Way NE5 . . . . .16 A3
Goschen St NE8 . . . . . . . .57 C4
GOSFORTH . . . . . . . . . . . . .9 A2
Gosforth Bsns Pk NE12 .10 A3
Gosforth Central Mid Sch
NE3 . . . . . . . . . . . . . . . . . . . .9 B2
Gosforth Ctr NE3 . . . . . . .18 A4
Gosforth East Mid Sch
NE3 . . . . . . . . . . . . . . . . . . . .9 B3
Gosforth High Sch NE3 . .9 A2
Gosforth Park Fst Sch
NE3 . . . . . . . . . . . . . . . . . . . .9 B3
Gosforth Park Villas
NE3 . . . . . . . . . . . . . . . . . . . .4 C4
Gosforth Park Way NE3 .10 B4
Gosforth St **20** NE10. . . . .47 C1
Gosforth Terr
Gateshead NE10 . . . . . . . .48 B1
Newcastle-u-T NE3 . . . . . . .9 C1
Gosforth West Mid Sch
NE3 . . . . . . . . . . . . . . . . . . . .8 C3
Goswick Ave NE7 . . . . . . .19 C3
Goswick Dr NE3 . . . . . . . . .9 A4
Govt Bldgs (DSS) NE98 .10 B1
Gowan Terr NE2 . . . . . . . .19 A1
Gower St NE6 . . . . . . . . . .48 C4
Gower Wlk NE10. . . . . . . . .59 B4
Gowland Ave NE4 . . . . . . .29 C2
Gracefield Cl NE5 . . . . . . .14 B3
Grace Gdns NE28 . . . . . . .21 B4
Grace Ho NE29 . . . . . . . . .24 C3
Grace St
Dunston NE11 . . . . . . . . . .56 B4
Newcastle-u-T, Byker
NE6 . . . . . . . . . . . . . . . . . . .33 A2
Newcastle-u-T, Walker
NE6 . . . . . . . . . . . . . . . . . . .33 B2
Gradys Yd NE15 . . . . . . . .12 B3
Grafton Cl **5** NE6 . . . . . . .32 C2
Grafton Ho **7** NE6 . . . . . .32 C2
Grafton St **11** NE6 . . . . . .32 C2
Gragareth Way NE37 . . . .69 C2
Graham Ave NE16 . . . . . . .55 A4
Graham Park Rd NE3 . . . .18 A3
Graham Rd NE31 . . . . . . . .35 B1
Grahamsley St NE8 . . . . .79 C2
Grainger Ct NE4 . . . . . . . .30 A1
Grainger Park Rd NE4 . . .30 A1
Grampian Gdns NE11 . . .57 A2
Granby Cl NE16 . . . . . . . . .62 C3
Granby Terr **4** NE16 . . . . .62 C2
Grandstand Rd NE2 . . . . .17 C2
Grange Ave NE12 . . . . . . .11 C2
Grange Cl NE28 . . . . . . . . .22 A2
Grange Cres
Gateshead NE10 . . . . . . . .60 C3
Ryton NE40 . . . . . . . . . . . . .39 B4
Grange Ct
Gateshead NE10 . . . . . . . .60 C3
**6** Jarrow NE32. . . . . . . .36 C3
Ryton NE40 . . . . . . . . . . . . .39 B4
Grange Dr NE40 . . . . . . . . .39 B4
Grange Farm Dr NE16 . .54 C1
Grange Fst Sch NE3 . . . . .8 C2
Grange La NE16 . . . . . . . .55 A1
Grange Manor NE16 . . . .55 A1
Grange Nook NE16 . . . . .54 C1
Grange Pl NE32 . . . . . . . . .36 C3
Grange Rd
Gateshead NE10 . . . . . . . .60 C3
Jarrow NE32 . . . . . . . . . . . .36 C3
Newburn NE15 . . . . . . . . . .25 C4
Newcastle-u-T, Fenham
NE4. . . . . . . . . . . . . . . . . . .29 B3
Newcastle-u-T, Gosforth
NE3. . . . . . . . . . . . . . . . . . . .9 A3
Ryton NE40 . . . . . . . . . . . . .25 A1
Grange Rd W NE32. . . . . .36 C3
Grange Terr **6** NE9 . . . . . .58 C4
Grange View NE40 . . . . . .39 B4
Grange Villas NE28 . . . . .22 A2
Grange Wlk **3** NE16 . . . .54 C1
Grantham Dr NE9. . . . . . . .64 C4
Grant St NE32 . . . . . . . . . .36 B3
Granville Cres NE12 . . . . .11 C3
Granville Dr
Longbenton NE12 . . . . . . . .11 C3
Newcastle-u-T NE3 . . . . . .13 B3
Granville Gdns NE2 . . . . .32 B4
Granville Lodge NE12 . . .11 C4

Granville Rd NE3 . . . . . . . .9 B3
Granville St NE8 . . . . . . . .79 C1
Grasmere DH3. . . . . . . . . .71 A2
Grasmere Ave
Gateshead NE10. . . . . . . . .60 B4
Hedworth NE32 . . . . . . . . .51 C3
Newburn NE15 . . . . . . . . . .25 C3
Newcastle-u-T NE5 . . . . . .34 A1
Grasmere Cres NE21 . . . .53 A4
Grasmere Ct NE15 . . . . . .25 C3
Grasmere Ho NE6. . . . . . .33 C1
Grasmere Pl NE3 . . . . . . . .9 A3
Grasmere Rd
Hebburn NE31 . . . . . . . . . .50 B4
Wallsend NE28 . . . . . . . . . .21 B1
Whickham NE16 . . . . . . . . .55 B3
Grasmere St W NE8. . . . .79 B1
Grasmere St NE8 . . . . . . .79 B1
Grasmoor Pl NE15 . . . . . .26 C3
Grassbanks NE10 . . . . . . .60 C2
Grassholm Pl NE12 . . . . .10 B3
Grasswell Dr NE5 . . . . . . .16 B3
Gray Ave NE13 . . . . . . . . . .2 C3
Grayling Rd NE11. . . . . . . .57 A3
Grays Terr **8** NE35. . . . . .52 A1
Graystones NE10 . . . . . . .61 A2
Gray's Wlk NE34 . . . . . . . .52 C2
Great North Rd
Newcastle-u-T, Gosforth
NE3. . . . . . . . . . . . . . . . . . . .9 A3
Newcastle-u-T, West
Jesmond NE2 . . . . . . . . . . .18 B2
Great Park Way NE13 . . . .4 A3
Grebe Cl NE11 . . . . . . . . . .77 A2
Grebe Ct **6** NE2 . . . . . . . .19 A1
Greely Rd NE5 . . . . . . . . . .15 A2
Greenacre Pk NE9 . . . . . .64 C3
Greenacres Cl NE40 . . . .38 C3
Greenbank
Blaydon NE21. . . . . . . . . . .41 B2
Jarrow NE32 . . . . . . . . . . . .36 C3
Greenbank Villas NE32 . .36 C3
Greenbourne Gdns
NE10. . . . . . . . . . . . . . . . . . .59 B3
Greencroft Ave NE6. . . . . .34 B4
Greendyke Ct NE5 . . . . . .14 B3
Greenesfield Bsns Ctr
NE8 . . . . . . . . . . . . . . . . . . .78 B3
Greenfield Ave NE5 . . . . .15 B2
Greenfield Pl NE40. . . . . . .25 B1
Greenfield Rd NE3 . . . . . . .4 B1
Greenfields Com Prim Sch
NE13. . . . . . . . . . . . . . . . . . . .2 C2
Greenfields Sch NE31. . . .36 B2
Greenfield Terr **2** NE10 .48 B1
Greenfinch Cl NE38 . . . . .71 B3
Greenford Rd NE6 . . . . . .48 C4
Green Gr NE40. . . . . . . . . .39 A3
Greenhead NE38 . . . . . . . .71 B4
Greenhill View NE5 . . . . .16 C2
Green La
Gateshead, Felling
NE10. . . . . . . . . . . . . . . . . . .47 C2
Gateshead, Pelaw NE10. .48 C1
Woolsington NE13 . . . . . . . .6 A4
Greenlands NE32 . . . . . . .51 B2
Green Lane Gdns NE10 .47 B2
Greenlaw NE5 . . . . . . . . . .27 C4
Greenlee Dr NE7. . . . . . . .20 B3
Green Pk NE28 . . . . . . . . .20 C3
Greenrigg NE21 . . . . . . . . .41 C1
Greenriggs Ave NE3 . . . . .5 A1
GREENSIDE . . . . . . . . . . .38 C1
Greenside Ave
Brunswick Village NE13 . . . .2 A2
Wallsend NE28 . . . . . . . . . .23 A3
Greenside Cres NE15 . . .28 B3
Greenside Prim Sch
NE40. . . . . . . . . . . . . . . . . . .38 B1
Greenside Rd
Crawcrook NE40. . . . . . . . .38 B3
Greenside NE40 . . . . . . . .38 B2
Green The
Gateshead NE10. . . . . . . . .60 A4
Newcastle-u-T NE3 . . . . . .17 A3
Walbottle NE15 . . . . . . . . .13 A1
Greentree Sq NE5 . . . . . .15 C2
Greenway
Newcastle-u-T, Fenham
NE4. . . . . . . . . . . . . . . . . . .29 B4
Newcastle-u-T NE5 . . . . . .14 B4
Greenwell Cl NE21 . . . . . .40 C1

Greenwell Terr NE40 . . . .38 A4
Greenwich Pl NE8 . . . . . .46 C4
Greenwood Ave NE6 . . . .21 B1
Greenwood Gdns
Dunston NE11. . . . . . . . . . .57 A1
Gateshead NE10. . . . . . . . .47 C2
Grenville Dr NE3. . . . . . . . .4 B1
Gretna Dr NE32 . . . . . . . . .52 B2
Gretna Rd NE15. . . . . . . . .28 C2
Gretton Pl NE7 . . . . . . . . .19 B3
Greyfriars La NE12 . . . . . .10 B2
Grey St
Brunswick Village NE13 . . . .2 A2
Wallsend NE28 . . . . . . . . . .22 A2
Greystead Cl NE5 . . . . . . .14 B3
Greystoke Ave
Newcastle-u-T NE2 . . . . . .32 B3
Whickham NE16 . . . . . . . . .55 A1
Greystoke Gdns
Gateshead NE9. . . . . . . . . .65 C2
Newcastle-u-T NE2 . . . . . .32 B4
Whickham NE16 . . . . . . . . .55 A1
Greystoke Pk NE3 . . . . . . .9 A4
Greystoke Wlk **2** NE16 .54 C1
Greywood Ave NE4 . . . . .29 C3
Grisedale Gdns NE9 . . . .65 B3
Grosvenor Ave
Newcastle-u-T NE2 . . . . . .19 A1
Whickham NE16 . . . . . . . . .55 A1
Grosvenor Cres NE31 . . .50 B4
Grosvenor Ct NE5 . . . . . . .14 B3
Grosvenor Gdns
Newcastle-u-T NE2 . . . . . .32 B4
Wallsend NE28 . . . . . . . . . .23 B3
Grosvenor Pl NE2 . . . . . . .19 A1
Grosvenor Rd NE2 . . . . . .19 A1
Grosvenor Villas **1**
NE2. . . . . . . . . . . . . . . . . . . .19 A1
Grosvenor Way NE5. . . . .14 B3
Grousemoor **2** NE37 . . .69 C3
Grove Ave NE3 . . . . . . . . .18 B4
Grove Cotts **9** DH3 . . . . .70 B4
Grove Ho NE3 . . . . . . . . . .18 B4
Grove Rd
Gateshead NE8. . . . . . . . . .58 C2
Walbottle NE15 . . . . . . . . .13 A2
Grove Terr NE16 . . . . . . . .62 C1
Grove The
Longbenton NE12 . . . . . . . .11 B2
Newcastle-u-T, Gosforth
NE3. . . . . . . . . . . . . . . . . . .18 B4
Newcastle-u-T, Jesmond
NE2. . . . . . . . . . . . . . . . . . .19 A2
Newcastle-u-T NE5 . . . . . .14 B1
Whickham NE16 . . . . . . . . .55 B2
Guelder Rd NE7 . . . . . . . .20 A3
Guildford Pl NE6. . . . . . . . .32 C3
Gullane Cl NE10 . . . . . . . .49 B2
Gunnerston Gr **1** NE3 . . .7 B1
Gunn St NE11. . . . . . . . . . .56 B4
Gut Rd NE28 . . . . . . . . . . .23 A1
Guyzance Ave NE3 . . . . . . .8 C2

## H

Haddricksmill Rd NE3 . . .18 C4
Haddricks Mill Rd NE3 . .18 C4
Hadrian Gdns NE21 . . . . .41 C1
Hadrian Ho **2** NE15. . . . .12 B2
Hadrian Pl
Gateshead NE9. . . . . . . . . .59 A3
Throckley NE15 . . . . . . . . .12 C2
Hadrian Rd
Jarrow NE32 . . . . . . . . . . . .51 C4
Newcastle-u-T NE4 . . . . . .29 C2
Wallsend NE28 . . . . . . . . . .22 B1
Hadrian Road Sta NE28 .22 C2
Hadrian Sch NE15 . . . . . .29 A2
Hadrians Ct NE11. . . . . . . .64 B3
Hadstone Pl **3** NE5. . . . .16 A1
Hagan Hall NE32 . . . . . . .51 B1
Haggerston Cl NE5 . . . . .15 C4
Haggerston Cres NE5 . . .15 C4
Haggerston Ct NE5 . . . . .15 C4
Haggerston Terr NE32. . .52 A4
Haggie Ave NE28 . . . . . . .22 B3
Haig Cres NE15 . . . . . . . . .28 C1
Haig St NE11 . . . . . . . . . . .56 B4
Haigh Terr NE9 . . . . . . . . .66 A1
Haig St NE11 . . . . . . . . . . .56 B4
Hailsham Ave NE12 . . . . .19 C3
Hainingwood Terr NE10 .49 A2
Halewood Ave NE3 . . . . . .16 C4

Half Fields Rd NE21. . . . .41 A1
Half Moon La NE8 . . . . . .79 B2
Halifax Pl NE11 . . . . . . . . .44 A1
Halifax Rd NE11 . . . . . . . .44 A1
Hall Ave NE4 . . . . . . . . . . .29 C2
Halleypike Cl NE7. . . . . . .20 B3
Hallgarth NE10 . . . . . . . . .60 C3
Hallgarth Rd NE21 . . . . . .41 A2
Hall Gdns NE10 . . . . . . . . .59 C3
Halling Cl NE6 . . . . . . . . . .48 C4
Hallow Dr NE15. . . . . . . . .12 B1
Hall Pk NE21 . . . . . . . . . . .40 C4
Hall Rd NE31 . . . . . . . . . . .35 C1
Hall Terr NE10 . . . . . . . . . .49 A2
Halterburn Cl NE3 . . . . . .17 B4
Halton Dr NE13 . . . . . . . . . .2 B2
Halton Way NE3 . . . . . . . . .4 A1
Hamar Cl NE29 . . . . . . . . .24 A4
Hambledon Gdns NE7. . .19 B3
Hambleton Gn NE9 . . . . .65 C1
Hamilton Ct **7** NE8 . . . . .58 C4
Hammerton Ct NE28 . . . .21 B1
Hampshire Ct NE4 . . . . . .77 A2
Hampshire Gdns NE28 . .22 C4
Hampstead Gdns NE32. .51 C2
Hampstead Rd NE4 . . . . .29 C1
Hampton Ct NE16 . . . . . . .43 A1
Hampton Dr NE10 . . . . . .59 B3
Hamsterley Cres
Gateshead NE9. . . . . . . . . .66 A3
Newcastle-u-T NE15 . . . . .26 C3
Handy Dr NE11 . . . . . . . . .44 A2
Hanlon Ct
Hebburn NE32 . . . . . . . . . .36 A3
Jarrow NE32 . . . . . . . . . . . .36 B4
Hannington Pl **3** NE6. . .32 B2
Hannington St **2** NE6. . .32 B2
Hanover Cl **2** NE5. . . . . .14 A2
Hanover Ct **5** NE9 . . . . . .65 B2
Hanover Dr NE21 . . . . . . .40 C1
Hanover Gdns **3** NE28 .23 B1
Hanover House NE32 . . . .51 A4
Hanover Sq NE1 . . . . . . . .78 A4
Hanover St NE1. . . . . . . . .78 A4
Hanover Wlk **1** NE5 . . . .14 A2
Harbottle Ave NE3 . . . . . . .8 B2
Harbottle Cres NE32 . . . .51 A2
Harbottle Ct NE6 . . . . . . .47 B4
Harbottle St **4** NE6. . . . .47 B4
Harcourt Pk **1** NE9 . . . . .58 C1
Harcourt St **2** NE9 . . . . .58 C1
Hardie Ave NE16 . . . . . . . .54 C4
Hardman Gdns NE40 . . . .25 B1
Hardwick Ct NE8 . . . . . . .46 C1
Hardwick Pl NE3. . . . . . . . .17 B3
Harebell Rd NE9 . . . . . . . .66 A4
Harehills Ave NE5. . . . . . .16 B1
Harehills Tower NE3 . . . .16 C3
Harelaw Gr NE5 . . . . . . . .14 B1
Hareside Cl NE15 . . . . . . .26 A4
Hareside Ct NE15 . . . . . . .26 A4
Hareside Wlk NE15 . . . . .26 A4
Harewood Cl NE16. . . . . .62 B4
Harewood Gn NE9 . . . . . .65 C2
Harewood Rd NE3 . . . . . . .9 A2
Hareydene NE5 . . . . . . . . . .6 A1
Hargill Dr NE38 . . . . . . . . .71 C1
Harle Cl NE5 . . . . . . . . . . .14 C1
Harlequin Lodge **9**
NE10. . . . . . . . . . . . . . . . . . .59 C4
Harle St NE28 . . . . . . . . . .23 C1
Harleston Way NE10 . . . .60 A2
Harley Terr NE3 . . . . . . . . . .9 B1
Harlow Ave NE3 . . . . . . . . .8 A3
HARLOW GREEN . . . . . . .65 C1
Harlow Green Com Inf Sch
NE9 . . . . . . . . . . . . . . . . . . .65 B2
Harlow Green Jun Sch
NE9 . . . . . . . . . . . . . . . . . . .65 B2
Harlow Green La NE9 . . .65 B2
Harlow Pl NE7 . . . . . . . . . .19 C3
Harnham Gdns NE5. . . . .16 A1
Harold St NE32 . . . . . . . . .37 A3
Harraby Gdns NE9 . . . . . .65 C3
Harras Bank DH3 . . . . . . .70 B3
Harraton Terr **15** DH3 . .70 B3
Harriet St **22** NE6 . . . . . .33 A2

**Harriet St**
Blaydon NE21 . . . . . . . . . . **41** B2
Newcastle-u-T NE6 . . . . . . **33** B2
**Harrington St 6** NE28 . .**21** C2
**Harrison Ct** DH3 . . . . . . . . **70** B3
**Harrison Gdns** NE8 . . . . . **57** C3
**Harrison Rd** NE28 . . . . . . **23** B3
**Harrow Gdns** NE13 . . . . . . **2** C1
**Hartburn** NE10 . . . . . . . . . **60** C2
**Hartburn Dr** NE5 . . . . . . . **14** B3
**Hartburn Pl** NE4 . . . . . . . **30** A3
**Hartburn Wlk** NE3 . . . . . . **7** B1
**Hartford Rd** NE3 . . . . . . . . **9** B3
**Hartford St 1** NE6 . . . . . **33** A4
**Harthope Dr** NE29 . . . . . . **24** C3
**Hartington St** NE8 . . . . . . **79** C1
**Hartland Dr** DH3 . . . . . . . **70** C3
**Hartleyburn Ave** NE31 . .**49** C3
**Hartside**
Birtley DH3 . . . . . . . . . . . . **70** C1
Newcastle-u-T NE15 . . . . . **27** A3
**Hartside Gdns** NE2 . . . . . **19** A1
**Hartside Pl** NE3 . . . . . . . . **4** C1
**Harvard Rd** NE3 . . . . . . . . **7** C2
**Harvey Cl** NE38 . . . . . . . . **69** B1
**Harvey Cres** NE10 . . . . . . **61** A4
**Harwood Cl** NE38 . . . . . . . **71** C1
**Hastings Ave**
Longbenton NE12 . . . . . . . **11** B3
Newcastle-u-T NE3 . . . . . . **7** B3
**Hastings Par** NE31 . . . . . **50** C3
**Haswell Cl** NE10 . . . . . . . **61** C3
**Hatfield Ave** NE31 . . . . . . **36** A2
**Haugh La**
Ryton NE15, NE40 . . . . . . **25** C2
Ryton, Ryton Haugh NE21 .**26** B1
**Haughton Cres**
Hedworth NE32 . . . . . . . . **51** A2
Newcastle-u-T NE5 . . . . . . **14** C1
**Haughton Ct** NE4 . . . . . . . **76** A3
**Hautmont Rd** NE31 . . . . . **50** B4
**Hauxley Dr** NE3 . . . . . . . . **8** A3
**Hauxley Gdns** NE3 . . . . . . **16** B2
**Havant Gdns** NE13 . . . . . . **2** B3
**Havelock Cl** NE8 . . . . . . . **79** B2
**Havelock Terr**
Gateshead NE8 . . . . . . . . **79** B2
Jarrow NE32 . . . . . . . . . . **36** C1
**Havercroft** NE10 . . . . . . . **61** A3
**Haversham Cl** NE7 . . . . . . **10** B1
**Hawesdale Cres** NE21 . .**53** A4
**Hawick Cres** NE6 . . . . . . . **47** A4
**Hawkhills Terr 6** DH3 . .**68** B1
**Hawksbury** NE16 . . . . . . . **54** C3
**Hawksfeld** NE10 . . . . . . . **66** C4
**Hawkshead Ct** NE3 . . . . . . **7** B3
**Hawkshead Pl** NE9 . . . . . **65** C4
**Hawksley** NE5 . . . . . . . . . **15** A2
**Hawks St** NE8 . . . . . . . . . **46** C4
**Hawk Terr** DH3 . . . . . . . . **71** A2
**Hawkwell Rise** NE15 . . . . **12** B1
**Hawthorn Ave** NE13 . . . . . **2** A2
**Hawthorn Cl** NE16 . . . . . . **55** A1
**Hawthorn Ct** NE3 . . . . . . **18** A4
**Hawthorn Dr**
Dunston NE11 . . . . . . . . . **56** B4
Hedworth NE32 . . . . . . . . **51** C2
**Hawthorne Ave** NE31 . . .**36** A2
**Hawthorne Gdns** NE9 . . .**58** B2
**Hawthorn Gdns**
**5** Gateshead NE10 . . . . . . **47** C1
Newcastle-u-T NE3 . . . . . . **17** A4
Ryton NE40 . . . . . . . . . . **40** A4
**Hawthorn Gr** NE28 . . . . . . **21** C2
**Hawthorn Mews** NE3 . . . **18** A4
**Hawthorn Pl** NE4 . . . . . . . **76** B4
**Hawthorn Prim Sch**
NE4 . . . . . . . . . . . . . . . . **76** A4
**Hawthorn Rd**
Blaydon NE21 . . . . . . . . . **41** B1
Newcastle-u-T NE3 . . . . . . **18** A4
**Hawthorn Rd W** NE3 . . . **18** A4
**Hawthorn St**
Jarrow NE32 . . . . . . . . . . **36** B3
Walbottle NE15 . . . . . . . . **13** A2
**Hawthorns The**
Gateshead NE8 . . . . . . . . **66** B1
Newcastle-u-T NE4 . . . . . . **76** A3

**Hawthorn Terr**
Crawcrook NE40 . . . . . . . . **38** A3
**8** Dunston NE11 . . . . . . . **56** B4
Gateshead NE8 . . . . . . . . **66** B1
Newcastle-u-T NE4 . . . . . . **76** A4
**12** Springwell NE9 . . . . . . **67** A1
**Hawthorn Wlk** NE4 . . . . . **76** B4
**Haydock Dr** NE10 . . . . . . **61** B3
**Haydon Cl** NE3 . . . . . . . . **8** A4
**Hayes Wlk** NE13 . . . . . . . **2** B2
**Hayfield La** NE16 . . . . . . **55** A2
**Hayhole Rd** NE29 . . . . . . **24** C2
**Hayleazes Rd** NE15 . . . . . **28** A3
**Haynyng The** NE10 . . . . . **60** A3
**Hazel** NE12 . . . . . . . . . . . **11** B3
**Hazeldene Ave** NE3 . . . . . **7** A1
**Hazeley Gr 4** NE3 . . . . . . **7** B1
**Hazeley Way** NE3 . . . . . . . **7** B1
**Hazel Gr** NE10 . . . . . . . . **61** A3
**Hazelmere Ave** NE3 . . . . . **5** A1
**Hazelmoor** NE31 . . . . . . . **35** B3
**Hazel Rd**
Blaydon NE21 . . . . . . . . . **41** C2
Gateshead NE8 . . . . . . . . **57** B4
**Hazel St** NE32 . . . . . . . . **36** B3
**Hazelwood** NE32 . . . . . . . **37** B2
**Hazelwood Ave** NE2 . . . . **18** C2
**Hazelwood Cl** NE9 . . . . . . **66** B2
**Hazelwood Com Prim Sch**
NE13 . . . . . . . . . . . . . . . . **2** B1
**Hazelwood Terr** NE28 . . .**23** B3
**HAZLERIGG** . . . . . . . . . . **4** A4
**Headlam Gn 2** NE6 . . . . **33** A1
**Headlam Ho 12** NE6 . . . . **33** A1
**Headlam St 4** NE6 . . . . . **33** A1
**Headlam View** NE28 . . . . **23** B2
**Heath Cl** NE11 . . . . . . . . . **57** A3
**Heathcote Gn** NE5 . . . . . . **15** C3
**Heath Cres** NE15 . . . . . . . **42** C4
**Heathdale Gdns** NE7 . . . . **19** C3
**Heatherdale Terr** NE9 . . .**65** C3
**Heather Hill 4** NE9 . . . . . **67** A1
**Heatherlaw**
Gateshead NE9 . . . . . . . . **59** B1
Washington NE37 . . . . . . . **69** B2
**Heather Pl**
Crawcrook NE40 . . . . . . . . **38** C4
Newcastle-u-T NE4 . . . . . . **76** B4
**Heatherslaw Rd** NE5 . . . .**29** A4
**Heatherwell Gn** NE10 . . .**59** B3
**Heathery La** NE3 . . . . . . . **9** C3
**Heathfield Cres** NE15 . . . **16** B3
**Heathfield Farm** NE40 . . .**38** C1
**Heathfield Gdns** NE40 . .**38** C1
**Heathfield Ho** NE9 . . . . . **58** B2
**Heathfield Pl**
Gateshead NE9 . . . . . . . . **58** B2
Newcastle-u-T NE3 . . . . . . **5** A1
**Heathfield Rd** NE9 . . . . . **58** B2
**Heathway** NE32 . . . . . . . . **51** B2
**Heathwell Gdns** NE16 . . .**55** A4
**Heathwell Rd** NE15 . . . . . **28** A3
**Heathwood Ave 1**
NE16 . . . . . . . . . . . . . . . **54** C3
**HEATON** . . . . . . . . . . . . . **33** B3
**Heaton Cl** NE6 . . . . . . . . **32** C3
**Heaton Gr** NE6 . . . . . . . . **32** C3
**Heaton Hall Rd** NE6 . . . . **32** C3
**Heaton Manor Sch** NE7 **19** B2
**Heaton Park Ct 9** NE6 .**32** C3
**Heaton Park Rd** NE6 . . . **32** C3
**Heaton Park View** NE6 . .**32** C3
**Heaton Pl** NE6 . . . . . . . . **32** C2
**Heaton Rd** NE6 . . . . . . . . **32** C3
**Heaton Terr** NE6 . . . . . . . **32** B2
**Heaton Wlk 4** NE6 . . . . . **32** C2
**HEBBURN** . . . . . . . . . . . **35** C1
**Hebburn Comp Sch**
NE31 . . . . . . . . . . . . . . . **50** A4
**HEBBURN HALL**
**PONDS** . . . . . . . . . . . . . **49** C4
**Hebburn Hospl** NE31 . . .**49** C4
**Hebburn Sta** NE31 . . . . . **35** B2
**Heddon Ave** NE13 . . . . . . **4** A4
**Heddon Cl**
Newcastle-u-T NE3 . . . . . . **8** B2
Ryton NE40 . . . . . . . . . . **25** B1
**Heddon View**
Blaydon NE21 . . . . . . . . . **41** A2
Ryton NE40 . . . . . . . . . . **25** B1
**Hedge Cl** NE11 . . . . . . . . **57** A3

**HEDGEFIELD** . . . . . . . . . **25** C1
**Hedgefield Ave** NE21 . . .**26** A1
**Hedgefield Cotts** NE21 . .**26** A1
**Hedgefield Ct** NE21 . . . . .**26** A1
**Hedgehope 6** NE37 . . . . **69** C2
**Hedgehope Rd** NE5 . . . . **15** B4
**Hedgeley Rd**
Hebburn NE31 . . . . . . . . **35** C2
Newcastle-u-T NE5 . . . . . . **27** C4
**Hedgeley Terr** NE6 . . . . . **34** A2
**Hedley Pl** NE28 . . . . . . . **21** C1
**Hedley St**
Gateshead NE8 . . . . . . . . **57** C4
Newcastle-u-T NE3 . . . . . . **9** A1
**Hedley Terr** NE3 . . . . . . . **9** A1
**HEDWORTH** . . . . . . . . . **51** B2
**Hedworth Ave** NE34 . . . . **52** C4
**Hedworthfield Prim Sch**
NE32 . . . . . . . . . . . . . . . **51** C1
**Hedworth La**
Boldon Colliery NE35 . . . . **52** A1
Hedworth NE32 . . . . . . . . **51** C2
**Hedworth Lane Prim Sch**
NE35 . . . . . . . . . . . . . . . **51** C1
**Hedworth Pl** NE9 . . . . . . **66** A4
**Hedworth View** NE32 . . .**51** C3
**Heighley St** NE15 . . . . . . **28** A1
**Helen St** NE21 . . . . . . . . **40** C2
**Helmsdale Ave 13** NE10 **47** C1
**Helmsley Dr** NE28 . . . . . **23** A2
**Helmsley Gn** NE9 . . . . . . **65** C2
**Helston Ct** NE15 . . . . . . **26** C3
**Helvellyn Ave** NE38 . . . . **71** C3
**Helvellyn Cl** NE21 . . . . . **53** B4
**Henderson Ave** NE16 . . .**54** C4
**Henderson Gdns** NE10 . .**61** A4
**Henderson Rd**
South Shields NE34 . . . . . **52** B4
Wallsend NE28 . . . . . . . . **21** C3
Wallsend NE28 . . . . . . . . **21** C4
**Hendersyde Cl** NE5 . . . . **15** C3
**Hendon Gdns** NE32 . . . . **51** C2
**Hendon Rd** NE8, NE9 . . . **59** A4
**Henley Gdns** NE28 . . . . . **23** C4
**Henlow Rd** NE15 . . . . . . **27** A3
**Henry St** NE3 . . . . . . . . . **9** A1
**Hensby Ct** NE5 . . . . . . . . **15** C4
**Henshaw Pl** NE5 . . . . . . **28** C3
**Henshelwood Terr 2**
NE2 . . . . . . . . . . . . . . . . **18** C1
**Hepburn Gdns** NE10 . . . **47** B1
**Hepple Way** NE3 . . . . . . . **8** B2
**Herbert St** NE8 . . . . . . . **46** C1
**Herd Cl** NE21 . . . . . . . . . **40** C1
**Herd House La** NE21 . . . .**40** B2
**Herdinghill** NE37 . . . . . . **69** B2
**Hereford Ct** NE3 . . . . . . . **7** C3
**Hereford Way** NE32 . . . . **51** A2
**Heritage Cl** NE8 . . . . . . . **77** C1
**Heron Cl** NE38 . . . . . . . . **71** C2
**Heron Pl** NE12 . . . . . . . . **10** B3
**Herrick St** NE5 . . . . . . . . **15** B3
**Hersham Cl** NE3 . . . . . . . **7** B1
**Hertford** NE9 . . . . . . . . . **65** A2
**Hesket Ct** NE3 . . . . . . . . **7** C3
**Hesleyside Dr** NE5 . . . . . **29** A4
**Heugh Hill** NE9 . . . . . . . **67** B2
**Hewitson Terr** NE10 . . . . **59** B4
**Hewley Cres** NE15 . . . . . **12** B1
**HEWORTH** . . . . . . . . . . . **60** B4
**Heworth Burn Cres**
NE10 . . . . . . . . . . . . . . . **60** A4
**Heworth Dene Gdns**
NE10 . . . . . . . . . . . . . . . **48** A1
**Heworth Grange Comp**
**Sch** NE10 . . . . . . . . . . **60** A4
**Heworth Sta (BR & Metro)**
NE10 . . . . . . . . . . . . . . . **60** A4
**Heworth Way** NE10 . . . . **61** C4
**Hewson Pl** NE9 . . . . . . . **59** A2
**Hexham** NE38 . . . . . . . . **71** B4
**Hexham Ave**
Hebburn NE31 . . . . . . . . **50** A3
Newcastle-u-T NE6 . . . . . . **34** A1
**Hexham Ct** NE11 . . . . . . **56** B2
**Hexham Ho 8** NE6 . . . . **34** B2
**Hexham Old Rd** NE21,
NE40 . . . . . . . . . . . . . . . **25** C1
**Hexham Rd**
Throckley NE15 . . . . . . . . **12** A2
Whickham NE16 . . . . . . . . **42** C1
**Hextol Gdns** NE15 . . . . . **28** A3

**Heyburn Gdns** NE15 . . . **29** B1
**Hibernian Rd** NE32 . . . . **36** C3
**Hibernia Rd** NE6 . . . . . . **48** C4
**Hickling Ct** NE5 . . . . . . . **16** A4
**Hiddleston Ave** NE7 . . . . **10** C1
**High Axwell** NE21 . . . . . . **41** C2
**High Back Cl** NE32 . . . . . **50** C4
**Highbridge** NE3 . . . . . . . **9** A3
**Highbury**
Gateshead NE10 . . . . . . . **60** A4
Newcastle-u-T NE2 . . . . . . **18** B2
**Highbury Ave** NE9 . . . . . **67** B2
**Highbury Cl** NE9 . . . . . . **67** B2
**Highclife Gdns** NE8 . . . . **58** C4
**High Croft Cl** NE31 . . . . . **49** C4
**High Dene** NE7 . . . . . . . . **19** C1
**High Dewley Burn** NE15 **12** B3
**Highfield**
Birtley DH3 . . . . . . . . . . . **68** B2
Sunniside NE16 . . . . . . . . **62** C3
**Highfield Ave** NE12 . . . . **11** B4
**Highfield Cl** NE15 . . . . . . **15** A3
**Highfield Ct** NE10 . . . . . . **60** A3
**Highfield Pl** NE13 . . . . . . **2** A1
**Highfield Rd**
Gateshead NE8 . . . . . . . . **46** C1
Newcastle-u-T NE5 . . . . . . **15** A3
**Highfield Terr** NE6 . . . . . **48** C4
**High Flatworth** NE29 . . .**23** C4
**Highgate Gdns** NE32 . . .**51** C2
**High Gate The** NE11 . . . . **16** C4
**High Gosforth Park**
**(Newcastle Race**
**Course)** NE3 . . . . . . . . **5** A2
**High Gr** NE40 . . . . . . . . . **39** C4
**Highgreen Chase** NE16 .**62** B4
**Highgrove** NE5 . . . . . . . . **14** B2
**Highheath 1** NE37 . . . . . **69** C2
**HIGH HEATON** . . . . . . . . **19** B3
**High Hedgefield Terr**
NE21 . . . . . . . . . . . . . . . **25** C1
**High Heworth La** NE10 . .**60** A3
**High House Gdns** NE10 . .**48** A1
**Highland Rd** NE5 . . . . . . **16** B3
**High Lane Row** NE31 . . . .**36** A3
**High Lanes** NE10 . . . . . . **60** B3
**High Laws** NE3 . . . . . . . . **19** A4
**Highlaws Gdns** NE9 . . . . **65** C2
**High Level Rd** NE8 . . . . . **78** B3
**High Mdws** NE3 . . . . . . . **16** C3
**High Moor Ct** NE5 . . . . . **16** C2
**High Quay** NE1 . . . . . . . . **32** B1
**High Reach** NE10 . . . . . . **48** C2
**Highridge** DH3 . . . . . . . . **68** B1
**High Ridge** NE13 . . . . . . . **4** B4
**High Row**
Newcastle-u-T NE15 . . . . . **27** A2
Ryton NE40 . . . . . . . . . . **40** A4
**High St Bk** NE3 . . . . . . . . **9** A1
**High St E** NE28 . . . . . . . **22** A1
**High St W** NE28, NE6. . .**21** B1
**High St**
Gateshead, Felling
NE10 . . . . . . . . . . . . . . . **59** C4
Gateshead NE8 . . . . . . . . **78** C3
Gateshead, Wrekenton
NE9 . . . . . . . . . . . . . . . . **66** A3
Jarrow NE32 . . . . . . . . . . **37** A3
Jarrow NE32 . . . . . . . . . . **37** B3
Newburn NE15 . . . . . . . . **26** A3
Newcastle-u-T NE3 . . . . . . **18** A4
**High View** NE28 . . . . . . . **21** C3
**High View N** NE28 . . . . . **21** C3
**High Well Gdns** NE10 . . .**48** A1
**Highwell La 4** NE5 . . . . **14** C1
**High West St** NE15 . . . . . **79** C2
**Highwood Rd** NE15 . . . . **28** A3
**Highworth Dr**
Newcastle-u-T NE7 . . . . . . **20** B3
**3** Springwell NE9 . . . . . . **67** A1
**Hilda St** NE8 . . . . . . . . . **79** A1
**Hilda Terr 7** NE15 . . . . . **12** B2
**Hilden Bldgs** NE7 . . . . . **20** A2
**Hilden Gdns** NE7 . . . . . . **20** A2
**Hillary Ave** NE12 . . . . . . **11** C4
**Hillcrest** NE32 . . . . . . . . **51** C2
**Hill Crest** NE10 . . . . . . . **60** A2
**Hillcrest Dr** NE11 . . . . . . **56** A3
**Hill Crest Gdns** NE2 . . . .**18** C4
**Hillcroft**
**3** Birtley DH3 . . . . . . . . **68** B1
Gateshead NE9 . . . . . . . . **58** C2

**Hill Dyke** NE9 . . . . . . . . **66** A2
**Hillfield St** NE8 . . . . . . . **79** B2
**Hillgate** NE8 . . . . . . . . . **78** B4
**Hill Head Dr** NE5 . . . . . . **14** B1
**Hillhead Gdns** NE11 . . . . **56** C2
**Hillhead Parkway** NE5 . .**14** A2
**Hillhead Rd** NE5 . . . . . . **14** B2
**Hillhead Way** NE5 . . . . . **14** C3
**Hill House Rd** NE15 . . . . **12** A2
**Hill Park Rd** NE32 . . . . . **37** A1
**Hill Rise** NE40 . . . . . . . . **38** B3
**Hills Ct** NE21 . . . . . . . . . **42** A4
**Hillside**
Birtley DH3 . . . . . . . . . . . **70** C4
Blaydon NE21 . . . . . . . . . **41** A2
Dunston NE11 . . . . . . . . . **56** B3
**Hillside Ave** NE15 . . . . . **28** A4
**Hillside Cres** NE15 . . . . . **42** C4
**Hillside Pl** NE9 . . . . . . . . **58** C2
**Hillsleigh Rd** NE5 . . . . . . **16** B2
**Hills St** NE8 . . . . . . . . . . **78** B3
**Hill St** NE32 . . . . . . . . . . **36** B3
**Hillsview Ave** NE3 . . . . . . **7** C1
**Hill Top**
Birtley DH3 . . . . . . . . . . . **70** C4
Blaydon NE21 . . . . . . . . . **41** A1
**Hill Top Ave** NE9 . . . . . . **59** A1
**Hill Top Gdns** NE9 . . . . . **58** C1
**Hilltop Ho** NE5 . . . . . . . . **15** B2
**Hill Top Sch** NE10 . . . . . **66** C4
**Hilton Ave** NE5 . . . . . . . **15** C2
**Hilton Prim Sch** NE15 . . **15** C2
**Hindley Cl** NE40 . . . . . . . **38** A3
**Hindley Gdns** NE4 . . . . . **29** B3
**Histon Ct** NE5 . . . . . . . . **15** C3
**Histon Way** NE5 . . . . . . . **15** C3
**Hither Gn** NE32 . . . . . . . **51** C2
**Hobart Ave** NE34 . . . . . . **52** B3
**Hobart Gdns** NE7 . . . . . . **10** B1
**Hodgkin Park Cres**
NE15 . . . . . . . . . . . . . . . **29** A1
**Hodgkin Park Rd** NE15 . .**29** A1
**Hodkin Gdns** NE9 . . . . . . **59** A2
**Holborn Pl** NE5 . . . . . . . **14** C1
**Holburn Cres** NE40 . . . . **25** B1
**Holburn Gdns** NE40 . . . . **25** C1
**Holburn Gdns** NE40 . . . . **25** C1
**Holburn La** NE40 . . . . . . **25** B2
**Holburn Lane Ct** NE40 . .**25** B2
**Holburn Pl** NE40 . . . . . . **25** C1
**Holburn Way** NE40 . . . . **25** B1
**Holburn Wlk** NE40 . . . . . **25** C1
**Holden Pl** NE5 . . . . . . . . **16** B2
**Holderness Rd**
Newcastle-u-T NE6 . . . . . . **19** C1
Wallsend NE28 . . . . . . . . **23** C3
**Hole La**
Sunniside NE16 . . . . . . . . **62** C3
Whickham NE16 . . . . . . . . **62** A4
**Holeyn Rd** NE15 . . . . . . . **12** A1
**Holland Park Dr** NE32 . .**51** C2
**Holland Pk** NE28 . . . . . . **20** C3
**Holley Park Prim Sch**
NE38 . . . . . . . . . . . . . . . **71** C3
**Hollings Cres** NE28 . . . . **21** C4
**Hollington Ave** NE12 . . . **10** C2
**Hollington Cl** NE12 . . . . **10** C2
**Hollinhill** NE39 . . . . . . . . **78** A4
**Hollinside Cl** NE16 . . . . . **54** C1
**Hollinside Gdns** NE15 . .**28** C2
**Hollinside Rd** NE11 . . . . **43** A2
**Hollow The** NE32 . . . . . . **51** A2
**Holly Ave**
Dunston NE11 . . . . . . . . . **56** B3
Newcastle-u-T, Fawdon
NE3 . . . . . . . . . . . . . . . . **8** A2
Newcastle-u-T, Jesmond
NE2 . . . . . . . . . . . . . . . . **19** A1
Ryton NE40 . . . . . . . . . . **25** A2
Wallsend NE28 . . . . . . . . **22** A1
Winlaton Mill NE21 . . . . . **53** B2
**Holly Ave W** NE2 . . . . . . **18** C1
**Holly Bush Gdns** NE40 . .**40** A4
**Holly Ct** NE40 . . . . . . . . **59** B4
**Holly Ct** NE5 . . . . . . . . . **15** C2
**Holly Gdns** NE9 . . . . . . . **58** B2
**Holly Hill** NE10 . . . . . . . **59** C4
**Hollyhock** NE31 . . . . . . . **50** A3
**Holly Park View** NE10 . .**59** C4
**Holly St** NE32 . . . . . . . . **36** B3
**Hollys The** DH3 . . . . . . . **68** A3
**Holly View** NE10 . . . . . . **59** B4
**Hollywell Gr** NE13 . . . . . . **6** A1

**Hollywood Ave**
Newcastle-u-T, Gosforth
NE3 . . . . . . . . . . . . . . . . . 9 B2
Wallsend NE6 . . . . . . . . . . 21 B1
**Hollywood Cres** NE3 . . . . . . 9 B2
**Hollywood Gdns** NE11 . . 57 A1
**Holme Ave**
Newcastle-u-T NE6 . . . . . . 21 A1
Whickham NE16 . . . . . . . . 55 A3
**Holme Gdns** NE28 . . . . . . 23 B2
**Holme Rise** NE16 . . . . . . 55 A3
**Holmesdale Rd** NE5 . . . 16 B3
**Holmland** NE15 . . . . . . . . 43 B4
**Holmside Ave** NE11 . . . . 56 C4
**Holmside Terr** NE16 . . . . 63 A2
**Holmwood Gr** NE2 . . . . . 18 B2
**Holwick Cl** NE38 . . . . . . . 71 C2
**HOLY CROSS** . . . . . . . . . 22 C3
**Holy Cross RC Prim Sch**
NE28 . . . . . . . . . . . . . . . . 23 A4
**Holyoake Gdns**
Birtley DH3 . . . . . . . . . . . 70 B4
Gateshead NE9 . . . . . . . . 58 B4
**Holystone Ave** NE3 . . . . . 8 C2
**Holystone Cres** NE7 . . . . 19 C3
**Holystone Ct** NE28 . . . . . 79 A1
**Holystone St** NE31 . . . . . 35 B2
**Holywell Ave** NE6 . . . . . . 48 A3
**Holywell Cl** NE21 . . . . . . 41 C1
**Holywell La** NE16 . . . . . . 62 C3
**Home Ave 2** NE9 . . . . . . 65 A4
**Homedowne Ho** NE3 . . . . . 9 A1
**Homeforth Ho** NE3 . . . . . . 9 A1
**Home Pk** NE28 . . . . . . . . 20 C3
**Homeside Pl 6** NE6 . . . . 32 C3
**Honeycrook Dr** NE7 . . . . 20 C3
**Honister Ave** NE2 . . . . . . 18 C3
**Honister Cl** NE15 . . . . . . 27 B3
**Honister Pl** NE15 . . . . . . 27 B3
**Honiton Ct** NE3 . . . . . . . . 6 C2
**Hood Sq** NE21 . . . . . . . . . 40 C1
**Hood St 4** NE16 . . . . . . . 42 C1
**Hopedene** NE10 . . . . . . . . 60 C1
**Hope Shield** NE38 . . . . . . 71 B1
**Hope St** NE32 . . . . . . . . . 37 A3
**Hopkins Wlk** NE34 . . . . . 52 C2
**Hopper Pl** NE8 . . . . . . . . 78 C3
**Hopper Rd** NE10 . . . . . . . 59 B3
**Hopper St**
Gateshead NE8 . . . . . . . . 78 C3
**8** Wallsend NE28 . . . . . . 21 C2
**Horatio St** NE1 . . . . . . . . 32 B1
**Hornbeam Pl** NE4 . . . . . . 76 B3
**Horncliffe Gdns** NE16 . . 55 B4
**Horncliffe Wlk** NE15 . . . . 26 B3
**Horning Ct** NE5 . . . . . . . . 15 C4
**Hornsea Cl** NE13 . . . . . . . . 2 B1
**Horse Crofts** NE21 . . . . . 41 B3
**Horsham Gr** NE29 . . . . . . 24 C4
**Horsley Ave** NE40 . . . . . . 38 A3
**Horsley Ct** NE3 . . . . . . . . 7 C2
**Horsley Gdns** NE11 . . . . 56 C4
**Horsley Rd** NE7 . . . . . . . 19 C2
**Horsley Terr** NE6 . . . . . . 34 A1
**Horwood Ave** NE5 . . . . . 14 C2
**Hospital Dr** NE31 . . . . . . 49 C4
**Hospital La** NE15 . . . . . . 26 C4
**Hospital Of King James**
The NE8 . . . . . . . . . . . . . 47 A1
**Hospl of St Mary the**
**Virgin The** NE4 . . . . . . . 76 B4
**Hotch Pudding Pl** NE15 . 15 A1
**Hotspur Prim Sch** NE2 . . 32 B2
**Hotspur St** NE6 . . . . . . . 32 B3
**Houghton Ave** NE5 . . . . 16 C3
**Houlet Garth 11** NE6 . . 33 A1
**Houndelee Pl** NE5 . . . . . 16 A1
**Hounslow Gdns** NE32 . . 51 C2
**Housesteads Gdns**
NE12 . . . . . . . . . . . . . . . . 10 A2
**Housesteads 6** NE28 . . 23 A4
**Houston St** NE4 . . . . . . . 76 B4
**Houston St** NE4 . . . . . . . 76 B4
**Howard Ho** NE3 . . . . . . . 18 A4
**Howard Pl** NE3 . . . . . . . . . 9 A1
**Howard St**
Gateshead, Mount Pleasant
NE8 . . . . . . . . . . . . . . . . . 47 A1
Gateshead, Windy Nook
NE10 . . . . . . . . . . . . . . . . 59 B2
Jarrow NE32 . . . . . . . . . . 37 A2
**Howat Ave** NE5 . . . . . . . . 16 C1

**Howdene Rd** NE15 . . . . . 28 A2
**HOWDON** . . . . . . . . . . . . 23 C2
**Howdon Green Ind Est**
NE28 . . . . . . . . . . . . . . . . 23 C2
**Howdon La** NE28 . . . . . . 23 B2
**HOWDON PANS** . . . . . . . 24 A1
**Howdon Rd**
North Shields, Howdon
Pans NE28 . . . . . . . . . . . 24 A2
North Shields, Redburn Dene
NE28, NE29 . . . . . . . . . . 24 C3
**Howdon Sta** NE28 . . . . . 23 B2
**Howe St**
Gateshead NE8 . . . . . . . . 46 C1
Hebburn NE31 . . . . . . . . 36 B2
**Howick Ave** NE3 . . . . . . . 8 B3
**Howlett Hall Rd** NE15 . . 28 A2
**Hownam Cl** NE3 . . . . . . . 17 B4
**Hoylake Ave** NE7 . . . . . . 11 A1
**Hoyle Ave** NE4 . . . . . . . . 29 C2
**Huddleston Rd** NE6 . . . . 33 B3
**Hudson St** NE8 . . . . . . . . 78 B3
**Hugh Gdns** NE4 . . . . . . . 44 A4
**Hugh St** NE28 . . . . . . . . . 21 C1
**Hull St** NE4 . . . . . . . . . . 30 A1
**Hulne Terr** NE15 . . . . . . . 27 A2
**Humber Gdns** NE8 . . . . . 47 A1
**Humbert St** NE32 . . . . . . 36 C2
**Hume St** NE6 . . . . . . . . . 32 B1
**Hunstanton Ct** NE9 . . . . 64 C3
**Huntcliffe Gdns** NE6 . . . 20 B1
**Hunter Ho** NE6 . . . . . . . . 48 C4
**Hunters Ct**
Newcastle-u-T NE3 . . . . . . 9 C1
Wallsend NE28 . . . . . . . . 22 A2
**Hunters Lodge** NE28 . . . 22 A2
**Hunter's Rd** NE3 . . . . . . 10 A1
**Huntingdon Cl** NE3 . . . . . 7 B4
**Hunt Lea** NE16 . . . . . . . . 54 A1
**Hurst Terr** NE6 . . . . . . . . 33 C2
**Hurworth Pl** NE32 . . . . . 36 C2
**Hutton Cl** NE38 . . . . . . . 69 B1
**Hutton Ho** NE29 . . . . . . . 24 C3
**Hutton St**
Boldon Colliery NE35 . . . . 52 B1
Gateshead NE8 . . . . . . . . . 8 B1
**Huxley Cres** NE8 . . . . . . 57 C3
**Hyde Park St** NE8 . . . . . 57 C4
**Hyde Pk** NE28 . . . . . . . . . 21 A3
**Hylton Rd** NE32 . . . . . . . 51 B3
**Hylton St** NE8 . . . . . . . . 47 A1
**Hylton Terr** NE10 . . . . . . 49 B2
**Hymers Ave** NE34 . . . . . 52 B4

## I

**Ilderton Pl** NE5 . . . . . . . 27 C4
**Ilford Pl** NE8, NE9 . . . . . 58 C4
**Ilford Rd**
Newcastle-u-T NE2 . . . . . 18 B3
Wallsend NE28 . . . . . . . . 23 A3
**Ilford Road Sta** NE2 . . . 18 B3
**Ilfracombe Ave** NE4 . . . . 29 C1
**Ilfracombe Gdns** NE9 . . 65 A3
**Illingworth Ho** NE29 . . . 24 C3
**Ilminster Ct** NE3 . . . . . . . 7 A2
**Inchberry Cl** NE4 . . . . . . 44 A4
**Inchcliffe Cres** NE5 . . . . 16 A2
**Industry Rd** NE6 . . . . . . 20 B2
**Ingleborough Cl 8**
NE37 . . . . . . . . . . . . . . . . 69 C2
**Inglemere Pl** NE15 . . . . . 28 B2
**Ingleside** NE16 . . . . . . . . 54 B2
**Inglewood Pl** NE3 . . . . . . 4 C1
**Ingoe Ave** NE3 . . . . . . . . 8 A3
**Ingoe St**
Newcastle-u-T NE15 . . . . 27 A2
North Shields NE29 . . . . . 24 A2
**Ingram Ave** NE3 . . . . . . . 8 A4
**Ingram St** NE5 . . . . . . . . 14 B4
**Ingram Terr** NE6 . . . . . . 34 B2
**Inleborough Dr** NE40 . . . 39 C4
**Innesmoor** NE31 . . . . . . . 35 B3
**Inskip Terr** NE8 . . . . . . . 58 B4
**Inst for Higher Rabbinical**
**Studies** NE8 . . . . . . . . 79 B1
**International Ctr for Life**
The * NE1 . . . . . . . . . . . 76 C4
**Inverness Rd** NE32 . . . . . 52 A2

**Invertay** NE3 . . . . . . . . . . 9 C1
**Invincible Dr** NE4 . . . . . . 76 A3
**Iolanthe Cres** NE6 . . . . . 33 C3
**Iona Cl** NE28 . . . . . . . . . 23 A4
**Iona Pl** NE6 . . . . . . . . . . 34 B2
**Iona Rd**
Brockley Whins NE32 . . . . 52 A3
Gateshead N10, NE9 . . . . 59 A3
**Iris Cl** NE21 . . . . . . . . . . 40 C2
**Iris Pl** NE4 . . . . . . . . . . . 29 B3
**Iris Terr** NE40 . . . . . . . . . 38 B3
**Irton St** NE3 . . . . . . . . . . . 9 A1
**Irvine Ho 7** NE12 . . . . . 11 B4
**Irwin Ave** NE28 . . . . . . . 22 A3
**Isabella Cl** NE4 . . . . . . . 44 A3
**Isabella Wlk** NE15 . . . . . 12 B1
**Ivanhoe View** NE9 . . . . . 65 C2
**Iveagh Cl** NE4 . . . . . . . . 43 C4
**Ivy Ave** NE40 . . . . . . . . . 25 A2
**Ivy Cl**
Newcastle-u-T NE4 . . . . . 76 B3
Ryton NE40 . . . . . . . . . . 25 A2
**Ivy La** NE9 . . . . . . . . . . . 65 B3
**Ivymount Rd** NE6 . . . . . . 19 C1
**Ivy Rd**
Longbenton NE12 . . . . . . 11 C4
Newcastle-u-T, Gosforth
NE3 . . . . . . . . . . . . . . . . 18 A4
Newcastle-u-T, Walkergate
NE6 . . . . . . . . . . . . . . . . 34 A4
**Ivy Road Prim Sch** NE12 11 C4
**Ivy St** NE13 . . . . . . . . . . . 2 C4
**Ivy Terr** NE40 . . . . . . . . . 38 A3

## J

**Jack Common Ho 3**
NE6 . . . . . . . . . . . . . . . . 32 C3
**Jacksons Pl** DH3 . . . . . . 68 B1
**Jackson St**
Gateshead NE8 . . . . . . . . 78 C3
Newcastle-u-T NE6 . . . . . 34 A2
**Jade Cl** NE15 . . . . . . . . . 27 A4
**James Pl St** NE6 . . . . . . 32 B2
**James St**
Newcastle-u-T, Elswick
NE4 . . . . . . . . . . . . . . . . 44 B4
Newcastle-u-T NE5 . . . . . 15 A2
**10** Whickham NE16 . . . . 54 C3
**James Terr** NE28 . . . . . . 21 C1
**Jane Eyre Terr** NE8 . . . . 47 A1
**Jane St 22** NE6 . . . . . . . 33 A2
**Jane Terr** NE6 . . . . . . . . 48 C4
**Janet Sq** NE6 . . . . . . . . . 33 A1
**Janet St**
**17** Newcastle-u-T, St
Lawrence NE6 . . . . . . . . 33 A1
Newcastle-u-T, St Peters
NE6 . . . . . . . . . . . . . . . . 47 B4
**Janus Cl** NE5 . . . . . . . . . 14 A4
**JARROW** . . . . . . . . . . . . . 37 B2
**Jarrow Cross CE Prim Sch**
NE32 . . . . . . . . . . . . . . . . 36 C2
**Jarrow Sch (Cornhill)**
NE32 . . . . . . . . . . . . . . . . 51 A1
**Jarrow Sch (Field**
**Terrace)** NE32 . . . . . . . 36 C1
**Jarrow Sta** NE32 . . . . . . 36 C3
**Jasmin Ave** NE5 . . . . . . . 14 A4
**Jasmine Cl** NE6 . . . . . . . 20 C1
**Jasmine Terr** DH3 . . . . . 70 C4
**Jasmine Villas 7** NE16 . 54 C3
**Jasper Ave** NE40 . . . . . . 39 A1
**Jedburgh Cl**
Gateshead NE8 . . . . . . . . 79 C1
Newcastle-u-T NE5 . . . . . 14 A4
**Jedburgh Ct** NE11 . . . . . 64 C2
**Jedburgh Gdns** NE15 . . 28 C3
**Jedmoor** NE31 . . . . . . . . 35 B3
**Jellicoe Rd** NE6 . . . . . . . 48 A3
**Jenifer Gr** NE7 . . . . . . . . 19 B4
**Jenison Ave** NE15 . . . . . 29 A1
**Jervis St** NE31 . . . . . . . . 36 A2
**Jesmond** . . . . . . . . . . . . . 18 C1
**Jesmond Dene Rd**
Newcastle-u-T, Jesmond
NE2 . . . . . . . . . . . . . . . . 19 A2
Newcastle-u-T, West
Jesmond NE2 . . . . . . . . 18 B3
**Jesmond Gdns** NE2 . . . . 19 A1

**Jesmond Park Ct 1**
NE7 . . . . . . . . . . . . . . . . 19 C1
**Jesmond Pk E** NE7 . . . . 19 C1
**Jesmond Pk W** NE7 . . . . 19 B2
**Jesmond Pl 1** NE2 . . . . 18 C1
**JESMOND VALE** . . . . . . . 32 B3
**Jesmond Vale** NE2 . . . . . 32 B3
**Jesmond Vale La** NE6 . . 32 C4
**Jesmond Vale Terr** NE6 . 32 C4
**Jessel St** NE3 . . . . . . . . . 65 A4
**Jetty The** NE10 . . . . . . . 48 C2
**Joan St** NE4 . . . . . . . . . . 43 C4
**Jobling Ave** NE21 . . . . . . 41 A2
**Joel Terr** NE10 . . . . . . . . 49 A2
**John Ave** NE40 . . . . . . . . 39 A1
**Johnson St**
**6** Dunston NE11 . . . . . . 44 B1
Gateshead NE8 . . . . . . . . 77 B1
Newcastle-u-T NE1 . . . . . 27 A2
**John St**
Gateshead, Old Fold
NE8 . . . . . . . . . . . . . . . . 47 A1
**1** Gateshead, Pelaw
NE10 . . . . . . . . . . . . . . . 48 B1
Newcastle-u-T NE4 . . . . . . 8 B1
Wallsend NE28 . . . . . . . . 21 C2
**Johnston Ave** NE31 . . . . 49 C3
**Joicey Rd** NE9 . . . . . . . . 58 B2
**Joicey Road Sch** NE9 . . 58 B2
**Joicey St** NE10 . . . . . . . . 48 C1
**Jonadab Rd** NE10 . . . . . 48 C2
**Jonadab St** NE10 . . . . . . 48 C1
**Jones St 4** DH3 . . . . . . . 70 B4
**Jonquil Cl** NE5 . . . . . . . . 14 A4
**Joseph Cl** NE4 . . . . . . . . 44 A4
**Joseph Hopper Aged**
**Miners' Homes** DH3 . . 68 B3
**Joseph Hopper Meml**
**Homes** NE9 . . . . . . . . . 59 B2
**Joseph Swan Sch** NE9 . 64 C3
**Joyce Cl** NE10 . . . . . . . . 61 C4
**Jubilee Ave** NE9 . . . . . . . 66 A1
**Jubilee Cres** NE3 . . . . . . . 8 B1
**Jubilee Ct**
Gateshead NE8 . . . . . . . . 57 B4
Hebburn NE31 . . . . . . . . 36 B2
**Jubilee Mews** NE3 . . . . . . 8 C1
**Jubilee Rd** NE3 . . . . . . . . . 8 C1
**Jubilee St 3** NE28 . . . . . 21 C2
**Jubilee Terr**
Crawcrook NE40 . . . . . . . 38 A3
Seaton Burn NE13 . . . . . . 2 B4
**7** Whickham NE16 . . . . 42 C1
**Jubilee Terrs** NE6 . . . . . 33 B2
**Julian Ave** NE6 . . . . . . . . 33 C3
**Julian Rd** NE10 . . . . . . . . 61 C4
**June Ave** NE21 . . . . . . . . 53 B2
**Juniper Cl** NE3 . . . . . . . . . 5 A1
**Juniper Ct** NE21 . . . . . . . 41 B3
**Juniper Wlk** NE5 . . . . . . 14 B4
**Jutland Ave** NE31 . . . . . 35 C2

## K

**Kane Gdns** NE10 . . . . . . 59 B2
**Kateregina** DH3 . . . . . . . 70 C4
**Kay's Cotts 5** NE10 . . . . 59 B3
**Kearton Ave** NE5 . . . . . . 14 A3
**Keats Rd** NE15 . . . . . . . . 26 B2
**Keats Wlk**
Biddick Hall NE34 . . . . . . 52 C3
Gateshead NE8 . . . . . . . . 46 C2
**Keebledale Ave** NE6 . . . 34 A3
**Keebledale Ho** NE6 . . . . 34 A3
**Keel Row** NE11 . . . . . . . . 43 A3
**Keir Hardie Ave** NE10 . . 61 C4
**Keith Cl** NE4 . . . . . . . . . . 44 A4
**Keldane Gdns** NE4 . . . . . 29 C2
**Kellfield Ave** NE9 . . . . . . 58 C2
**Kellfield Rd** NE9 . . . . . . . 58 C2
**Kells Gdns** NE9 . . . . . . . 58 C1
**Kells La** NE9 . . . . . . . . . . 58 B1
**Kells Lane Prim Sch**
NE9 . . . . . . . . . . . . . . . . 58 B1
**Kellsway** NE10 . . . . . . . . 60 B1
**Kellsway Ct** NE10 . . . . . . 60 B1
**Kelly Rd** NE31 . . . . . . . . 50 A3
**Kelso Cl** NE5 . . . . . . . . . 14 A4
**Kelso Gdns**
Newcastle-u-T NE15 . . . . 28 C2
Wallsend NE28 . . . . . . . . 23 B4
**Kelson Way** NE5 . . . . . . 14 A4

**Kelso Pl** NE8 . . . . . . . . . 77 B1
**Kelston Way** NE5 . . . . . . 16 A2
**Kelvin Gdns 3** NE11 . . . 44 B1
**Kelvin Gr** NE8 . . . . . . . . . 57 C4
**Kelvin Grove Com Prim**
**Sch** . . . . . . . . . . . . . . . . 58 A4
**Kempton Gdns** NE8 . . . . 57 B3
**Kendal** DH3 . . . . . . . . . . 71 A2
**Kendal Cres** NE6 . . . . . . 59 A1
**Kendale Wlk** NE5 . . . . . . 14 C3
**Kendal Gdns** NE28 . . . . . 23 B4
**Kendal Gn 24** NE6 . . . . 32 C2
**Kendal Ho 27** NE6 . . . . 32 C2
**Kendal Pl** NE6 . . . . . . . . 32 C2
**Kendal St 1** NE6 . . . . . . 32 C1
**Kenilworth Ct** NE4 . . . . . 76 A4
**Kenilworth Rd** NE4 . . . . 76 A4
**Kenilworth View 7**
NE9 . . . . . . . . . . . . . . . . 65 B2
**Kenley Rd** NE5 . . . . . . . . 28 B4
**Kenmoor Way** NE5 . . . . . 14 A3
**Kenmore Cl** NE10 . . . . . . 61 A4
**Kenmore Cres** NE40 . . . 39 A2
**Kennet Ave** NE32 . . . . . . 51 B3
**Kennford** NE9 . . . . . . . . . 65 B2
**Kennington Gr** NE6 . . . . 33 C1
**Kensington Ave** NE3 . . . . 9 A3
**Kensington Ct**
**5** Gateshead NE10 . . . . 59 B4
Hebburn NE31 . . . . . . . . 35 B1
**Kensington Gdns** NE28 . 20 C3
**Kensington Terr 2**
NE11 . . . . . . . . . . . . . . . 56 B4
**Kensington Villas 5**
NE5 . . . . . . . . . . . . . . . . 14 C3
**Kent Ave**
**3** Dunston NE11 . . . . . . 56 C4
Hebburn NE31 . . . . . . . . 35 B1
Wallsend NE28 . . . . . . . . 23 A2
**Kent Ct** NE3 . . . . . . . . . . . 7 B4
**Kentmere** DH3 . . . . . . . . 71 A1
**Kentmere Ave** NE6 . . . . . 34 A3
**KENTON** . . . . . . . . . . . . . 16 C4
**Kenton Ave** NE3 . . . . . . . 17 B3
**Kenton Bank** NE5 . . . . . . . 7 A1
**KENTON BANKFOOT** . . . . 6 B2
**KENTON BAR** . . . . . . . . . 16 B4
**Kenton Bar Prim Sch**
NE3 . . . . . . . . . . . . . . . . 16 B4
**Kenton Cres** NE3 . . . . . . 17 A4
**Kenton La** NE3 . . . . . . . . 16 C4
**Kenton Park Sh Ctr** NE3 17 B4
**Kenton Rd** NE3 . . . . . . . . 17 B3
**Kenton Sch** NE3 . . . . . . . 16 C4
**Kent St** NE32 . . . . . . . . . 36 B2
**Kenwood Gdns** NE9 . . . . 65 B2
**Kepier Chare Com Prim**
**Sch** NE40 . . . . . . . . . . . 38 B3
**Keppel St** NE11 . . . . . . . 44 B1
**Kestrel Cl** NE38 . . . . . . . 71 C1
**Kestrel Ct 16** DH3 . . . . . 70 B4
**Kestrel Mews** NE16 . . . . 54 C3
**Kestrel Pl** NE12 . . . . . . . 10 B3
**Keswick Gdns** NE28 . . . 23 B3
**Keswick Gr** NE5 . . . . . . . 28 B4
**Keswick St** NE8 . . . . . . . 79 B1
**Ketton Cl** NE12 . . . . . . . . 10 C2
**Keyes Gdns** NE2 . . . . . . 18 C3
**Kidderminster Dr** NE5 . . 14 A3
**Kidlandlee Gn** NE5 . . . . . 15 B4
**Kidlandlee Pl** NE5 . . . . . 15 B4
**Kielder** NE38 . . . . . . . . . . 71 B4
**Kielder Cl** NE15 . . . . . . . 15 B4
**Kielder Gdns** NE32 . . . . 51 A3
**Kielder Pl** NE5 . . . . . . . . 15 B4
**Kielder Rd** NE15 . . . . . . . 27 A3
**Kielder Way** NE3 . . . . . . . 8 C3
**Kilburne Cl** NE7 . . . . . . . 20 C3
**Kilburn Gdns** NE29 . . . . 24 B3
**Kilburn Gn** NE9 . . . . . . . 65 C1
**Killin Cl** NE5 . . . . . . . . . . 14 A4
**Killingworth Rd** NE3 . . . 10 A1
**Killowen St 5** NE9 . . . . . 64 C4
**Kiln Rise** NE16 . . . . . . . . 62 B4
**Kilnshaw Pl** NE5 . . . . . . . 5 A1
**Kimberley Gdns** NE2 . . . 32 B4
**Kinfauns Terr 5** NE9 . . . 58 C1
**King Edward Pl** NE8 . . . . 47 A1
**King Edward Rd**
Newcastle-u-T NE6 . . . . . 19 C1

**King Edward Rd** continued
Ryton NE40 . . . . . . . . . . . . . .40 A4
King Edward St NE8 . . . . . .47 A1
Kingfisher Bvd NE15 . . . . .27 B1
Kingfisher Ct NE11 . . . . . . .77 A2
Kingfisher Lodge NE32 . .36 B2
Kingfisher Rd NE12 . . . . . .10 B3
King George Ave NE11 . .56 B4
King George Rd NE3 . . . . .7 C2
Kingham Ct NE3 . . . . . . . . .19 A4
King James St NE8 . . . . . .79 C1
King John St NE6 . . . . . . . .32 C4
King John Terr NE6 . . . . . .32 C4
Kings Ave NE3 . . . . . . . . . . .36 A1
Kingsbridge NE12 . . . . . . .10 A3
Kingsbridge Cl NE29 . . . . .24 C4
Kings Cl NE8 . . . . . . . . . . . .47 A1
Kingsdale Rd NE12 . . . . . .10 A3
King's Dr NE40 . . . . . . . . . .39 A1
**Kingsley Ave**
Biddick Hall NE34 . . . . . . .52 C3
Newcastle-u-T NE5 . . . . . . .5 A1
**Kingsley Pl**
8 Dunston NE11 . . . . . . . .44 B1
8 Newcastle-u-T NE6 . . .32 C3
Wallsend NE28 . . . . . . . . . .23 A3
Whickham NE16 . . . . . . . . .55 A4
Kingsley Terr NE40 . . . . . .38 A4
Kings Meadow NE32 . . . .51 B1
**Kingsmeadow Com Comp**
Sch NE11 . . . . . . . . . . . . . .56 A4
Kings Meadows NE4 . . . .76 A3
Kingsmere Gdns NE6 . . .48 C4
Kings Road N NE28 . . . . .21 C4
Kings Road S NE28 . . . . .21 C3
**King St**
Birtley DH3 . . . . . . . . . . . . .70 A4
Gateshead, Bensham
NE8 . . . . . . . . . . . . . . . . . . .57 B4
Gateshead, Pelaw NE10 . .48 C1
Newcastle-u-T NE1 . . . . . .78 B4
Kings Terr 28 NE6 . . . . . .67 A1
Kingston Ave NE6 . . . . . . .47 C4
Kingston Gn NE6 . . . . . . . .33 B1
**KINGSTON PARK** . . . . . . .7 A2
Kingston Park Ave NE3 . .7 A2
Kingston Park Ctr NE3 . . .7 A2
**Kingston Park Prim Sch**
NE3 . . . . . . . . . . . . . . . . . . . .7 A2
Kingston Park Rd NE3 . . .8 A3
Kingston Park Sta NE3 . .7 A2
Kingston Rd NE8 . . . . . . . .59 A4
Kings Vale NE28 . . . . . . . .22 A4
**Kingsway**
Newcastle-u-T NE4 . . . . . .29 C4
Sunniside NE16 . . . . . . . . .62 B2
Kingsway Ave NE3 . . . . . . .9 A3
Kingsway Ho NE11 . . . . . .64 B4
**Kingsway Interchange**
NE11 . . . . . . . . . . . . . . . . . .64 C3
Kingsway N NE11 . . . . . . .57 B1
Kingsway S NE11 . . . . . . .64 B3
Kings Wlk NE5 . . . . . . . . . .14 A4
Kingswood Ave NE2 . . . . .18 B3
Kingswood Cl NE35 . . . . .52 A1
Kinnaird Ave NE3 . . . . . . .28 B2
Kinross Cl DH3 . . . . . . . . .70 C2
Kinross Ct NE10 . . . . . . . .49 A2
Kinross Dr NE3 . . . . . . . . . .8 A1
Kinver Dr NE5 . . . . . . . . . .14 A3
**Kipling Ave**
Hebburn NE31 . . . . . . . . . .36 A2
Whickham NE16 . . . . . . . . .55 A4
Kipling Ct NE16 . . . . . . . . .55 A4
Kirby Cl NE34 . . . . . . . . . . .52 B4
Kirkdale Ct 2 NE34 . . . . .52 C4
Kirkdale Gn NE4 . . . . . . . .76 B4
Kirkham Ave NE3 . . . . . . . .7 A3
Kirkheaton Pl NE5 . . . . . .29 A4
Kirkleatham Gdns NE6 . .20 B2
Kirkley Cl NE3 . . . . . . . . . . .8 C2
Kirkley Lodge NE3 . . . . . . .8 C2
Kirk St NE6 . . . . . . . . . . . . .33 A1
Kirkston Ave NE15 . . . . . .27 B3
Kirkstone DH3 . . . . . . . . . .70 C2
Kirkstone Ave NE32 . . . . .51 C3
Kirkstone Cl NE21 . . . . . .53 B4
Kirkstone Gdns NE7 . . . . .19 B3

Kirkstone Rd NE10 . . . . . .60 B4
Kirkwood Dr NE3 . . . . . . . .8 A1
Kirkwood Gdns NE10 . . .61 A4
Kirkwood Pl NE3 . . . . . . . .4 B1
Kirton Ave NE4 . . . . . . . . .29 C2
Kitchener St NE9 . . . . . . . .58 C4
Kitchener Terr NE32 . . . . .36 C1
Kittiwake Dr NE38 . . . . . . .71 B3
Knaresdale DH3 . . . . . . . .70 C1
Knarsdale Pl 3 NE5 . . . .14 C1
Knightsbridge NE3 . . . . . . .9 A2
Knightsbridge Ct NE3 . . . .9 A2
Knightside Gdns NE11 . .56 C3
Knightside Wlk NE5 . . . . .14 A3
Knoll Rise NE11 . . . . . . . . .56 B3
Knop Law Fst Sch NE5 . .14 A3
Knott Pl NE15 . . . . . . . . . .28 C1
Knoulberry NE37 . . . . . . . .69 C2
Knoulberry Rd NE37 . . . .69 C2
Knowle Pl NE12 . . . . . . . . .10 C1
Knowsley Ct NE3 . . . . . . . .6 C1
Kristin Ave NE32 . . . . . . . .51 B4
Kyle Cl NE4 . . . . . . . . . . . . .76 B4
Kyle Rd NE8 . . . . . . . . . . . .57 B4
Kyloe Cl NE3 . . . . . . . . . . . .7 C3
Kyloe Pl NE5 . . . . . . . . . . .15 B3
Kyloe Villas NE5 . . . . . . . .15 B3

**L**

**Laburnum Ave**
Gateshead NE10 . . . . . . . .60 C3
Newcastle-u-T NE6 . . . . . .34 A4
Wallsend NE28 . . . . . . . . . .21 C2
**Laburnum Gdns**
6 Gateshead, Felling
NE10 . . . . . . . . . . . . . . . . . .47 C1
Gateshead, Low Fell NE9 .58 B2
Jarrow NE32 . . . . . . . . . . . .50 C4
**Laburnum Gr**
Hebburn NE31 . . . . . . . . . .50 A3
Sunniside NE16 . . . . . . . . .62 C2
Whickham NE16 . . . . . . . . .54 C3
Laburnum Ho NE28 . . . . .22 A1
Laburnum Rd NE21 . . . . .41 B2
Ladybank NE5 . . . . . . . . . .13 C4
Ladyhaugh Dr NE16 . . . . .62 B4
Ladykirk Rd NE4 . . . . . . . .29 C1
Ladywell Rd NE21 . . . . . .41 B2
Laing Dr NE28 . . . . . . . . . .23 C3
Laith Rd NE3 . . . . . . . . . . . .7 C1
Lake App NE21 . . . . . . . . .42 B1
Lakeside NE21 . . . . . . . . . .42 B1
Lake View NE31 . . . . . . . . .50 A4
Laleham Ct NE3 . . . . . . . . .7 B3
Lambden Ct NE29 . . . . . . .24 C3
Lambert Rd NE37 . . . . . . .69 B3
Lambert Sq NE3 . . . . . . . . .8 B1
Lambeth Pl NE8 . . . . . . . . .58 C4
Lambley Cl NE16 . . . . . . . .62 B2
Lambley Cres NE31 . . . . .49 C3
**Lambourn Ave**
Longbenton NE12 . . . . . . .11 A3
North Shields NE29 . . . . . .24 C4
Lamb St NE6 . . . . . . . . . . . .34 B1
**LAMBTON** . . . . . . . . . . . . .71 C3
Lambton Ave NE16 . . . . . .55 B4
Lambton Cl NE40 . . . . . . .38 B4
Lambton Rd NE31 . . . . . . .36 A3
Lambton St NE8 . . . . . . . . .78 B3
Lambton Terr NE32 . . . . . .51 A4
Lampeter Ct NE15 . . . . . .15 C4
Lamport St NE31 . . . . . . . .35 A3
Lanark Dr NE32 . . . . . . . . .52 A2
Lancaster Ct NE3 . . . . . . . .7 B3
Lancaster Rd NE11 . . . . . .44 A1
Lancaster Way NE32 . . . .50 C1
Lancefield Ave NE6 . . . . .48 B4
Lancet Ct NE8 . . . . . . . . . .79 C2
Lanchester Ave NE9 . . . .66 C3
Lanchester Cl NE10 . . . . .61 B2
Lancing Ct NE3 . . . . . . . . . .7 A3
Landscape Terr NE40 . . . .39 A1
Landseer Gdns NE9 . . . . .59 A3
Landswood Terr NE21 . . .53 C3
Lane Head NE40 . . . . . . . .24 A1
Lanercost Ave NE21 . . . . .41 A2
Lanercost Dr NE5 . . . . . . .29 A4
**Lanercost Gdns**
Gateshead NE10 . . . . . . . .59 B2
Throckley NE15 . . . . . . . . .12 B2

Lanesborough Ct NE3 . . . .8 B1
Langdale DH3 . . . . . . . . . .71 A1
Langdale Cl NE12 . . . . . . .10 B2
Langdale Cres NE21 . . . .53 A4
Langdale Gdns NE6 . . . . .34 B2
Langdale Rd NE9 . . . . . . . .58 C1
Langdon Rd NE5 . . . . . . . .14 C2
Langford Dr NE35 . . . . . . .52 B2
Langham Rd NE15 . . . . . .28 B1
Langholm Rd NE3 . . . . . . . .9 A3
Langhorn Cl NE6 . . . . . . . .32 C3
Langleeford Rd NE5 . . . . .15 B4
Langley Ave NE10 . . . . . . .61 A2
Langley Mere 8 NE12 . .11 B4
**Langley Rd**
Newcastle-u-T, Walker
NE6 . . . . . . . . . . . . . . . . . . .34 A2
Newcastle-u-T, West Denton
NE5 . . . . . . . . . . . . . . . . . . .28 A4
Langley Terr NE32 . . . . . .51 A3
Langton St NE8 . . . . . . . . .79 C1
Langton Terr NE7 . . . . . . .19 C2
Lansbury Cl DH3 . . . . . . . .68 A2
Lansbury Dr DH3 . . . . . . . .68 A1
Lansbury Gdns NE10 . . . .61 C4
Lansbury Rd NE16 . . . . . .55 B2
**Lansdowne Cres** NE3 . . . .9 A1
Lansdowne Gdns NE2 . .32 B4
**Lansdowne Pl** NE3 . . . . . . .9 A1
Lansdowne Rd NE12 . . . .11 B4
**Lansdowne Terr** NE3 . . . . .9 A1
**Lansdowne Terr E** NE3 . . .9 A1
Lanthwaite Rd NE9 . . . . . .65 B4
Lapwing Cl NE38 . . . . . . . .71 B3
L'Arbre Cres NE16 . . . . . .54 B3
Larch Cl NE9 . . . . . . . . . . .66 B2
Larches The NE4 . . . . . . . .76 A3
Larch Rd NE21 . . . . . . . . . .41 C3
Larch St 2 NE11 . . . . . . .62 C2
**Larchwood Ave**
Newcastle-u-T, Fawdon
NE3 . . . . . . . . . . . . . . . . . . . .8 A3
Newcastle-u-T, Walkergate
NE6 . . . . . . . . . . . . . . . . . . .33 C4
Wideopen NE13 . . . . . . . . . .2 C1
Larchwood Gdns NE11 . .57 A1
Larkrise Cl NE7 . . . . . . . . .20 B3
Larkspur NE9 . . . . . . . . . . .66 A4
**Larkspur Com Prim Sch**
NE9 . . . . . . . . . . . . . . . . . . .66 A4
Larkspur Rd NE16 . . . . . .55 A2
Larkspur Terr NE2 . . . . . .18 C1
Larne Cres NE9 . . . . . . . . .58 C1
Lartington Gdns NE3 . . . .10 A1
La Sagesse Sch NE2 . . . .18 C3
Laski Gdns NE10 . . . . . . . .61 A4
Lauderdale Ave NE28 . . .22 A4
Launceston Cl NE3 . . . . . .7 B4
Laurel Ave NE3 . . . . . . . . .10 A1
Laurel Cres NE6 . . . . . . . .21 A1
Laurel Rd NE21 . . . . . . . . .41 C2
**Laurel St**
Throckley NE15 . . . . . . . . .12 B3
Wallsend NE28 . . . . . . . . . .22 A1
Laurel Way NE40 . . . . . . . .38 C3
Laurel Wlk NE3 . . . . . . . . . .9 A1
Laurelwood Gdns NE11 .57 A1
**Lavender Gdns**
Gateshead NE9 . . . . . . . . .58 B2
Newcastle-u-T NE2 . . . . . .18 B1
Lavender Rd NE16 . . . . . .54 C2
Lavender Row 2 NE9 . . .59 A1
Lavender Wlk NE31 . . . . .50 A3
Laverick NE10 . . . . . . . . . .60 B2
Laverock Ct 12 NE6 . . . . .33 A1
Laverock Pl 3 NE5 . . . . . .7 B1
Lavers Rd DH3 . . . . . . . . .68 B1
Lawns The NE2 . . . . . . . . .19 A2
Lawnsway NE32 . . . . . . . .51 B1
Lawn The NE40 . . . . . . . . .25 A2
Lawrence Ave NE21 . . . . .41 B3
Lawrence Ct NE21 . . . . . .41 B3
Lawrence Hill Ct NE10 . .61 B4
Lawson Ave NE32 . . . . . .51 C3
Lawson St NE28 . . . . . . . .22 A1
Lawson Terr NE4 . . . . . . . .44 A4
Laxford DH3 . . . . . . . . . . . .70 C2
Laybourn Gdns 5 NE34 .52 B4
Layburn Gdns NE15 . . . .27 C4
Layfield Rd NE3 . . . . . . . . . .4 C1
Lea Ave NE32 . . . . . . . . . . .51 B2
Leabank NE15 . . . . . . . . . .27 B4

Lead Rd NE40 . . . . . . . . . .39 A1
Leafield Cl DH3 . . . . . . . . .68 C2
Lea Gn DH3 . . . . . . . . . . . .71 A1
Leacroft Ct NE3 . . . . . . . . .8 B1
Lealholm Rd NE7 . . . . . . .10 B1
Leam Gdns NE10 . . . . . . .61 A4
**Leam La**
Gateshead NE10 . . . . . . . .61 A2
Jarrow NE32 . . . . . . . . . . . .51 B3
**LEAM LANE** . . . . . . . . . . .60 C2
**Leamside**
Gateshead NE10 . . . . . . . .60 B2
Jarrow NE32 . . . . . . . . . . . .51 B3
Leasyde Wlk NE16 . . . . . .54 B1
Leazes Parkway NE15 . .12 B1
Leazes The NE15 . . . . . . .12 A1
Lecondale NE10 . . . . . . . .60 B1
Lecondale Ct NE10 . . . . . .60 B1
Leeming Gdns NE9 . . . . .59 A2
Legion Gr NE15 . . . . . . . .28 A3
Legion Rd NE15 . . . . . . . .28 A3
Leicester St NE6 . . . . . . . .33 C1
Leicester Way NE32 . . . . .50 C1
Leighton St 7 NE6 . . . . .32 B2
Leighton Terr DH3 . . . . . .68 A1
**LEMINGTON** . . . . . . . . . . .27 A3
Lemington Gdns NE5 . . .29 A3
Lemington Rd NE15 . . . . .26 C2
**Lemington Riverside Prim**
Sch NE15 . . . . . . . . . . . . .27 B2
Lenore Terr NE40 . . . . . . .39 A2
Leopold St NE32 . . . . . . . .36 C2
Lesbury Ave NE28 . . . . . .23 A3
Lesbury Chase NE3 . . . . .8 C3
Lesbury Gdns NE13 . . . . .2 C2
Lesbury Rd NE6 . . . . . . . .32 C4
**Lesbury St**
Newcastle-u-T NE15 . . . . .27 A2
North Shields NE28 . . . . . .24 A1
Lesley Ct NE3 . . . . . . . . . . .9 A1
Leslie Ave NE31 . . . . . . . .35 C1
Leslie Cl NE40 . . . . . . . . . .40 A4
Leslie Cres NE3 . . . . . . . .18 A3
Letch Way NE15 . . . . . . . .27 A3
Leuchars Ct DH3 . . . . . . .70 B3
Lewis Dr NE4 . . . . . . . . . . .30 A2
Leybourne Hold DH3 . . . .68 B2
Leyburn Dr NE7 . . . . . . . .19 B3
Leyburn Pl DH3 . . . . . . . . .68 A2
Leyton Pl NE8 . . . . . . . . . .59 A4
Liberty Ho NE2 . . . . . . . . .18 C1
Lichfield Ave NE6 . . . . . . .48 A4
Lichfield Cl NE3 . . . . . . . . .7 C3
Lichfield Way NE32 . . . . .50 C1
Liddell Terr NE8 . . . . . . . .57 C4
Lieven St NE13 . . . . . . . . . .4 A4
Liffey Rd NE31 . . . . . . . . . .50 B3
Lightbourne Rd NE6 . . . .34 B2
**Lightfoot Sports Ctr The**
NE6 . . . . . . . . . . . . . . . . . . .48 B4
Lightwood Ave NE15 . . . .42 C4
Lilac Cl NE5 . . . . . . . . . . . .13 C4
**Lilac Gdns**
Gateshead NE9 . . . . . . . . .58 B2
Whickham NE16 . . . . . . . . .54 C2
Lilac Rd NE6 . . . . . . . . . . . .21 B1
Lilburn Gdns NE3 . . . . . . .19 A4
Lilburn Pl NE23 . . . . . . . . .16 A1
Lilian Ave NE28 . . . . . . . . .21 B1
Lily Ave NE2 . . . . . . . . . . . .18 C1
Lily Bank NE28 . . . . . . . . .22 A2
Lily Cl NE21 . . . . . . . . . . . .40 C2
Lily Cres NE2 . . . . . . . . . . .18 C1
Lily Est NE15 . . . . . . . . . . .12 B3
Lily Terr NE5 . . . . . . . . . . .15 B3
Limecroft NE32 . . . . . . . . .51 B1
Lime Gr NE40 . . . . . . . . . . .25 A1
Limekiln Ct NE28 . . . . . . .22 B2
Limekiln Rd NE28 . . . . . .22 B2
**Lime St**
Blaydon NE21 . . . . . . . . . .41 C1
Newcastle-u-T NE1, NE6 .32 B1
Throckley NE15 . . . . . . . . .12 B3
Limetrees Gdns NE9 . . . .58 B3
Limewood Gr NE13 . . . . .2 A1
Linacre Ct NE3 . . . . . . . . . .6 C2
Linbridge Dr NE5 . . . . . . .14 C1
Lincoln Ave NE28 . . . . . . .21 B3
Lincoln Ct NE31 . . . . . . . .35 B1
Lincoln Gn NE3 . . . . . . . . . .4 C1
Lincoln St NE8 . . . . . . . . . .79 B1

Lincoln Way NE32 . . . . . .51 A1
Lincrest Ct NE5 . . . . . . . . .15 A2
Lindale Ave NE16 . . . . . . .54 C1
Lindale Rd NE4 . . . . . . . . .29 C4
Linden NE9 . . . . . . . . . . . . .66 B4
**Linden Ave**
Newcastle-u-T, Fenham
NE4 . . . . . . . . . . . . . . . . . . .29 B3
Newcastle-u-T, Gosforth
NE3 . . . . . . . . . . . . . . . . . . .18 A4
Linden Gr 1 NE11 . . . . . .56 C4
**Linden Rd**
Blaydon NE21 . . . . . . . . . .41 C2
Longbenton NE12 . . . . . . .11 B2
Newcastle-u-T NE3 . . . . . .18 A4
Linden Sch NE12 . . . . . . .11 B4
**Linden Terr**
Longbenton NE12 . . . . . . .11 B2
25 Springwell NE9 . . . . . .67 A1
Linden Way NE9 . . . . . . . .66 B2
Lindfield Ave NE5 . . . . . . .16 A1
**Lindisfarne Cl**
Newcastle-u-T, Jesmond
NE2 . . . . . . . . . . . . . . . . . . .19 A2
Newcastle-u-T NE5 . . . . . .15 A1
**Lindisfarne Com Prim Sch**
NE8 . . . . . . . . . . . . . . . . . . .46 C2
Lindisfarne Dr NE8 . . . . . .79 C2
Lindisfarne Pl NE28 . . . . .22 B3
**Lindisfarne Rd**
Hebburn NE31 . . . . . . . . . .50 A3
Jarrow NE32 . . . . . . . . . . . .51 C4
Newcastle-u-T NE2 . . . . . .19 A2
**Lindisfarne Recess**
NE32 . . . . . . . . . . . . . . . . . .51 C4
Lindrick Ct NE10 . . . . . . . .61 B3
Lindum Rd NE9 . . . . . . . . .58 B4
Lingcrest NE9 . . . . . . . . . .59 B1
Lingey Gdns NE10 . . . . . .61 B4
**Lingey House Prim Sch**
NE10 . . . . . . . . . . . . . . . . . .61 A3
Lingey La NE10 . . . . . . . . .61 A3
Lingshaw NE10 . . . . . . . . .61 A3
Lingside NE32 . . . . . . . . . .51 B1
Linhope Ave NE3 . . . . . . . .8 A3
Linhope PRU NE5 . . . . . .15 A2
Linhope Rd NE5 . . . . . . . .15 A2
**Link Rd**
Hazlerigg NE13 . . . . . . . . . .4 A4
Newcastle-u-T NE5 . . . . . .16 C2
Links Gn NE3 . . . . . . . . . . .9 B2
Links Green Wlk NE3 . . . .9 B2
Links Wlk NE5 . . . . . . . . . .15 A2
Linkway NE32 . . . . . . . . . .51 C1
Linnel Dr NE15 . . . . . . . . .27 C3
Linnet Ct NE38 . . . . . . . . .71 C3
Linnetsfield NE6 . . . . . . . .34 A4
Linney Gdns NE34 . . . . . .52 C4
Linskill Pl NE3 . . . . . . . . . .17 A3
Linthorpe Rd NE3 . . . . . . . .9 A4
Linton Rd NE9 . . . . . . . . . .65 A3
Lintzford Gdns NE15 . . . .27 C3
Linum Pl NE4 . . . . . . . . . . .29 C4
Linwood Pl NE3 . . . . . . . . .4 C1
Lishman Terr NE40 . . . . . .38 C1
Lisle Ct 11 NE28 . . . . . . .21 C2
Lisle Gr NE28 . . . . . . . . . .23 B3
Lisle St NE28 . . . . . . . . . . .21 C2
Lismore Pl NE15 . . . . . . . .29 B2
Lismor Terr 11 NE9 . . . . .67 A1
Lister Ave NE11 . . . . . . . . .44 B1
Listers La NE9 . . . . . . . . . .58 C4
Lister St NE15 . . . . . . . . . .28 A1
Litchfield Cres 2 NE21 . .41 A1
Litchfield La NE21 . . . . . .41 A1
Litchfield St 1 NE21 . . . .41 A1
Litchfield Terr 3 NE21 . .41 A1
Littledene NE9 . . . . . . . . . .58 B3
Little Dene NE2 . . . . . . . . .18 B3
Little Way NE15 . . . . . . . . .43 A4
Littondale NE28 . . . . . . . . .21 A4
Lloyd Ct NE11 . . . . . . . . . .44 A2
Lloyd St 6 NE40 . . . . . . . .38 B3
Lobban Ave NE31 . . . . . . .49 C3
Lobelia Ave NE10 . . . . . . .47 A2
Lobelia Cl NE5 . . . . . . . . . .13 C3
Lobley Gdns NE11 . . . . . .56 C2
**LOBLEY HILL** . . . . . . . . . .56 C1
**Lobley Hill Prim Sch**
NE11 . . . . . . . . . . . . . . . . . .56 C2
Lobley Hill Rd NE8, NE11 .57 B3
Lockerbie Gdns NE15 . . .27 C3

Lodges Rd The NE9 . . . . .65 A3
Lodore Gr NE32 . . . . . . . .51 C3
Lodore Rd NE2 . . . . . . . . .18 B3
Logan Rd NE6 . . . . . . . . .21 A1
Lombard St NE1 . . . . . . . .78 B4
London Ave NE37 . . . . . . .67 C1
Long Bank
  Birtley DH3 . . . . . . . . . . .68 B3
  Gateshead NE9 . . . . . . . .66 A1
LONGBENTON . . . . . . . . .11 A4
Longbenton Com Coll
  NE12 . . . . . . . . . . . . . . .11 A3
Longbenton Sta NE12 . . .10 B1
Longborough Ct NE7 . . .19 B4
Long Crag NE37 . . . . . . . .69 C1
Longdean Cl NE31 . . . . . .35 A1
Longfield Terr NE6 . . . . . .48 C4
Long Headlam 11 NE6 . .33 A2
Longhirst
  Gateshead NE10 . . . . . . .60 C3
  Newcastle-u-T NE5 . . . . .15 A2
Longhirst Dr NE13 . . . . . .2 B1
Long Meadow Cl NE40 . .38 C3
Longniddry Ct NE5 . . . . . .64 C3
Longridge NE21 . . . . . . . .40 C2
Longridge Ave NE7 . . . . .20 B2
Long Ridge Rd NE21,
  NE40 . . . . . . . . . . . . . . .39 C2
Longrigg NE10 . . . . . . . . .60 C3
Long Rigg NE16 . . . . . . . .42 C2
Longstaff Gdns NE34 . . .52 B4
Longstone Sq NE5 . . . . . .14 B1
Longwood Cl NE16 . . . . . .62 C3
Lonnen Ave NE4 . . . . . . . .29 B3
Lonnen Dr NE16 . . . . . . . .54 C4
Lonnen The NE40 . . . . . . .25 C1
Lonsdale DH3 . . . . . . . . .71 A1
Lonsdale Ct NE34 . . . . . .52 C1
Lonsdale Gdns NE28 . . . .23 B4
Lonsdale Terr NE2 . . . . . .18 C2
Loraine Terr NE15 . . . . . .27 A2
Lordenshaw NE5 . . . . . . .15 A2
Lord Lawson of Beamish
  Com Sch DH3 . . . . . . . . .70 C3
Lord St NE1 . . . . . . . . . . .76 C4
Lorton Rd NE9 . . . . . . . . .65 B4
Losh Terr NE6 . . . . . . . . .34 A1
Lothian Cl DH3 . . . . . . . .70 C1
Lothian Ct NE5 . . . . . . . . .16 A3
Lotus Cl NE5 . . . . . . . . . .13 C3
Lotus Pl NE4 . . . . . . . . . .29 B3
Lough Ct NE9 . . . . . . . . . .59 A1
Louie Terr NE9 . . . . . . . . .58 C1
Loup St NE21 . . . . . . . . . .41 B3
Lovaine St NE15 . . . . . . .25 C4
Loveless Gdns NE10 . . . .61 A4
Lovett Wlk NE8 . . . . . . . .77 C2
Lowdham Ave NE29 . . . . .24 C4
Loweswater Rd
  Gateshead NE9 . . . . . . . .65 B4
  Newcastle-u-T NE5 . . . . .28 C4
Loweswood Cl NE7 . . . . . .19 B1
LOW FELL . . . . . . . . . . . .58 B1
Lowfield Terr NE6 . . . . . . .48 B4
Lowfield Wlk NE16 . . . . . .54 C2
Low Fold NE6 . . . . . . . . . .32 C1
Lowgate NE5 . . . . . . . . . .12 B1
Low Gosforth Ct NE3 . . . .5 A1
LOW GREENSIDE . . . . . .38 C2
Low Heworth La NE10 . .48 B1
Lowick Cl DH3 . . . . . . . . .70 C1
Lowick Ct NE3 . . . . . . . . .18 C4
Lowlean Ct NE5 . . . . . . . .15 A1
Lownds Terr NE6 . . . . . . .33 C2
Low Reach NE10 . . . . . . .48 C2
Lowrey's La NE9 . . . . . . . .58 B1
Low Row NE40 . . . . . . . . .40 A3
Lowthian Cres NE6 . . . . .33 C1
LOW WALKER . . . . . . . . .34 C2
Low Well Gdns NE10 . . . .48 A1
Lucy St NE21 . . . . . . . . . .41 C3
Ludlow Ct NE3 . . . . . . . . . .7 C3
Luke's La NE10, NE31 . . .50 B1
Lukes Lane Com Sch
  NE31 . . . . . . . . . . . . . . .50 C3
Lulworth Ave NE32 . . . . .37 B1
Lumley Ave NE16 . . . . . . .43 A1
Lumley Ct NE31 . . . . . . . .36 A4
Lumley Gdns NE8 . . . . . .47 A1
Lumley Terr NE32 . . . . . . .51 B4
Lumley Wlk NE11 . . . . . . .77 A1
Lune Gn NE32 . . . . . . . . .51 B2

Lupin Cl NE5 . . . . . . . . . .14 A4
Luss Ave NE32 . . . . . . . . .52 A3
Lutterworth Cl NE12 . . . .10 C2
Lutterworth Pl NE12 . . . .10 C1
Lutterworth Rd NE12 . . . .10 C1
Lychgate Ct NE8 . . . . . . .78 C3
Lyden Gate NE9 . . . . . . . .65 B3
Lydford Ct NE3 . . . . . . . . . .7 A2
Lydford Way DH3 . . . . . . .70 C3
Lydney Cl NE15 . . . . . . . .12 A1
Lynden Gdns NE5 . . . . . .15 B3
LYNDHURST . . . . . . . . . .65 B3
Lyndhurst Ave
  Gateshead NE9 . . . . . . . .65 B4
  Newcastle-u-T NE2 . . . . .18 C2
Lyndhurst Cres NE9 . . . . .65 B4
Lyndhurst Dr NE9 . . . . . . .65 B3
Lyndhurst Gdns NE2 . . . .18 B2
Lyndhurst Gn NE9 . . . . . .65 A4
Lyndhurst Gr NE9 . . . . . . .65 A4
Lyndhurst Rd NE12 . . . . . .11 A2
Lyndhurst Terr 11 NE16 . .42 C1
Lynfield Ct NE5 . . . . . . . . .15 C3
Lynfield Pl NE5 . . . . . . . . .15 C3
Lynholme Ct 9 NE8 . . . . .58 C4
Lynholm Gr NE12 . . . . . . .11 B4
Lynmouth Pl NE7 . . . . . . .19 C3
Lynmouth Rd NE9 . . . . . .65 A3
Lynmouth Rd NE7 . . . . . .19 C2
Lynnholme Gdns
  Gateshead, Deckham
  NE9 . . . . . . . . . . . . . . . .58 C4
  4 Gateshead NE9 . . . . .58 B4
Lynn Rd NE28 . . . . . . . . .21 B1
Lynnwood Ave NE4 . . . . .30 A1
Lynnwood Terr NE4 . . . . .30 A1
Lynton Ave NE32 . . . . . . .37 C1
Lynton Ct NE5 . . . . . . . . .15 C3
Lynton Pl NE5 . . . . . . . . .15 C3
Lynton Way NE5 . . . . . . . .15 C3
Lynwood Ave NE21 . . . . .41 B3
Lynwood Bsns Dev Ctr
  NE4 . . . . . . . . . . . . . . . .30 A1
Lyon St NE31 . . . . . . . . . .35 B3
Lytchfeld NE10 . . . . . . . . .61 A3
Lytham Gn NE10 . . . . . . .49 A2
Lytham Pl NE6 . . . . . . . . .33 C1
Lythe Way NE12 . . . . . . . .11 A2

**M**

Mabel St NE21 . . . . . . . . .41 B3
MacAdam St NE8 . . . . . . .57 B3
McCracken Cl NE3 . . . . . . .9 A4
McCracken Dr NE13 . . . . .2 C3
McCutcheon Ct NE6 . . . .48 A3
MacDonald Rd NE4 . . . . .43 C4
McErlane Sq NE10 . . . . . .48 C1
McEwan Gdns NE4 . . . . .30 A1
McGowen Ct 6 NE6 . . . .33 A1
McIlvenna Gdns NE28 . .21 C4
McIntyre Hall NE31 . . . . .36 A3
McIntyre Rd NE31 . . . . . .36 A3
McKendrick Villas NE5 . .16 B1
Macmillan Gdns NE10 . . .61 C4
McNamara Rd NE28 . . . .23 A3
Maddox Rd NE12 . . . . . . .11 B2
Madeira Cl NE15 . . . . . . .14 A4
Madras St NE34 . . . . . . . .52 C4
Mafeking St
  5 Gateshead NE9 . . . . .58 C4
  Newcastle-u-T NE6 . . . . .48 B3
Magenta Cres NE5 . . . . . .14 A4
Magnolia Cl NE4 . . . . . . .29 B3
Maiden La NE40 . . . . . . . .38 C2
Maiden St NE4 . . . . . . . . .76 B3
Main Cres NE28 . . . . . . . .21 A4
Main Rd NE3 . . . . . . . . . . .6 C2
Main St NE40 . . . . . . . . . .38 B4
Makendon St NE31 . . . . .35 C3
Makepeace Terr 8 NE9 .67 A1
Malaga Cl NE15 . . . . . . . .13 C4
Malaya Dr NE6 . . . . . . . . .34 C1
Malcolm St NE6 . . . . . . . .32 B2
Maling Ct NE6 . . . . . . . . .47 A4
Maling St NE6 . . . . . . . . . .32 B1
Mallard Cl NE38 . . . . . . . .71 B4
Mallard Lodge 11 NE10 .59 C4
Mallowburn Cres NE3 . . .16 A4
Malone Gdns DH3 . . . . . .68 C2
Malory Pl NE8 . . . . . . . . . .79 C2
Malton Cl NE15 . . . . . . . .27 C2

Malton Ct NE32 . . . . . . . .36 B3
Malton Gdns NE28 . . . . . .21 C4
Malton Gn NE9 . . . . . . . .65 C1
Malvern Cl
  Dunston NE11 . . . . . . . . .56 C2
  Newcastle-u-T NE5 . . . . .26 C3
Malvern Gdns NE11 . . . . .56 C3
Malvern Rd NE28 . . . . . . .23 B3
Malvern St NE4 . . . . . . . .76 A4
Mandarin Lodge 8
  NE10 . . . . . . . . . . . . . . .59 C4
Mandela Way NE11 . . . . .43 C3
Mangrove Cl NE5 . . . . . . .14 A4
Manisty Ho NE4 . . . . . . . .44 A4
Manor Ave
  Longbenton NE7 . . . . . . .11 A1
  Newburn NE15 . . . . . . . .26 A4
Manor Cl NE3 . . . . . . . . . . .9 B1
Manor Dr NE7 . . . . . . . . .11 A1
Manorfields NE12 . . . . . . .11 B2
Manor Gdns
  Gateshead NE10 . . . . . . .61 B4
  Longbenton NE7 . . . . . . .11 A1
Manor Gr
  Longbenton NE7 . . . . . . .11 A1
  Newburn NE15 . . . . . . . .26 A3
Manor House Cl 11 NE6 .33 A1
Manor House Farm Cotts
  NE5 . . . . . . . . . . . . . . . .16 B4
Manor House Rd NE2 . . .19 A1
Manor Pl NE7 . . . . . . . . .11 A1
Manor Rd NE7 . . . . . . . . .11 A1
Manor Terr
  Blaydon NE21 . . . . . . . . .40 C1
  Winlaton Mill NE21 . . . . .53 B3
Manorway NE32 . . . . . . . .51 B1
Manor Wlk NE7 . . . . . . . .11 A1
Mansell Pl NE3 . . . . . . . . .16 C3
Mansion Hts NE11 . . . . . .56 A3
Maple Ave NE11 . . . . . . . .56 C3
Maple Cl NE15 . . . . . . . . .27 C2
Mapledene Rd NE3 . . . . . .8 A2
Maple Gr
  Gateshead, Felling
  NE10 . . . . . . . . . . . . . . .60 A4
  Gateshead, Saltwell NE8 .58 A3
Maple Rd NE21 . . . . . . . .41 B2
Maple Row NE11 . . . . . . .43 A2
Maple St
  Jarrow NE32 . . . . . . . . . .36 B3
  Newcastle-u-T NE4 . . . . .76 B4
Maple Terr NE4 . . . . . . . .76 B4
Maplewood NE6 . . . . . . . .33 C4
Mapperley Dr NE15 . . . . .27 C3
Marblet Ct NE11 . . . . . . . .57 A3
Marconi Way NE11 . . . . . .43 A2
Marcross Cl NE15 . . . . . .13 C2
Mardale Gdns NE9 . . . . . .65 B3
Mardale Rd NE15 . . . . . . .15 C1
Mareburn Cres NE10 . . . .60 A4
Margaret Collins Ho
  NE6 . . . . . . . . . . . . . . . .33 B2
Marian Ct NE8 . . . . . . . . .79 A1
Marian Dr NE10 . . . . . . . .49 B3
Maria St NE4 . . . . . . . . . .44 A4
Marie Curie Dr NE4 . . . . .44 B4
Marigold Ave NE10 . . . . .47 A2
Marina View
  Hebburn NE31 . . . . . . . .35 B2
  Wallsend NE28 . . . . . . . .23 A2
Marine Dr NE31 . . . . . . . .50 C3
Mariners Wharf NE1 . . . .32 B1
Market La NE11, NE16 . . .55 C4
Market Sq NE32 . . . . . . . .36 C3
Market St NE1 . . . . . . . . .78 C2
Market Way NE11 . . . . . . .57 C2
Marlboro Ave NE16 . . . . .55 A4
Marlborough Ct 5 NE3 . . .9 A3
Marlborough Ave NE3 . . . .9 A3
Marlborough Cres
  Gateshead NE9 . . . . . . . .66 A3
  Newcastle-u-T NE1 . . . . .76 C4
Marlborough Ct
  Jarrow NE32 . . . . . . . . . .36 C1
  Newcastle-u-T NE3 . . . . . .7 B3
Marleen Ave NE6 . . . . . . .33 A4
Marleen Ct 2 NE6 . . . . . .33 A4
Marlfield Ct NE5 . . . . . . . .15 C3
Marlowe Gdns NE8 . . . . . .79 C1
Marlowe Wlk NE34 . . . . . .52 C3
Marlow Pl NE12 . . . . . . . .11 A2
Marlow Way NE16 . . . . . .54 B1
Marmion Rd NE6 . . . . . . .34 B4

Marondale Ave NE6 . . . . .34 A3
Marquis Ave NE5 . . . . . . .14 A4
Marquis Cl NE12 . . . . . . .11 B1
Marquis Ct NE11 . . . . . . .64 B3
Marquisway NE11 . . . . . . .64 B2
Marr Rd NE31 . . . . . . . . . .36 A1
Marsden Gr NE9 . . . . . . . .66 B3
Marsden La NE5 . . . . . . . .15 B3
Marsham Ct NE15 . . . . . .27 C3
Marsham Rd 3 NE5 . . . . .14 C3
Marsh Ct NE11 . . . . . . . . .57 A3
Marske Terr NE6 . . . . . . . .48 B4
Marston Wlk 1 NE16 . . . .54 B1
Martello Gdns NE7 . . . . . .20 B2
Martin Ct NE38 . . . . . . . . .71 B2
Martin Hall NE32 . . . . . . .37 A2
Martin Rd NE28 . . . . . . . .23 B2
Martin Way NE13 . . . . . . . .2 A2
Mary Agnes St NE3 . . . . . .8 B1
Mary Ave DH3 . . . . . . . . .68 A2
Maryhill Cl NE4 . . . . . . . .44 A4
Mary's Pl NE6 . . . . . . . . .34 C2
Mary St
  Blaydon NE21 . . . . . . . . .41 B3
  Blaydon, Winlaton NE21. .40 C2
Mary Terr NE5 . . . . . . . . .15 B3
Masefield Ave NE16 . . . . .43 A1
Masefield Dr NE34 . . . . . .52 C2
Masefield Pl NE8 . . . . . . .79 C2
Mason Rd NE28 . . . . . . . .21 B4
Mason St
  Brunswick Village NE13 . . .2 A1
  4 Newcastle-u-T NE6 . . .33 A1
Mason View NE13 . . . . . . .2 A1
Matfen Ave NE13 . . . . . . . .4 A4
Matfen Cl NE15 . . . . . . . .27 C2
Matfen Pl
  Newcastle-u-T, Fawdon
  NE3 . . . . . . . . . . . . . . . . .8 B2
  Newcastle-u-T, Fenham
  NE4 . . . . . . . . . . . . . . . .30 A3
Mather Rd NE4 . . . . . . . . .76 B4
Matlock Gdns NE5 . . . . . .15 A3
Matlock Rd NE32 . . . . . . .37 A1
Matthew Bank NE2 . . . . . .18 C3
Matthew Cl NE6 . . . . . . . .32 C2
Matthew St 13 NE6 . . . . .32 C2
Maude Gdns 7 NE28 . . . .21 C1
Maudlin Pl 2 NE5 . . . . . .16 B1
Maud St NE15 . . . . . . . . .27 A2
Maurice Rd NE28 . . . . . . .34 C4
Maurice Road Ind Est
  NE28 . . . . . . . . . . . . . . .34 C4
Maxwell St NE8 . . . . . . . .57 C3
May Ave
  Ryton NE40 . . . . . . . . . . .25 A2
  Winlaton Mill NE21. . . . . .53 B3
Maybury Villas NE12 . . . .10 B1
Mayfair Ct NE31 . . . . . . . .35 B1
Mayfair Gdns NE8 . . . . . .58 C4
Mayfair Rd NE2 . . . . . . . .18 B2
Mayfield Cl NE16 . . . . . . .55 A1
Mayfield Ave NE15 . . . . . .12 C1
Mayfield Gdns
  Jarrow NE32 . . . . . . . . . .36 B2
  Throckley NE15 . . . . . . . .12 C1
  Wallsend NE28 . . . . . . . .21 B3
Mayfield Pl NE13 . . . . . . . .2 A1
Mayfield Rd NE3 . . . . . . . .18 A4
Mayfield Terr NE5 . . . . . . .16 C1
Mayoral Way NE11 . . . . . .64 B3
May St
  Birtley DH3 . . . . . . . . . . .70 B4
  Blaydon NE21 . . . . . . . . .41 A1
Maytree House NE4 . . . . .76 A4
Maywood Cl NE3 . . . . . . .16 C4
Meacham Way NE16 . . . .54 C1
Mead Ave NE12 . . . . . . . .11 A1
Meadowbrook Dr NE10 .61 B3
Meadow Cl
  Blaydon NE21 . . . . . . . . .40 B1
  Dunston NE11 . . . . . . . . .44 A1
  Longbenton NE12 . . . . . .10 C3
  Ryton NE40 . . . . . . . . . . .25 B1
Meadowcroft Mews
  NE8 . . . . . . . . . . . . . . . .79 A1
Meadowdale Cres NE5 . .16 B3
Meadow Dr NE13 . . . . . . .2 C2
Meadowfield Ave NE3. . . .8 B2
Meadowfield Cres NE40 .38 C2
Meadowfield Est NE9 . . .67 A1
Meadowfield Gdns NE6 . .21 B1

Meadowfield Rd NE3 . . . .17 C4
Meadow La
  Crawcrook NE40 . . . . . . .38 C4
  Dunston NE11 . . . . . . . . .44 B1
Meadow Rd
  Newcastle-u-T NE15 . . . .27 B4
  Wallsend NE28 . . . . . . . .23 A1
Meadow Rise
  Gateshead NE9 . . . . . . . .59 B1
  Newcastle-u-T NE5 . . . . .15 C4
Meadows The
  Ryton NE40 . . . . . . . . . . . .8 A2
  Ryton NE40 . . . . . . . . . . .25 B1
Meadow View NE29 . . . . .24 C4
Meadow Well Sta NE29 .24 C4
Meadow Well Way
  NE29 . . . . . . . . . . . . . . .24 C4
Meadow Wlk NE40 . . . . . .25 B1
Mead Wlk NE6 . . . . . . . . .34 A2
Medburn Rd NE15 . . . . . .27 A3
Medlar NE9 . . . . . . . . . . . .66 B4
Medomsley Gdns NE9 . . .66 C4
Medway NE32 . . . . . . . . . .51 B2
Medway Ave NE31 . . . . . .50 A3
Medway Cres NE8 . . . . . .59 A4
Medwood Ct NE3 . . . . . . . .7 C1
Melbourne Ct NE8 . . . . . .78 B3
Melbourne Gdns NE34 . .52 B3
Melbury Rd NE7 . . . . . . . .19 B1
Meldon Ave NE3 . . . . . . . . .8 A3
Meldon Cl NE28 . . . . . . . .22 C3
Meldon Ct NE40 . . . . . . . .38 A3
Meldon Gdns NE11 . . . . .56 C1
Meldon St NE28 . . . . . . . .24 A1
Meldon Terr
  Greenside NE40 . . . . . . .38 B1
  Newcastle-u-T NE6 . . . . .32 C4
Melkington Ct NE5 . . . . . .15 C3
Melkridge Gdns NE7 . . . .20 B3
Mellendean Cl NE5 . . . . .15 C3
Melmerby Cl NE3 . . . . . . . .9 B3
Melness Rd NE13 . . . . . . .2 A1
Melock Ct NE13 . . . . . . . . .2 A1
Melrose Ave
  Gateshead NE9 . . . . . . . .58 C1
  Hebburn NE31 . . . . . . . .50 A3
Melrose Cl
  Newcastle-u-T, Bell's Close
  NE15 . . . . . . . . . . . . . . .27 C2
  Newcastle-u-T NE3 . . . . . .4 B2
Melrose Gdns NE28 . . . . .23 B4
Melrose Gr NE32 . . . . . . .52 A4
Meltham Ct NE15 . . . . . . .13 C2
Melton Ave NE6 . . . . . . . .34 A1
MELTON PARK . . . . . . . . .4 C1
Melville Dr NE7 . . . . . . . . .19 B4
Melvin Pl 5 NE5 . . . . . . . .15 C2
Mendham Cl NE10 . . . . . .60 A2
Mendip Gdns NE11 . . . . . .57 A2
Mendip Way NE12 . . . . . .10 A2
Merchants Wharf 10
  NE6 . . . . . . . . . . . . . . . .47 B4
Mercia Way NE15 . . . . . . .27 C1
Meredith Gdns NE8 . . . . .79 C1
Meresyde NE10 . . . . . . . .60 C3
Meresyde Ct NE10 . . . . . .60 C3
Merganser Lodge 10
  NE10 . . . . . . . . . . . . . . .59 C4
Meridan Way NE7 . . . . . . .20 B3
Merlay Hall NE6 . . . . . . . .48 C4
Merle Gdns 16 NE6 . . . . .33 A1
Merlin Cres NE28 . . . . . . .23 A3
Merlin Ct 17 NE10 . . . . . .47 C1
Merlin Pl NE12 . . . . . . . . .10 B3
Mersey Rd NE8 . . . . . . . .59 A4
Mersey Rd
  Gateshead NE8 . . . . . . . .59 A4
  Hebburn NE31 . . . . . . . .50 B3
Merton Ct NE4 . . . . . . . . .43 C4
Methuen St NE9 . . . . . . . .58 C4
MetroCentre The NE11. .43 B2
Metro Ctr Sta NE11 . . . . .43 C2
Metrocentre Indoor Theme
  Pk* NE11 . . . . . . . . . . . .43 B2
Metro Ret Pk NE11 . . . . .43 A2
Mews The
  Blaydon NE21 . . . . . . . . .42 A2
  Gateshead NE10 . . . . . . .61 A4
Michaelgate NE6 . . . . . . .33 C4

Mickle Cl NE37 . . . . . . . . . .**69** C2
Middle Garth **1** NE5 . . . .16 B2
Middle Gate NE5 . . . . . . . . .14 B1
Middle Row NE40 . . . . . . . .40 A3
Middle St NE6 . . . . . . . . . . .34 B2
Middle St NE6 . . . . . . . . . . .34 A2
Middleton Ave NE4 . . . . . .29 C2
Middlewood Pk NE4 . . . . .29 C3
Midhurst Rd NE12 . . . . . . .11 B3
Midway NE6 . . . . . . . . . . . . .34 B2
Milburn Dr NE15 . . . . . . . .28 C2
Mildmay Rd NE2 . . . . . . . . .18 B2
Milecastle Ct NE5 . . . . . . .14 B2
Milecastle Fst Sch NE5 .14 A2
Milfield Ave NE28 . . . . . . .22 A4
Milford Gdns . . . . . . . . . . . . .4 B1
Milford Rd NE15 . . . . . . . . .29 A1
Millbank Rd NE6 . . . . . . . . .48 C4
Millbeck Gdns NE9 . . . . . .65 C2
Millbrook NE10 . . . . . . . . . .60 A3
Mill Cres NE31 . . . . . . . . . . .49 B2
Mill Dene View NE32 . . . .37 A1
Miller's La NE16 . . . . . . . . .43 A1
Millers Rd NE6 . . . . . . . . . .33 A3
Miller St NE8 . . . . . . . . . . . .57 C4
Millfield Ave NE4 . . . . . . . .16 C3
Millfield Cl NE15 . . . . . . . . .26 A3
Millfield Ct NE16 . . . . . . . . .55 B3
Millfield Gdns NE10 . . . . .59 B4
Millfield La NE15 . . . . . . . . .26 A4
Millfield Rd NE16 . . . . . . . .55 A2
Millford NE10 . . . . . . . . . . . .61 A2
Millford Ct NE10 . . . . . . . . .61 A2
Millgrove View NE3 . . . . . .17 A3
Mill Hill Rd NE5 . . . . . . . . .28 A4
Milling Ct NE8 . . . . . . . . . . .77 C2
Mill La

  Hebburn NE10, NE31 . . . . .50 A2
  Newcastle-u-T NE4 . . . . . .76 A4
  Winlaton Mill NE21 . . . . . .53 A3
Millom Pl NE9 . . . . . . . . . . .65 C4
Mill Rd NE8 . . . . . . . . . . . . .78 C4
Mill Rise NE3 . . . . . . . . . . . .18 C4
Mills Gdns NE28 . . . . . . . . .21 C3
Mill View NE10 . . . . . . . . . .59 B3
Millway NE9 . . . . . . . . . . . . .58 C3
Milner Cres NE21 . . . . . . . .40 C1
Milne Way NE3 . . . . . . . . . . .8 A2
Milsted Ct NE15 . . . . . . . . .13 C2
Milton Ave NE31 . . . . . . . .35 C2
Milton Pl **22** NE9 . . . . . . .67 A1
Milton Rd NE15 . . . . . . . . .55 A4
Milton Sq NE8 . . . . . . . . . . .46 C2
Milton St

  Greenside NE40 . . . . . . . . .38 A1
  Jarrow NE32 . . . . . . . . . . . .36 C4
Milvain Ave NE4 . . . . . . . . .29 C2
Milvain Cl NE15 . . . . . . . . .79 C1
Milvain St NE8 . . . . . . . . . .79 C1
Milverton Ct NE3 . . . . . . . . .7 A2
Mimosa Dr NE31 . . . . . . . .50 A3
Mimosa Pl NE4 . . . . . . . . . .29 B4
Mindrum Terr

  Newcastle-u-T NE4 . . . . . .34 A1
  North Shields NE29 . . . . . .24 B4
Miners Cotts NE15 . . . . . . .28 B3
Miner's Cotts NE16 . . . . . .55 B2
Minerva Cl NE5 . . . . . . . . . .14 A4
Mingarry DH3 . . . . . . . . . . .71 A2
Minorca Pl NE3 . . . . . . . . . .17 A3
Minster Ct NE8 . . . . . . . . . .78 C3
Minster Gr NE15 . . . . . . . . .13 C3
Minster Par NE32 . . . . . . . .37 A3
Mirk La NE8 . . . . . . . . . . . . .78 B4
Mistletoe Rd NE2 . . . . . . . .18 C1
Mitcham Cres NE7 . . . . . . .19 C4
Mitchell Ave NE2 . . . . . . . .18 C2
Mitchell's Bldgs NE9 . . . . .67 B1
Mitchell St

  Birtley DH3 . . . . . . . . . . . . .70 B4
  Crawcrook NE40 . . . . . . . . .38 A3
  Newcastle-u-T NE6 . . . . . .34 C1
Mitford Dr NE15 . . . . . . . . .14 C3
Mitford Gdns

  Dunston NE11 . . . . . . . . . . .56 C1
  Wideopen NE13 . . . . . . . . . .2 C2
Mitford Pl NE3 . . . . . . . . . . .8 B2
Mitford St NE28 . . . . . . . . .24 A2
Mitford Terr NE32 . . . . . . .51 A2

Moat Gdns NE10 . . . . . . . .61 B4
Modder St NE6 . . . . . . . . . .48 B3
Moffat Ave NE32 . . . . . . . .52 A4
Molineux Cl **6** NE6 . . . . .32 C2
Molineux Ct **8** NE6 . . . . .32 C2
Molineux St NE6 . . . . . . . . .32 C2
Mollyfair Cl NE40 . . . . . . . .38 C4
Monarch Rd NE4 . . . . . . . . .77 A2
Monarch Terr NE21 . . . . . .41 B2
Monastery Ct **11** NE32 . . .50 B4
Monkchester Gn NE6 . . . .33 C1
Monkchester Rd NE6 . . . . .48 A4
Monk Ct NE8 . . . . . . . . . . . .79 C2
Monkridge NE15 . . . . . . . .13 C2
Monkridge Ct NE3 . . . . . . .18 C4
Monkridge Gdns NE11 . .56 C3
Monksfeld NE10 . . . . . . . . .60 A3
Monkside NE6 . . . . . . . . . . .33 B4
Monkside Cl NE38 . . . . . . .71 C2
Monks Park Way NE12 . .10 B2
Monkswray NE32 . . . . . . . .37 C2
MONKTON . . . . . . . . . . . . . .50 C4
Monkton NE10 . . . . . . . . . .60 B2
Monkton Ave NE34 . . . . . .52 C4
Monkton Bsns Pk NE31 .50 B2
Monkton Bsns Pk S

  NE10 . . . . . . . . . . . . . . . . . .50 B1
Monkton Hall NE32 . . . . . .50 B4
Monkton Hall Hospl

  NE31 . . . . . . . . . . . . . . . . . .50 B4
Monkton Inf Sch NE34 .52 C3
Monkton Jun Sch NE34 52 B4
Monkton La

  Hebburn NE32 . . . . . . . . . . .50 B4
  Jarrow NE31, NE32 . . . . . . .50 B2
Monkton Rd NE32 . . . . . . .36 C3
Monkton Terr NE32 . . . . . .37 A2
Monmouth Gdns NE28 . .23 B4
Monroe Pl NE5 . . . . . . . . . .16 B2
Mons Ave NE31 . . . . . . . . . .35 C2
Montagu Ave NE3 . . . . . . .17 B2
Montagu Ct NE3 . . . . . . . . .17 B2
Montague Ct NE9 . . . . . . . .58 B4
Montague St NE15 . . . . . . .27 B2
Montagu Prim Sch NE5 16 C2
Montpellier Pl NE3 . . . . . .17 A3
Montrose Cres NE9 . . . . . .59 A3
Montrose Dr NE10 . . . . . . .61 B3
Monument Terr **11** DH3 .70 B4
Moor Cres NE3 . . . . . . . . . .18 A3
Moorcroft Cl NE15 . . . . . . .27 B3
Moorcroft Rd NE15 . . . . . .27 C2
Moor Ct NE3 . . . . . . . . . . . .17 C2
Moore Ave NE11 . . . . . . . . .56 B4
Moore Cres DH3 . . . . . . . . .68 B2
Moore St NE8 . . . . . . . . . . .46 C1
Moorfield NE3 . . . . . . . . . . .16 B3
Moorfoot Gdns NE11 . . . .56 C3
Moorhead NE5 . . . . . . . . . .16 C1
Moorhead Mews NE5 . . .16 C1
Moorings The **8** NE6 . . .47 B4
Moor La NE5 . . . . . . . . . . . .16 B4
Moorland Cres NE6 . . . . . .33 C3
Moorland Ho NE5 . . . . . . .16 A2
Moorlands NE32 . . . . . . . . .51 C1
Moor Pl NE3 . . . . . . . . . . . .18 A3
Moor Rd N NE3 . . . . . . . . . .18 B4
Moor Rd S NE2, NE3 . . . . .18 B3
Moorside NE3 . . . . . . . . . . .51 B1
Moorside Ct NE5 . . . . . . . .16 C1
Moorside N NE4 . . . . . . . . .30 A4
Moorside Pl NE4 . . . . . . . . .30 A4
Moorside S NE4 . . . . . . . . .30 A3
Moorvale La NE5 . . . . . . . .16 C2
Moor View NE40 . . . . . . . . .38 C4
Moorview Cres NE5 . . . . . .16 C2
Moorway Dr NE15 . . . . . . .27 C3
Moralee Cl NE7 . . . . . . . . . .20 B3
Moray Cl DH3 . . . . . . . . . . .70 C4
Morecambe Par NE31 . . .50 C2
Morgans Way NE21 . . . . . .40 C2
Morgy Hill E **3** NE40 . . .38 B3
Morgy Hill W **2** NE40 . .38 B3
Morland Gdns NE9 . . . . . .59 A3
Morley Ave NE10 . . . . . . . .49 A2
Morley Ct **10** NE6 . . . . . . .33 A3
Morley Hill Rd NE5 . . . . . .28 A4
Morley Terr **6** NE10 . . . .59 C4
Mornington Ave NE3 . . . .17 A3
Morpeth Ave

  Jarrow NE32 . . . . . . . . . . . .51 A3
  Wideopen NE13 . . . . . . . . . .2 C3

Morpeth Cl NE38 . . . . . . . .71 C4
Morpeth Terr NE29 . . . . . .24 B4
Morris Gdns NE10 . . . . . . .61 A4
Morrison St NE8 . . . . . . . . .77 C2
Morris Rd NE16 . . . . . . . . .55 A4
Morris St

  Birtley DH3 . . . . . . . . . . . . .70 B4
  Gateshead NE8 . . . . . . . . . .57 B4
Morrit Ct NE7 . . . . . . . . . . .11 A1
Morston Dr NE15 . . . . . . . .27 C2
Mortimer Ave NE5 . . . . . . .15 A3
Morton St NE6 . . . . . . . . . .33 B2
Morven Dr NE10 . . . . . . . . .49 A1
Morven Lea NE21 . . . . . . . .41 A4
Morwick Pl **3** NE5 . . . . . .16 B1
Moss Bank NE9 . . . . . . . . . .65 C3
Moss Cl NE15 . . . . . . . . . . .27 A4
Moss Cres NE40 . . . . . . . . .38 C4
Mosspool NE21 . . . . . . . . . .40 C2
Moss Side NE9 . . . . . . . . . .66 A3
Mostyn Gn NE3 . . . . . . . . . .8 A1
Moulton Ct NE5 . . . . . . . . .16 A2
Moulton Pl NE5 . . . . . . . . .16 A2
Mountbatten Ave NE31 .50 A4
Mount Ct DH3 . . . . . . . . . . .68 C1
Mountfield Gdns NE3 . . . .8 A4
Mountfield Prim Sch

  NE3 . . . . . . . . . . . . . . . . . . . .7 C1
Mount Gr NE11 . . . . . . . . .56 B3
Mount La NE9 . . . . . . . . . . .69 A4
Mount Lonnen NE9 . . . . . .69 A4
MOUNT PLEASANT . . . . . .46 C1
Mount Pleasant

  Birtley DH3 . . . . . . . . . . . . .68 B1
  **5** Blaydon NE21 . . . . . . . .41 A1
  **10** Newcastle-u-T NE6 . . .33 A2
Mount Pleasant Bglws **4**

  DH3 . . . . . . . . . . . . . . . . . . . .68 B1
Mount Pleasant Ct

  NE15 . . . . . . . . . . . . . . . . . . .12 B2
Mount Pleasant Gdns

  NE8 . . . . . . . . . . . . . . . . . . . .46 C1
Mount Rd

  Birtley DH3 . . . . . . . . . . . . .68 C1
  Gateshead NE9 . . . . . . . . . .69 A4
Mountside Gdns NE11 . .56 B3
Mount The

  Ryton NE40 . . . . . . . . . . . . .25 A1
  Throckley NE15 . . . . . . . . .12 A2
Mount View

  **17** Crawcrook NE40 . . . . .38 B3
  Whickham NE16 . . . . . . . . .55 A4
Mourne Gdns NE11 . . . . . .56 C2
Mowbray Rd NE12 . . . . . . .11 C4
Mowbray St NE6 . . . . . . . . .32 B3
Muirfield Dr NE10 . . . . . . .60 A2
Muirfield Rd NE7 . . . . . . . .11 A1
Mulben Cl NE4 . . . . . . . . . .44 A4
Mulberry Gdns NE10 . . . .47 B2
Mulberry Pk NE9 . . . . . . . .58 B1
Mulberry Pl NE4 . . . . . . . . .76 B3
Mulberry St NE10 . . . . . . .47 B2
Mulcaster Gdns NE28 . . .21 B3
Mulgrave Terr NE8 . . . . . . .78 B3
Mulgrave Villas NE8 . . . . .79 B2
Mullen Dr NE40 . . . . . . . . .39 C4
Mullen Gdns NE28 . . . . . .21 B4
Mullen Rd NE28 . . . . . . . . .21 C4
Mull Gr NE32 . . . . . . . . . . .52 A3
Mundella Terr NE6 . . . . . . .32 C3
Mundle Ave NE21 . . . . . . .41 B1
Murrayfield Rd NE5 . . . . . .16 B3
Murray Gdns **1** NE11 . . .56 C3
Murray Rd NE28 . . . . . . . . .23 A3
Murray St NE21 . . . . . . . . .41 B3
Muscott Gr NE15 . . . . . . . .28 B2
Musgrave Prim Sch

  NE9 . . . . . . . . . . . . . . . . . . .58 B2
Musgrave Rd NE9 . . . . . . .58 B2
Musgrave Terr

  Gateshead NE10 . . . . . . . . .48 C1
  Newcastle-u-T NE6 . . . . . .33 C2
Muswell Hill NE15 . . . . . . .28 B1
Mutual St NE28 . . . . . . . . .21 C1
Myreside Pl NE12 . . . . . . .10 C3
Myrtle Ave NE11 . . . . . . . .56 B4
Myrtle Gr

  Gateshead NE11 . . . . . . . . .58 B1
  Newcastle-u-T NE2 . . . . . .18 C2
  Wallsend NE28 . . . . . . . . . .22 B1
Myrtle Rd NE21 . . . . . . . . .41 B1

**N**

Nafferton Pl NE5 . . . . . . . .29 A4
Nailsworth Cl NE35 . . . . . .52 A2
Nairn Cl DH3 . . . . . . . . . . . .70 C2
Nairn St NE32 . . . . . . . . . . .52 A3
Nansen Cl NE5 . . . . . . . . . .15 A2
Napier Ct NE16 . . . . . . . . . .62 C4
Napier Rd NE16 . . . . . . . . .42 C1
Napier St NE32 . . . . . . . . . .36 C3
Napier Way NE21 . . . . . . . .42 A2
Narvik Way NE29 . . . . . . . .23 C4
Navenby Cl NE3 . . . . . . . . . .9 B4
Naworth Dr NE5 . . . . . . . . .14 C3
Naworth Terr NE32 . . . . . .51 C4
Naylor Ave NE21 . . . . . . . . .53 B2
Naylor Bldgs NE21 . . . . . . .53 B2
Naylor Ct NE21 . . . . . . . . . .42 A4
Neale Terr **1** DH3 . . . . . . .70 B4
Nearlane Cl NE13 . . . . . . . .2 C4
Nedderton Cl NE5 . . . . . . .13 C4
Neill Dr NE16 . . . . . . . . . . .62 C2
Neilson Rd NE10 . . . . . . . .47 A3
Nelson Ave NE3 . . . . . . . . . .8 B1
Nelson Cres NE29 . . . . . . .24 B2
Nelson Rd NE6 . . . . . . . . . .49 A4
Nelson St

  Dunston NE11 . . . . . . . . . . .44 B2
  Gateshead NE8 . . . . . . . . . .78 C3
  Greenside NE40 . . . . . . . . .38 B1
Nelson Terr NE29 . . . . . . . .24 B3
Neptune Rd

  Newcastle-u-T, Denton

    Burn NE15 . . . . . . . . . . . . .27 C3
  Newcastle-u-T, Lemington

    NE15 . . . . . . . . . . . . . . . . .27 B2
  Wallsend NE28 . . . . . . . . . .34 C4
Ness Ct NE21 . . . . . . . . . . .40 C2
Nest Rd NE10 . . . . . . . . . . .47 C2
Netherby Dr NE5 . . . . . . . .29 A4
Nether Farm Rd NE10 . .48 B1
Netherton Gdns NE13 . . . .2 B2
Netherwitton Way NE3 . .4 B1
Neville Cres DH3 . . . . . . . .68 B2
Neville Rd NE15 . . . . . . . . .27 C3
Neville's Cross Rd NE31 36 A1
Neville St NE1 . . . . . . . . . . .78 A4
Newarth Cl NE15 . . . . . . . .27 C3
Newbank Wlk NE21 . . . . . .40 C1
Newbiggin Hall Ctr NE5 .6 B1
Newbiggin La NE15 . . . . . .15 A4
Newbold St NE6 . . . . . . . . .33 B1
Newbolt Ct NE8 . . . . . . . . .46 C2
Newbrough Cres NE2 . . .18 C2
NEWBURN . . . . . . . . . . . . . .26 A3
Newburn Bridge Rd NE15,

  NE21 . . . . . . . . . . . . . . . . . .25 C2
Newburn Hall Motor

  Mus* NE15 . . . . . . . . . . . .26 A4
NEWBURN HAUGH . . . . . .41 B4
Newburn Haugh Ind Est

  NE15 . . . . . . . . . . . . . . . . . .27 A2
Newburn Ind Est NE21 .26 B2
Newburn Lane End

  NE15 . . . . . . . . . . . . . . . . . .12 B2
Newburn Manor Fst Sch

  NE15 . . . . . . . . . . . . . . . . . .26 A3
Newburn Rd

  Newburn NE15 . . . . . . . . . .26 A4
  Throckley NE15 . . . . . . . . .12 C1
Newbury Ave NE8 . . . . . . .57 C4
Newbury Cl NE15 . . . . . . . .27 B3
Newby Pl NE9 . . . . . . . . . . .65 C4
Newcastle Arena NE4 . . .76 C3
Newcastle Bank NE1 . . . .68 A3
Newcastle Bsns Pk NE4 76 A3
Newcastle Coll Trevelyan

  Bldg NE4 . . . . . . . . . . . . . .76 B4
Newcastle Discovery

  Mus* NE1 . . . . . . . . . . . . . .76 C4
Newcastle General Hospl

  NE4 . . . . . . . . . . . . . . . . . . .30 A2
Newcastle International

  Airport NE13 . . . . . . . . . . . .3 B1
Newcastle Rd DH3 . . . . . . .68 B2
Newcastle Trade Ctr

  NE4 . . . . . . . . . . . . . . . . . . .76 B3
Newcastle Upon Tyne

  Central Sta NE1 . . . . . . . . .78 A4
Newdene Wlk NE15 . . . . . .27 B2
Newfield Wlk NE16 . . . . . .54 C2
Newham Ave NE13 . . . . . . .4 A4

Newington Rd NE6 . . . . . .32 B2
Newlands NE3 . . . . . . . . . . . .5 A1
Newlands Rd NE2 . . . . . . .18 B3
Newlands Sch NE5 . . . . . .18 B4
Newlyn Dr NE32 . . . . . . . . .37 B2
Newlyn Rd NE3 . . . . . . . . . .7 C1
Newman Pl **10** NE8 . . . . .58 C4
Newman Terr NE8 . . . . . . .58 C4
Newmarch St NE32 . . . . . .36 B3
Newminster Rd NE4 . . . . .29 B3
Newnham Way NE16 . . . . .54 B1
Newquay Gdns **4** NE9 . .65 B2
New Rd

  Dunston NE11 . . . . . . . . . . .57 A2
  Gateshead NE10 . . . . . . . . .61 B1
New South Terr DH3 . . . . .70 C4
Newton Ave NE28 . . . . . . .23 A3
Newton Cl NE15 . . . . . . . . .27 C3
Newton Pl NE7 . . . . . . . . . .19 C2
Newton Rd NE7 . . . . . . . . .19 C2
Newton St

  Dunston NE11 . . . . . . . . . . .44 B2
  Gateshead NE8 . . . . . . . . . .57 C4
Nichol Ct NE4 . . . . . . . . . . .29 B1
Nichol St NE4 . . . . . . . . . . .29 B1
Nidsdale Ave NE6 . . . . . . . .34 B3
Nile Ct NE15 . . . . . . . . . . . .27 A4
Nile St NE8 . . . . . . . . . . . . .46 C1
Ninth Ave

  Gateshead NE11 . . . . . . . . .64 B3
  Newcastle-u-T NE6 . . . . . .33 A4
Ninth Ave E NE11 . . . . . . .64 B3
Nithdale Cl NE6 . . . . . . . . .34 C4
Nixon St NE8 . . . . . . . . . . . .46 C4
Noble Gdns NE34 . . . . . . . .52 B4
Noble St

  **3** Gateshead NE10 . . . . .47 C1
  Newcastle-u-T NE4 . . . . . .44 B3
Noel Ave NE21 . . . . . . . . . .53 B2
Noel Terr NE21 . . . . . . . . . .53 C3
Nolan Hall NE32 . . . . . . . .36 C2
Norbury Gr NE6 . . . . . . . . .33 B1
Norfolk Ave DH3 . . . . . . . .70 C1
Norfolk Gdns NE28 . . . . . .22 C4
Norfolk Pl DH3 . . . . . . . . . .70 C1
Norfolk Rd NE8 . . . . . . . . .46 C4
Norfolk Sq **11** NE6 . . . . . .32 C2
Norfolk Way NE15 . . . . . . .27 C3
Norham Cl NE13 . . . . . . . . .2 A1
Norham Dr NE5 . . . . . . . . .14 C3
Norham Pl NE2 . . . . . . . . . .18 C1
Norham Rd NE8 . . . . . . . . .8 C2
Norham Terr NE32 . . . . . . .51 A3
Norhurst NE16 . . . . . . . . . .54 A1
Norland Rd NE15 . . . . . . . .28 A2
Norman Terr NE28 . . . . . . .23 C2
Normount Ave **2** NE4 . .29 C1
Normount Gdns NE4 . . . . .29 C2
Normount Rd NE4 . . . . . . .29 C2
North Ave

  Longbenton NE12 . . . . . . .11 B2
  Newcastle-u-T, Gosforth

    NE3 . . . . . . . . . . . . . . . . . .18 A4
  Newcastle-u-T NE5 . . . . . .15 A2
Northbourne Ho NE9 . . . .58 B1
Northbourne Rd NE31,

  NE32 . . . . . . . . . . . . . . . . . .36 B2
Northbourne St

  Gateshead NE8 . . . . . . . . . .58 B4
  Newcastle-u-T NE4 . . . . . .44 B4
North Cl

  **4** Newcastle-u-T NE6 . . .33 A3
  Ryton NE40 . . . . . . . . . . . . .25 A1
Northcote NE16 . . . . . . . . .54 C1
Northcote Ave NE5 . . . . . .14 A1
North Croft NE12 . . . . . . . .11 C3
North Cross St NE3 . . . . . . .9 A1
North Cl **5** NE32 . . . . . . .36 C3
North Dene DH3 . . . . . . . . .68 B3
North Dr NE31 . . . . . . . . . .49 B4
North East Bus Mus*

  NE10 . . . . . . . . . . . . . . . . . .61 A2
North Eastern Ct NE16 . .56 A4
Northern Counties Sch

  NE2 . . . . . . . . . . . . . . . . . . .18 B1
North Farm Rd NE31 . . . .35 B1
North Fawdon Prim Sch

  NE3 . . . . . . . . . . . . . . . . . . . .8 A3
Northfield Cl NE16 . . . . . . .54 B1
Northfield Rd NE3 . . . . . . .17 C4
Northfields Cl **28** NE6 . .33 A4

Northfields Ho 22 NE6 . .33 A3
North Gr NE40 . . . . . . . .25 B1
North Jesmond Ave
NE2 . . . . . . . . . . . . . . . .18 C2
Northlands NE21 . . . . . .41 A1
Northlea NE15 . . . . . . . .27 C4
North Lodge Apartments
11 NE21 . . . . . . . . . . . . .41 A1
Northmoor Rd NE6 . . . .33 C4
North Rd
Boldon Colliery NE35 . .52 A1
Wallsend NE28 . . . . . . .21 C2
Northside DH3 . . . . . . . .68 C2
NORTH SIDE . . . . . . . . .68 C2
North Side NE8 . . . . . . .77 B2
North St
Birtley DH3 . . . . . . . . . .71 A3
Blaydon NE21 . . . . . . . .40 C2
Jarrow NE32 . . . . . . . . .36 C3
North Terr NE28 . . . . . .22 C2
Northumberland Ave
Longbenton NE12 . . . . .11 B3
Newcastle-u-T NE3 . . . .17 B3
Wallsend NE28 . . . . . . .23 A4
Northumberland Ct
NE31 . . . . . . . . . . . . . . .35 B1
Northumberland Dock Rd
NE28 . . . . . . . . . . . . . . .24 A1
Northumberland Gdns
Newcastle-u-T, Jesmond
Vale NE2 . . . . . . . . . . . .32 B4
Newcastle-u-T NE5 . . . .13 C3
Northumberland Pl
DH3 . . . . . . . . . . . . . . . .70 C1
Northumberland Rd
Newcastle-u-T, Lemington
NE15 . . . . . . . . . . . . . . .27 A2
Ryton NE40 . . . . . . . . . .25 A2
Northumberland St
Gateshead NE8 . . . . . . .77 C1
Wallsend NE28 . . . . . . .22 A2
Northumberland Terr
25 Newcastle-u-T NE6 . .32 C2
Wallsend NE28 . . . . . . .23 A2
Northumberland Villas
NE28 . . . . . . . . . . . . . . .22 C2
Northumbria Lodge
NE5 . . . . . . . . . . . . . . . .16 C1
Northumbria Univ, Coach
Lane Campus NE7 . . . .20 A4
Northumbria Wlk
Newcastle-u-T, East
Denton NE5 . . . . . . . . .15 B2
Newcastle-u-T NE5 . . . .15 A1
North View
Gateshead NE9 . . . . . . .65 C3
Hazlerigg NE13 . . . . . . . .4 A4
Jarrow NE32 . . . . . . . . .36 B2
4 Longbenton NE12 . . . .11 B4
Newcastle-u-T NE6 . . . .32 C3
Newcastle-u-T NE6 . . . .33 A4
Wallsend NE28 . . . . . . .22 A2
Whickham NE11 . . . . . .54 C3
North View Terr NE8 . . .47 B1
NORTH WALBOTTLE . . .13 B3
North Walbottle Rd
Newcastle-u-T NE5 . . . .13 C4
Walbottle NE15 . . . . . . .13 B2
Northway
Gateshead NE9 . . . . . . .59 A3
Throckley NE15 . . . . . . .12 B2
North West Side NE8 . . .77 B2
Norton Way NE15 . . . . .27 C2
Norwich Ave NE13 . . . . . .2 B1
Norwich Way NE32 . . . .51 A1
Norwood Ave
Newcastle-u-T, Brunton
Park NE3 . . . . . . . . . . . . .4 C1
Newcastle-u-T, Heaton
NE6 . . . . . . . . . . . . . . . .19 C1
Norwood Ct
Gateshead NE9 . . . . . . .66 A2
Longbenton NE12 . . . . .11 B2
Norwood Gdns 4 NE9 . .58 C4
Norwood Rd
Gateshead NE11 . . . . . .57 A1
Newcastle-u-T NE15 . . .27 B4
November Ctyd NE8 . . . .77 B2
Nuneaton Way NE5 . . . .13 C4
Nunn Gdns 12 NE16 . . . .54 C3
Nuns La NE8 . . . . . . . . .78 C3
Nuns Moor Cres NE4 . . .29 C3

Nuns Moor Rd NE4 . . . .29 C3
Nunwick Way NE7 . . . . .20 B4
Nursery Gdns NE5 . . . . .28 C4
Nursery La NE10 . . . . . .59 B3
Nutley Pl NE15 . . . . . . .28 B1

**O**

Oak Ave NE11 . . . . . . . .56 B3
Oakdale Cl NE15 . . . . . .27 B2
Oakenshaw NE15 . . . . . .27 C2
Oakfield Ave NE16 . . . . .55 A2
Oakfield Cl NE16 . . . . . .55 A2
Oakfield Dr NE16 . . . . . .55 A2
Oakfield Gdns
Newcastle-u-T NE15 . . .29 B1
Wallsend NE28 . . . . . . .21 A3
Oakfield Inf & Jun Schs
NE9 . . . . . . . . . . . . . . . .65 A3
Oakfield Rd
Dunston NE11 . . . . . . . .56 C2
Newcastle-u-T NE3 . . . .17 C3
Whickham NE16 . . . . . .54 C1
Oakfield Terr
Gateshead NE10 . . . . . .48 C1
Newcastle-u-T NE3 . . . .17 C4
Oak Gr
Longbenton NE12 . . . . .11 B4
Wallsend NE28 . . . . . . .22 B1
Oakham Ave NE16 . . . . .54 B2
Oakhurst Dr NE3 . . . . . .17 B3
Oakhurst Terr NE12 . . . .11 B3
Oakland Rd NE2 . . . . . .18 B2
Oaklands
Newcastle-u-T NE3 . . . .18 A3
Whickham NE16 . . . . . .55 B4
Oaklands Ave NE3 . . . . .18 A3
Oakridge NE16 . . . . . . .54 B2
Oak Sq NE8 . . . . . . . . . .77 C1
Oak St
Jarrow NE32 . . . . . . . . .36 B3
Seaton Burn NE13 . . . . . .2 C4
1 Throckley NE15 . . . . .12 B2
Oaks The NE40 . . . . . . .39 A1
Oak Terr NE21 . . . . . . . .41 B1
Oaktree Ave NE6 . . . . . .21 B1
Oakwellgate NE8 . . . . . .78 C4
Oakwood
Gateshead NE10 . . . . . .60 A1
Hebburn NE31 . . . . . . . .35 A3
Oakwood Ave
Gateshead NE9 . . . . . . .65 B3
Wideopen NE13 . . . . . . .2 C1
Oakwood Cl NE16 . . . . .67 A1
Oakwood Gdns NE11 . . .57 A1
Oakwood Pl 2 NE5 . . . .16 A1
Oban Ave NE28 . . . . . . .23 A4
Oban Ct NE6 . . . . . . . . .33 A1
Oban Gdns 9 NE6 . . . . .33 A1
Oban St
Brockley Whins NE32 . .52 A3
Gateshead NE10 . . . . . .47 B1
Octavia Ct NE28 . . . . . .23 A4
Octavian Way NE11 . . . .64 A3
October Ctyd NE8 . . . . .77 B2
Office Row NE38 . . . . . .71 C1
Off Quay Bldg The NE6 .32 C1
Ogle Ave NE13 . . . . . . . .4 A4
Ogle Gr NE32 . . . . . . . .50 C3
O'Hanlon Cres NE28 . . .21 B4
Oil Mill Rd NE6 . . . . . . .34 C3
Okehampton Ct 2 NE9 .65 B2
OLD BENWELL . . . . . . . .28 C1
Old Durham Rd NE8,
NE9 . . . . . . . . . . . . . . . .59 A2
Old Farm Ct NE16 . . . . .62 C2
Oldfield Rd NE6 . . . . . . .48 B2
Old Fold Rd NE10, NE8 .47 A2
OLD FORT . . . . . . . . . . .47 B1
Old Main St NE40 . . . . .38 A3
Old Vicarage Wlk 21
NE6 . . . . . . . . . . . . . . . .33 A2
Old Well Ave 4 NE21 . . .41 A1
Old Well La NE21 . . . . . .41 A1
Olive Gdns NE9 . . . . . . .58 C2
Olive Pl NE4 . . . . . . . . .29 B3
Oliver Ave NE4 . . . . . . .29 C2
Oliver Cres DH3 . . . . . . .68 B2
Ollerton Gdns NE10 . . . .59 B2
Ongar Way NE12 . . . . . .10 C3
Onslow Gdns NE9 . . . . .58 B1
Orange Gr NE16 . . . . . . .55 B4

Orchard Cl NE16 . . . . . .62 C3
Orchard Ct
Greenside NE40 . . . . . . .38 B1
Ryton NE40 . . . . . . . . . .25 A1
Orchard Gdns
Gateshead NE9 . . . . . . .65 B4
Wallsend NE28 . . . . . . .21 B4
Orchard-Leigh NE15 . . .27 C2
Orchard Pk 8 DH3 . . . . .70 B4
Orchard Pl NE2 . . . . . . .19 A1
Orchard Rd NE16 . . . . . .55 B3
Orchard Rise NE15 . . . . .26 C3
Orchard St
Birtley DH3 . . . . . . . . . .70 B4
Newcastle-u-T NE1 . . . .78 A4
Orchard Terr
Newcastle-u-T NE15 . . .27 A2
8 Throckley NE15 . . . . .12 B2
Orchard The
Newcastle-u-T NE15 . . .27 B2
Whickham NE16 . . . . . .55 B3
Ord Ct NE4 . . . . . . . . . .29 B3
Orde Ave NE28 . . . . . . .22 C3
Ordley Cl NE15 . . . . . . .27 C2
Ord St NE4 . . . . . . . . . .76 C3
Oriole Ho NE12 . . . . . . .11 B3
Ormiscraig NE15 . . . . . .27 C2
Ormiston NE15 . . . . . . .27 C2
Ormonde Ave NE15 . . . .28 B2
Ormonde St NE32 . . . . .36 C3
Ormsby Gn NE5 . . . . . . .28 B4
Ormskirk Cl NE15 . . . . .27 B2
Orpington Ave NE6 . . . .33 C2
Orton Cl NE4 . . . . . . . . .44 A4
Orwell Gn NE3 . . . . . . . .16 C3
Osbaldeston Gdns NE3 .17 C3
Osborne Ave NE2 . . . . . .18 C2
Osborne Rd NE2 . . . . . .18 C2
Osborne Terr NE8 . . . . .79 A1
Oslo Cl NE29 . . . . . . . . .23 C4
Osprey House 4 NE2 . . .18 C1
Oswald Terr NE8 . . . . . .79 A1
Oswald Wlk NE3 . . . . . . .9 C1
Oswin Ave NE12 . . . . . .11 B4
Otterburn Ave NE3 . . . .17 B4
Otterburn Ct NE8 . . . . .79 A1
Otterburn Gdns
Dunston NE11 . . . . . . . .56 C3
Gateshead NE9 . . . . . . .58 A1
Whickham NE16 . . . . . .55 A3
Otterburn Terr NE2 . . . .18 C1
Ottercap Cl NE15 . . . . . .27 B2
Ottershaw NE15 . . . . . . .27 C2
Ottovale Cres NE21 . . . .40 C1
Ottringham Cl NE15 . . . .27 B2
Oulton Cl NE5 . . . . . . . .15 C4
Our Lady & St Anne's RC
Prim Sch NE4 . . . . . . . .76 C4
Ousby Ct NE3 . . . . . . . . .7 B3
Ouseburn Rd
Newcastle-u-T, Jesmond
Vale NE2, NE6 . . . . . . . .32 B4
Newcastle-u-T, St Ann's
NE1 . . . . . . . . . . . . . . . .32 B2
Ouse St NE1 . . . . . . . . .32 B1
Ouston Cl NE10 . . . . . . .61 B3
Ouston St NE15 . . . . . . .28 A1
Oval Park View NE10 . . .59 C3
Oval The
Longbenton NE12 . . . . .11 C2
Newcastle-u-T NE6 . . . .47 C4
Woolsington NE13 . . . . . .6 A4
Overdene NE15 . . . . . . .28 A3
Overfield Rd NE3 . . . . . . .8 A1
Overhill Terr NE8 . . . . . .79 A1
Overstone Ave NE40 . . .38 B2
Overton Cl NE15 . . . . . .27 B2
Ovett Gdns NE8 . . . . . . .47 A2
Ovingham Gdns NE13 . . .2 B2
Ovington Gr 10 NE5 . . . .29 B4
Owlet Cl NE21 . . . . . . . .40 C1
Oxberry Gdns NE10 . . . .59 B3
Oxclose Com Sch NE38 .71 C4
Oxclose Village Prim Sch
NE38 . . . . . . . . . . . . . . .69 C1
Oxford Ave NE28 . . . . . .21 B3
Oxford Cres NE31 . . . . .36 A2
Oxford Pl DH3 . . . . . . . .70 B1
Oxford Terr NE8 . . . . . . .79 B1
Oxford Way NE32 . . . . . .51 A1
Oxley Mews 7 NE35 . . . .52 A1

Oxted Pl NE6 . . . . . . . . .48 A3

**P**

Paddock The
Gateshead NE10 . . . . . .60 B2
Walbottle NE15 . . . . . . .13 A1
Woolsington NE13 . . . . . .6 A4
Pader Cl NE23 . . . . . . . . .2 B1
Padstow Gdns NE9 . . . . .65 A2
Padstow Rd NE29 . . . . .24 C4
Page St NE31 . . . . . . . . .36 A3
Paignton Ave NE4 . . . . .30 A1
Palace St NE4 . . . . . . . .76 B4
Pallinsburn Ct NE5 . . . .15 C3
Palm Ave NE4 . . . . . . . .29 B3
Palmer Community Hospl
NE32 . . . . . . . . . . . . . . .36 C3
Palmer Cres NE31 . . . . .36 A2
Palmer Gdns NE10 . . . . .61 B4
Palmer St NE32 . . . . . . .36 B3
Palmerston Ave NE6 . . .33 C3
Palmerston Wlk 5 NE8 . .79 A2
Pankhurst Gdns NE10 . .61 C4
Parade Cl NE6 . . . . . . . .34 B1
Parade The NE6 . . . . . . .34 B1
PARADISE . . . . . . . . . . .43 B4
Park Ave
Blaydon, Bleach Green
NE21 . . . . . . . . . . . . . . .41 A2
Blaydon NE21 . . . . . . . .41 B2
Dunston NE11 . . . . . . . .56 A3
Newcastle-u-T, Fawdon
NE3 . . . . . . . . . . . . . . . . .8 A3
Newcastle-u-T, Gosforth
NE3 . . . . . . . . . . . . . . . . .8 C2
Wallsend NE28 . . . . . . .21 C2
Park Cl NE4 . . . . . . . . . .76 A4
Park Ct
Gateshead, Chowdene
NE11 . . . . . . . . . . . . . . .64 B3
Gateshead NE8 . . . . . . .78 C3
Wallsend NE6 . . . . . . . .21 B1
Parkdale Rise NE16 . . . .54 C3
Park Dr
Longbenton NE12 . . . . .11 C4
Newcastle-u-T NE3 . . . . .4 C1
Whickham NE16 . . . . . .55 B4
Parker Ave NE3 . . . . . . .17 C3
Parker Ct NE11 . . . . . . .44 A2
Parkfield NE32 . . . . . . . .51 B1
Park Field NE40 . . . . . . .25 A1
Parkgate La NE21 . . . . . .53 A4
Parkhead Com Prim Sch
NE21 . . . . . . . . . . . . . . .53 B4
Parkhead Gdns NE21 . . .53 A4
Park Head Rd NE7 . . . . .19 B1
Parkhead Sq NE21 . . . . .41 B1
Parkin Gdns NE10 . . . . .60 A3
Parkinson's Cotts NE40 .40 A4
Park La
Blaydon NE21 . . . . . . . .53 A4
Gateshead NE8 . . . . . . .46 C3
Parkland
Longbenton NE12 . . . . .11 B2
Ryton NE21 . . . . . . . . . .40 C4
Parkland Ave NE21 . . . . .53 A4
Parklands NE10 . . . . . . .61 B4
Parklands Ct NE10 . . . . .49 B1
Parklands Way NE10 . . .61 B4
Park Rd
Gateshead NE10, NE8 . .47 A2
Hebburn NE31 . . . . . . . .35 C1
Jarrow NE32 . . . . . . . . .36 B2
Newburn NE15 . . . . . . .26 A4
Newcastle-u-T NE4 . . . .76 A3
Wallsend NE28 . . . . . . .22 A1
Park Rise NE15 . . . . . . . .27 A3
Park Row 8 NE10 . . . . .59 C4
Parkside
Dunston NE11 . . . . . . . .56 B4
Hebburn NE31 . . . . . . . .49 C4
Throckley NE15 . . . . . . .12 C1
Wallsend NE28 . . . . . . .22 B1
Parkside Ave
Blaydon NE21 . . . . . . . .41 B1
Newcastle-u-T NE7 . . . .10 C1
Parkside Ct NE13 . . . . . . .2 C2
Parkside Terr NE28 . . . .21 B4
Park Terr
Blaydon NE21 . . . . . . . .41 C2

**Park Terr** continued
Dunston NE11 . . . . . . . .56 B4
Wallsend NE28 . . . . . . .21 C2
Whickham NE16 . . . . . .42 C1
Park View
Blaydon NE21 . . . . . . . .53 B4
Jarrow NE32 . . . . . . . . .51 A4
Longbenton, Forest Hall
NE12 . . . . . . . . . . . . . . .11 B4
Newcastle-u-T NE6 . . . .34 B1
Wallsend NE28 . . . . . . .21 C2
Wideopen NE13 . . . . . . .2 C2
Park View Cl NE40 . . . . .25 B1
Park View Gdns NE40 . .25 B1
Park Villas NE28 . . . . . .21 C2
Parkville NE6 . . . . . . . . .32 B3
Parkway NE14 . . . . . . . .54 A2
Parliament St NE31 . . . .35 A3
Parmontley St NE15 . . .28 A1
Parson's Ave NE6 . . . . . .34 A1
Parsons' Gdns 5 NE11 . .44 B1
Partridge Cl NE38 . . . . .71 B4
PATH HEAD . . . . . . . . . .41 A3
Pathside NE32 . . . . . . . .51 B2
Path The 8 NE9 . . . . . . .65 A4
Patience Ave NE13 . . . . . .2 C4
Patina Ct NE15 . . . . . . . .29 A4
Patterdale Gdns NE7 . . .19 C4
Patterdale Terr NE8 . . . .58 B4
Patterson St NE21 . . . . .42 A4
Pattinson Gdns
Gateshead, Carr Hill
NE9 . . . . . . . . . . . . . . . .59 A3
Gateshead, Old Fold
NE10 . . . . . . . . . . . . . . .47 B2
Pauline Gdns NE15 . . . .28 B3
Paulsway NE32 . . . . . . . .37 C2
Pavilion The NE16 . . . . .42 B1
Paxford Cl NE7 . . . . . . .10 B1
Peacock Ct NE11 . . . . . .57 A3
Pearth Edge 2 NE9 . . . . .67 A1
Peareth Ct NE8 . . . . . . .78 C3
Peareth Hall Rd NE37,
NE9 . . . . . . . . . . . . . . . .67 B2
Pearson Pl NE32 . . . . . .37 A4
Peartree Gdns NE6 . . . .21 B1
Peary Cl NE5 . . . . . . . . .15 A2
Pease Ave NE15 . . . . . . .29 A2
Peel Ct NE13 . . . . . . . . . .2 B4
Peel Gdns NE34 . . . . . . .52 A4
Peel La NE1 . . . . . . . . . .76 C4
Peel St NE1 . . . . . . . . . .76 C4
PELAW . . . . . . . . . . . . . .48 B1
Pelaw Ind Est NE10 . . . .61 C4
Pelaw Sta NE10 . . . . . . .48 C1
Pelaw Way NE10 . . . . . .48 C1
Peldon Cl NE7 . . . . . . . .10 A1
Pelham St NE1 . . . . . . . .7 B3
Pembridge NE38 . . . . . .69 C1
Pembroke Ave
Birtley DH3 . . . . . . . . . .70 C1
Newcastle-u-T NE6 . . . .33 C3
Pembroke Ct NE3 . . . . . .7 B3
Pembroke Gdns NE28 . .23 B4
Pembrooke Ave NE6 . . .33 C3
Pendower Way NE15 . . .29 A1
Penfold Cl NE7 . . . . . . .20 A4
Pennine Gdns NE11 . . . .56 C2
Pennine Way NE12 . . . .10 B2
Penn St NE4 . . . . . . . . . .76 B3
Pennyfine Rd NE16 . . . .63 B2
Penrith Gdns NE9 . . . . .65 C4
Penrith Gdns NE9 . . . . .65 C4
Penrith Rd NE31 . . . . . .50 B4
Penrose Gn NE3 . . . . . . .8 A1
Pensford Ct NE3 . . . . . . .7 A2
Penshaw Gn NE5 . . . . . .16 B3
Penshaw View
Birtley DH3 . . . . . . . . . .71 A3
Gateshead NE10 . . . . . .61 B4
Hebburn NE31 . . . . . . . .50 A4
Jarrow NE31 . . . . . . . . .51 A4
Penshaw Way DH3 . . . . .71 A4
Pensher St E NE10 . . . . .47 B1
Pensher St NE10 . . . . . .47 B1
Pent Cl NE40 . . . . . . . . .38 C2
Pentland Gdns NE11 . . .56 C3
Penyghent Way NE37 . . .69 C2

Penzance Par NE31 . . . . . .50 C2
Peppercorn Ct NE1 . . . . . .78 B4
Percy Cres NE29 . . . . . . . .24 B3
Percy Ct NE29 . . . . . . . . . .24 B3
Percy Gdns
Dunston NE11 . . . . . . . . . .56 C3
Longbenton NE12 . . . . . . .11 B4
Percy Hedley Sch NE12 .11 B3
PERCY MAIN . . . . . . . . . .24 B3
Percy Main Prim Sch
NE29 . . . . . . . . . . . . . . . . . .24 B2
Percy Main Sta NE29 . .24 B3
Percy Main Village Sta
NE29 . . . . . . . . . . . . . . . . . .24 A3
Percy St
Jarrow NE32 . . . . . . . . . . .37 A3
Newcastle-u-T, Lemington
NE15 . . . . . . . . . . . . . . . . . .27 A2
Wallsend NE28 . . . . . . . . .22 A2
Percy Terr
Newburn NE15 . . . . . . . . .26 A3
Newcastle-u-T NE3 . . . . . .9 C1
Percy Way NE15 . . . . . . .13 B1
Peregrine Pl NE12 . . . . . .10 B3
Perry St NE8, NE9 . . . . . .58 B4
Perth Ave NE32, NE34 . . .52 A3
Perth Cl NE28 . . . . . . . . . .23 A4
Perth Ct NE11 . . . . . . . . . .64 C3
Perth Gdns NE28 . . . . . . .23 A4
Peterborough Cl NE8 . .79 B2
Peterborough Way
NE32 . . . . . . . . . . . . . . . . . .51 A1
Petherton Ct NE3 . . . . . . .7 A2
Peth La NE40 . . . . . . . . . .25 B2
Petteril NE38 . . . . . . . . . .71 C1
Pexton Way NE15 . . . . . .26 B4
Pheasantmoor 3 NE37 .69 C3
Philiphaugh NE28 . . . . . .34 C4
Philip's Ct 3 NE9 . . . . . .59 A1
Philipson St NE6 . . . . . . .34 A2
Phillips Ave NE16 . . . . . .54 C4
Phoenix Rd NE38 . . . . . .69 A2
Picherwell NE10 . . . . . . . .59 C3
Pickering Ct NE32 . . . . . .36 B3
Pickering Gn NE9 . . . . . .65 C2
Picktree Lodge NE38 . . .71 A1
Pikestone Cl NE38 . . . . . .71 C3
Pilgrim St NE1 . . . . . . . . .78 B4
Pilgrimsway
Gateshead NE9 . . . . . . . . .59 A3
Jarrow NE32 . . . . . . . . . . .37 C2
Pilton Rd NE5 . . . . . . . . . .15 A3
Pilton Wlk 4 NE5 . . . . . .15 A3
Pimlico Ct NE9 . . . . . . . . .65 A4
Pine Ave NE3 . . . . . . . . . . .8 A3
Pine Rd NE21 . . . . . . . . . .41 B2
Pine St
Birtley DH3 . . . . . . . . . . . .68 B1
Greenside NE40 . . . . . . . .39 A1
Jarrow NE32 . . . . . . . . . . .36 B2
Seaton Burn NE13 . . . . . . .2 C4
Throckley NE15 . . . . . . . .12 B3
Pines The
Greenside NE40 . . . . . . . .39 A1
Newcastle-u-T NE4 . . . . . .76 A3
Pinetree Way NE11 . . . . .43 A2
Pinewood NE31 . . . . . . . .35 A3
Pinewood Ave NE13 . . . . .2 C1
Pinewood Cl
Newcastle-u-T, Kingston
Park NE3 . . . . . . . . . . . . . . .6 C3
Newcastle-u-T, Walkerville
NE6 . . . . . . . . . . . . . . . . . . .21 A1
Pinewood Gdns NE11 . .56 C1
Pink La NE1 . . . . . . . . . . . .76 C4
Pinner Pl NE6 . . . . . . . . . .48 A4
Pintail Ct 10 NE34 . . . . . .52 C4
Pipershaw NE37 . . . . . . . .69 B2
Pipe Track La NE4 . . . . . .54 C4
Pipewellgate NE1 . . . . . .78 B3
Planesway NE10 . . . . . . . .60 A1
Planetree Ave NE4 . . . . . .29 B4
Plantation Ave NE16 . . . .54 C4
Plantation Gr NE10 . . . . .49 B2
Plantation St NE28 . . . . . .34 C4
Plantation The NE6 . . . . .48 B4
Plawsworth Gdns NE9 . .66 A3
Pleasant Pl 5 DH3 . . . . . .68 B1
Plenmeller Pl NE16 . . . . .62 B3

Plessey Terr NE7 . . . . . . .19 C2
Plover Cl 5 NE38 . . . . . . .71 B3
Plover Lodge DH3 . . . . . .68 B2
Plummer St NE4 . . . . . . . .76 C3
Point Pleasant Ind Est
NE28 . . . . . . . . . . . . . . . . . .23 A1
Point Pleasant Terr
NE28 . . . . . . . . . . . . . . . . . .22 C1
Polmaise St NE21 . . . . . .41 B2
Polpero Cl DH3 . . . . . . . . .70 C3
Polwarth Cres NE3 . . . . . .9 A4
Polwarth Dr NE3 . . . . . . . .4 C1
Polwarth Pl NE3 . . . . . . . .4 C1
Polwarth Rd NE3 . . . . . . . .4 C1
Pontdyke NE10 . . . . . . . . .67 A4
Ponteland Cl NE38 . . . . . .71 B4
Ponteland Rd
Newcastle-u-T, Blakelaw
NE5 . . . . . . . . . . . . . . . . . . .16 B3
Newcastle-u-T, Kenton
Bankfoot NE3 . . . . . . . . . . .6 C2
Woolsington NE13 . . . . . . .6 B3
Pooley Cl NE5 . . . . . . . . . .15 C1
Pooley Rd NE5 . . . . . . . . .15 C1
Poplar Ave NE6 . . . . . . . .21 A1
Poplar Cl NE31 . . . . . . . . .50 A3
Poplar Cres
Birtley DH3 . . . . . . . . . . . .68 A1
Dunston NE11 . . . . . . . . . .56 B3
Gateshead NE8 . . . . . . . . .79 B2
Poplar Gr NE9 . . . . . . . . . .9 A1
Poplar Rd NE21 . . . . . . . .41 B1
Poplar St NE15 . . . . . . . . .12 B3
Poplars The
Newcastle-u-T, Elswick
NE4 . . . . . . . . . . . . . . . . . . .76 A3
Newcastle-u-T, Gosforth
NE3 . . . . . . . . . . . . . . . . . . .18 A3
Popplewell Gdns NE9 . . .65 B4
Porlock Ho NE32 . . . . . . .37 B1
Porlock Rd NE32 . . . . . . .37 B1
Portland Gdns 1 NE9 . . .65 A2
Portland Rd NE15 . . . . . . .12 C2
Portland St
Gateshead NE10 . . . . . . . .48 C1
Newcastle-u-T NE4 . . . . . .44 B4
Portman Pl NE6 . . . . . . . .48 A3
Portmarnock NE37 . . . . . .67 C2
Portmeads Rd DH3 . . . . .70 C4
Portmeads Rise DH3 . . . .70 C4
PORTOBELLO . . . . . . . . .71 A4
Portobello Ind Est DH3 .71 A4
Portobello Prim Sch
DH3 . . . . . . . . . . . . . . . . . . .70 C2
Portobello Terr DH3 . . . .71 A2
Portobello Way DH3 . . . .70 C1
Portree Cl DH3 . . . . . . . . .70 C1
Portrush Way NE7 . . . . . .11 A1
Portugal Pl NE28 . . . . . . .21 C1
Potter St
Jarrow NE32 . . . . . . . . . . .36 B3
Wallsend NE28 . . . . . . . . .23 B1
Pottersway NE9 . . . . . . . .59 A3
Pottery Bank NE6 . . . . . .48 B3
Pottery La NE1 . . . . . . . . .76 C3
Potts St NE6 . . . . . . . . . . .33 A2
Powburn Gdns NE4 . . . . .29 C4
Poynings Cl NE5 . . . . . . . .7 A1
Praetorian Dr NE28 . . . . .21 C1
Precinct The NE21 . . . . . .41 C3
Prefect Pl NE9 . . . . . . . . .58 C3
Prendwick Ave NE31 . . . .49 C3
Prendwick Ct NE31 . . . . .49 C3
Prensgarth Way NE34 . .52 B3
Prestmede NE10 . . . . . . . .60 A3
Prestwick NE10 . . . . . . . .60 A1
Prestwick Dr NE10 . . . . . .61 B3
Prestwick Gdns NE3 . . . .17 A4
Prestwick Terr NE20 . . . . .3 A1
Pretoria St NE15 . . . . . . . .28 B1
Price St NE1 . . . . . . . . . . . .35 A3
Priestley Ct NE34 . . . . . . .52 C3
Priestley Gdns NE10 . . . .61 A3
PRIMROSE . . . . . . . . . . . .51 B3
Primrose Gdns NE28 . . . .21 B4
Primrose Hill NE9 . . . . . .58 C1
Primrose Hill Hospl
NE32 . . . . . . . . . . . . . . . . . .51 B4
Primrose Hill Terr NE32 .51 B3
Primrose Terr
Birtley DH3 . . . . . . . . . . . .70 C4
Jarrow NE32 . . . . . . . . . . .51 B4

Prince Consort Ind Est
NE31 . . . . . . . . . . . . . . . . . .35 A3
Prince Consort La NE31 35 B2
Prince Consort Rd
Gateshead NE8 . . . . . . . . .79 C1
Hebburn NE31 . . . . . . . . .35 A3
Jarrow NE32 . . . . . . . . . . .37 A2
Prince Philip Cl NE15 . .29 A1
Prince Rd NE28 . . . . . . . .21 C3
Princes Ave NE3 . . . . . . . .8 C3
Princes Cl NE3 . . . . . . . . .8 C4
Prince's Mdw NE3 . . . . . .8 B1
Princes Pk
Dunston NE11 . . . . . . . . . .57 A2
Gateshead NE8 . . . . . . . . .57 B1
Princes Rd NE3 . . . . . . . . .4 B1
Princess Dr NE8 . . . . . . . .77 A1
Princess St
Gateshead NE10 . . . . . . . .48 C1
Sunniside NE16 . . . . . . . .62 C2
Princesway NE11 . . . . . . .57 B1
Princesway Central
NE11 . . . . . . . . . . . . . . . . . .64 A4
Princesway S NE11 . . . . .64 A3
Prinn Pl NE16 . . . . . . . . . .62 C2
Priors Way NE28 . . . . . . .22 C2
Priory Ct
Gateshead NE8 . . . . . . . . .78 C3
Gateshead, Wardley
NE10 . . . . . . . . . . . . . . . . . .61 A4
Priory Gn 20 NE6 . . . . . . .32 C1
Priory Pl
Brunswick Village NE13 . . .2 A1
Newcastle-u-T NE6 . . . . . .33 A1
Priory Rd NE32 . . . . . . . . .37 A4
Priory Way NE15 . . . . . . .14 A4
Proctor Ct NE6 . . . . . . . . .34 B1
Proctor St NE6 . . . . . . . . .34 B1
Prospect Ave NE28 . . . . .21 C3
Prospect Avenue N
NE28 . . . . . . . . . . . . . . . . . .21 C4
Prospect Terr NE9 . . . . . .66 B1
Providence Pl 18 NE10 . .47 C1
Provident Terr NE28 . . . .21 B2
Provost Gdns NE4 . . . . . .43 C4
Prudhoe Ct NE3 . . . . . . . .7 B3
Prudhoe Gr NE32 . . . . . . .51 A3
Pullman Ct NE9 . . . . . . . .58 A1
Purbeck Rd NE12 . . . . . . .10 C2
Purley Cl NE28 . . . . . . . . .23 A4
Purley Gdns NE3 . . . . . . .17 A4

Quality Row NE6 . . . . . . .32 B1
Quality Row Rd NE6 . . . .32 B1
Quarryfield Rd NE8 . . . . .78 C4
Quarry Rd
Hebburn NE31 . . . . . . . . .35 C1
Newcastle-u-T NE5 . . . . . .27 A2
Quarry Row 19 NE10 . . . .47 C1
Quay Corner Ave NE32 . .37 B4
Quayside
Newcastle-u-T NE1 . . . . . .78 B4
Newcastle-u-T, St Lawrence
NE1, NE6 . . . . . . . . . . . . . .32 B1
Quay View NE28 . . . . . . . .23 B2
Queen Ann Ct 21 NE6 . . .33 A3
Queen Elizabeth Ave
NE9 . . . . . . . . . . . . . . . . . . .59 A2
Queen Elizabeth Ct
NE34 . . . . . . . . . . . . . . . . . .52 B3
Queen Elizabeth Hospl
NE9 . . . . . . . . . . . . . . . . . . .59 A2
Queensbridge NE12 . . . .10 A3
Queensbury Dr NE15 . . . .13 C2
Queensbury Gate NE12 .10 B2
Queen's Cres
Hebburn NE31 . . . . . . . . .49 C4
Wallsend NE28 . . . . . . . . .21 C3
Queens Ct
Gateshead NE8 . . . . . . . . .77 C1
Newcastle-u-T, Brunton Park
NE3 . . . . . . . . . . . . . . . . . . . .4 C2
Walbottle NE15 . . . . . . . . .13 B1
Queens Dr
Sunniside NE16 . . . . . . . .62 C2
Whickham NE16 . . . . . . . .55 B1
Queens Gdns NE12 . . . . .11 B2
Queens La NE1 . . . . . . . . .78 A4
Queensland Ave NE34 . .52 B4

Queens Rd
Newcastle-u-T NE5 . . . . . .15 B3
Walbottle NE15 . . . . . . . . .13 B1
Queen's Rd NE2 . . . . . . . .19 A1
Queen St
Birtley DH3 . . . . . . . . . . . .70 A4
Gateshead NE8 . . . . . . . . .57 B4
Newcastle-u-T NE1 . . . . . .78 B4
Queens Terr NE28 . . . . . .22 A3
Queen's Terr NE2 . . . . . . .19 A1
Queensway
Newcastle-u-T, Brunton
Park NE3 . . . . . . . . . . . . . . .4 B1
Newcastle-u-T, Fenham
NE4 . . . . . . . . . . . . . . . . . . .29 B4
Queensway N NE11 . . . . .57 B2
Queensway N NE11 . . . . .57 B1
Queensway S NE11 . . . . .64 A3
Queen Victoria St NE10. .48 C1
Quentin Ave NE3 . . . . . . . .7 B1
Quigley Terr DH3 . . . . . . .68 A2

Rabbit Banks Rd NE8 . . .78 A3
Raby Cres 9 NE6 . . . . . . .33 A2
Raby Cross 10 NE6 . . . . . .33 A1
Rabygate 7 NE6 . . . . . . . .33 A2
Raby Gdns NE32 . . . . . . . .51 A4
Raby Rd NE38 . . . . . . . . . .69 C1
Raby St
Gateshead NE8 . . . . . . . . .58 B4
16 Newcastle-u-T, Byker
NE6 . . . . . . . . . . . . . . . . . . .32 C2
Newcastle-u-T, St Lawrence
NE6 . . . . . . . . . . . . . . . . . . .33 A1
Radcliffe Cotts 5 NE15 . .12 B2
Radcliffe Pl 3 NE5 . . . . . .16 B2
Radcliffe St NE3 . . . . . . . .70 B3
Radnor Gdns NE28 . . . . .23 B3
Radnor St NE1 . . . . . . . . .21 C4
Rae Ave NE28 . . . . . . . . . .21 C4
Raeburn Gdns NE9 . . . . .59 A3
Raglan NE38 . . . . . . . . . . .69 C1
Raglan St NE32 . . . . . . . .37 A3
Railton Gdns NE9 . . . . . . .59 A2
Railway Cotts DH3 . . . . .70 A4
Railway St
Dunston NE11 . . . . . . . . . .44 B2
Dunston NE11 . . . . . . . . . .77 A1
Hebburn NE31 . . . . . . . . .36 A3
Jarrow NE32 . . . . . . . . . . .36 B3
Newcastle-u-T NE4 . . . . . .76 B3
Railway Terr
Newcastle-u-T NE4 . . . . . .76 B3
Wallsend NE28 . . . . . . . . .22 B1
Rainton Cl NE10 . . . . . . . .61 B2
Ralph St NE31 . . . . . . . . . .36 A3
Ramparts The NE15 . . . . .28 A4
Ramsay St NE21 . . . . . . . .41 A3
Ramshaw Cl NE7 . . . . . . .20 C3
Randolph St NE32 . . . . . .37 A3
Ranmere Rd NE15 . . . . . .28 B1
Rannoch Cl NE10 . . . . . . .61 B4
Rannoch Ho NE2 . . . . . . .19 A2
Rapperton Ct 7 NE5 . . . .15 A3
Ratho Ct NE10 . . . . . . . . .60 A2
Ravel Ct NE32 . . . . . . . . . .37 A4
Ravenburn Gdns NE15 . .28 A2
Ravensburn Wlk 6
NE15 . . . . . . . . . . . . . . . . . .12 B2
Ravenscar Cl NE16 . . . . . .54 B1
Ravenscourt Pl NE8 . . . . .79 A1
Ravensdale Cres 3
NE9 . . . . . . . . . . . . . . . . . . .58 C2
Ravenshill Rd NE4 . . . . . .27 B4
Ravenside Rd NE4 . . . . . .29 C4
Ravenswood 5 NE6 . . . . .20 A1
Ravenswood Cl NE12 . . .11 C4
Ravenswood Gdns NE9 .65 A3
Ravenswood Prim Sch
NE6 . . . . . . . . . . . . . . . . . . .20 A1
Ravenswood Rd NE6 . . . .20 A1
Ravensworth Apartments
6 NE11 . . . . . . . . . . . . . . .56 C4
Ravensworth Ave NE9. . .66 A2
Ravensworth Ct NE38 . . .23 A2
Ravensworth Ct
Dunston NE11 . . . . . . . . . .77 A1
Newcastle-u-T NE9 . . . . . .7 B3

Ravensworth Rd
Birtley DH3 . . . . . . . . . . . .68 A3
Dunston NE11 . . . . . . . . . .77 A1
Ravensworth St NE28 . . .23 A2
Ravensworth Terr
Dunston NE11 . . . . . . . . . .56 C4
Jarrow NE32 . . . . . . . . . . .51 A3
Sunniside NE16 . . . . . . . .62 C2
Ravensworth Terrace Prim
Sch DH3 . . . . . . . . . . . . . . .70 B4
Raven Terr 7 DH3 . . . . . .68 B1
Rawling Rd NE8 . . . . . . . .57 C4
Rawlston Way NE5. . . . . .16 A3
Raylees Gdns NE11 . . . . .56 C3
Rayleigh Dr NE13 . . . . . . .2 B3
Rayleigh Gr NE8 . . . . . . . .57 C4
Readhead Dr NE6 . . . . . .48 B4
Reay Gdns NE5 . . . . . . . . .15 B3
Reay Pl NE3 . . . . . . . . . . . .8 B1
Reay St NE10 . . . . . . . . . .49 A2
Rectory Ave NE3 . . . . . . . .18 C4
Rectory Ct 6 NE16 . . . . . .55 A3
Rectory Dr NE3 . . . . . . . . .18 C4
Rectory Gr NE3 . . . . . . . . .9 B1
Rectory La
Blaydon NE21 . . . . . . . . . .53 A4
Whickham NE16 . . . . . . . .55 A3
Rectory Pl NE8 . . . . . . . . .79 A1
Rectory Rd
Gateshead, Carr Hill
NE10 . . . . . . . . . . . . . . . . . .59 B3
Gateshead, Shipcote NE8,
NE9 . . . . . . . . . . . . . . . . . . .58 A4
Newcastle-u-T NE3 . . . . . .18 B4
Rectory Rd E NE10 . . . . .59 C3
Rectory Terr NE3 . . . . . . .18 C4
Red Admiral Ct NE11 . . .57 A3
Red Bglws NE9 . . . . . . . . .66 C1
Redburn Rd NE5 . . . . . . . .15 A4
Redcar Rd
Newcastle-u-T NE6 . . . . . .20 B1
Wallsend NE28 . . . . . . . . .23 B3
Redcliffe Way NE15 . . . . .15 C3
Redcroft Gn NE5 . . . . . . . .15 C3
Rede Ave NE31 . . . . . . . . .35 C2
Redemarsh NE10 . . . . . . .60 B2
Redesdale Ave NE3 . . . . . .8 B2
Redesdale Cl
Longbenton NE12 . . . . . . .11 A4
Newcastle-u-T NE15 . . . . .27 C3
Redesdale Gdns NE11 . . .56 B3
Redesdale Prim Sch
NE28 . . . . . . . . . . . . . . . . . .21 A4
Rede St
Gateshead NE11 . . . . . . . .57 B1
Jarrow NE32 . . . . . . . . . . .36 B1
Redewater Gdns NE16 . .54 C2
Redewater Rd NE4 . . . . . .29 C4
Redwood Cl NE5 . . . . . . . .15 B1
Redwood Ct NE7 . . . . . . .20 B3
Redheugh Bridge Rd NE1,
NE4 . . . . . . . . . . . . . . . . . . .76 C3
Redheugh Ct NE8 . . . . . . .57 A4
Red House Rd NE31 . . . .36 B2
Redland Ave NE3 . . . . . . . .7 C2
Redmayne Ct 9 NE10 . . .66 B1
Redmayne Ct 11 NE10 . .59 C4
Rednam Pl NE5 . . . . . . . . .15 C2
Redruth Gdns NE9 . . . . . .65 A2
Redshank Cl NE38 . . . . . .71 B2
Redwing Ct NE16 . . . . . . .33 C3
Redwood Gdns NE11 . . . .57 A1
Reedham Ct NE5 . . . . . . .15 C4
Reedside NE40 . . . . . . . . .25 B1
Reedsmouth Pl NE5 . . . . .28 C4
Reestones Pl NE3 . . . . . . .7 B1
Reeth Way NE15 . . . . . . . .12 A1
Regency Dr NE16 . . . . . . .54 B2
Regent Ave NE3 . . . . . . . . .8 B2
Regent Centre Sta NE3 . .9 A2
Regent Ct
Gateshead NE8 . . . . . . . . .79 C2
Hebburn NE31 . . . . . . . . .35 B1
Regent Ctr The NE3 . . . . .9 A2
Regent Dr NE16 . . . . . . . .62 A4
Regent Farm Ct NE3 . . . .9 A1
Regent Farm Fst Sch
NE3 . . . . . . . . . . . . . . . . . . . .8 B2
Regent Farm Rd NE3 . . . .8 C2

**Regent Rd**
Jarrow NE32 . . . . . . . . . .37 A2
Newcastle-u-T NE3 . . . . .9 A1
Wallsend NE28 . . . . . . . .21 B3
**Regent Rd N** NE3 . . . . . . . .9 A1
**Regents Cl** NE28 . . . . . . . .20 C4
**Regents Pk** NE28 . . . . . . . .20 C3
**Regent Terr** NE8 . . . . . . . .79 B2
**Reginald St** NE8 . . . . . . . .47 A1
**Regrave Cl** NE8 . . . . . . . .47 A2
**Reid Ave** NE28 . . . . . . . .21 C3
**Reid Park Cl** NE2 . . . . . .19 A2
**Reid Park Ct** NE2 . . . . . .19 A2
**Reid Park Rd** NE2 . . . . . .19 A2
**Relton Ave** NE6 . . . . . . . .47 C4
**Remus Cl** NE13 . . . . . . . .2 B1
**Rendel St** NE11 . . . . . . . .44 B1
**Rendle Rd** NE4 . . . . . . . .49 A4
**Renforth Cl** NE8 . . . . . . . .47 A2
**Renforth St** NE11 . . . . . .56 B4
**Renfrew Gn** NE5 . . . . . . .15 C3
**Renfrew Pl** DH3 . . . . . . . .70 C2
**Rennington** NE10 . . . . . .60 C1
**Rennington Pl** 5 NE5..16 B2
**Renwick Ave** NE3 . . . . . . .7 C2
**Renwick Ct** NE8 . . . . . . . .57 B4
**Renwick St** NE6 . . . . . . . .33 B2
**Resida Cl** NE15 . . . . . . . .27 A4
**Retreat The** NE15 . . . . . .26 A3
**Revell Terr** NE15 . . . . . .16 C1
**Reyrolle Cl** NE31 . . . . . . .35 B1
**Rheydt Ave** NE28 . . . . . .21 A2
**Rhodes St** NE6 . . . . . . . .34 B1
**Rhuddlan Cl** NE5 . . . . . .15 C4
**Rhyl Par** NE31 . . . . . . . . .35 C2
**Ribbledale Gdns** NE7 ..19 C3
**Ribblesdale** NE28 . . . . . .21 A4
**Ribble Wlk** NE32 . . . . . . .51 B2
**Richard Browell Rd**
 NE15 . . . . . . . . . . . . . .12 C1
**Richardson Ave** 2
 NE34 . . . . . . . . . . . . . .52 B4
**Richardson Dees Prim Sch**
 NE28 . . . . . . . . . . . . . .22 B2
**Richardson St**
 3 Newcastle-u-T NE6...33 A4
 Wallsend NE28 . . . . . . . .22 A2
**Richmond Ave**
 Gateshead NE10 . . . . . . . .49 B1
 Whickham NE16 . . . . . . . .43 A1
**Richmond Ct**
 1 Gateshead, Low Fell
 NE9 . . . . . . . . . . . . . .65 A4
 Gateshead NE8 . . . . . . . .79 C1
 Jarrow NE32 . . . . . . . . . .36 B3
**Richmond Gdns** NE28..22 C3
**Richmond Lodge** NE3..18 B4
**Richmond Mews** NE3 ..17 C3
**Richmond Pk** NE28 . . . . . .20 C3
**Richmond Terr**
 13 Gateshead, Felling
 NE10 . . . . . . . . . . . . . .59 C4
 Gateshead NE8 . . . . . . . .79 B1
 Walbottle NE15 . . . . . . . .13 A1
**Rickgarth** NE10 . . . . . . . .60 B1
**Rickleton Way** NE38 ..71 C1
**Riddell Ave** NE15 . . . . . . .29 A1
**Ridge Ct** NE13 . . . . . . . .4 B4
**Ridge The** NE40 . . . . . . .39 B4
**Ridgeway**
 Birtley DH3 . . . . . . . . . . .68 B2
 Gateshead NE10 . . . . . . . .61 A2
 Newcastle-u-T NE8 . . . . . .54 C4
**Ridge Way The** NE3 ..17 A4
**Ridgewood Cres** NE3 ..10 A1
**Ridgewood Gdns** NE3...9 C1
**Ridgewood Villas** NE3 ..9 C1
**Riding Barns Way** NE16 .62 B2
**Riding Cl** NE40 . . . . . . . .38 A3
**Riding Lea** NE21 . . . . . . .40 C1
**Ridings Ct** NE40 . . . . . . .38 A3
**Riding The** NE3 . . . . . . . .16 C3
**Ridley Ave** NE28 . . . . . . .23 C4
**Ridley Cl** NE3 . . . . . . . . .8 A4
**Ridley Gdns** NE16 . . . . . . .42 C1
**Ridley St** NE8 . . . . . . . . .58 A4
**Ridley Terr** NE10 . . . . . . .60 A4
**Ridsdale Ave** NE5 . . . . . .14 C1
**Ridsdale Cl** NE28 . . . . . .22 A4
**Ridsdale Ct** NE8 . . . . . . .79 A1
**Riley St** NE32 . . . . . . . . .36 B3

**Riley Street Ind Est**
 NE32 . . . . . . . . . . . . . .36 B3
**Ringlet Cl** NE11 . . . . . . . .57 A3
**Ringwood Gn** NE12 ..11 A3
**Ripley Ave** NE29 . . . . . . .24 C4
**Ripley Cl** NE9 . . . . . . . . .65 C1
**Ripley Terr** NE6 . . . . . . . .33 C2
**Ripon Dr**
 Newcastle-u-T NE2 ..32 B4
 Wallsend NE28 . . . . . . . .22 C3
**Ripon St** NE8 . . . . . . . . .79 B1
**Rise The**
 Newcastle-u-T NE3 ..16 C4
 Ryton NE21 . . . . . . . . . .40 C4
**River La** NE40 . . . . . . . .25 A2
**Riversdale Ct** NE15 ..27 A2
**Riversdale Way** NE15 ..27 A2
**Riverside Bsns Pk** NE28 23 B1
**Riverside Ct** NE11 . . . . . .77 A1
**Riverside Lodge** NE15..25 A3
**Riverside The** NE31 ..35 A3
**Riverside Way** NE11,
 NE16 . . . . . . . . . . . . . .43 B3
**River View**
 Blaydon NE21 . . . . . . . . .41 A2
 Ryton NE40 . . . . . . . . . .25 C1
**Riverview Lodge** NE4 ..43 C4
**Roachburn Rd** NE5 ..14 C2
**Robert Allan Ct** NE13 ..2 A2
**Robert Owen Gdns**
 NE10 . . . . . . . . . . . . . .59 B3
**Roberts St** NE15 . . . . . . . .28 B1
**Roberts Terr** NE32 ..36 C1
**Robinson Gdns** NE28..23 B3
**Robinson St** 5 NE6 ..33 A2
**Robinswood** 8 NE9 ..58 B1
**Robsheugh Pl** NE5 ..29 A4
**Robson St**
 7 Gateshead NE8 ..58 B1
 Newcastle-u-T NE6 ..32 C2
**Rochdale St** NE18 . . . . . . . .21 C1
**Rochester Gdns** NE11..56 C4
**Rochester Sq** NE32 ..51 A1
**Rochester St** NE6 . . . . . . . .48 C4
**Rochester Terr** 1 NE10 60 A4
**Rockcliffe Gdns** NE15..28 A3
**Rockcliffe Way** NE9 ..66 B1
**Rock Gr** 4 NE6 . . . . . . . .34 B1
**Rockmore Rd** NE21 ..41 B1
**Rockwood Gdns** NE40..38 A1
**Rockwood Hill Rd** NE40 .38 B1
**Rockwood Terr** NE40..38 B1
**Rodney St** NE6 . . . . . . . .32 C1
**Rodsley Ave** NE8 . . . . . . . .58 A1
**Roeburn Way** NE3 . . . . . . .17 A3
**Roehedge** NE10 . . . . . . . .61 A2
**Rogan Ave** 8 NE37 ..69 C2
**Rogerson Terr** NE5 ..14 C3
**Roger St** NE6 . . . . . . . . . .32 C2
**Rokeby Ave** NE15 . . . . . . .27 B2
**Rokeby Dr** NE3 . . . . . . . .17 A4
**Rokeby St** NE15 . . . . . . . .27 B2
**Rokeby Terr** NE6 . . . . . . .20 A1
**Rokeby View** NE9 . . . . . . .65 B1
**Rokerby Ave** NE16 ..55 B2
**Roland Rd** NE28 . . . . . . . .22 C2
**Rollesby Ct** NE5 . . . . . . .15 C4
**Rolling Mill Rd** NE32..36 B4
**Roman Ave** NE6 . . . . . . . .33 C2
**Roman Ct** NE28 . . . . . . . .22 C4
**Roman Road Prim Sch**
 NE10 . . . . . . . . . . . . . .60 C1
**Roman Way The** NE5 ..27 B4
**Romford Pl** NE9 . . . . . . . .58 C4
**Romiley Gr** NE10 . . . . . . . .61 C3
**Romney Gdns** NE9 ..59 A3
**Romsey Gr** NE15 . . . . . . . .27 A4
**Ronald Dr** NE15 . . . . . . . .28 B2
**Ronald Gdns** NE31 ..49 C4
**Ronsdorf Ct** NE8 . . . . . . . .36 C2
**Rooksleigh** 6 NE21..41 A1
**Rookwood Dr** NE13 ..2 C4
**Rookwood Rd** NE5 ..28 B4
**Ropery La**
 Hebburn NE31 . . . . . . . . .35 B2
 Wallsend NE28 . . . . . . . .23 B2
**Ropery Rd** NE8 . . . . . . . .57 A4
**Ropery The** NE6 . . . . . . . .47 C4
**Rose Ave** NE16 . . . . . . . .55 A3
**Rosebank Hall** NE28 ..23 A2
**Roseberry Terr** 1 NE35 32 A1
**Rosebery Ave** NE8 ..58 C4

**Rose Bery Cres** NE2....32 B4
**Rosebery Pl** NE2........32 B4
**Rosebud Cl** 8 NE16....42 C1
**Rose Ct** NE31 . . . . . . . .35 B1
**Rosedale** NE28 . . . . . . . .21 A4
**Rosedale Ct** NE5 . . . . . . . .14 B2
**Rosedale Rd** NE40 . . . . . . . .38 B3
**Roseden Ct** NE12 . . . . . . . .11 A3
**Rosefinch Lodge** NE9..58 B1
**Rose Gdns** NE28 . . . . . . . .21 C4
**ROSEHILL** . . . . . . . . . . . .22 C2
**Rosehill Rd** NE28 . . . . . . . .23 A2
**Rosehill Way** NE5 . . . . . . . .16 A1
**Roselea** NE32 . . . . . . . . .51 B1
**Rosemary Gdns** NE9 ..66 B2
**Rosemount** NE15 . . . . . . . .15 A2
**Rosemount Ave** NE16 ..61 A3
**Rosemount Way** NE7..11 A1
**Rose St**
 Gateshead NE8 . . . . . . . .77 C2
 Hebburn NE31 . . . . . . . . .35 B1
**Rose Terr**
 Greenside NE40 . . . . . . . .39 B2
 Newcastle-u-T NE5 ..16 C1
**Rose Villa La** NE16 ..55 A3
**Rosewell Pl** NE16 . . . . . . . .62 B4
**Rosewood Ave** NE3 ..9 C2
**Rosewood Cres** NE6 ..21 A1
**Rosewood Gdns**
 Gateshead NE9 . . . . . . . .59 A1
 Newcastle-u-T NE3 ..17 A4
**Rosewood Terr**
 Birtley DH3 . . . . . . . . . . .68 A1
 Wallsend NE28 . . . . . . . .23 B2
**Roseworth Ave** NE3 ..18 B3
**Roseworth Cl** NE3 ..18 B4
**Roseworth Cres** NE3..18 B3
**Roseworth Terr**
 Newcastle-u-T NE3 ..18 A4
 Whickham NE16 . . . . . . . .55 A3
**Ross Ave** NE11 . . . . . . . .44 B1
**Rossdale** 8 NE38 ..38 B3
**Rossendale Pl** NE12..10 A2
**Rosslyn Ave**
 Gateshead NE8 . . . . . . . .58 C2
 Newcastle-u-T NE3 ..7 C1
**Rosslyn Pl** DH3 . . . . . . . .70 C2
**Ross Way** NE3 . . . . . . . .8 A4
**Rotary Way** NE29 . . . . . . . .24 C3
**Rothay Pl** NE5 . . . . . . . .16 A2
**Rothbury Ave**
 Gateshead NE10 . . . . . . . .48 C1
 Hebburn NE32 . . . . . . . . .50 C4
 Newcastle-u-T NE3 ..8 C2
**Rothbury Gdns**
 Dunston NE11 . . . . . . . . .56 C1
 Wallsend NE28 . . . . . . . .23 A3
 Wideopen NE13 . . . . . . . .2 C2
**Rothbury Terr**
 Newcastle-u-T NE6 ..33 A4
 North Shields NE29 ..47 B4
**Rotherfield Gdns** 8
 NE9 . . . . . . . . . . . . . .65 B2
**Rothley Ave** NE5 . . . . . . . .29 A3
**Rothley Cl** NE3 . . . . . . . .9 B1
**Rothwell Rd** NE3 . . . . . . . .9 A1
**Roundhill** NE32 . . . . . . . .51 C1
**Roundhill Ave** NE16 ..16 A2
**Roundstone Cl** NE7 ..20 B4
**Roundway The** NE12 ..10 C3
**Rowanberry Rd** NE12 ..10 C2
**Rowan Ct** 4 NE34 ..52 C4
**Rowan Dr** NE3 . . . . . . . .8 A2
**Rowans The** NE9 . . . . . . . .66 B2
**Rowantree Rd** NE6 ..21 B1
**Rowanwood Gdns** NE11 57 A1
**Rowedge Wlk** NE5 ..15 B2
**Rowes Mews** NE6 . . . . . . . .47 B4
**Rowlandson Cres** NE10 59 C4
**Rowlandson Terr** 12
 NE10 . . . . . . . . . . . . . .59 C4
**Rowsley Rd** NE32 . . . . . . . .37 A1
**Row's Terr** NE3 . . . . . . . .9 C1
**Roxburgh Pl** 2 NE6..32 C3
**Royal Cres** NE4 . . . . . . . .29 C4
**Royal Ind Est** NE32 ..36 A4
**Royal Quays Outlet**
 Shopping NE29 . . . . . . . .24 C2
**Royston Terr** NE6 . . . . . . . .48 C4
**Rudby Cl** NE3 . . . . . . . . .9 B4
**Rudchester Pl** NE5....29 A4

**Ruddock Sq** 1 NE6....47 B4
**Rugby Gdns**
 Gateshead NE9 . . . . . . . .66 A3
 Wallsend NE28 . . . . . . . .22 C3
**Runhead Est** NE40 . . . . . . . .39 C4
**Runhead Gdns** NE40..25 B1
**Runhead Terr** NE40 ..25 C1
**Runnymede Rd** NE16..54 C2
**Runnymede Way** NE3 ..16 C4
**Runswick Ave** NE12 ..10 A2
**Rupert Terr** NE15 . . . . . . . .26 A4
**Rushall Pl** NE12 . . . . . . . .10 C2
**Rushie Ave** NE15 . . . . . . . .29 A1
**Rushley Cres** NE21 ..41 B3
**Rushsyde Cl** NE11 ..54 A1
**Rushyrig** NE37 . . . . . . . . .69 C2
**Ruskin Ave** 7 NE11 ..44 B1
**Ruskin Dr** NE7 . . . . . . . .20 C3
**Ruskin Rd**
 Birtley DH3 . . . . . . . . . . .70 B4
 Gateshead NE10, NE9 ..59 A3
 Whickham NE16 . . . . . . . .54 C4
**Russel Ct** NE2 . . . . . . . .19 A2
**Russell Ct** NE8 . . . . . . . .77 C1
**Russell Sq** NE13 . . . . . . . .2 B4
**Russell St** NE32 . . . . . . . .37 A3
**Russell Terr** DH3 . . . . . . . .68 A2
**Ruth Ave** NE21 . . . . . . . .41 B2
**Rutherford St** NE28 ..23 C3
**Ruthven Ct** NE2 . . . . . . . .19 A2
**Rutland Ave** NE6 . . . . . . . .34 B3
**Rutland Rd**
 Hebburn NE31 . . . . . . . . .50 B3
 Wallsend NE28 . . . . . . . .21 B1
**Rutland Sq** DH3 . . . . . . . .68 A1
**Ryall Ave** NE13 . . . . . . . .4 A4
**Ryal Terr** NE6 . . . . . . . . .34 A1
**Ryal Wlk** NE3 . . . . . . . . .16 B4
**Rydal** NE10 . . . . . . . . . .61 C4
**Rydal Cres** NE21 . . . . . . . .53 A4
**Rydal Rd**
 Newcastle-u-T, Gosforth
 NE3 . . . . . . . . . . . . . .9 B1
 Newcastle-u-T, Lemington
 NE15 . . . . . . . . . . . . . .27 B4
**Rydal St** NE8 . . . . . . . . .79 B1
**Rydal Terr** NE13 . . . . . . . .4 B4
**Ryde Terr** NE11 . . . . . . . .77 A1
**Rye Cl** NE15 . . . . . . . . .12 C1
**Ryedale Ct** 7 NE34..52 C4
**Rye Hill**
 Newcastle-u-T NE4 ..76 B4
 Newcastle-u-T NE4 ..76 C4
**Ryhope Gdns** NE9 . . . . . . . .66 B4
**RYTON** . . . . . . . . . . . . . .39 B4
**Ryton Hall Dr** NE40 ..25 A2
**RYTON HAUGH** . . . . . . . . .26 B1
**Ryton Ind Est** NE21 ..26 A1
**Ryton Terr** NE6 . . . . . . . .48 B4
**RYTON WOODSIDE** ..39 A2

## S

**Sackville Rd** NE6 . . . . . . . .20 A1
**Sacred Heart Lower Sch**
 NE4 . . . . . . . . . . . . . .30 A2
**Sacred Heart RC High Sch**
 NE4 . . . . . . . . . . . . . .29 B3
**Sacred Heart RC Mid Sch**
 NE4 . . . . . . . . . . . . . .29 C3
**Sacred Heart RC Prim Sch**
 NE4 . . . . . . . . . . . . . .29 B3
**Sacriston Gdns** NE9..66 A2
**Saffron Pl** NE6 . . . . . . . .34 B1
**Saga Ct** NE6 . . . . . . . . .21 A1
**Sage Cl** NE15 . . . . . . . .27 A4
**Sage Gateshead The**
 NE8 . . . . . . . . . . . . . .78 C4
**St Agnes' Gdns N** NE40..38 A4
**St Agnes' Gdns** NE40..38 A4
**St Agnes RC Prim Sch**
 NE40 . . . . . . . . . . . . . .38 A4
**St Agnes' Terr** NE40..38 A4
**St Aidan's Prim Sch**
 NE8 . . . . . . . . . . . . . .77 C1
**St Aidan's Rd** NE28 ..21 B1
**St Aidan's St** NE8 . . . . . . . .79 A1
**St Alban's Cres**
 Gateshead NE10 . . . . . . . .59 B3
 Newcastle-u-T NE6 ..20 B2
**St Alban's Pl** NE10 ..59 B3

**St Alban's RC Prim Sch**
 NE10 . . . . . . . . . . . . . .48 C1
**St Alban's RC Sch** NE6..34 A3
**St Alban's Terr** NE31 ..79 C1
**St Aloysius RC Inf Sch**
 NE31 . . . . . . . . . . . . . .35 C3
**St Aloysius RC Jun Sch**
 NE31 . . . . . . . . . . . . . .35 C3
**St Aloysius View** NE31..35 B2
**St Andrew's Ct** NE7 ..11 A1
**St Andrew's Dr** NE9 ..64 C3
**St Andrew's St** NE31 ..35 A3
**St Anne's RC Prim Sch**
 NE9 . . . . . . . . . . . . . .65 C2
**ST ANN'S** . . . . . . . . . . . . .32 B1
**St Ann's Cl** NE1 . . . . . . . .32 B1
**ST ANTHONY'S** . . . . . . . . .48 A3
**St Anthony's CE Prim Sch**
 NE6 . . . . . . . . . . . . . .48 B3
**St Anthony's Ct** NE6 ..34 A2
**St Anthony's Ho** NE6..48 B3
**St Anthony's Rd** NE6..48 A3
**St Anthony's Wlk** NE6..48 B3
**St Asaph Cl** NE12 . . . . . . . .20 B4
**St Augustine's RC Prim**
 Sch NE10 . . . . . . . . . . . .60 C2
**St Austell Cl** NE5 . . . . . . . .16 A4
**St Austell Gdns** NE5 ..65 A2
**St Bartholomew's CE Prim**
 Sch NE12 . . . . . . . . . . . .11 B1
**St Bede's Dr** NE8 . . . . . . . .79 C2
**St Bede's Ho** NE9 . . . . . . . .58 C3
**St Bede's RC Prim Sch**
 Jarrow NE32 . . . . . . . . . .37 A3
 Newcastle-u-T NE15 ..28 B2
**St Buryan Cres** NE5 ..15 B2
**St Catherines Gr** NE2 ..32 B3
**St Catherine's RC Prim**
 Sch NE2 . . . . . . . . . . . .32 B4
**St Charles' RC Prim Sch**
 NE3 . . . . . . . . . . . . . .8 C2
**St Christopher Way**
 NE29 . . . . . . . . . . . . . .24 A2
**St Clements Ct**
 3 Longbenton NE12 ..10 B2
 Newcastle-u-T NE3 ..8 A1
**St Columba's RC Prim Sch**
 NE28 . . . . . . . . . . . . . .21 B2
**St Cuthbert's Ct**
 Gateshead NE8 . . . . . . . .79 A2
 Newcastle-u-T NE3 ..8 B1
**St Cuthbert's Dr** NE10..60 B3
**St Cuthbert's Gn** NE5..29 A3
**St Cuthbert's High Sch**
 NE15 . . . . . . . . . . . . . .28 C2
**St Cuthberts Lower Sch**
 NE15 . . . . . . . . . . . . . .28 C2
**St Cuthbert's Pl** NE8..79 A1
**St Cuthbert's Rd**
 Gateshead NE8 . . . . . . . .79 A2
 Gateshead, Windmill Hills
 NE8 . . . . . . . . . . . . . .78 B3
 Newcastle-u-T, Benwell
 NE5 . . . . . . . . . . . . . .28 C3
 Newcastle-u-T, Fenham
 NE5 . . . . . . . . . . . . . .29 A4
 Wallsend NE28 . . . . . . . .22 C3
**St Cuthberts Way** NE21..41 C3
**St David's Way** NE32 ..51 B1
**St Edmund Campion RC**
 Sch NE9 . . . . . . . . . . . .66 B4
**St Edmund's Ct** NE8 ..46 C1
**St Edmund's Dr** NE10..60 B3
**St Edmund's Rd** NE8..79 C1
**St Etienne Ct** 12 NE10..59 C4
**St Gabriel's Ave** NE6 ..19 C1
**St George's Cl** NE2 ..18 C2
**St Georges Cl** NE10 ..61 A3
**St George's Rd** NE15..27 C1
**St George's RC Prim Sch**
 NE15 . . . . . . . . . . . . . .27 B1
**St George's Rd** NE15 ..27 C1
**St George's Terr**
 Newcastle-u-T, Lemington
 NE15 . . . . . . . . . . . . . .27 C1

**St George's Terr** *continued*
Newcastle-u-T, West
Jesmond NE2 . . . . . . . . . . . . .**18** C2
**St Helen's Cres** NE9 . . . . . .**58** A1
**St Helens Terr** NE9 . . . . . . .**58** B1
**St Hilda's Ave** NE28 . . . . . .**22** C3
**St Ives Way** NE5 . . . . . . . . . .**16** A4
**St James Bvld** NE1, NE4 .**76** C4
**St James' Cres** NE15 . . . .**43** C4
**St James Ct** NE8 . . . . . . . . .**47** A1
**St James Gate** NE1 . . . . . .**76** C4
**St James' Gdns** 6 NE15 **29** B1
**St James Lodge** 4 NE4 .**29** B1
**St James' Mall** NE31 . . . . .**35** B1
**St James RC Prim Sch**
NE31 . . . . . . . . . . . . . . . . . . . .**50** B4
**St James Rd** NE8 . . . . . . . .**46** C2
**St James' Rd** NE15 . . . . . .**29** B1
**St James Sq** NE8 . . . . . . . .**46** C2
**St James St** NE1 . . . . . . . . . .**9** C1
**St James' Terr** NE29 . . . .**24** B3
**St John Boste RC Prim**
**Sch** NE38 . . . . . . . . . . . . . . .**69** C1
**St John's Ave** NE11 . . . . . .**35** B1
Newcastle-u-T NE4 . . . . . .**44** A4
North Shields NE29 . . . . . .**24** B3
**St John's Gn** NE29 . . . . . .**24** B3
**St John's Mall** NE31 . . . . .**35** B1
**St Johns Pl** NE10 . . . . . . . .**59** C4
**St John's Rd** NE4 . . . . . . . .**44** A4
**St John's St** NE29 . . . . . . .**24** B3
**St John's Terr**
Jarrow NE32 . . . . . . . . . . . . .**36** C3
North Shields NE29 . . . . . .**24** B3
**St John's Wlk**
Hebburn NE31 . . . . . . . . . . .**35** C1
Newcastle-u-T NE4 . . . . . .**44** A4
North Shields NE29 . . . . . .**24** B3
**St John the Baptist's RC**
**Prim Sch** NE10 . . . . . . . .**59** C4
**St John Vianney RC Prim**
**Sch** NE5 . . . . . . . . . . . . . . . .**14** B1
**St Joseph's Ct**
8 Birtley DH3 . . . . . . . . . .**68** B1
Hebburn NE31 . . . . . . . . . . .**49** C3
**St Joseph's RC Comp Sch**
NE31 . . . . . . . . . . . . . . . . . . . .**49** C2
**St Joseph's RC Inf Sch**
DH3 . . . . . . . . . . . . . . . . . . . . .**68** B1
**St Joseph's RC Jun Sch**
DH3 . . . . . . . . . . . . . . . . . . . . .**70** B4
**St Joseph's RC Prim Sch**
Blaydon NE21 . . . . . . . . . . .**41** A3
Gateshead NE8 . . . . . . . . . .**79** C2
Hedworth NE32 . . . . . . . . . .**51** A1
Newcastle-u-T NE15 . . . . .**43** C4
**St Joseph's Way** NE32 .**51** B1
**St Julien Gdns**
Newcastle-u-T NE7 . . . . . .**20** B2
Wallsend NE28 . . . . . . . . . .**23** C3
**St Just Pl** NE5 . . . . . . . . . . .**16** A4
**St Keverne Sq** NE5 . . . . .**16** A4
**St Lawerence's RC Prim**
**Sch** NE6 . . . . . . . . . . . . . . . .**33** A2
**ST LAWRENCE** . . . . . . . .**32** C1
**St Lawrence Rd** NE6 . . . .**47** B4
**St Lawrence Sq** NE6 . . . .**32** C1
**St Lukes Ct** NE31 . . . . . . . .**49** C4
**St Luke's Rd** NE29 . . . . . .**24** B3
**St Margarets Ave** NE12 . .**11** B2
**St Margaret's Rd** NE15 . .**42** C4
**St Mark's Ct** 11 NE6 . . . . .**33** A3
**St Marks Ct** NE5 . . . . . . . .**15** A4
**St Mark's Ct** NE29 . . . . . .**24** B2
**St Mark's RC Prim Sch**
NE5 . . . . . . . . . . . . . . . . . . . . .**15** A4
**St Mark's St** 18 NE6 . . . .**33** A3
**St Mary's Coll** NE4 . . . . . .**29** C3
**St Mary's Ct** NE8 . . . . . . . .**79** C2
**St Mary's Gn** 4 NE16 . . . .**55** A3
**St Mary's Pl** NE15 . . . . . . .**12** C2
**St Mary's RC Cath** NE1 .**76** C4
**St Mary's RC Comp Sch**
NE7 . . . . . . . . . . . . . . . . . . . . .**10** B1

**St Mary's RC Prim Sch**
Brockley Whins NE32 . . . . .**51** C3
Whickham NE16 . . . . . . . . .**55** B3
**St Mary's & St Thomas**
**Aquinas RC Prim Sch**
NE21 . . . . . . . . . . . . . . . . . . . .**40** C4
**St Matthew's RC Prim Sch**
NE32 . . . . . . . . . . . . . . . . . . . .**51** A2
**St Michael's Mount** 3
NE6 . . . . . . . . . . . . . . . . . . . . .**33** A3
**St Michaels RC Prim Sch**
NE4 . . . . . . . . . . . . . . . . . . . . .**78** A4
**St Michael's Rd** NE6 . . . .**32** C1
**St Michael's Way** NE11 . .**43** B1
**St Michaels Workshops** 10
NE6 . . . . . . . . . . . . . . . . . . . . .**32** C1
**St Nicholas Ave**
Newcastle-u-T, Gosforth
NE3 . . . . . . . . . . . . . . . . . . . . .**18** A4
Newcastle-u-T, South
Gosforth NE3 . . . . . . . . . . .**18** B4
**St Nicholas Hospl** NE3 . . .**8** B1
**St Nicholas' St** NE1 . . . . . .**78** A4
**St Omers Rd** NE11 . . . . . . .**44** B2
**St Oswald's Ave** NE6 . . . .**33** C2
**St Oswalds C of E Prim**
**Sch** NE31 . . . . . . . . . . . . . . .**36** A3
**St Oswald's Gn** NE6 . . . . .**33** C3
**St Oswald's RC Prim Sch**
Gateshead NE9 . . . . . . . . . .**66** A3
Newcastle-u-T NE3 . . . . . . . .**9** B3
**St Oswald's Rd**
Hebburn NE31 . . . . . . . . . . .**36** A3
Wallsend NE28 . . . . . . . . . .**22** C4
**St Patrick's Cl** NE10 . . . . .**59** C4
**St Patrick's Wlk** NE10 . . .**59** C4
**St Paul's CE Prim Sch**
NE4 . . . . . . . . . . . . . . . . . . . . .**76** B1
**St Pauls Ct** NE8 . . . . . . . . .**77** C1
**St Pauls Monastery** ★
NE32 . . . . . . . . . . . . . . . . . . . .**37** B3
**ST Paul's Rd** NE32 . . . . . . .**37** A3
**ST PETER'S** . . . . . . . . . . . . .**47** B4
**St Peter's Ct** NE6 . . . . . . .**33** A1
**St Peter's Quayside E**
NE6 . . . . . . . . . . . . . . . . . . . . .**47** C4
**St Peter's Quayside W** 9
NE6 . . . . . . . . . . . . . . . . . . . . .**47** C4
**St Peter's RC Prim Sch**
NE9 . . . . . . . . . . . . . . . . . . . . .**58** C2
**St Peter's Rd**
Newcastle-u-T NE6 . . . . . .**33** A1
Wallsend NE28 . . . . . . . . . .**22** B3
**St Peter's Wharf** NE6 . . .**47** B4
**St Philip Nert RC Prim Sch**
NE11 . . . . . . . . . . . . . . . . . . . .**56** C4
**St Rollox St** NE31 . . . . . . . .**35** B1
**St Ronans View** NE9 . . . . .**65** B2
**St Simon St** NE34 . . . . . . .**52** C4
**St Stephen's RC Prim Sch**
NE12 . . . . . . . . . . . . . . . . . . . .**10** C1
**St Stephen's Way** NE29 . .**24** B3
**St Teresa's RC Prim Sch**
NE6 . . . . . . . . . . . . . . . . . . . . .**32** C4
**St Thomas More RC Sch**
NE21 . . . . . . . . . . . . . . . . . . . .**41** A3
**St Thomas St** 6 NE9 . . . .**58** C1
**St Vincent Ct** NE6 . . . . . . .**46** C1
**St Vincents Cl** NE15 . . . . .**27** C4
**St Vincent's RC Sch**
NE6 . . . . . . . . . . . . . . . . . . . . .**48** A4
**St Vincent St** NE8 . . . . . . .**46** C1
**St Wilfrid's RC Prim Sch**
NE10 . . . . . . . . . . . . . . . . . . . .**47** A2
**Saker Pl** 1 NE28 . . . . . . . .**21** C1
**Salcombe Ave** NE32 . . . . .**37** B2
**Salcombe Gdns** NE9 . . . . .**65** A2
**Salem St** NE32 . . . . . . . . . .**37** A3
**Salisbury Gdns** NE2 . . . . .**32** B4
**Salisbury Ho** NE6 . . . . . . . .**32** B2
**Salisbury St** NE10 . . . . . . .**48** C1
**Salisbury Way** NE32 . . . . .**51** A1
**Salkeld Gdns** NE9 . . . . . . .**58** C4
**Salkeld Rd** NE9 . . . . . . . . . .**58** C2
**Saltburn Gdns** NE28 . . . . .**23** C3
**Salters Cl** NE3 . . . . . . . . . . . .**9** C2
**Salters Ct** NE3 . . . . . . . . . . . .**9** C2
**Salters' La** NE3, NE12 . . . .**10** A3
**Salters' Rd** NE3 . . . . . . . . . .**17** C4
**Saltford** NE9 . . . . . . . . . . . . .**65** B2
**SALTMEADOWS** . . . . . . . .**46** C4

**Saltmeadows Rd** NE10,
NE8 . . . . . . . . . . . . . . . . . . . . .**47** A4
**Saltwell Park Mansion**
Mus** ★ NE8 . . . . . . . . . . . . . .**58** A2
**Saltwell Pl** NE8 . . . . . . . . . .**57** C4
**Saltwell Rd** NE8 . . . . . . . . .**57** C4
**Saltwell Rd S** NE9 . . . . . . .**64** C4
**Saltwell St** NE8 . . . . . . . . . .**57** C4
**Saltwell View** NE8 . . . . . . .**58** A3
**Sanderling Cl** NE40 . . . . . .**39** C4
**Sanderlings** 3 NE28 . . . . .**21** C1
**Sanders Gdns** DH3 . . . . . . .**68** B1
**Sanderson Hospl** NE3 . . . .**17** C4
**Sanderson Rd** NE2 . . . . . . .**18** C2
**Sanderson St** NE4 . . . . . . .**44** B3
**Sandford Mews** NE13 . . . . .**2** A1
**Sandhill** NE1 . . . . . . . . . . . . .**78** B4
**Sandiacres** NE32 . . . . . . . .**51** B1
**Sandmere Pl** NE15 . . . . . . .**28** B1
**Sandoe Gdns** NE15 . . . . . .**28** C1
**Sandown Ct** NE28 . . . . . . .**23** B4
**Sandown Gdns**
Gateshead NE8 . . . . . . . . . .**57** C4
Wallsend NE28 . . . . . . . . . .**23** A4
**Sandpiper Cl**
Ryton NE40 . . . . . . . . . . . . .**39** C4
Washington NE38 . . . . . . . .**71** B2
**Sandpiper Pl** NE12 . . . . . .**10** B3
**Sandray Cl** DH3 . . . . . . . . . .**70** C1
**Sandringham Ave** NE12 .**11** B2
**Sandringham Ct**
6 Gateshead NE10 . . . . . .**59** B4
2 Longbenton NE12 . . . . .**10** B3
**Sandringham Dr** NE16 . .**54** C3
**Sandringham Mews** 8
NE28 . . . . . . . . . . . . . . . . . . . .**23** A4
**Sandringham Rd**
Newcastle-u-T, South
Gosforth NE3 . . . . . . . . . . .**18** C4
Newcastle-u-T, West Denton
NE5 . . . . . . . . . . . . . . . . . . . . .**27** C4
**Sands Ind Est The** NE16 **42** C1
**Sands Rd** NE16 . . . . . . . . . .**42** C1
**Sandstone Ct** NE34 . . . . . .**52** B3
**Sandwich St** NE6 . . . . . . . .**48** B3
**Sandy Cres** NE6 . . . . . . . . .**48** A4
**Sandygate Mews** NE16 . .**62** C1
**Sandy La**
Gateshead NE9 . . . . . . . . . .**66** B1
Wideopen NE1, NE13 . . . . .**8** C4
**Sandy Lane Ind Area** NE3 **5** B4
**Satley Gdns** NE10 . . . . . . .**66** A2
**Savory Rd** NE28 . . . . . . . . .**23** A3
**Saxilby Dr** NE3 . . . . . . . . . . . .**9** B4
**Saxondale Rd** NE3 . . . . . . . .**7** C1
**Saxon Way** NE32 . . . . . . . .**37** A3
**Saxton Gr** NE7 . . . . . . . . . . .**19** B4
**Scafell** DH3 . . . . . . . . . . . . . .**70** C1
**Scafell Dr** NE5 . . . . . . . . . . .**16** B3
**Scafell Gdns** NE11 . . . . . . .**56** C2
**Scalby Cl** NE3 . . . . . . . . . . . . .**9** B4
**Scarborough Ct** NE6 . . . . .**33** B2
**Scarborough Par** NE31 . . .**50** C2
**Scarborough Rd** NE6 . . . . .**33** B2
**Sceptre Ct** NE4 . . . . . . . . . .**76** A4
**School Ave** NE11 . . . . . . . . .**56** B4
**School Cl** NE9 . . . . . . . . . . . .**59** C2
**School La** NE16 . . . . . . . . . .**55** B3
**School St**
Birtley DH3 . . . . . . . . . . . . . .**70** B4
Hebburn NE31 . . . . . . . . . . .**36** A3
Whickham NE16 . . . . . . . . .**54** C3
**Scotby Gdns** NE9 . . . . . . . .**65** C3
**Scotland Ct** NE21 . . . . . . . .**40** C1
**SCOTSWOOD** . . . . . . . . . .**42** C4
**Scotswood Rd** NE15,
NE4 . . . . . . . . . . . . . . . . . . . . .**43** A4
**Scotswood View** NE11 . . .**43** B2
**Scott Ct** NE34 . . . . . . . . . . . .**52** C3
**Scott's Ave** 15 NE40 . . . . .**38** B3
**Scott's Ct** NE10 . . . . . . . . .**61** A2
**Scrogg Rd** NE6 . . . . . . . . . .**34** A2
**Seaburn Gdns** NE9 . . . . . . .**66** B3
**Seaham Gdns** NE9 . . . . . . .**66** A2
**Seascale Pl** NE9 . . . . . . . . .**65** C4
**Seaton Burn Coll** NE13 . . . .**2** C4
**Seaton Cl** NE10 . . . . . . . . . .**61** A2
**Seaton Gdns** NE9 . . . . . . . .**66** A3
**Seaton Pl**
Brunswick Village NE13 . . . .**2** A2
Newcastle-u-T NE6 . . . . . .**48** A3

**Second Ave**
Dunston NE11 . . . . . . . . . . .**57** A2
Newcastle-u-T NE6 . . . . . .**33** A3
North Shields NE29 . . . . . .**25** C4
**Second St** NE8 . . . . . . . . . . .**79** A1
**Sedgemoor Ave** NE15 . . . .**42** C4
**Sedgewick Pl** NE8 . . . . . . .**79** B1
**Sedley Rd** NE28 . . . . . . . . . .**21** C1
**Sefton Ave** NE6 . . . . . . . . . .**20** A1
**Segedunum Cres** NE28 . . .**22** B4
**Segedunum Way** NE28 . . .**21** C1
**Segendum Roman Fort**
Ctr** ★ NE28 . . . . . . . . . . . . . .**22** A1
**Seine Ct** NE32 . . . . . . . . . . .**37** A2
**Selborne Ave** NE9 . . . . . . .**64** C4
**Selborne Gdns** NE2 . . . . . .**32** B4
**Selby Ct**
2 Jarrow NE32 . . . . . . . . . .**36** C3
Newcastle-u-T NE6 . . . . . .**48** B4
**Selby Gdns**
Newcastle-u-T NE6 . . . . . .**34** A4
Wallsend NE28 . . . . . . . . . .**21** C3
**Selkirk Cres** DH3 . . . . . . . . .**68** B2
**Selkirk St** NE32 . . . . . . . . . .**52** A3
**Selsey Cl** NE10 . . . . . . . . . .**60** A2
**Selwyn Cl** NE5 . . . . . . . . . . .**16** B4
**Serin Ho** NE5 . . . . . . . . . . . .**15** B3
**Seton Ave** NE34 . . . . . . . . .**52** B4
**Seton Wlk** NE34 . . . . . . . . .**52** B4
**Settlingstone Cl** NE7 . . . . .**20** C3
**Seventh Ave**
Gateshead NE11 . . . . . . . . .**64** B4
Newcastle-u-T NE6 . . . . . .**33** A3
**Severn Ave** NE31 . . . . . . . .**50** A3
**Severn Dr** NE32 . . . . . . . . . .**51** B2
**Severn Gdns** NE8 . . . . . . . .**59** A4
**Severus Rd** NE4 . . . . . . . . .**29** C3
**Seymour St** NE11 . . . . . . . .**77** A1
**Seymour St** NE11 . . . . . . . .**77** A1
**Shadon Way** DH3 . . . . . . . .**71** A3
**Shaftesbury Ave** NE32 . .**37** C1
**Shaftesbury Gr** NE6 . . . . . .**32** C3
**Shaftesbury Wlk** NE8 . . . .**77** C2
**Shafto Cl** NE15 . . . . . . . . . .**28** C1
**Shafto Cl** NE40 . . . . . . . . . .**38** B3
**Shaftoe Cl** NE3 . . . . . . . . . . . .**8** B3
**Shafto St**
Newcastle-u-T NE15 . . . . .**28** B1
Wallsend NE28 . . . . . . . . . .**22** C3
**Shakespeare Ave** NE31 . .**35** C2
**Shakespeare St**
Jarrow NE32 . . . . . . . . . . . .**36** C4
Newcastle-u-T NE1 . . . . . .**79** A3
**Shamrock Ct** NE15 . . . . . . .**27** A4
**Shandon Way** NE3 . . . . . . . .**7** C1
**Shannon Ct** NE3 . . . . . . . . . .**7** A3
**Shap La** NE5 . . . . . . . . . . . . .**15** B1
**Sharpendon St** NE31 . . . . .**35** C3
**Sharperton Dr** NE3 . . . . . . . .**4** A1
**Shawbrow Cl** NE7 . . . . . . . .**20** C3
**Shawdon Cl** NE5 . . . . . . . . .**16** A4
**Shaw Gdns** NE10 . . . . . . . .**61** A4
**Shearlegs Rd** NE8 . . . . . . .**46** C3
**Shearwater Ave** NE12 . . . .**10** B3
**Shearwater Cl** NE5 . . . . . . .**15** C4
**Sheen Ct** NE3 . . . . . . . . . . . . .**6** C1
**Sheldon Gr** NE3 . . . . . . . . . .**17** B3
**Sheldon St** NE32 . . . . . . . . .**36** C3
**Shelford Gdns** NE15 . . . . .**27** C3
**Shelley Ave** NE9 . . . . . . . . .**67** A1
**Shelley Dr** NE8 . . . . . . . . . . .**46** C2
**Shelley Rd** NE15 . . . . . . . . .**26** B3
**Shepton Cotts** NE16 . . . . .**63** A3
**Sheraton** NE10 . . . . . . . . . .**60** C1
**Sherburn Grange N**
NE32 . . . . . . . . . . . . . . . . . . . .**36** B1
**Sherburn Grange S**
NE32 . . . . . . . . . . . . . . . . . . . .**36** B1
**Sherburn Terr** NE9 . . . . . . .**66** A2
**Sherburn Way** NE10 . . . . .**61** B3
**Sherfield Dr** NE7 . . . . . . . . .**20** B2
**Sheridan Gr** NE38 . . . . . . . .**71** C1
**Sheridan Rd** NE34 . . . . . . .**52** C3
**SHERIFF HILL** . . . . . . . . . .**59** A2
**Sheriffs Cl** NE10 . . . . . . . . .**59** A4
**Sheriffs Hall Villas** 7
NE9 . . . . . . . . . . . . . . . . . . . . .**58** C1
**Sheriff's Highway** NE9 . . .**58** C1
**Sherringham Ave** NE3 . . .**16** C4
**Sherwood** NE9 . . . . . . . . . . . .**4** C2
**Sherwood View** NE28 . . . .**21** B4
**Shibdon Bank** NE21 . . . . . .**41** C2

**Shibdon Bsns Pk** NE21 . .**42** A3
**Shibdon Cres** NE21 . . . . . .**41** C2
**Shibdon Ct** NE21 . . . . . . . . .**41** B3
**Shibdon Park View**
NE21 . . . . . . . . . . . . . . . . . . . .**41** C2
**Shibdon Pond Nature**
**Reserve** ★ NE21 . . . . . . . . .**42** A2
**Shibdon Rd**
Blaydon NE21 . . . . . . . . . . .**41** C3
Blaydon NE21 . . . . . . . . . . .**42** A2
**Shibdon Way** NE21 . . . . . .**42** B2
**Shield Ave** NE16 . . . . . . . . .**43** A1
**Shieldclose** 2 NE37 . . . . .**69** C2
**Shield Gr** NE3 . . . . . . . . . . . . .**9** B2
**Shield La** 1 NE6 . . . . . . . . .**33** A2
**Shields Rd**
Gateshead NE10 . . . . . . . . .**60** B4
Newcastle-u-T NE6 . . . . . .**33** A3
**Shields Rd W** 5 NE6 . . . . .**32** B2
**Shilmore Rd** NE3 . . . . . . . . . .**8** A1
**Shincliffe Gdns** NE9 . . . . .**66** B3
**SHIPCOTE** . . . . . . . . . . . . . .**58** A4
**Shipcote La** NE8 . . . . . . . . .**58** B4
**Shipcote Terr** NE8 . . . . . . .**58** B4
**Shipley Art Gallery** ★
NE8 . . . . . . . . . . . . . . . . . . . . .**58** B4
**Shipley Ave** NE4 . . . . . . . . .**29** C2
**Shipley Ct** NE8 . . . . . . . . . . .**79** C1
**Shipley Pl** 16 NE6 . . . . . . .**32** C2
**Shipley Rise** 9 NE6 . . . . . .**33** A2
**Shipley St** NE15 . . . . . . . . . .**27** A2
**Shipley Wlk** 26 NE6 . . . . .**32** C2
**Shipton Cl** NE35 . . . . . . . . .**52** A1
**Shirlaw Cl** NE5 . . . . . . . . . . .**15** A4
**Shirwood Ave** NE16 . . . . . .**55** A4
**Shopping Ctr The** NE5 . . .**14** A2
**Shop Spouts** NE21 . . . . . . .**41** B3
**Shoreham Ct** NE3 . . . . . . . . .**7** A3
**Shortridge Terr** NE2 . . . . .**19** A1
**Shot Factory La** NE4 . . . . .**76** C3
**Shotley Gdns** NE9 . . . . . . . .**58** C3
**Shrewsbury Cl** NE12 . . . . .**20** B4
**Shrewsbury St** NE11 . . . . .**56** B4
**Shrigley Gdns** NE3 . . . . . . . .**8** A1
**Shunner Ct** NE37 . . . . . . . .**69** C2
**Side** NE1 . . . . . . . . . . . . . . . . .**78** B4
**Sidmouth Rd** NE9 . . . . . . . .**65** A3
**Silage Rd** NE29 . . . . . . . . . .**59** A1
**Silksworth Gdns** NE9 . . . .**66** A2
**Silloth Ave** NE5 . . . . . . . . . .**28** B4
**Silver St** 3 NE9 . . . . . . . . .**58** C4
**Silverdale Ave** NE10 . . . . .**61** C4
**Silverdale Terr** NE8 . . . . . .**58** B4
**Silverdale Way**
Brockley Whins NE34 . . . . .**52** B3
Whickham NE16 . . . . . . . . .**62** A4
**Silverhill Dr** NE5 . . . . . . . . .**28** C3
**Silverhill Sch The** NE5 . . .**29** A3
**Silver Lonnen** NE5 . . . . . . .**28** C4
**Silvermere Dr** NE40 . . . . . .**39** C4
**Silverton Gdns** NE40 . . . . .**38** C1
**Silverwood Gdns** NE11 . . .**57** A1
**Simonburn** NE38 . . . . . . . . .**71** B4
**Simonburn Ave** NE4 . . . . .**29** C4
**Simon Pl** NE13 . . . . . . . . . . . .**2** A1
**SIMONSIDE** . . . . . . . . . . . . .**37** C1
**Simonside Ave** NE28 . . . . .**23** A4
**Simonside Ind Est** NE32 **37** C1
**Simonside Pl** 2 NE6 . . . . .**33** A3
**Simonside Prim Sch**
Brockley Whins NE32 . . . . .**51** C4
Newcastle-u-T NE5 . . . . . . . .**6** A1
**Simonside Rd** NE21 . . . . . .**41** B1
**Simonside Terr** NE6 . . . . . .**33** A4
**Simonside View**
Jarrow NE32 . . . . . . . . . . . .**51** B4
13 NE16 . . . . . . . . . . . . . . .**54** C3
**Simonside Wlk** NE11 . . . . .**56** C1
**Simpsons Memorial**
**Homes** NE40 . . . . . . . . . . . .**38** C4
**Simpson St** NE40 . . . . . . . .**40** A4
**Simpson Terr** NE15 . . . . . .**13** C1
**Sinderby Cl** NE3 . . . . . . . . . . .**9** B4
**Sir Charles Parsons Sch**
NE6 . . . . . . . . . . . . . . . . . . . . .**34** A3
**Sir GB Hunter Memorial**
**Hospl** NE28 . . . . . . . . . . . . .**22** A2
**Sir Godfrey Thomson Ct**
NE10 . . . . . . . . . . . . . . . . . . . .**59** B4
**Siskin Ho** NE12 . . . . . . . . . .**11** C4
**Sixth Ave**
Gateshead NE11 . . . . . . . . .**64** A4

**Sixth Ave** continued
Newcastle-u-T NE6 . . . . . . . . .33 A3
**Skaylock Dr** NE38 . . . . . . . . .71 C3
**Skegness Par** NE31 . . . . . .50 C2
**Skelder Ave** NE12 . . . . . . . . .10 C2
**Skelton Cl** NE3 . . . . . . . . . . . .7 C4
**Skiddaw Pl** NE9 . . . . . . . . . .65 C4
**Skinnerburn Rd** NE1,
NE4 . . . . . . . . . . . . . . . . . . . . . .76 C3
**Skipper Cl** NE11 . . . . . . . . . .57 A3
**Skipton Gn** NE9 . . . . . . . . . .65 C2
**Skye Gr** NE32 . . . . . . . . . . . .52 A2
**Slake Rd** NE32 . . . . . . . . . . .37 B4
**Slaley Cl** NE10 . . . . . . . . . . .61 B3
**Slatyford La** NE5 . . . . . . . . .28 B4
**Slingsby Gdns** NE7 . . . . . . .26 B3
**Slipway The** NE10 . . . . . . . .48 C2
**Smeaton Ct** ⬛ NE28 . . . . .23 B1
**Smeaton St** ⬛ NE28 . . . . .23 B1
**Smithburn Rd** NE10 . . . . . . .60 A3
**Smithyford** NE9 . . . . . . . . . .65 B1
**Smithy La** NE11, NE9 . . . . . .65 A1
**Snowdon Gdns** NE11 . . . .56 C2
**Snowdrop Cl** NE21 . . . . . . . .40 C2
**Softley Pl** NE15 . . . . . . . . . . .28 A3
**Solway Rd** NE31 . . . . . . . . . .50 B4
**Solway St** NE6 . . . . . . . . . . .47 B4
**Somerford** NE9 . . . . . . . . . . .67 A2
**Somersby Dr** NE3 . . . . . . . . . .7 C1
**Somerset Gdns** NE28 . . . .21 B3
**Somerset Rd** NE31 . . . . . . . .50 B3
**Somerton Ct** NE3 . . . . . . . . . .7 A2
**Somervyl Ave** NE12 . . . . . .10 A2
**Sorrell Cl** NE4 . . . . . . . . . . . .29 B3
**Soulby Cl** NE3 . . . . . . . . . . . . .7 A2
**Sourmilk Hill La** NE9 . . . . .58 C2
**Souter Rd** NE3 . . . . . . . . . . . .8 B1

**South Ave**
Ryton NE40 . . . . . . . . . . . . . . . .25 A1
Whickham NE16 . . . . . . . . . . .55 A1
**South Bend** NE3 . . . . . . . . . . .4 B1
**SOUTH BENWELL** . . . . . . . .43 C4
South Benwell Prim Sch
NE4 . . . . . . . . . . . . . . . . . . . . . . .44 A4
**South Benwell Rd** NE15 . .43 B4
**South Cl** NE40 . . . . . . . . . . . .39 B4
**Southcote** NE16 . . . . . . . . . .54 C1
**South Croft** NE12 . . . . . . . . .11 C3
**South Cross St** NE3 . . . . . . . .9 A1
**South Dr**
Hebburn NE31 . . . . . . . . . . . .49 C4
Woolsington NE13 . . . . . . . . . .4 C4
**Southend Par** NE31 . . . . . . .50 C2
**Southend Rd** NE9 . . . . . . . . .59 A1
**Southend Terr** NE9 . . . . . . . .59 A2
**Southern Rd** NE6 . . . . . . . . .48 B4
**Southern Way** NE40 . . . . . . .39 B4
**Southfield Gdns** NE16 . . . .55 B2
**Southfield Gn** NE16 . . . . . . .55 B2
**Southfield Rd**
Longbenton NE12 . . . . . . . . .11 B2
Whickham NE16 . . . . . . . . . . .55 B2
**Southfields Ho** ⬛ NE6 . .48 C2
**Southfield Terr**
Newcastle-u-T NE6 . . . . . .48 C4
Whickham NE16 . . . . . . . . . . .55 B2
**Southfork** NE15 . . . . . . . . . . .27 A4
**Southgate** CE12 . . . . . . . . . .10 A2
**SOUTH GOSFORTH** . . . . . . .18 C4
South Gosforth Fst Sch
NE3 . . . . . . . . . . . . . . . . . . . . . . .18 C4
South Gosforth Sta NE3 18 C4
**South Gr** NE40 . . . . . . . . . . . .39 C4
**South Hill Rd** NE8 . . . . . . . . .79 A1
**Southlands**
Gateshead NE9 . . . . . . . . . . .66 A2
Hedworth NE32 . . . . . . . . . . .51 C1
Newcastle-u-T NE7 . . . . . . . .19 B2
**South Lea** NE21 . . . . . . . . . . .41 B1
**Southmead Ave** NE5 . . . . .16 A1
**Southmoor Rd** NE6 . . . . . . .34 A3
**South Par** NE11 . . . . . . . . . . .57 A4
**Southport Par** NE31 . . . . . . .50 C2
**South Ridge** NE3 . . . . . . . . . .8 A4
**South Row** NE8 . . . . . . . . . . .46 C4
**South Shore Rd**
Gateshead, East Gateshead
NE8 . . . . . . . . . . . . . . . . . . . . . . .47 A3
Gateshead, Saltmeadows
NE8 . . . . . . . . . . . . . . . . . . . . . . .46 C4
**South St**
Gateshead NE8 . . . . . . . . . . .79 C1

**South St** continued
Hebburn NE31 . . . . . . . . . . . .36 A3
Newcastle-u-T, Coxlodge
NE3 . . . . . . . . . . . . . . . . . . . . . . . .8 C2
Newcastle-u-T NE1 . . . . . . . .78 A4
South Street Prim Sch
NE8 . . . . . . . . . . . . . . . . . . . . . . .79 C1
**South Terr** NE28 . . . . . . . . . .22 C2
**South Tyneside Coll**
NE31 . . . . . . . . . . . . . . . . . . . . . .49 B2
**South View**
Birtley DH3 . . . . . . . . . . . . . . .70 C4
Crawcrook NE40 . . . . . . . . . .38 B4
⬛ Gateshead NE10 . . . . . . .59 C4
Hazlerigg NE13 . . . . . . . . . . . .4 A4
Jarrow NE32 . . . . . . . . . . . . . .36 B2
Longbenton NE7 . . . . . . . . . .11 A1
Newcastle-u-T NE5 . . . . . . . .27 C4
⬛ Springwell NE9 . . . . . . . .67 A1
**South View Terr**
Whickham NE16 . . . . . . . . . .55 A2
Whickham, Swalwell
NE16 . . . . . . . . . . . . . . . . . . . . . .55 A4
**South View W** NE6 . . . . . . . .32 B2
**Southway**
Gateshead NE9 . . . . . . . . . . .59 A2
Newcastle-u-T NE15 . . . . . . .27 C3
**Southwood Gdns** NE3 . . .17 A4
**Sovereign Cl** NE4 . . . . . . . .76 A4
**Sovereign Pl** NE4 . . . . . . . .76 A4
**Spalding Cl** NE7 . . . . . . . . . .20 A4
**Spa Well Cl** NE21 . . . . . . . . .53 A4
**Spa Well Turn** NE21 . . . . . .54 A3
**Speedwell** NE9 . . . . . . . . . . .59 B1
**Spencer Gr** NE16 . . . . . . . . .54 C4
**Spencers Bank** ⬛ NE16 42 C1
**Spencer St**
Hebburn NE31 . . . . . . . . . . . .36 A3
Newcastle-u-T NE6 . . . . . . . .33 A4
**Spencer Terr** NE15 . . . . . . .13 C1
**Spenfield Rd** NE15 . . . . . . .16 B3
**Spenser St** NE32 . . . . . . . . .36 A3
**Spenser Wlk** NE34 . . . . . . .52 C3
**Spinneyside Gdns** NE11 56 B3
**Spinney The** NE7 . . . . . . . . .26 A2
**Spinney The** NE7 . . . . . . . . .19 C2
**Spires La** NE6 . . . . . . . . . . . .33 A2
**Spital Terr** NE3 . . . . . . . . . . . .9 B1
**Split Crow Rd** NE10, NE8 59 A4
**Spoors Cotts** NE16 . . . . . . .54 C2
**Spoor St** NE11 . . . . . . . . . . . .57 A1
**Springbank Ho** NE2 . . . . . .32 B3
**Springbank Rd** NE2 . . . . . .32 B3
**Springfeld** NE10 . . . . . . . . . .67 A4
**Springfell** DH3 . . . . . . . . . . . .70 C3
**Springfield Ave** NE6 . . . . . .66 A1
**Springfield Gdns** NE28 . .21 A3
**Springfield Pl** NE9 . . . . . . . .58 C2
**Springfield Rd**
Blaydon NE21 . . . . . . . . . . . . .41 B1
Newcastle-u-T NE5 . . . . . . . .16 B2
**Springfield Terr** ⬛
NE10 . . . . . . . . . . . . . . . . . . . . . .59 B3
**Springhill Gdns** NE15 . . . .29 B3
**Springs The** DH3 . . . . . . . . .71 A3
**Springsyde Cl** NE16 . . . . . .54 A1
**SPRINGWELL** . . . . . . . . . . . . .67 A2
**Springwell Ave**
Gateshead NE9 . . . . . . . . . . .66 B3
Jarrow NE32 . . . . . . . . . . . . . .37 A2
Newcastle-u-T NE6 . . . . . . . .48 A4
**Springwell Cl** NE21 . . . . . . .41 C1
**Springwell Rd**
Gateshead NE9 . . . . . . . . . . .66 B3
Jarrow NE32 . . . . . . . . . . . . . .37 A2
Springwell NE9 . . . . . . . . . . .67 A1
Springwell Sta* NE9 . . .67 A3
**Springwell Terr**
Gateshead NE9 . . . . . . . . . . .66 C3
⬛ Springwell NE9 . . . . . . . .67 A1
Springwell Village Prim
Sch NE9 . . . . . . . . . . . . . . . . . .67 A1
**Springwood** NE31 . . . . . . . .35 A3
**Square Ho** ⬛ NE10 . . . . . . .59 B3
**Square The** ⬛ NE16 . . . . .55 A4
**Squires Gdns** NE10 . . . . . . .59 C3
**Stable La** NE10 . . . . . . . . . . . .8 A4
**Stadium Ind Pk** NE10 . . . .47 A3
**Stadium Rd** NE10 . . . . . . . . .47 A3
**Stadium Villas** NE28 . . . . .22 A2
**Stafford Villas** ⬛ NE9 . . .67 A1
**Staindrop** NE10 . . . . . . . . . . .60 C1

**Staines Rd** NE6 . . . . . . . . . . .47 C4
**Stainton Dr** NE10 . . . . . . . . .59 C4
**Stainton Gdns** NE9 . . . . . . .66 A2
**Staithes Ave** NE12 . . . . . . . .11 A2
**Staithes Rd** NE11 . . . . . . . . .77 A2
**Staithes St** NE6 . . . . . . . . . . .34 C2
**Staith La** NE21 . . . . . . . . . . . .40 C4
**Stalks Rd** NE13 . . . . . . . . . . . .2 B2
**Stamfordham Cl** NE28 . . .21 B2
**Stamfordham Mews** ⬛
NE5 . . . . . . . . . . . . . . . . . . . . . . .16 B1
**Stamfordham Rd** NE5 . . . .14 A4
**Stamp Exchange** NE1 . . . .78 A4
**Standfield Gdns** NE10 . . . .61 B4
**Staneway** NE10 . . . . . . . . . . .60 A1
**Stanfield Ct** NE7 . . . . . . . . . .20 C3
**Stang Wlk** NE12 . . . . . . . . . .11 A1
**Stanhope** NE38 . . . . . . . . . . .69 C1
**Stanhope Rd** NE32 . . . . . . . .37 B1
**Stanhope St** NE40 . . . . . . . .38 B1
**Stanley Gdns** NE9 . . . . . . . .66 A2
**Stanley Gr** NE7 . . . . . . . . . . .19 C3
**Stanley St**
Jarrow NE32 . . . . . . . . . . . . . .37 A3
Newcastle-u-T NE4 . . . . . . . .44 B4
Wallsend NE28 . . . . . . . . . . . .23 A3
**Stanmore Rd** NE6 . . . . . . . . .20 A1
**STANNERS** . . . . . . . . . . . . . . . .28 B2
**Stannington Ave** NE6 . . . .32 C3
**Stannington Gr** ⬛ NE6 . .32 C3
**Stannington Pl** ⬛ NE6 . . .32 C3
**Stanton Cl** NE10 . . . . . . . . . .61 C3
**Stanway Dr** NE7 . . . . . . . . . . .19 B3
**Stapeley Cl** ⬛ NE3 . . . . . . . .7 B1
**Stapeley View** NE3 . . . . . . . .7 B1
**Stapleford Cl** NE5 . . . . . . . . .15 C1
**Staple Rd** NE32 . . . . . . . . . . .37 A3
**STARGATE** . . . . . . . . . . . . . . . .40 A3
**Stargate Gdns** NE9 . . . . . . .66 A2
**Stargate Ind Est** NE40 . . .40 A3
**Stargate La** NE40 . . . . . . . . .40 A4
**Starling Wlk** NE16 . . . . . . . .63 A2
**Station App**
Gateshead NE11, NE9 . . . . .64 B3
Longbenton NE12 . . . . . . . . .11 B2
Newcastle-u-T NE6 . . . . . . . .47 B4
**Station Bank** NE40 . . . . . . . .25 A2
**Station La** DH2, DH3 . . . . . .70 A4
**Station Rd**
Boldon Colliery NE35 . . . . . .52 A2
Gateshead, Bill Quay
NE10 . . . . . . . . . . . . . . . . . . . . . .49 A2
Gateshead, Low Fell NE9 . . .58 A1
Hebburn NE31 . . . . . . . . . . . .35 B2
Longbenton NE12 . . . . . . . . .11 B3
Newburn NE15 . . . . . . . . . . . .26 A3
Newcastle-u-T, Kenton
Bankfoot NE3 . . . . . . . . . . . . . .6 C2
Newcastle-u-T, South
Gosforth NE3 . . . . . . . . . . . . . .9 C1
Newcastle-u-T, Wincombe
NE6 . . . . . . . . . . . . . . . . . . . . . . .34 B1
North Shields NE29 . . . . . . .24 B4
Wallsend NE28 . . . . . . . . . . . .21 C2
Wallsend NE28 . . . . . . . . . . . .22 A1
Wallsend, Willington Quay
NE28 . . . . . . . . . . . . . . . . . . . . . .23 B1
**Station Rd N** NE12 . . . . . . . .11 B4
**Station St** NE32 . . . . . . . . . . .36 C3
**Stavordale Terr** NE9 . . . . . .58 C3
**Staward Terr** NE6 . . . . . . . . .48 B4
**Staynebrigg** NE10 . . . . . . . .60 C2
**Stead St** NE28 . . . . . . . . . . . .23 B3
**Steenbergs** ⬛ NE1 . . . . . . .32 B2
**STELLA** . . . . . . . . . . . . . . . . . . .40 C4
**Stella Bank** NE21 . . . . . . . . .26 A1
**Stella Hall Dr** NE21 . . . . . . .40 C4
**Stella La** NE21 . . . . . . . . . . . .40 C4
**Stella Rd**
Blaydon NE21 . . . . . . . . . . . . .41 A4
Ryton NE21 . . . . . . . . . . . . . . .41 A4
**Stephen Ct** NE32 . . . . . . . . .37 A2
Stephenson Meml Prim
Sch NE28 . . . . . . . . . . . . . . . . .23 B2
**Stephenson Rd** NE7 . . . . . .19 C1
**Stephenson's La** NE1 . . . .78 A4
**Stephenson St**
Gateshead NE8 . . . . . . . . . . .57 C4
Wallsend NE28 . . . . . . . . . . . .23 C1
**Stephenson Terr**
Gateshead NE8 . . . . . . . . . . .59 C4
Newcastle-u-T NE15 . . . . . . .13 C1

**Stephenson Terr** continued
Throckley NE15 . . . . . . . . . . . .12 B2
**Stephenson Way** NE21 . . .53 A4
**Stephen St** NE6 . . . . . . . . . .32 B2
**Stepney Bank** NE1 . . . . . . . .32 B2
**Stepney Rd** ⬛ NE1, NE2 .32 B2
**Sterling Cotts** NE10 . . . . . .59 B3
**Stileford** NE10 . . . . . . . . . . . .60 C3
**Stirling Ave** NE32 . . . . . . . . .52 A4
**Stirling Ct** NE11 . . . . . . . . . . .64 C2
**Stocksfield Ave** NE5 . . . . . .29 A3
Stocksfield Avenue Prim
Sch NE5 . . . . . . . . . . . . . . . . . .28 C3
**Stocksfield Gdns** NE9 . . . .65 C2
**Stockwell Gn** NE6 . . . . . . . .34 A4
**Stoker Ave** NE34 . . . . . . . . . .52 B4
**Stokesley Gr** NE7 . . . . . . . . .19 B3
**Stonechat Cl** ⬛ NE38 . . . .71 B3
**Stonechat Mount** NE21 .40 C4
**Stonechat** NE12 . . . . . . . . . .10 B3
**Stonecroft Gdns** NE7 . . . .20 B3
**Stonecrop** NE9 . . . . . . . . . . .59 B1
**Stonefold** NE15 . . . . . . . . . . .15 C3
**Stoneleigh Ave** NE12 . . . .10 B3
**Stoneleigh Pl** ⬛ NE12 . .10 B2
**Stone St** NE10 . . . . . . . . . . . .59 B2
**Stonethwaite** NE29 . . . . . . .24 C3
**Stonegate Cl** NE10 . . . . . . .48 A1
**Stonegate Gdns** NE10 . .48 A1
**Stonegate La** NE10 . . . . . . .48 A1
**Stoneyhurst Rd** NE3 . . . . . .18 C4
**Stoneyhurst Rd W** NE3 . .18 B4
**Stoney La** NE9 . . . . . . . . . . . .67 A1
**Stoneylea Cl** NE40 . . . . . . . .38 A3
**Stoneylea Rd** NE5 . . . . . . . .28 A4
**Store St**
Blaydon NE21 . . . . . . . . . . . . .41 A1
Newcastle-u-T NE15 . . . . . . .27 A2
**Storey La** NE21 . . . . . . . . . . .40 C4
**Stormont Gn** NE3 . . . . . . . . .17 A3
**Stothard St** NE32 . . . . . . . . .37 A3
**Stotts Rd** NE6 . . . . . . . . . . . .34 B4
**Stowell Terr** NE10 . . . . . . . .60 A4
**Straker St** NE32 . . . . . . . . . .37 B2
**Stratford Gdns** NE9 . . . . . .58 B2
**Stratford Gr** NE6 . . . . . . . . .32 B3
**Stratford Grove Terr**
NE6 . . . . . . . . . . . . . . . . . . . . . . .32 B3
**Stratford Gr W** NE6 . . . . . .32 B3
**Stratford Rd** NE6 . . . . . . . . .32 B3
**Stratford Villas** NE6 . . . . . .32 B3
**Strathearn Way** NE3 . . . . . . .8 A3
**Strathmore Cres** NE4 . . . .29 C2
**Strathmore Rd**
Gateshead NE10, NE9 . . . . .59 A3
Newcastle-u-T NE3 . . . . . . . . .9 A3
**Strawberry Gdns** NE28 . .31 B4
**STREET GATE** . . . . . . . . . . . . .63 A3
**Street Gate Pk** NE16 . . . . . .63 B3
**Stretford Ct** NE9 . . . . . . . . . .65 B1
**Struddars Farm Ct**
NE21 . . . . . . . . . . . . . . . . . . . . . .42 B2
**Stuart Ct** NE3 . . . . . . . . . . . . . .7 A2
**Stuart Gdns** NE15 . . . . . . . .12 B2
**Stuart Terr** NE10 . . . . . . . . . .47 C1
**Stubbs Ave** NE16 . . . . . . . . .54 C4
**Studdon Wlk** NE3 . . . . . . . . . .7 B1
**Studley Gdns** ⬛ NE9 . . . .58 B1
**Studley Villas** NE12 . . . . . .11 C3
**Sturdee Gdns** NE2 . . . . . . .18 C3
**Styford Gdns** NE15 . . . . . . .27 C3
**Suffolk Gdns** NE28 . . . . . . .22 C4
**Suffolk Pl**
Birtley DH3 . . . . . . . . . . . . . . .70 C1
Gateshead NE8 . . . . . . . . . . .46 C4
**Suffolk Rd** NE31 . . . . . . . . . .50 B3
**Suffolk St** NE32 . . . . . . . . . . .36 C2
**Sugley Dr** NE15 . . . . . . . . . . .27 B2
**Sugley St** NE15 . . . . . . . . . . .27 B2
**Sugley Villas** NE15 . . . . . . .27 B2
**Sullivan Wlk** NE31 . . . . . . . .35 C1
**Summerfield Rd** NE9 . . . . .58 B3
**Summerhill**
Blaydon NE21 . . . . . . . . . . . . .41 A3
Hedworth NE32 . . . . . . . . . . .51 C1
Newcastle-u-T NE4 . . . . . . . .76 A4
**Summerhill Ave** NE3 . . . . . . .5 A1
**Summerhill Terr** NE4 . . . . .76 C4
**Summer St** NE10 . . . . . . . . . .47 C1
**Sunbury Ave** NE2 . . . . . . . . .18 C2

**Sunderland Rd**
Gateshead, Felling
NE10 . . . . . . . . . . . . . . . . . . . . . .60 A4
Gateshead, Heworth
NE10 . . . . . . . . . . . . . . . . . . . . . .60 B4
Gateshead, Wardley
NE10 . . . . . . . . . . . . . . . . . . . . . .61 B3
**Sunderland St** NE1 . . . . . . .76 C4
**Sundew Rd** NE9 . . . . . . . . . .66 A4
**Sundridge Dr** NE10 . . . . . . .61 B3
**Sunhill** NE16 . . . . . . . . . . . . . .62 C2
**Sunnidale** NE16 . . . . . . . . . .54 A1
**Sunningdale Ave**
Newcastle-u-T NE6 . . . . . . . .34 A2
Wallsend NE28 . . . . . . . . . . . .22 A2
**Sunningdale Cl** NE10 . . . . .59 C3
**SUNNISIDE** . . . . . . . . . . . . . . .62 B2
**Sunniside Cl** NE16 . . . . . . . .62 C3
**Sunniside Gdns**
Gateshead NE9 . . . . . . . . . . .66 A2
Newcastle-u-T NE15 . . . . . . .28 C2
**Sunniside Rd** NE16 . . . . . . .62 C3
Sunniside Sta* NE16 . .62 C1
**Sunnybank Ave** NE15 . . . .29 B1
**Sunnycrest Ave** NE6 . . . . .34 A2
**Sunnygill Terr** NE40 . . . . . .38 B2
**Sunnyway** NE5 . . . . . . . . . . .16 A2
**Sun St** ⬛ NE16 . . . . . . . . . .62 C2
**Surrey Rd** NE31 . . . . . . . . . . .50 B3
**Surrey St** NE32 . . . . . . . . . . .36 B2
**Surrey Terr** DH3 . . . . . . . . . .70 B1
**Sussex Gdns** NE28 . . . . . . .22 C3
**Sussex St** NE32 . . . . . . . . . . .36 B2
**Sutherland Ave** NE4 . . . . . .29 C3
**Sutherland St** NE8 . . . . . . . .79 C1
**Sutton St** NE6 . . . . . . . . . . . .33 C3
**Swainby Cl** NE3 . . . . . . . . . . . .9 B4
**Swaledale Gdns** NE7 . . . . .19 C3
**Swallow Tail Dr** NE11 . . . . .57 A4
**SWALWELL** . . . . . . . . . . . . . . .43 B1
**Swalwell Bank** NE16 . . . . . .54 C4
Swalwell Cty Prim Sch
NE16 . . . . . . . . . . . . . . . . . . . . . .55 A4
**Swan Ave** NE28 . . . . . . . . . . .22 B3
**Swan Ct** NE11 . . . . . . . . . . . . .77 A1
**Swan Dr** NE11 . . . . . . . . . . . . .77 A1
**Swan Rd** NE6 . . . . . . . . . . . . .49 A4
**Swan St** NE8 . . . . . . . . . . . . . .78 C3
**Swanton Cl** NE5 . . . . . . . . . .15 C4
**Swanway** NE9 . . . . . . . . . . . .59 A3
**Swards Rd** NE10 . . . . . . . . . .60 A3
**Swarland Ave** NE7 . . . . . . . .10 C1
**Swarth Cl** NE37 . . . . . . . . . . .69 C2
**Swinbourne Terr** NE32 . .51 A3
**Swinburne Pl**
Birtley DH3 . . . . . . . . . . . . . . .70 B3
Gateshead NE8 . . . . . . . . . . .78 C3
**Swinburne St**
Gateshead NE8 . . . . . . . . . . .78 B3
Jarrow NE32 . . . . . . . . . . . . . .37 C2
**Swindale Cl** NE21 . . . . . . . . .53 B4
**Swindon St** NE31 . . . . . . . . .35 B2
**Swindon Terr** NE6 . . . . . . . .19 C1
**Swinhoe Gdns** NE13 . . . . . . .2 B2
**Swinley Gdns** NE15 . . . . . . .28 A2
**Swyntoft** NE10 . . . . . . . . . . . .61 A3
**Sycamore Cl** NE2 . . . . . . . . .19 A2
**Sycamore Gr**
Gateshead NE10 . . . . . . . . . .60 A4
Springwell NE9 . . . . . . . . . . .67 A1
**Sycamore Rd** NE21 . . . . . . .41 B2
**Sycamore St**
Throckley NE15 . . . . . . . . . . . .12 B3
Wallsend NE28 . . . . . . . . . . . .22 A1
**Sycamores The** NE4 . . . . . .76 A3
**Sydney Ct** NE8 . . . . . . . . . . . .78 B3
**Sydney Gdns** NE34 . . . . . . .52 B3
**Syron** NE16 . . . . . . . . . . . . . . .54 B3

**T**

**Talbot Cotts** DH3 . . . . . . . . .70 B4
**Talbot Gn** NE5 . . . . . . . . . . . .28 C4
**Talbot House Sch** NE15 .13 A2
**Talbot Terr** ⬛ DH3 . . . . . . .70 B4
**Talisman View** ⬛ NE9 . . .65 B2
**Tamarisk Way** NE9 . . . . . . . .59 B1
**Tamerton Dr** DH3 . . . . . . . . .70 C2
**Tanfield Pl** NE9 . . . . . . . . . . .66 A2

**Tanfield Rd**
Gateshead NE9. . . . . . . . . .**66** A2
Newcastle-u-T NE15 . . . . .**28** B2
**Tankerville Pl 3** NE2 . . . .**18** C1
**Tankerville Terr** NE2 . . . .**18** C1
**Tantallon** DH3 . . . . . . . . . .**70** C2
**Tantobie Rd** NE15. . . . . . .**28** B2
**Tarlton Cres** NE10 . . . . . .**59** B4
**Tarset Pl** NE3 . . . . . . . . . . . **8** B2
**Tarset St** NE1. . . . . . . . . . .**32** B1
**Tasmania Rd** NE44 . . . . . .**52** B3
**Taunton Ave** NE32 . . . . . .**37** C1
**Tavistock Pl** NE32. . . . . . .**37** B1
**Tavistock Rd** NE2 . . . . . . .**18** C2
**Taylor Ave** NE13 . . . . . . . . **2** C2
**Taylor Gdns** NE10 . . . . . . .**48** C1
**Teal Cl**
Longbenton NE7 . . . . . . . .**11** A1
**6** Washington NE38 . . .**71** B3
**TEAMS** . . . . . . . . . . . . . . . .**77** B1
**Team St** NE8. . . . . . . . . . . .**77** B1
**TEAM VALLEY** . . . . . . . . .**57** C1
**Team Valley Bsns Ctr**
NE11 . . . . . . . . . . . . . . . .**57** C2
**Team Valley Trad Est**
NE11 . . . . . . . . . . . . . . . .**64** B4
**Teasdale Ho** NE5 . . . . . . . . **6** B1
**Tebay Dr** NE5 . . . . . . . . . .**28** A4
**Tedco Bsns Ctr** NE32 . . .**36** A4
**Teddington Cl** NE3. . . . . . . **6** C3
**Tedham Rd** NE15 . . . . . . . .**27** A3
**Teesdale Gdns** NE7 . . . . .**19** C3
**Teesdale Gn** NE12 . . . . . . .**11** B4
**Tees Rd** NE31. . . . . . . . . . .**50** A3
**Teindland Cl** NE4 . . . . . . . .**44** A4
**Telford Ct** NE28. . . . . . . . .**24** A2
**Telford St**
Gateshead NE8. . . . . . . . .**57** C3
North Shields NE28 . . . . .**24** A2
**Tempest St** NE21 . . . . . . . .**40** C4
**Temple Gn** NE8 . . . . . . . . .**57** B4
**Temple St**
Gateshead NE10. . . . . . . .**47** C1
Newcastle-u-T NE1 . . . . . .**76** C4
**Tenbury Cres** NE12. . . . . .**11** A3
**Tennant St**
Hebburn NE31 . . . . . . . . .**35** B1
**3** South Shields NE34. . .**52** C4
**Tennyson Ave** NE31 . . . . .**36** A2
**Tennyson Cres** NE16 . . . .**54** C4
**Tennyson Ct** NE8 . . . . . . . .**46** C2
**Tennyson Gn** NE3 . . . . . . .**17** A3
**Tenter Garth** NE15 . . . . . .**12** A2
**Tenth Ave**
Gateshead NE11. . . . . . . .**64** B2
Newcastle-u-T NE6 . . . . . .**33** A4
**Tenth Ave W** NE11 . . . . . .**64** B2
**Terrace The**
**6** Boldon Colliery
NE35. . . . . . . . . . . . . . . .**52** A1
Longbenton NE12 . . . . . . .**11** A2
**Tetford Pl** NE12. . . . . . . . .**11** A3
**Teviot St** NE8 . . . . . . . . . . .**71** C1
**Teviotdale Gdns** NE7 . . . .**19** C3
**Teviot St** NE8 . . . . . . . . . .**58** C4
**Teviot Way** NE32. . . . . . . .**36** B1
**Tewkesbury Rd** NE15. . . . .**27** A3
**Thames Ave** NE32 . . . . . . .**51** B2
**Thames Gdns** NE28 . . . . .**21** C1
**Thames Rd** NE31 . . . . . . . .**50** B3
**Thames St** NE8 . . . . . . . . .**46** C1
**Tharsis Rd** NE31. . . . . . . . .**35** B1
**Thatcher Cl** NE16 . . . . . . . .**54** C1
**Theresa Russell Ho** NE6 .**33** A2
**Theresa St** NE21 . . . . . . . .**41** B3
**Third Ave**
Gateshead NE11. . . . . . . .**57** B2
Newcastle-u-T NE6 . . . . . .**33** A3
**Third St** NE28. . . . . . . . . . .**22** B1
**Thirlington Cl** NE5. . . . . . .**15** C3
**Thirlmere**
Birtley DH3 . . . . . . . . . . . .**71** A2
Gateshead NE10. . . . . . . .**61** C4
**Thirlmere Cres** NE21 . . . .**53** A4
**Thirlmere Ct** NE31 . . . . . . .**50** B4
**Thirlmere Way** NE15 . . . . .**15** C1
**Thirlmoor** NE37 . . . . . . . . .**69** C2
**Thirlwall Cl** NE12 . . . . . . . .**10** A2
**Thirlwell Gr** NE32. . . . . . . .**51** A3**

**Thirlwell Rd** NE8 . . . . . . . .**46** C3
**Thirston Way** NE3 . . . . . . . . **7** B1
**Thistle Ave** NE4 . . . . . . . . .**38** C4
**Thistle Ct** NE31 . . . . . . . . .**35** B1
**Thistledon Ave** NE16. . . . .**54** B2
**Thistley Cl** NE6 . . . . . . . . . .**33** C4
**Thistley Gn** NE10 . . . . . . . .**49** A1
**Thomas Bell Ho 3**
NE34. . . . . . . . . . . . . . . .**52** C4
**Thomas Bewick Sch**
NE5. . . . . . . . . . . . . . . . .**14** A2
**Thomas Dr** NE31 . . . . . . . .**35** B2
**Thomas Hepburn Com**
Comp Sch NE10 . . . . . .**60** A3
**Thomas Horsley Ho**
NE15. . . . . . . . . . . . . . . .**28** C1
**Thomas St**
Gateshead NE9. . . . . . . . .**66** B1
Newcastle-u-T NE5 . . . . . .**15** A2
Whickham NE16 . . . . . . . .**54** C3
**Thomas Walling Prim Sch**
NE5. . . . . . . . . . . . . . . . .**16** A2
**Thompson Gdns** NE28 . . .**21** C2
**Thompson Pl** NE10 . . . . . .**59** C4
**Thornborough Ho 18**
NE6. . . . . . . . . . . . . . . . .**33** A2
**Thornbury 3** NE21 . . . . . .**41** A1
**Thornbury Cl**
Boldon Colliery NE35 . . . .**52** A1
Newcastle-u-T NE3 . . . . . . **6** C1
**Thorn Cl** NE13 . . . . . . . . . . . **2** A1
**Thorndale Rd** NE15 . . . . . .**28** A1
**Thorne Ave** NE10 . . . . . . . .**61** A4
**Thorne Brake** NE10 . . . . . .**60** C3
**Thorne Terr** NE6 . . . . . . . . .**33** C3
**Thornfield Rd** NE3 . . . . . . .**17** C4
**Thornhaugh Ave** NE16 . . .**54** B2
**Thornhill Cl** NE11. . . . . . . .**56** C4
**Thornhill Rd** NE12 . . . . . . .**11** B2
**Thornlea Gdns** NE9 . . . . . .**58** B2
**Thornleigh Rd** NE2 . . . . . .**18** C1
**Thornley Ave** NE10. . . . . . .**61** A2
**Thornley Cl** NE16 . . . . . . . .**62** B4
**Thornley Rd** NE5. . . . . . . . .**28** A4
**Thornley Wood* NE21 . . . .**53** A2
**Thornton Cotts** NE40. . . . .**25** A4
**Thornton Cres** NE21 . . . . .**41** B3
**Thorntree Dr** NE15. . . . . . .**28** B3
**Thorntree Wlk** NE32 . . . . .**51** C2
**Thornwood Gdns** NE11. . . .**57** A2
**Thornygarth** NE10 . . . . . . .**60** A3
**Thorpe Dr** NE40 . . . . . . . . .**25** C1
**Three Mile Ct** NE3 . . . . . . . **9** A4
**THROCKLEY**. . . . . . . . . . .**12** B1
**Throckley Fst Sch** NE15 .**12** A2
**Thropton Ave** NE7 . . . . . . .**10** C1
**Thropton Cl** NE10. . . . . . . .**61** B2
**Thropton Cres** NE3 . . . . . . **8** C2
**Thropton Terr** NE7 . . . . . . .**19** C2
**Thursby** DH3 . . . . . . . . . . . .**71** A2
**Thursby Gdns** NE9 . . . . . . .**65** C3
**Tiberius Cl 6** NE28 . . . . . .**21** C1
**Tidings The** NE10 . . . . . . . .**49** A2
**Till Ave** NE21 . . . . . . . . . . .**41** A2
**Tilley Rd** NE38 . . . . . . . . . .**69** B2
**Tillmouth Gdns** NE4 . . . . .**29** A2
**Tillmouth Park Rd** NE15 .**12** B1
**Till St 7** NE6 . . . . . . . . . . .**47** B4
**Tilson Way** NE3 . . . . . . . . . . **8** A2
**Times Sq** NE1 . . . . . . . . . . .**76** C4
**Timlin Gdns** NE28 . . . . . . .**23** C3
**Tindale Dr** NE16 . . . . . . . . .**54** C2
**Tintern Cres** NE6 . . . . . . . .**32** C3
**Tirril Pl** NE5 . . . . . . . . . . . .**15** B1
**Titan Ho 7** NE6 . . . . . . . . .**34** B2
**Titan Rd** NE6 . . . . . . . . . . . .**34** B1
**Titlington Gr** NE31 . . . . . . .**49** C3
**Tiverton Ave 1** NE4 . . . . .**29** C2
**Tiverton Gdns** NE9 . . . . . .**65** A3
**Toberty Gdns** NE10 . . . . . .**61** A4
**Togstone Pl 4** NE5 . . . . . .**16** A1
**Toll Bridge Rd** NE21. . . . . .**42** B3
**Tonbridge Ave** NE29 . . . . .**24** C4
**Toner Ave** NE31. . . . . . . . . .**49** C4
**Toner Avenue Prim Sch**
NE31. . . . . . . . . . . . . . . .**49** C3
**Topcliffe Ho** NE9. . . . . . . . .**65** C2
**Toppings St** NE35. . . . . . . .**52** A1
**Tor Mere Cl** NE37 . . . . . . . .**69** C2
**Torquay Gdns** NE9 . . . . . . .**65** A3
**Torquay Par** NE31. . . . . . . .**50** C3**

**Torver Cl** NE13. . . . . . . . . . . **2** B1
**Torver Pl** NE9. . . . . . . . . . . .**65** C4
**Tosson Terr** NE6 . . . . . . . . .**20** A1
**Tower Ct** NE11. . . . . . . . . . .**77** A1
**Tower Gdns** NE40. . . . . . . .**25** A1
**Towers Ave** NE2 . . . . . . . . .**18** C2
**Towers Pl** NE34. . . . . . . . . .**37** C1
**Tower View** NE15 . . . . . . . .**29** A2
**Towneley Cotts** NE40. . . . .**38** C4
**Townfield Gdns** NE15 . . . .**26** A4
**Trafford** NE9 . . . . . . . . . . . .**65** B1
**Trafford Wlk** NE5 . . . . . . . .**14** C3
**Transbritannia Ct** NE21 .**42** A4
**Tranwell Cl** NE3 . . . . . . . . . . **8** A4
**Tredegar Cl** NE5 . . . . . . . . .**15** C4
**Treetops The** NE32 . . . . . .**50** C4
**Treherne Rd** NE2 . . . . . . . .**18** B3
**Trent Ave** NE31 . . . . . . . . . .**50** B3
**Trent Dr** NE32 . . . . . . . . . . .**51** A3
**Trent Gdns** NE8. . . . . . . . . .**59** A4
**Trentham Ave** NE7 . . . . . . .**10** C1
**Trevelyan Dr** NE5 . . . . . . . .**15** B4
**Trevethick St** NE8 . . . . . . .**57** C4
**Trewhitt Rd** NE6 . . . . . . . . .**33** A4
**Tribune Pl** NE9 . . . . . . . . . .**59** A3
**Trimdon Gr** NE9 . . . . . . . . .**66** B3
**Trinity Ct** NE8. . . . . . . . . . . .**78** C3
**Trinity Ctyd** NE6 . . . . . . . . .**47** C4
**Trinity Maritime Mus***
NE1. . . . . . . . . . . . . . . . .**78** B1
**Trinity Sch (Deneview**
Site) NE3. . . . . . . . . . . .**19** A4
**Trinity Sch (Kenton**
Site) NE3. . . . . . . . . . . .**17** C2
**Trinity Sch (Oakfield Coll)**
NE4. . . . . . . . . . . . . . . . .**29** B2
**Trinity Sq** NE8 . . . . . . . . . .**78** C3
**Trojan Ave** NE6 . . . . . . . . . .**33** C3
**Troutbeck Ave** NE6 . . . . . .**47** A4
**Troutbeck Gdns** NE9 . . . . .**65** B3
**Troutbeck Way** NE34. . . . .**52** B3
**Troutdale Pl** NE12 . . . . . . .**10** A2
**Troves Cl** NE4 . . . . . . . . . . .**44** A4
**Trowbridge Way** NE3. . . . . **8** A1
**Truro Way** NE32 . . . . . . . . .**51** B1
**Tudor Way** NE3 . . . . . . . . . . **6** C2
**Tudor Wlk** NE3 . . . . . . . . . . . **7** A2
**Tudor Wynd** NE6. . . . . . . . .**20** B2
**Tulip Cl** NE21 . . . . . . . . . . . .**41** A2
**Tulip St** NE8. . . . . . . . . . . . .**47** B1
**Tumulus Ave** NE6 . . . . . . . .**34** B4
**Tundry Way** NE21 . . . . . . . .**42** B4
**Tunstall Ave** NE6. . . . . . . . .**33** B2
**Turbinia Gdns** NE7 . . . . . .**20** B2
**Turfside**
Gateshead NE10. . . . . . . .**61** A3
Hedworth NE32 . . . . . . . .**51** C1
**Turnberry Cl** NE10 . . . . . . .**61** B2
**Turnberry Way** NE3 . . . . . . **9** C2
**Turnbull The** NE1. . . . . . . . .**78** A4
**Turner Cl** NE40 . . . . . . . . . .**39** C4
**Turner Cres** NE3 . . . . . . . . . **8** B1
**Turnstone Dr** NE38. . . . . . .**71** B3
**Turret Rd** NE15 . . . . . . . . . .**28** A3
**Tweed Gr** NE15 . . . . . . . . . .**27** A3
**Tweedmouth Ct** NE3 . . . . .**18** C4
**Tweed St**
Hebburn NE31 . . . . . . . . .**35** C1
Jarrow NE32 . . . . . . . . . .**36** B1
Newcastle-u-T NE4 . . . . . .**30** A1
**Tweedy Terr** NE6. . . . . . . . .**34** A1
**Twizell Ave** NE21. . . . . . . . .**41** A2
**Two Ball Lonnen** NE4 . . . .**29** B4
**Tyndal Gdns 4** NE11. . . . .**44** B1
**Tyne App** NE32 . . . . . . . . . .**36** B4
**Tynebank** NE21 . . . . . . . . . .**41** A2
**Tynedale Ave** NE28. . . . . . .**21** C4
**Tynedale Ct** NE28 . . . . . . . .**23** B4
**Tynedale Ho** NE15 . . . . . . .**28** C1
**Tynedale Terr** NE12 . . . . . .**11** B2
**Tynegate Office Precinct**
NE8. . . . . . . . . . . . . . . . .**79** C2
**Tyne Gdns** NE40 . . . . . . . . .**40** A4
**Tynell Wlk** NE3 . . . . . . . . . . . **6** C1
**Tyne Main Rd** NE10 . . . . . .**48** A4
**Tynemouth Cl 3** NE6 . . . .**32** C2
**Tynemouth Ct 7** NE6 . . . .**33** A4
**Tynemouth Gr 9** NE6 . . . .**33** A3
**Tynemouth Rd**
Jarrow NE32 . . . . . . . . . .**51** A2
Newcastle-u-T NE6 . . . . . .**33** A3
Wallsend NE28 . . . . . . . . .**23** B3**

**Tynemouth Way 8** NE6 .**33** A3
**Tyne Point Ind Est** NE32 **37** C1
**Tyne Rd E** NE8 . . . . . . . . . .**77** C2
**Tyne Riverside Ctry Pk***
NE15. . . . . . . . . . . . . . . .**25** B4
**Tyneside Rd** NE4 . . . . . . . .**76** B3
**Tyne St**
Blaydon NE21. . . . . . . . . .**41** A1
Gateshead, Bill Quay
NE10. . . . . . . . . . . . . . .**48** C2
Gateshead, Felling Shore
NE10. . . . . . . . . . . . . . .**48** A2
Gateshead, Pelaw NE10. .**48** B2
Jarrow NE32 . . . . . . . . . .**36** C4
Newcastle-u-T NE1 . . . . . .**32** B1
Newcastle-u-T NE21 . . . . .**41** B1
**Tynevale Ave** NE21 . . . . . .**41** B1
**Tynevale Terr**
Gateshead NE8. . . . . . . . .**77** C1
Newcastle-u-T NE15 . . . . .**27** A2
**Tyne View**
Blaydon NE21. . . . . . . . . .**41** B1
Hebburn NE31 . . . . . . . . .**35** A3
Newcastle-u-T NE15 . . . . .**27** B2
**Tyne View Ave** NE16 . . . . .**55** B4
**Tyne View Com Prim Sch**
NE8. . . . . . . . . . . . . . . . .**77** C2
**Tyne View Gdns** NE10 . . . .**48** B1
**Tyne View Pl** NE8 . . . . . . . .**77** C1
**Tyne View Prim Sch** NE8 **34** B1
**Tyne View Terr** NE28. . . . . .**24** A1
**Tyne Vw** NE15. . . . . . . . . . .**12** B1
**Tynewold Cl** NE8. . . . . . . . .**77** C1**

## U

**Uldale Ct** NE3 . . . . . . . . . . . . **7** C3
**Ullswater Ave** NE32 . . . . . .**51** C3
**Ullswater Cres** NE21 . . . . .**53** A4
**Ullswater Way** NE5 . . . . . .**28** C4
**Ulverstone Terr** NE6 . . . . .**33** C3
**Ulverston Gdns** NE9 . . . . .**65** C4
**Underhill Terr** NE9 . . . . . . .**67** B1
**Underwood** NE10 . . . . . . . .**60** C2
**Union Hall Rd** NE15 . . . . . .**27** B3
**Union Rd** NE6 . . . . . . . . . . .**33** A2
**Union St**
Jarrow NE32 . . . . . . . . . .**36** C4
Wallsend NE28 . . . . . . . . .**34** C4
**Uplands The**
Birtley DH3 . . . . . . . . . . . .**68** C1
Newcastle-u-T NE3 . . . . . .**17** A4
**Uplands Way** NE9 . . . . . . . .**67** A2
**Upper Precinct The**
NE21. . . . . . . . . . . . . . . .**41** C3
**Upton St** NE8 . . . . . . . . . . .**77** C1
**Urswick Ct** NE3. . . . . . . . . . . **6** C1
**Ushaw Rd** NE31. . . . . . . . . .**36** A2
**Usk Ave** NE32 . . . . . . . . . . .**51** B3
**Uxbridge Terr 3** NE10 . .**47** C1**

## V

**Vale Ho** NE2 . . . . . . . . . . . .**32** B4
**Valentia Ave** NE6 . . . . . . . .**33** C3
**Valeshead Ho 17** NE28 . .**21** C2
**Valeside** NE15 . . . . . . . . . .**12** A2
**Vale Wlk** NE2 . . . . . . . . . . .**32** B4
**Valley Cres** NE21. . . . . . . . .**40** C2
**Valley Dr**
Dunston NE11. . . . . . . . . .**56** B3
Gateshead NE9. . . . . . . . .**58** B3
Whickham NE16 . . . . . . . .**54** C4
**Valley Gdns**
Gateshead NE9. . . . . . . . .**58** C3
Wallsend NE28 . . . . . . . . .**22** B3
**Valley Gn** NE40 . . . . . . . . . .**38** B2
**Valley Shopping Village**
NE11 . . . . . . . . . . . . . . . .**64** B4
**Valley View**
Birtley DH3 . . . . . . . . . . . .**68** C1
Jarrow NE32 . . . . . . . . . .**51** A4
Newcastle-u-T, Jesmond
NE2. . . . . . . . . . . . . . . .**19** A1
Newcastle-u-T, Lemington
NE15. . . . . . . . . . . . . . .**27** A2
**Valley View Prim Sch**
NE32. . . . . . . . . . . . . . . .**51** A4
**Vallum Pl** NE9 . . . . . . . . . . .**59** A2
**Vallum Rd**
Newcastle-u-T NE6 . . . . . .**33** C2
Throckley NE15 . . . . . . . .**12** C2
**Vance Bsns Pk** NE11 . . . .**57** A3**

**Vance Ct** NE21. . . . . . . . . . .**42** A4
**Vancouver Dr** NE7 . . . . . . .**20** B2
**Vauxhall Rd** NE6 . . . . . . . . .**34** B4
**Velville Ct** NE3 . . . . . . . . . . . **6** C2
**Ventnor Ave** NE4. . . . . . . . .**30** A1
**Ventnor Cres** NE9 . . . . . . . .**58** A1
**Ventnor Gdns** NE9 . . . . . . .**58** A2
**Verdun Ave** NE31 . . . . . . . .**35** C2
**Viaduct St** NE28 . . . . . . . . .**22** C2
**Vicars' La** NE7 . . . . . . . . . . .**10** B1
**Victoria Ave**
Gateshead NE10. . . . . . . .**59** B3
Longbenton NE12 . . . . . . .**11** B3
Wallsend NE28 . . . . . . . . .**21** C2
**Victoria Bglws** NE11 . . . . .**77** A1
**Victoria Ct**
Gateshead NE8. . . . . . . . .**77** C1
Hebburn NE31 . . . . . . . . .**35** B1
**Victoria House** NE8 . . . . . .**77** C1
**Victoria Ind Est** NE31 . . . .**49** B3
**Victoria Mews**
Newcastle-u-T NE2 . . . . . .**32** B4
Whickham NE16 . . . . . . . .**54** C3
**Victoria Rd** NE8 . . . . . . . . . .**57** B4
**Victoria Rd E** NE31 . . . . . . .**36** A2
**Victoria Rd W** NE31 . . . . . .**49** C4
**Victoria Sq 4** NE10 . . . . . .**59** C4
**Victoria St**
Crawcrook NE40. . . . . . . .**38** B4
Dunston NE11. . . . . . . . . .**77** A1
Hebburn NE31 . . . . . . . . .**35** A2
Newcastle-u-T NE4 . . . . . .**76** B4
**Victoria Terr**
**5** Gateshead, Felling
NE10 . . . . . . . . . . . . . . .**59** C4
Gateshead, Wrekenton
NE9. . . . . . . . . . . . . . . .**66** A3
Jarrow NE32 . . . . . . . . . .**36** B2
**14** Springwell NE9 . . . . .**67** A1
**3** Throckley NE15 . . . . . .**12** B2
**Viewforth Gn 1** NE5. . . . .**16** A1
**Vigodale** DH3. . . . . . . . . . . .**71** A1
**Vigo La** NE38 . . . . . . . . . . . .**71** C1
**Viking Ind Est** NE32 . . . . . .**36** B4
**Viking Precinct 8**
NE32. . . . . . . . . . . . . . . .**36** C3
**Village Ctr** NE37 . . . . . . . . .**67** C1
**Village East** NE40 . . . . . . . .**25** A2
**Village Farm** NE15 . . . . . . .**13** B1
**Village Hts** NE8 . . . . . . . . . .**79** B2
**Village Pl** NE6 . . . . . . . . . . .**33** B1
**Villa Pl** NE8. . . . . . . . . . . . . .**79** B1
**Villas The** NE13 . . . . . . . . . . **2** C1
**Villa View** NE9 . . . . . . . . . . .**58** C2
**Vimy Ave** NE31. . . . . . . . . . .**35** C2
**Vindolanda 2** NE28. . . . . .**23** A4
**Vine Cl** NE8. . . . . . . . . . . . . .**77** C1
**Vine St** NE28 . . . . . . . . . . . .**22** A1
**Viola Terr** NE16 . . . . . . . . . .**55** A3
**Violet Cl** NE4 . . . . . . . . . . . .**43** C4**

## W

**Wagon Way** NE28 . . . . . . . .**22** B1
**Wagonway Rd** NE31. . . . . .**35** C3
**Wagtail Cl** NE21 . . . . . . . . .**53** B4
**WALBOTTLE** . . . . . . . . . . .**13** A2
**Walbottle Campus Tech**
Coll NE15 . . . . . . . . . . . .**13** A2
**Walbottle Hall Gdns**
NE15. . . . . . . . . . . . . . . .**13** B1
**Walbottle Rd**
Newburn NE15 . . . . . . . . .**26** A4
Walbottle NE15 . . . . . . . .**13** A1
**Walbottle Village Fst Sch**
NE15. . . . . . . . . . . . . . . .**13** A1
**Waldridge Cl** NE37. . . . . . .**69** C2
**Waldridge Gdns** NE9. . . . .**66** B4
**WALKER**. . . . . . . . . . . . . . .**34** A2
**Walker Ct 11** NE16 . . . . . .**54** C3
**Walkerdene Ho** NE6 . . . . .**34** C4
**WALKERGATE** . . . . . . . . . .**33** C4
**Walkergate Hospl** NE6 . .**33** C4
**Walker Gate Ind Est**
NE6. . . . . . . . . . . . . . . . .**34** C2
**Walkergate Prim Sch**
NE6. . . . . . . . . . . . . . . . .**33** C4
**Walkergate Sta** NE6. . . . . .**33** C4
**Walker Gr** NE6. . . . . . . . . . .**34** A4
**Walker Park Cl** NE6 . . . . . .**48** C4
**Walker Park Gdns** NE6 . .**48** C4**

Walker Rd NE6 . . . . . . . . 48 A3
Walker Riverside Ind Pk
NE6. . . . . . . . . . . . . . . . 49 A4
Walker Riverside Pk★
NE6. . . . . . . . . . . . . . . . 49 A4
Walker Tech Coll NE6. . 34 A2
Walker Terr NE6 . . . . . . . 79 B2
Walker View NE10. . . . 59 C4
WALKERVILLE . . . . . . . . 21 A1
Wallace Ave NE6. . . . . . . 55 B4
Wallace Gdns NE9 . . . . . 66 C3
Wallace St NE11. . . . . . . 77 A1
Wallace Terr NE40 . . . . 25 A2
Wall Cl NE3. . . . . . . . . . . . 8 B1
Wallinfen NE10 . . . . . . . 60 B1
Wallington Ave NE13. . . 2 A2
Wallington Ct NE3 . . . . . 7 B3
Wallington Dr NE15. . . 27 C4
WALLSEND. . . . . . . . . . . . 22 B2
Wallsend Jubilee Prim Sch
NE28. . . . . . . . . . . . . . . 22 B2
Wallsend Rd
North Shields NE29 . . . . 24 A3
North Shields NE29 . . . . 24 B4
Wallsend St Peter's CE
Prim Sch NE28 . . . . . . 22 C2
Wallsend Sta NE28 . . . . 22 A1
Wall St NE3 . . . . . . . . . . . 8 B1
Wall Terr NE6. . . . . . . . . 33 C3
Walmer Terr NE9 . . . . . . 66 B1
Walnut Gdns NE8 . . . . . 57 B4
Walnut Pl NE3 . . . . . . . . 17 A3
Walpole St NE6. . . . . . . 33 C4
Walsh Ave NE1 . . . . . . . . 35 C3
Walter St
Brunswick Village NE13 . . . 2 A2
Jarrow NE32 . . . . . . . . . . 36 C2
Waltham Cl NE28 . . . . . . 21 A4
Waltham Pl 4 NE5 . . . . 15 C2
Walton Rd NE5 . . . . . . . . 15 B1
Walworth Gr NE32 . . . . 51 A3
Wandsworth Rd NE6 . . . 32 C3
Wansbeck NE38 . . . . . . 71 C1
Wansbeck Cl NE16. . . . 62 B3
Wansbeck Ho NE15 . . . 27 A2
Wansbeck Rd
Jarrow NE32 . . . . . . . . . . 36 C1
Newcastle-u-T NE3 . . . . . . 8 B2
Wansbeck Rd S NE3 . . . . 8 B2
Wansbeck Road Sta NE3 8 B2
Wansfell Ave NE5. . . . . . 16 B3
Wansford Ave NE5 . . . . 15 C1
Wansford Way
Whickham NE16 . . . . . . 54 B1
Whickham NE16. . . . . . 62 B4
Wantage Ave NE29 . . . . 24 B4
Warbeck Cl NE3 . . . . . . . 6 C2
Warburton Cres NE9 . . 58 C4
Warcop Ct NE3 . . . . . . . . 7 C3
Wardenlaw NE10 . . . . . 60 B1
Wardill Gdns NE9 . . . . 59 A3
Wardle Gdns NE10 . . . . 60 A3
Wardle St NE3 . . . . . . . . . 9 C1
Wardle Terr NE40 . . . . 38 B4
WARDLEY . . . . . . . . . . . . 61 B4
Wardley Cl NE10 . . . . . . 61 C4
Wardley Dr NE10 . . . . . . 61 C4
Wardley La NE10, NE31 . . 49 B1
Wardley Prim Sch NE10 61 A4
Wardroper Ho NE6. . . . 48 C4
Warenford Pl NE5 . . . . 29 A3
Warenmill Cl NE15. . . . 26 C3
Wark Cres NE32 . . . . . . 51 A2
Wark Ct NE3 . . . . . . . . . . 18 C4
Warkworth Ave NE28 . . 22 A4
Warkworth Cres
Newburn NE15 . . . . . . . 26 A3
Newcastle-u-T NE3 . . . . . . 8 C2
Warkworth Dr NE13. . . . 2 C2
Warkworth Gdns NE10 . . 59 B4
Warkworth St
3 Newcastle-u-T, Byker
NE6. . . . . . . . . . . . . . . . 33 A2
Newcastle-u-T, Lemington
NE15 . . . . . . . . . . . . . 27 A2
Warkworth Terr NE32 . . 51 A3
Warkworth Woods NE3 . . 4 B2
Warren Ave NE6 . . . . . . 34 B4
Warrenmor NE10 . . . . . 60 C3
Warrens Wlk NE21 . . . . 40 C1

Warrington Rd
Newcastle-u-T, Elswick
NE4. . . . . . . . . . . . . . . . 76 A4
Newcastle-u-T, Fawdon
NE3 . . . . . . . . . . . . . . . . 7 C2
Warton Terr NE6 . . . . . 33 A4
Warwick Ave NE16 . . . . 55 A1
Warwick Cl NE16 . . . . . 54 C1
Warwick Ct
Gateshead NE8. . . . . . . . 79 C2
Newcastle-u-T NE3 . . . . . . 7 B3
Warwick Dr NE16 . . . . . 55 A1
Warwick Hall Wlk NE7 . . 22 B4
Warwick Rd
Hebburn NE31 . . . . . . . . 50 B3
Newcastle-u-T NE5 . . . . 27 C4
Wasdale Rd NE5 . . . . . . 28 C4
Washington Gdns NE9 . . 66 A3
Washington Service Area
DH3, NE38 . . . . . . . . . 71 A3
Washingwell Com Prim
Sch NE16. . . . . . . . . . . 55 B2
Washingwell La NE16 . . 55 C2
Washingwell Pk NE16 . . 55 B2
Waskdale Cres NE21 . . 53 A4
Waskerley Cl NE16 . . . . 62 C3
Waskerley Gdns NE9 . . 66 B3
Waterbeach Pl NE5 . . . 15 C2
Waterbury Rd NE3 . . . . . 4 B1
Watergate NE1 . . . . . . . . 78 B4
Waterloo St
Blaydon NE21 . . . . . . . . . 40 C1
Newcastle-u-T NE1 . . . . 76 C4
Watermark The NE11 . . 43 B3
Watermill NE40 . . . . . . 25 A1
Watermill La NE10 . . . . 60 A4
Watermill Pk NE10 . . . . 59 C3
Water Row NE15. . . . . . 26 C3
Waterside Dr NE11. . . . 44 A2
Waterside Pk NE31 . . . . 35 A2
Water St NE4 . . . . . . . . . 76 B3
Waterville Rd NE29 . . . 24 C4
Watling Pl NE9 . . . . . . . 59 A2
Watson Gdns NE28. . . . 23 B3
Watson St
Gateshead NE8. . . . . . . . 77 C1
Jarrow NE32 . . . . . . . . . . 37 A4
Watt St NE8 . . . . . . . . . . 57 C3
Waverdale Ave NE6 . . . 34 B3
Waverley Cres NE15 . . 27 B3
Waverley Prim Sch
NE15. . . . . . . . . . . . . . 27 C2
Waverley Rd
Gateshead NE9. . . . . . . . 65 C1
Newcastle-u-T NE4 . . . . 76 B4
Wayside NE15 . . . . . . . . 28 C1
Wealcroft NE10 . . . . . . 60 B1
Wealcroft Ct NE10 . . . . 60 B1
Weardale Ave
Longbenton NE12 . . . . . . 11 B4
Newcastle-u-T NE6 . . . . 34 B2
Wallsend NE28 . . . . . . . . 21 C4
Wear Rd NE31 . . . . . . . . 50 A3
Wear St NE32. . . . . . . . . 36 C3
Weathercock La NE9 . . 58 B1
Weatherside NE21 . . . . 41 A1
Webb Gdns NE10 . . . . . 61 B4
Wedgewood Cotts NE15 27 B2
Wedmore Rd NE5. . . . . 14 B3
Weidner Rd NE15, NE4 . . 29 B2
Welbeck Gn NE6. . . . . . 33 C1
Welbeck Prim Sch NE6 33 B1
Welbeck Rd NE6. . . . . . 33 C1
Weldon Cres NE7 . . . . . 19 C2
Weldon Rd NE12 . . . . . . 10 C2
Weldon Way NE3 . . . . . . 8 C2
Welford Ave NE3 . . . . . . 8 B1
Well Bank Rd NE37 . . . . 67 C1
Wellburn Rd NE37 . . . . 67 C1
Well Close Wlk NE16 . . 54 C2
Wellesley St NE32. . . . 36 C1
Wellfield Cl NE15 . . . . 12 A1
Wellfield Ct NE40 . . . . 38 A3
Wellfield La NE15 . . . . 15 C2
Wellfield Rd
Newcastle-u-T NE4 . . . . 29 B1
Newcastle-u-T NE4 . . . . 29 C1

Wellfield Terr
3 Gateshead NE9 . . . . . 59 B3
Newcastle-u-T NE10 . . . 49 A1
Wellgarth Rd NE37. . . . 67 C1
Wellington Ct 2 NE10 . 59 B4
Wellington Rd
Dunston NE11. . . . . . . . 44 A1
Dunston NE11. . . . . . . . 44 B1
Wellington St
Gateshead, Felling
NE10. . . . . . . . . . . . . . 59 B4
Gateshead NE8. . . . . . . . 78 B3
Hebburn NE31 . . . . . . . . 35 B1
Newcastle-u-T, Lemington
NE15 . . . . . . . . . . . . . 27 B2
Wells Cl NE12. . . . . . . . 20 B4
Wells Gdns NE9. . . . . . 65 A2
Wellshede NE10 . . . . . . 61 A3
Wells St NE35. . . . . . . . 52 A1
Wellway NE32 . . . . . . . . 51 A2
Welwyn Cl NE28 . . . . . . 21 A4
Wenlock Pl 6 NE34. . . . 52 C4
Wensley Cl NE5. . . . . . . 16 A4
Wensleydale Dr NE12 . . 11 B4
Wentworth Cl NE10 . . . . 59 C3
Wentworth Grange NE3 18 B4
Wentworth Pl NE4 . . . . 76 B4
Werhale Gn NE10 . . . . . 59 C4
Wesley Ct
Blaydon NE21. . . . . . . . . 41 C3
1 Gateshead, Felling
NE10. . . . . . . . . . . . . . 59 B4
Wesley Gr NE40. . . . . . 38 A3
Wesley Mount NE40. . . 38 A3
Wesley St NE9 . . . . . . . 58 B1
Wesley Way NE15 . . . . 12 B2
Westacre Gdns NE5. . . 29 A3
West Acres NE21 . . . . . 41 C2
Westacres Ave NE16 . . 55 A1
Westacres Cres NE15 . . 29 A2
West Ave
Longbenton NE12 . . . . . 11 B2
Newcastle-u-T, Gosforth
NE3 . . . . . . . . . . . . . . . 18 A4
Newcastle-u-T NE5 . . . . 15 A2
Westbourne Ave
Gateshead NE8. . . . . . . . 58 A4
Newcastle-u-T, Gosforth
NE3 . . . . . . . . . . . . . . . . 9 A3
3 Newcastle-u-T, Walker
NE6. . . . . . . . . . . . . . . 34 B2
Newcastle-u-T, Walker
NE6. . . . . . . . . . . . . . . 34 A3
Westbourne Gdns 2
NE6. . . . . . . . . . . . . . . 34 B2
Westburn Gdns NE28 . . 21 A4
Westburn Mews NE40. . 38 A3
Westbury Ave NE6 . . . . 34 B3
Westbury Ct NE12. . . . . 10 B1
Westcliffe Way NE34 . . 52 B3
West Copperas NE15. . . 28 A3
West Cres NE10. . . . . . . 61 B4
Westcroft Rd NE12. . . . 11 C4
WEST DENTON . . . . . . 14 B1
West Denton Cl NE15 . . 27 B4
West Denton Prim Sch
NE5. . . . . . . . . . . . . . . 14 B1
West Denton Rd NE15. . 27 B4
West Denton Ret Pk
NE5. . . . . . . . . . . . . . . 15 B2
West Denton Way NE5 . . 14 C1
Westerdale NE28 . . . . . 21 A4
Westerdale Pl NE6. . . . 34 C2
WESTERHOPE . . . . . . 14 C3
Westerhope Gdns 11
NE5. . . . . . . . . . . . . . . 16 B1
Westerhope Prim Sch
NE5. . . . . . . . . . . . . . . 14 C1
Western Ave
Gateshead NE11. . . . . . 64 A4
Newcastle-u-T, Elswick
NE4 . . . . . . . . . . . . . . . 29 C1
Newcastle-u-T NE5 . . . . 14 B1
Western Com Prim Sch
NE28 . . . . . . . . . . . . . 22 A2
Western Dr NE4 . . . . . . 30 A1
Westernmoor NE37 . . . 69 B2
Western Rd
Jarrow NE32 . . . . . . . . . . 36 B2
Wallsend NE28 . . . . . . . . 23 A3
Western View NE9 . . . . 66 A1
Western Way
Blaydon NE21. . . . . . . . . 42 A2

Western Way continued
Ryton NE40. . . . . . . . . . . 39 B4
West Farm Ave NE12 . . 10 B2
West Farm Rd
Newcastle-u-T NE6 . . . . 33 C3
Wallsend NE28 . . . . . . . . 23 A3
West Farm Wynd NE12 . . 10 A2
Westfield
Gateshead NE10. . . . . . . 60 A2
Hedworth NE32 . . . . . . 51 B1
Newcastle-u-T NE3 . . . . 17 C2
Westfield Ave
Brunswick Village NE13. . . 2 A2
Crawcrook NE40. . . . . . 38 B3
Newcastle-u-T NE3 . . . . 18 A3
Westfield Cres
Crawcrook NE40. . . . . . 38 B3
Newcastle-u-T NE3 . . . . 18 A3
Westfield Ct
Jarrow NE32 . . . . . . . . . . 36 C2
Wallsend NE28 . . . . . . . . 34 C4
Westfield Dr NE3 . . . . 18 A3
Westfield Gr NE3 . . . . . 17 C3
Westfield Lodge NE9. . . 64 C4
Westfield Pk
Newcastle-u-T NE3 . . . . 18 A3
Wallsend NE28. . . . . . . . 21 B2
Westfield Rd
Gateshead NE8. . . . . . . . 58 A4
Newcastle-u-T NE15 . . . 29 A1
Westfield Sch NE3 . . . . 17 C3
Westfield Terr
Gateshead NE8. . . . . . . . 58 A4
1 Springwell NE9 . . . . . 66 C1
Westgarth NE5 . . . . . . . 15 A4
West Gate Com Coll
NE4 . . . . . . . . . . . . . . . 29 B2
Westholme Gdns NE15 . . 29 B2
WEST JESMOND . . . . 18 B2
West Jesmond Ave NE2 18 C2
West Jesmond Prim Sch
NE2. . . . . . . . . . . . . . . 18 C1
West Jesmond Sta NE2 18 C2
Westlands
Hedworth NE32 . . . . . . 51 C1
Newcastle-u-T, High Heaton
NE7. . . . . . . . . . . . . . . 19 B2
Newcastle-u-T NE5 . . . . 14 A1
West Lea NE21. . . . . . . 53 B4
Westline Ind Est DH2 . . 70 A2
Westmacott St NE15 . . 25 C4
West Mdws NE5 . . . . . . 14 A3
Westminster Cres NE31 50 A2
Westminster Dr NE11 . . 56 B2
Westminster St NE8 . . 57 C4
Westminster Way NE12 . . 20 B4
Westmoreland St NE28 . . 22 A2
Westmorland Ave 2
NE28 . . . . . . . . . . . . . 23 C1
Westmorland Ct NE31. . . 35 B1
Westmorland Gdns NE9 58 B1
Westmorland Ho NE9 . . 58 A1
Westmorland La NE1 . . 76 C4
Westmorland Rd
Newcastle-u-T, Elswick NE1,
NE4 . . . . . . . . . . . . . . . 76 A4
Newcastle-u-T NE4 . . . . 76 C4
Westmorland Wlk NE4. . 44 B3
Weston Ave NE10 . . . . 54 B1
Westover Gdns NE9. . . 58 B3
West Par
Hebburn NE31 . . . . . . . . 35 B1
Newcastle-u-T NE4 . . . . 76 B4
West Park Gdns NE21 . . 41 B1
West Park Rd NE8, NE9 . . 58 A3
West Pk NE11. . . . . . . . 44 B1
West Rd NE15, NE5 . . . 29 A2
West Rig The NE3 . . . . 16 C4
West Row DH3. . . . . . . 71 A3
West Spencer Terr
NE15 . . . . . . . . . . . . . 13 C1
West St
5 Birtley DH3 . . . . . . . . 70 B4
Gateshead NE8. . . . . . . . 78 B3
Hebburn NE31 . . . . . . . . 36 A3
Wallsend NE28 . . . . . . . . 21 B2
Whickham NE16 . . . . . . 54 C3
West Thorn Wlk NE16 . . 54 C2
West Thorp NE5 . . . . . . . 6 A1
West Vallum NE15 . . . . 28 A3
West View
Blaydon NE21 . . . . . . . . 41 B3

West View continued
Gateshead NE9. . . . . . . . 66 A4
5 Longbenton NE12 . . . 11 B4
Newcastle-u-T, Elswick
NE4 . . . . . . . . . . . . . . . 44 B4
Newcastle-u-T, Lemington
NE15 . . . . . . . . . . . . . 27 A2
Wideopen NE13 . . . . . . . 2 B3
West Walker Prim Sch
NE6. . . . . . . . . . . . . . . 48 C4
Westward Ct NE5 . . . . . 14 C3
Westway
Blaydon NE21 . . . . . . . . 41 A2
Throckley NE15 . . . . . . 12 C3
West Way NE11 . . . . . . 56 C3
Westway Ind Est NE15 . . 12 B3
Westwell Cl NE3 . . . . . . 19 A4
Westwood Ave NE6 . . . 19 C1
Westwood Gdns
6 Gateshead NE9. . . . . 66 B3
Newcastle-u-T NE3 . . . . 16 C2
Westwood Rd NE3 . . . . . 4 C1
Westwood View NE40 . . 38 B3
Wetheral Gdns NE9 . . . 65 B3
Wetheral Terr NE6 . . . 48 B4
Wetherby Gr NE8 . . . . 57 C3
Weyhill Ave NE29 . . . . 24 B4
Weymouth Gdns NE9 . . 65 B2
Whaggs La NE16 . . . . . 55 A2
Whalton Ave NE3 . . . . . 8 B2
Whalton Cl NE10 . . . . . 61 B3
Whalton Ct NE3 . . . . . . 8 B2
Wharfdale Pl NE6. . . . . 34 C3
Wharfedale Gn NE9 . . . 65 C1
Wharmlands Gr NE5 . . 28 A3
Wharmlands Rd NE15 . . 28 A3
Wharrier St NE6 . . . . . 48 B4
Wharrier Street Prim Sch
NE6. . . . . . . . . . . . . . . 48 B4
Wheatear Cl 1 NE38. . . 71 B3
Wheatfield Ct NE5 . . . . 15 A3
Wheatfield Gr NE12. . . 11 A3
Wheatfield Rd NE5 . . . 15 A3
Whernside Cl 4 NE37 . . 69 C2
Whernside Wlk NE40 . . 39 C1
WHICKHAM . . . . . . . . . 55 A3
Whickham Ave 6
NE16. . . . . . . . . . . . . . 54 C3
Whickham Bank 6
NE16. . . . . . . . . . . . . . 54 C3
Whickham Gdns 14 NE6 33 A1
Whickham Highway NE11,
NE16. . . . . . . . . . . . . . 56 A3
Whickham Ind Est NE16 54 B4
Whickham Lodge NE16 . . 55 B3
Whickham Lodge Rise
NE16. . . . . . . . . . . . . . 55 B3
Whickham Parochial CE
Prim Sch NE16 . . . . . . 54 B1
Whickham Pk NE16 . . . 55 B3
Whickham Rd NE31 . . . 35 C2
Whickham Sch NE16. . . 54 C2
Whickham View
Gateshead NE9. . . . . . . . 65 B4
Newcastle-u-T NE15 . . . 28 B2
Whinbrooke NE10 . . . . 60 C2
Whinbush Pl NE15 . . . . 28 B1
Whinlatter Gdns NE9 . . 65 B4
Whinlaw NE9. . . . . . . . . 66 A4
Whinmoor Pl NE5 . . . . 16 C1
Whinneyfield Rd NE6 . . 34 A3
Whinshaw NE10 . . . . . . 60 B3
Whinstone Mews NE12. . 11 B2
Whitbeck Ct NE5 . . . . . 15 B1
Whitbeck Rd NE5 . . . . 28 B4
Whitburn Gdns NE9 . . 66 B3
Whitby Cl NE8 . . . . . . . 79 C1
Whitby Cres NE12. . . . 11 A2
Whitby Gdns NE28 . . . 22 C4
Whitchurch Cl NE35 . . 52 A1
Whitebeam Pl NE4. . . . 76 B3
Whitebridge Cl NE3 . . . 9 A3
Whitebridge Ct NE3 . . . 9 A3
Whitebridge Parkway
NE3 . . . . . . . . . . . . . . . . 9 B4
Whitebridge Pk NE3 . . . 9 B4
Whitebridge Wlk NE3. . . 9 B4
Whitefield Gr NE10 . . . 59 C4
Whitefield Terr NE6. . . 20 B1
Whitefriars Way NE12. . 10 B2

Whitegate CI NE11........44 B2
**Whitehall Rd**
 Gateshead NE8...........79 B1
 Gateshead, Shipcote NE8..57 C4
 Walbottle NE15 .........13 A2
Whitehill NE10 ...........60 B1
Whitehill Dr NE10.........59 C1
WHITEHILLS..............59 C1
Whitehouse Cres NE9....66 C4
Whitehouse La NE9.......66 C4
**Whitehouse Mews**
 NE28...................22 A2
**Whitehouse Rd**
 Newcastle-u-T, Delaval
 NE15..................43 B4
 Newcastle-u-T, Old Benwell
 NE15..................43 A4
White House Way NE10 .60 A1
Whitelees CI NE3 .........7 C3
Whiteley CI NE40 .........38 C1
Whiteley Rd NE21........42 A4
**White Mere Com Prim Sch**
 NE10...................61 B3
White Mere Gdns NE10 .61 B4
White Oaks NE10 .........60 A1
Whites Gdns NE31.......35 B2
White St NE6.............34 C2
Whitethorn Cres NE5 ...16 C2
Whitethroat CI **6** NE38 .71 B3
Whitewell CI NE40.......25 A1
Whitewell La NE40.......25 A1
Whitewell Rd NE21.......41 B2
Whitfield Dr NE12........11 A2
**Whitfield Rd**
 **6** Longbenton NE12 .....11 B4
 Newcastle-u-T NE15 .....28 A1
Whitgrave Rd NE5.......16 B3
Whitley Ct **7** NE9........66 B3
Whitmore Rd NE21.......41 B3
Whittingham Ct NE8....79 A1
Whittingham Rd NE15...15 B4
Whittington Gr NE5.....29 A4
Whittleburn NE10........60 B1
Whitton PI NE7...........19 C4
Whitton Way NE3.........8 C2
Whitwell Terr NE40......25 A2
**Whitworth CI**
 Gateshead NE8..........57 C3
 Newcastle-u-T NE15 .....34 B1
Whitworth PI NE6........34 B1
Whitworth Rd NE37.....69 B3
**Whorlton Grange Cotts**
 NE5...................14 C4
Whorlton PI **1** NE15...14 C3
Whorlton Terr NE5......13 C4
Whyndyke NE10 ..........60 B1
Wickets The NE13........13 B2
Wickham Ind Est NE16..42 C1
Widdrington Gdns NE13 .2 C2
Widdrington Rd NE21...41 B2
Widdrington Terr NE21..40 C4
WIDEOPEN...............2 C1
Widnes PI NE12..........11 A3
Wigeon CI NE38.........71 C2
Wigmore Ave NE6........48 A4
**Wilberforce St**
 Jarrow NE32............37 A3
 Wallsend NE28..........34 C4
Wilberforce Wlk NE8 ...77 C2
Wilbury PI NE15.........16 A2
Wilfred St NE6...........32 B2
Wilfrid St DH3............70 B3
Wilkes CI NE5............15 A2
Wilkinson Ave NE31.....49 A4
Wilkinson Ct **4** NE32...36 C3
Willerby Dr NE3 ..........9 B4
**William Armstrong Dr**
 NE4...................44 B3
William IV Yd NE8.......78 B4
William St W NE31......35 B2

Williams Pk NE12........11 A2
**William St**
 Gateshead NE10.........47 C1
 Hebburn NE31...........35 B3
 Newcastle-u-T NE3 .......9 C1
 Whickham NE16 .........54 C3
William Terr NE31........35 B3
**William Whiteley Homes**
 NE40...................38 C1
WILLINGTON.............23 A4
WILLINGTON QUAY ....23 C2
Willington Terr NE28....22 C3
**Willow Ave**
 Dunston NE11...........56 B4
 Newcastle-u-T NE4 ......29 B4
Willowbank Gdns NE2 ..18 C4
Willow CI NE16 ..........55 A2
Willow Ct NE40..........25 B2
Willowfield Ave NE3 .....8 A2
**Willow Gr**
 Gateshead NE10.........60 A4
 Wallsend NE28..........22 B1
Willow Grange NE32....36 B3
Willow Rd NE21 .........41 C2
Willows CI NE13..........2 A1
**Willows The**
 Hebburn NE31...........50 A4
 Hedworth NE32 .........51 B1
 Newcastle-u-T NE4 ......76 A3
 Throckley NE15 ..........12 B1
Wills Mews NE7.........20 C2
Wills Oval NE7...........20 C2
Wilmington CI NE3 ......6 C2
Wilson Ave DH3 ..........68 B1
Wilson Gdns NE3........17 C3
Wilson's La NE9 .........58 B1
**Wilson St**
 Dunston NE11...........56 B4
 Wallsend NE28..........21 C2
Wilson Terr **1** NE12....11 B4
Wilsway NE15 ...........12 A2
Wilton Ave NE6..........48 A4
Wilton Cotts **5** NE35 ..52 A1
Wilton Gdns N NE35 ....52 A1
Wilton Gdns S NE35....52 A1
Wiltshire Dr NE28........21 A4
Wiltshire Gdns NE28 ...21 B3
Wimbourne Gr **1** NE5 ..15 A3
Wimslow CI NE28.......21 A3
Wincanton PI NE29.....24 C4
Winchcombe PI NE7....19 B3
Winchester CI NE32.....51 A1
Winchester Wlk NE13....2 B2
WINCOMBLEE.............34 C1
Wincomblee Rd NE6....49 A4
Windermere DH3 ........70 C2
Windermere Ave NE10 .60 B4
**Windermere Cres**
 Blaydon NE21...........53 A4
 Hebburn NE31...........50 B4
 Hedworth NE32 .........51 C3
Windermere Gdns NE16 55 B3
Windermere Rd NE5....28 C4
Windermere St W NE8 .79 B1
Windermere St NE8.....79 B1
Windhill Rd NE6.........48 B3
WINDMILL HILLS........79 B2
**Windmill Hills Prim Sch**
 NE8...................79 B2
**Windmill Way**
 Gateshead NE8..........79 A2
 Hebburn NE31...........35 C4
Windshields Wlk NE15 .12 A1
**Windsor Ave**
 Gateshead NE8..........58 A4
 Newcastle-u-T NE3 ......18 C4
**Windsor CI**
 Wallsend NE28..........23 B4
 Whickham NE16.........40 C4
Windsor Cotts NE28.....23 B4
**Windsor Cres**
 Hebburn NE31...........36 A2
 Newcastle-u-T NE5 ......15 B3

**Windsor Ct**
 **7** Gateshead NE10.....59 B4
 Newcastle-u-T, Kingston Park
 NE3....................7 C3
 Newcastle-u-T, South
 Gosforth NE3 ...........9 C1
Windsor Dr NE28 ........23 B4
Windsor Gdns NE10.....59 B4
Windsor Pk NE28 .......21 A3
**Windsor Rd**
 Birtley DH3.............68 A2
 Springwell NE9..........66 B2
Windsor St **2** NE28....21 C2
**Windsor Terr**
 Crawcrook NE40........38 C4
 Newcastle-u-T, South
 Gosforth NE3 ..........18 C4
 **1** Springwell NE9......67 A1
Windsor Way NE3........7 B3
Windsor Wlk NE3.........7 B3
Windt St NE13.............2 A1
WINDY NOOK............59 C2
**Windy Nook Prim Sch**
 NE10..................59 C2
Windy Nook Rd N10,
 NE9...................59 A2
Windy Ridge NE10 .......59 A2
**Windy Ridge Villas**
 NE10..................59 B3
Wingate CI NE15.........27 C2
Wingate Gdns NE9......66 B3
Wingrove Ave NE4......30 A2
Wingrove Gdns NE4 ....30 A3
**Wingrove Prim Sch**
 NE4...................30 A2
Wingrove Rd N NE4.....30 A3
Wingrove Terr **11** NE9 ..67 A1
Winifred Gdns NE28 ....22 A1
WINLATON...............41 A1
WINLATON MILL........53 B2
Winship Terr **15** NE6 ...33 A2
Winskell Rd NE34.......52 C4
**Winslow CI**
 Boldon Colliery NE35...52 B2
 Newcastle-u-T NE6 .....34 B2
Winslow Gdns NE9......58 A1
Winslow PI NE6 .........34 B2
Winster NE38............71 C1
Winston Ct NE9..........67 A1
Winton Way NE3..........8 A1
Wirralshir NE10 .........60 C2
Wiseton Ct NE7.........10 A1
Wishart Ho NE4 .........44 A4
Wishaw Rise NE15......27 C3
Witham Ho NE32........51 B2
Witham Rd NE31........50 B3
Witherington CI NE7....20 C3
Witton Ct NE3 ............7 C2
**Witton Gdns**
 **1** Gateshead NE9......66 B2
 Jarrow NE32............51 B3
Witton Rd NE31.........36 A4
Witty Ave NE31..........36 A1
Woburn CI NE28 ........21 A3
Woburn Way NE5.......15 B2
Wolseley CI NE8 .........77 C1
Wolseley Gdns NE2 ....32 B4
Wolsingham Gdns **5**
 NE9...................66 B3
Wolsingham Rd NE3...17 C4
Wolsingham St NE4....76 A3
Wolveleigh Terr NE3 ....9 B1
Wolviston Gdns **4** NE9 .66 B3
**Woodbine Ave**
 Newcastle-u-T NE3 .....18 A4
 Wallsend NE28..........21 C2
Woodbine CI NE4........44 B4
Woodbine PI NE8........79 B1
Woodbine Rd NE3 .......9 A1
Woodbine St NE8.......79 B1
**Woodbine Terr**
 Birtley DH3.............70 C4

**Woodbine Terr** *continued*
 Gateshead, Bensham
 NE8...................79 B1
 Gateshead, Bill Quay
 NE10..................48 C1
 Gateshead, Felling NE10 .59 A4
Woodbine Villas NE8....79 B1
Woodbrook Ave NE5....28 B4
Woodburn NE10 .........60 A1
Woodburn Ave NE4 ....29 C4
Woodburn Gdns NE11..56 C2
Woodburn St NE15......27 A3
Woodchurch CI NE12 ...20 B4
Woodend Way NE3 ......7 B4
Woodford NE9............65 A1
Woodgate Gdns NE10 ..49 A1
Woodgate La NE10......49 A2
Wood Gr NE15...........27 C3
Woodhead Rd NE6.......34 A4
Woodhorn Gdns NE13...2 B2
**Woodhouses La**
 Whickham, Fellside
 NE16..................54 A2
 Whickham, Swalwell
 NE16..................54 C4
Woodland Cres NE15 ...43 B4
Woodland Mews NE2 ...19 A2
**Woodlands**
 Newcastle-u-T NE3 .....18 A3
 Throckley NE15 .........12 A3
Woodlands CI NE15 .....12 A3
**Woodlands Park Dr**
 NE21..................41 C2
**Woodlands Park Villas**
 NE13....................4 C4
Woodlands Pk NE13 .....2 C1
Woodlands Rd NE15 ....27 B3
Woodlands Terr NE10 ..59 B4
Woodlea CI NE29 .......24 C3
Woodlea Gdns NE3 ......9 C2
Woodlea Sq NE29.......24 C3
Woodleigh View NE5....16 C3
Woodman St NE28......23 C3
Woodmans Way NE16...62 A4
Woodpack Ave NE16 ...54 B2
Woods Gn NE10 .........49 B1
**Woodside Ave**
 Newcastle-u-T NE6 .....34 C3
 Throckley NE15 .........12 C2
Woodside CI NE40 ......25 A1
Woodside Cres NE12....11 C4
Woodside Ct NE12......11 C4
Woodside Gdns NE11 ..56 B3
**Woodside La**
 Greenside NE40.........39 A3
 Ryton NE40.............39 A4
Woodside Way NE40 ...25 A1
Woodside Rd NE21 .....27 C3
Wood St NE11...........56 B4
Woods Terr NE8.........79 C1
**Woodstock Rd**
 Gateshead NE9..........65 C2
 Newcastle-u-T NE15 ....28 B1
**Wood Terr**
 Gateshead NE10.........49 A2
 Jarrow NE32............50 C4
Woodthorne Rd NE2 ...18 C3
Woodvale Dr NE31......49 B4
**Woodvale Gdns**
 Gateshead NE9..........59 B2
 Newcastle-u-T NE15 ....27 C3
Woodvale Rd NE21.....22 C2
Woodville Rd NE15 .....27 B4
Woodwynd NE10 ........60 B2
Wooler Ave NE29 .......24 B4
Wooler Cres NE8 ........57 B4
Wooler Gn NE15.........26 C3
Wooler Sq NE13 ..........2 C3
**Woolerton Dr**
 Gateshead N10, NE9 ....59 B2
 Gateshead NE9..........59 A2
Wooler Wlk NE32........50 C4
Wooley St NE28.........21 C1

Woolmer Ct NE7........20 C3
Woolsington Gdns NE13 .6 A4
Woolsington Pk S NE13 .6 A4
Wooperton Gdns NE5 ..29 A3
Worcester Gn NE8 ......79 B2
Worcester Way NE13....2 C3
**Wordsworth Ave**
 Hebburn NE31...........35 C2
 Whickham NE16........55 A4
Wordsworth Cres NE9 ..67 A1
Wordsworth St NE8....46 C2
Worley Ave NE9.........65 A4
Worley Mews NE9.......65 A4
Worsley CI NE28........21 A4
Worthing CI NE28.......21 A3
Wraysbury Ct NE3 .......7 B3
Wreigh St NE31.........35 B2
Wreken Gdns NE10 .....61 B4
WREKENTON............66 A3
Wrekenton Row NE9....66 A3
Wren CI NE38...........71 C3
Wroxham Ct NE5 .......15 C4
Wuppertal Ct NE32 ....36 C2
Wychcroft Way NE5.....16 A2
Wych Elm Cres NE7.....20 A3
Wycliffe Ave NE3 ........17 A3
Wye Ave NE32...........51 B3
Wye Rd NE31............50 A3
Wylam Gdns NE28......23 A4
Wylam St NE32..........36 C3
Wylam View NE21.......41 A2
Wynbury Rd NE9........58 C1
Wyncote Ct NE7.........19 C2
Wyndfall Way NE3......17 B3
Wyndham Ave NE3......17 A3
**Wyndham Prim Sch**
 NE3...................17 B3
Wyndley CI NE16........54 B1
Wyndley Ho NE3........17 A3
Wyndley PI NE3..........17 A3
Wyndrow PI NE3........17 A3
Wyndsail PI NE3.........17 B3
**Wynd The**
 Newcastle-u-T NE3 .....17 B4
 Throckley NE15 .........12 B1
Wyndtop PI NE3.........17 B3
Wyndward PI NE3.......17 B3
Wynn Gdns NE10 .......48 B1
Wynyard Gdns NE9.....66 A2
Wynyard St NE11 .......56 B4
Wythburn PI NE9 .......65 C4

# Y

Yatesbury Ave NE5......15 C3
Yeadon Ct NE3 ...........7 A3
Yeavering CI NE3 ........17 C4
Yelverton Cres NE6 .....48 B3
Yetholm PI NE5...........15 B4
Yetholm Rd NE8 .........77 B1
Yetlington Dr NE3 ......17 B4
Yewburn Way NE12.....11 A2
Yewcroft Ave NE15......28 B2
Yewdale Gdns NE9......65 B4
Yewtree Gdns NE6......21 B1
Yewtrees NE10 ..........60 A1
Yewvale Rd NE5 .........16 B1
York Ave NE32...........51 A3
York Ct **9** NE28.........21 C1
Yorkdale PI NE6 .........34 B2
York Dr NE28 ............21 C1
York Rd DH3..............70 B1
**York St**
 Gateshead NE10.........48 C1
 Jarrow NE32............36 B2
York Terr NE10..........59 C4
Yorkwood NE31.........35 A3
Younghall CI NE40......38 C1

# Z

Zion Terr NE21...........41 A2

# List of numbered locations

In some busy areas of the maps it is not always possible to show the name of every place.

Where not all names will fit, some smaller places are shown by a number. If you wish to find out the name associated with a number, use this listing.

*The places in this list are also listed normally in the Index.*

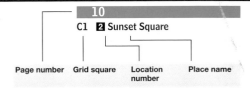

**10**

C1 **2** Sunset Square

Page number · Grid square · Location number · Place name

## 7

B1 **1** Gunnerston Gr
**2** Dunnykirk Ave
**3** Laverock Pl
**4** Hazeley Gr
**5** Stapeley Ct
**6** Dugdale Ct
**7** Castle Cl
**8** Bellingham Ct

## 10

B2 **1** Stoneleigh Pl
**2** Sandringham Ct
**3** St Clements Ct

## 11

B4 **1** Wilson Terr
**2** Burn Ave
**3** Fairfield Ave
**4** North View
**5** West View
**6** Whitfield Rd
**7** Irvine Ho
**8** Langley Mere

## 12

B2 **1** Oak St
**2** Hadrian Rd
**3** Victoria Terr
**4** Field Terr
**5** Radcliffe Cotts
**6** Ravensburn Wlk
**7** Hilda Terr
**8** Orchard Terr
**9** Crescent The

## 14

A1 **1** Angram Wlk
**2** Askrigg Wlk
**3** Audland Wlk
**4** Austwick Wlk
A2 **1** Hanover Wlk
**2** Hanover Cl
**3** Elgar Ave
C1 **1** Birkshaw Wlk
**2** Bickerton Wlk
**3** Knarsdale Pl
**4** Highwell La
C3 **1** Whorlton Pl
**2** Aged Miners' Homes
**3** Marsham Rd
**4** Counden Rd
**5** Kensington Villas

## 15

A2 **1** Frankham St
**2** Barents Cl
**3** Forestborn Ct
A3 **1** Wimbourne Gn
**2** Buxton Gn
**3** Chatsworth Gdns
**4** Pilton Wlk
**5** Boyd Terr
**6** Belmont Cotts
**7** Rapperton Ct
B2 **3** Fairspring
**4** Fenton Wlk

**6** Fourstones
**7** Fordmoss Wlk
C1 **1** Finsmere Pl
**2** Cotehill Rd
**3** Buttermere Cl
C2 **1** Amersham Pl
**2** Abercrombie Pl
**3** Chandra Pl
**4** Waltham Pl
**5** Melvin Pl
**6** Curzon Pl
**7** Blakelaw Rd

## 16

A1 **1** Viewforth Gn
**2** Oakwood Pl
**3** Hadstone Pl
**4** Togstone Pl
**5** Deepbrook Rd
B1 **1** Bondicarr Pl
**2** Maudlin Pl
**3** Morwick Pl
**4** Doxford Gdns
**5** Embleton Gdns
**6** Chevington Gdns
**7** Stamfordham Mews
**8** Cheeseburn Gdns
**9** Westerhope Gdns
B2 **1** Middle Garth
**2** Crossbrook Rd
**3** Radcliffe Pl
**4** Birling Pl
**5** Rennington Pl

## 18

C1 **1** Jesmond Pl
**2** Henshelwood Terr
**3** Tankerville Pl
**4** Osprey House

## 19

A1 **1** Grosvenor Villas
**2** Collingwood Terr
**3** Fenwick Terr
**4** Fenwick Cl
**5** Farquhar St
**6** Grebe Ct
C1 **1** Jesmond Park Ct
**2** Glenridge Ave

## 21

C1 **1** Saker Pl
**2** Forum The
**3** Sanderlings
**4** Elsdon Terr
**5** Eden Ct
**6** Tiberius Cl
**7** Maude Gdns
**8** York Ct
C2 **1** Burn Ave
**2** Windsor St
**3** Jubilee St
**4** Cobden St
**5** Blenkinsop St
**6** Harrington St
**7** Douglass St
**8** Hopper St
**9** Albert Ave

**10** Clifton Ave
**11** Lisle Ct
**12** Valeshead Ho

## 23

A4 **1** Stanwix
**2** Vindolanda
**3** Corstopitum
**4** Carvoran
**5** Chesters
**6** Housteads
**7** Dovecrest Ct
**8** Sandringham Mews
**9** Garden Pk
**10** Iona Ct
B1 **1** Carlyle St
**2** Smeaton St
**3** Hanover Gdns
**4** Carlyle Ct
**5** Smeaton Ct
**6** Byron Ave
**7** Addison Ct
C1 **1** Eldon Ct
**2** Westmorland Ave
**3** Gladstone St

## 29

B1 **1** Dolphin Ct
**2** Bond St
**3** St James Lodge
**4** Atkinson Terr
**5** St James' Gdns
**7** David Adams Ho
**8** Benwell Grange Cl
**9** Benwell Grange
B4 **9** Angerton Gdns
**10** Ovington Gr
C1 **1** Tiverton Ave
**2** Normount Ave
**3** Adelaide Ho
**4** Clennel Ho
**5** Adelaide Ctr The

## 32

B2 **1** Stepney Rd
**2** Hannington St
**3** Hannington Pl
**4** Claypath St
**5** Shields Rd W
**6** Back Stephen St
**7** Leighton St
**8** Steenbergs
C1 **1** Kendal St
**2** Gordon Ho
**3** Gordon Rd
**4** Chevron The
**5** Dibley Sq
**6** Dibley St
**7** Brinkburn Sq
**8** Brock Sq
**9** Byker Bsns Development Ctr
**10** St Michaels Workshops
C2 **1** Southfields Ho
**2** Addison Cl
**3** Tynemouth Cl
**4** Heaton Wlk
**5** Grafton Cl

**6** Molineux Cl
**7** Grafton Ho
**8** Molineux Ct
**9** Back Heaton Park Rd
**10** Belvedere Ho
**11** Grafton St
**12** Flora St
**13** Matthew St
**14** Edwin St
**15** Addison Rd
**16** Raby St
**17** Brinkburn St
**18** Shipley Pl
**19** Norfolk Sq
**20** Priory Gn
**21** Brinkburn La
**22** Brinkburn Ct
**23** Shipley Wlk
**24** Kendal Gn
**25** Brinkburn Pl
**26** Kendal Pl
**27** Kendal Ho
**28** Dalton Cres
**29** Northumberland Terr
C3 **1** Stannington Pl
**2** Roxburgh Pl
**3** Jack Common Ho
**4** Alison Ct
**5** Stannington Gr
**6** Homeside Pl
**7** Eversley Pl
**8** Kingsley Pl
**9** Heaton Park Ct

## 33

A1 **1** Manor House Cl
**2** Headlam Gn
**3** St Michael's Mount
**4** Mason St
**5** Avondale Rise
**6** McGowen Ct
**7** Beresford Gdns
**8** Clydesdale Mount
**9** Oban Gdns
**10** Raby Cross
**11** Houlet Garth
**12** Laverock Ct
**13** Bolam Coyne
**14** Whickham Gdns
**15** Garmondsway
**16** Merle Gdns
**17** Janet St
A2 **1** Shield La
**2** Denmark St
**3** Warkworth St
**4** Headlam St
**5** Robinson St
**6** Glendale Terr
**7** Rabygate
**8** Raby Cres
**9** Shipley Rise
**10** Mount Pleasant
**11** Long Headlam
**12** Headlam Ho
**13** Felton Gn
**14** Felton Ho
**15** Winship Terr
**16** Felton Wlk
**17** Byker Cres
**18** Thornborough Ho
**19** Bamburgh Terr

**20** Benson Pl
**21** Old Vicarage Wlk
**22** Harriet Pl
**23** Jane St
A3 **1** Fourth Ave
**2** Brough St
**3** Brough Ct
**4** North Cl
**5** Elvet Way
**6** Elvet Ct
**7** Tynemouth Ct
**8** Tynemouth Way
**9** Tynemouth Gr
**10** Denmark Ct
**11** St Mark's Cl
**12** Belvedere Ct
**13** St Mark's St
**14** Algernon Cl
**15** Algernon Rd
**16** Morley Ct
**17** Algernon Ct
**18** Charles Ct
**19** Chillingham Ct
**20** Brough Way
**21** Queen Ann Ct
**22** Northfields Ho
**23** Northfields Cl
A4 **1** Hartford St
**2** Marleen Ct
**3** Richardson St
**4** Cleghorn St

## 34

B2 **1** Eastbourne Ct
**2** Westbourne Gdns
**3** Westbourne Ave
**4** Andrew Ct
**5** Dawson St
**6** Aston Wlk
**7** Titan Ho
**8** Hexham Ho

## 36

C3 **1** Beverley Ct
**2** Selby Ct
**3** Ellen Ct
**4** Wilkinson Ct
**5** North Ct
**6** Grange Ct
**7** Bede Precinct
**8** Viking Precinct
**9** Arndale Arc
**10** Ellison St
**11** Monastery Ct

## 38

B3 **1** Rossdale
**2** Morgy Hill W
**3** Morgy Hill E
**4** Clifford Gdns
**5** George St
**6** Lloyd St
**7** Emma View
**8** David Terr
**9** Catherine View
**10** Claude St
**11** Benjamin St
**12** Dick St
**13** Scott's Ave

14 Bradley View
15 Fell View W
16 Fell View
17 Mount View

## 41
A1 1 Litchfield St
2 Litchfield Cres
3 Litchfield Terr
4 Old Well Ave
5 Mount Pleasant
6 Rooksleigh
7 Garth The
8 Thornbury
9 Commercial St
10 Garden Terr
11 North Lodge Apartments

## 42
C1 1 Lyndhurst Terr
2 Crowley Villas
3 Spencers Bank
4 Hood St
5 Brewery La
6 Brewery Bank
7 Jubilee Terr
8 Rosebud Cl

## 44
B1 1 Baker Gdns
2 Fowler Gdns
3 Kelvin Gdns
4 Tyndal Gdns
5 Parsons' Gdns
6 Johnson St
7 Ruskin Ave
8 Kingsley Pl

## 47
B4 1 Ruddock Sq
2 Finchale Terr
3 Glanton Ct
4 Harbottle St
5 Lilburn Cl
6 Fenning Pl
7 Till St
8 Moorings The
9 St Peter's Quayside W
10 Merchants Wharf
C1 1 Bennett Gdns
2 Noble St
3 Uxbridge Terr
4 Eastern Gdns
5 Hawthorn Gdns
6 Laburnum Gdns
7 Avenue The
8 Field St
9 Gordon Ct
10 Church Ct
11 Carlisle Ct
12 St Etienne Ct
13 Helmsdale Ave
14 Brandling Ct
15 Brandling La
16 Collingwood St
17 Merlin Ct

18 Providence Pl
19 Quarry Row
20 Gosforth St

## 48
B1 1 John St
2 Greenfield Terr
3 Durham St
4 Ashfield Terr
5 George St

## 52
A1 1 Roseberry Terr
2 Gladstone Terr
3 Coronation Terr
4 Brockley Terr
5 Wilton Cotts
6 Terrace The
7 Oxley Mews
8 Grays Terr
B4 2 Richardson Ave
C4 1 Edendale Ct
2 Kirkdale Ct
3 Tennant St
4 Rowan Ct
5 Laybourn Gdns
6 Wenlock Pl
7 Ryedale Ct
8 Thomas Bell Ho
9 Clive St
10 Pintail Ct

## 54
B1 1 Marston Wlk
C1 2 Greystoke Wlk
3 Grange Wlk
C3 1 Heathwood Ave
2 Eleanor Terr
3 Axwell Park Cl
4 Bank Top Hamlet
5 Edith Terr
6 Whickham Bank
7 Jasmine Villas
8 William St
10 James St
11 Walker Ct
12 Nunn Gdns
13 Simonside View

## 55
A3 1 Deans Cl
2 Abbots Way
3 Square The
4 St Mary's Gn
5 Carnation Terr
6 Rectory Ct
7 Church Gn

## 56
B4 1 Glebe Terr
2 Kensington Terr
3 Briarwood Cres
5 Crescent The
6 Whickham Ave
8 Hawthorn Terr
C3 1 Murray Gdns
C4 1 Linden Gr

3 Kent Ave
4 Derwent Twr
5 Brompton Workshops
6 Ravensworth Apartments
7 Debden Ho

## 58
B1 1 Alum Well Rd
2 Studley Gdns
3 Elder Gr
4 Rock Gr
5 Robson St
6 Robinswood
9 Carters Lo
B4 1 Cotterdale Ave
3 Ellwood Gdns
4 Lynnholme Gdns
5 Dryden Ct
6 Bowes Lyon Ct
C1 1 Harcourt Pk
2 Harcourt St
3 Beaconsfield Cres
5 Kinfauns Terr
6 St Thomas St
7 Sheriffs Hall Villas
C2 1 Crossway Villas
2 Beverley Ct
3 Ravensdale Cres
4 Egremont Dr
5 Ravenswood
6 Fells The
C4 3 Silver Ct
4 Norwood Gdns
5 Mafeking St
6 Grange Terr
7 Hamilton Ct
8 Ellison Villas
9 Lynholme Ct
10 Newman Pl
11 Deckham St

## 59
A1 1 Charnwood Gdns
2 Lavender Row
3 Philip's Ct
4 Beacon Ct
5 Fell Ct
B3 1 Springfield Terr
2 Coldwell Terr
3 Wellfield Terr
4 Square Hos
5 Kay's Cotts
6 Co-operative Cres
B4 1 Wesley Ct
2 Wellington St
3 Ellerbeck Cl
4 Hollybush Rd
5 Kensington Ct
6 Sandringham Ct
7 Windsor Ct
C4 1 Redmayne Ct
3 Croudace Row
4 Park Row
5 Victoria Sq
6 Victoria Terr
7 Morley Terr
7 Crowhall Towers
8 Mandarin Lodge
9 Harlequin Lodge

10 Merganser Lodge
11 Mallard Lodge
12 Rowlandson Terr
13 Richmond Terr
14 Benson Terr
15 South View

## 60
A4 1 Rochester Terr

## 62
C2 1 Beech St
2 Larch St
3 Sun St
4 Granby Terr
5 Dewhurst Terr

## 65
A2 1 Portland Gdns
A4 1 Richmond Ct
2 Home Ave
3 Ellison Pl
4 Chowdean Terr
5 Earls Dene
6 Forster Ct
7 Coronation Terr
8 Path The
B2 1 Bodmin Ct
2 Okehampton Ct
4 Newquay Gdns
5 Hanover Ct
6 Talisman View
7 Kenilworth View
8 Rotherfield Gdns

## 66
B2 1 Witton Gdns
2 Galloping Green Cotts
3 Galloping Green Farm Cl
B3 1 Burnhope Gdns
2 Simonside Pl
3 Waskerley Gdns
4 Wolviston Gdns
5 Wolsingham Gdns
6 Westwood Gdns
7 Whitley Ct
C1 1 Westfield Terr
2 Clifton Ct
3 Ashfield Terr
4 Belmont Terr

## 67
A1 1 Windsor Terr
2 Pearath Edge
3 Highworth Dr
4 Heather Hill
5 Ferndale Terr
6 Albion Terr
7 Fell Pl
8 Makepeace Terr
9 Claremont Terr
10 Lismor Terr
11 Wingrove Terr
12 Hawthorn Terr
13 Belle View Terr

14 Victoria Terr
15 Alexandra Terr
16 South View
17 Springwell Terr
18 Blackberries The
19 Stafford Villas
20 Westfield Cres
21 Coronation Terr
22 Milton Pl
23 Kings Terr
24 Carlton Terr
25 Linden Terr

## 68
B1 1 Birtley Villas
2 Huddart Terr
3 Hillcroft
4 Mount Pleasant Bglws
5 Pleasant Pl
6 Hawkhills Terr
7 Raven Terr
8 St Joseph's Ct
9 Esk Terr
10 Dove Ct

## 69
B3 1 Donkin Rd
C2 1 Highheath
2 Shieldclose
3 Ingleborough Cl
4 Whernside Cl
5 Drumaldrace
6 Hedgehope
7 Dairnbrook
8 Rogan Ave
C3 2 Grousemoor
3 Pheasantmoor

## 70
B4 1 Neale Terr
2 Craig St
3 Bertram St
4 Jones St
5 West St
6 Dunelm Cl
7 Constables Garth
8 Orchard Pk
9 Grove Cotts
10 Daisy Cotts
11 Monument Terr
12 Talbot Terr
13 Coop Bldgs
14 Arndale Ho
16 Harraton Terr
16 Kestrel Ct

## 71
B3 1 Wheatear Cl
2 Fieldfare Cl
3 Stonechat Cl
4 Cormorant Cl
5 Plover Cl
6 Whitethroat Cl
7 Glenholme Cl
8 Teal Cl